Revivalism and Social Christianity

Revivalism and Social Christianity

The Prophetic Faith of Henri Nick and André Trocmé

CHRISTOPHE CHALAMET

☙PICKWICK *Publications* • Eugene, Oregon

REVIVALISM AND SOCIAL CHRISTIANITY
The Prophetic Faith of Henri Nick and André Trocmé

Copyright © 2013 Christophe Chalamet. All rights reserved. Except for brief quotations in critical publications or reviews, no part of this book may be reproduced in any manner without prior written permission from the publisher. Write: Permissions, Wipf and Stock Publishers, 199 W. 8th Ave., Suite 3, Eugene, OR 97401.

Pickwick Publications
An Imprint of Wipf and Stock Publishers
199 W. 8th Ave., Suite 3
Eugene, OR 97401

www.wipfandstock.com

ISBN 13: 978-1-61097-858-3

Cataloging-in-Publication data:

Chalamet, Christophe.

Revivalism and social Christianity : the prophetic faith of Henri Nick and André Trocmé.

xviii + 214 p. ; 23 cm. Includes bibliographical references and index.

ISBN 13: 978-1-61097-858-3

1. Trocmé, André, 1901–1971. 2. Nick, Henri. 3. Protestants—France—History. 4. Pacifists—France—History. I. Title.

BX4805.2 .C43 2013

Manufactured in the U.S.A.

For Megan, Leila, and Max

Blessed are the peacemakers;
for they will be called children of God.
Blessed are those who are persecuted for righteousness' sake,
For theirs is the kingdom of heaven.

Matthew 5:9–10 (NRSV)

Contents

List of Images and Map / ix
Acknowledgments / xi
Abbreviations / xiii
Introduction / xv

Part One
The Meanings of Conversion—Henri Nick / 1

Part Two
André Trocmé's First Steps in Spiritual and Social Christianity / 46

Part Three
The "Conspiracy of Good" in Le Chambon-sur-Lignon / 125

Part Four
After the War / 169

Epilogue / 182

Appendix
Declaration Read by Pastors André Trocmé and Édouard Theis in the Church of Le Chambon on Sunday, June 23, 1940 / 189

Bibliography / 193
Index Nominum / 207

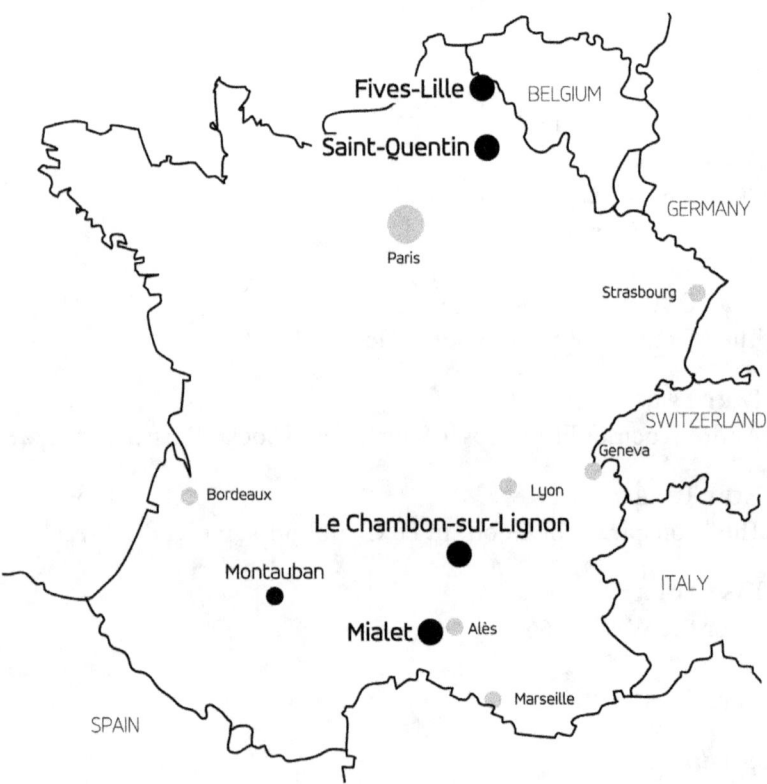

Map of France

Images and Map

André Trocmé in 1925 / x

André Trocmé, summer of 1948 / x

Henri Nick and André Trocmé among other pastors and their wives (northern France) / xiv

Henri Nick during World War I / 45

Temple (Protestant church) of Saint-Quentin / 45

André Trocmé, arrival in Le Chambon (1934) / 124

Marcel Heuzé (parish bulletin, Reformed church in Marseille, 1945) / 188

Magda and André Trocmé in 1938 / 192

Map of France / viii

André Trocmé in 1925

André Trocmé, summer of 1948

Acknowledgments

I COULD NOT HAVE written this study without the support of Fordham University, where I had the good fortune of working during eight years, until May 2011. I would especially like to thank my former department chair, Terrence W. Tilley, as well as Nancy Busch, dean of Fordham's Graduate School of Arts and Sciences, and James S. Wilson, director of faculty development. My thanks go to my friends and colleagues in the theology department at Fordham, including Joyce O'Leary and Anne-Marie Sweeney.

I owe a debt of gratitude to several librarians and archivists: Wendy Chmielewski, of the "Peace Collection" at Swarthmore College; Michele Hiltzik, of the Rockefeller Archive Center, in Tarrytown, New York; Florence Poinsot and Sophie Vié, librarians at the Société de l'histoire du protestantisme français (SHPF) in Paris; Timorah Perel and Irena Steinfeldt, of Yad Vashem.

Michel Cornier brought some of his father's papers to the United States so I could consult them. I am grateful to him for entrusting these documents to me. Richard Unsworth and Pierre Boismorand have been generous to me with regard to photographs of Trocmé, among other things.[1] Alain Robert provided the map of France that is included in the book. I have benefited from a conversation in Manhattan, in the early stages of this project, with Gérard Bollon, a specialist of the history of Le Chambon during the war.

In France, I have been helped in various ways by Étienne Sévin ("Fraternité" of Clamart), Jacky Mosse ("Foyer du peuple," in Fives), Clotilde Herbert ("Les Amis du Cambrésis"), Simone Doise (formerly Simone

---

1. Richard Unsworth's book *A Portrait of Pacifists: Le Chambon, the Holocaust, and the Lives of André and Magda Trocmé* (Syracuse University Press, 2012) was published after the completion of my manuscript. I was not able to profit from it.

Acknowledgments

Mairesse, née Pévenage) and Nicolas Offenstadt. Grégoire Humbert, with whom I am editing the correspondance of Gounelle and Nick in their early ministry, has assisted me in several ways in my discovery of Henri Nick.

Right from the beginning of my work on this book, I received support from Nelly Trocmé Hewett, André Trocmé's daughter, and wish to thank her for her friendship. She read the entire manuscript and helped me avoid a number of errors. Thanks to her, I was able to meet Rudy Appel as well as Hanne and Max Liebmann, who were rescued in Le Chambon during the Second World War. I consider myself fortunate to have encountered them. On November 12, 2009, Nelly Trocmé, Rudy Appel, Hanne and Max Liebmann came to Fordham's Rose Hill campus, in the Bronx, to talk about Le Chambon.

One of the highlights of my time in New York City was my encounter with George M. Houser, a pioneer of the Civil Rights Movement. I am glad some of my undergraduate students and colleagues had the opportunity to meet him at Fordham.

I had the pleasure of presenting some of my work on Henri Nick and André Trocmé at the American Academy of Religion's annual meeting in Montreal, on November 9, 2009, and at "Maryhouse," which is part of Dorothy Day's "Catholic Worker," on the Lower East Side of Manhattan, on January 15, 2010. I wish to thank Jane Sammon for her invitation. Speaking with portraits of Gandhi and Martin Luther King Jr. hanging on the wall behind me, I knew what I was about to present would not fall on deaf ears.

There is one person who appears in this book who has marked my (paternal) family: Marcel Heuzé, the brother of my grandmother Cécile Chalamet, née Heuzé. This book is scholarly in nature, but in writing it I also hoped to honor his, as well as Henri Nick's and André Trocmé's, memory.

I dedicate this work to my wife Megan and our children Leila and Max. May we remember and honor those who precede us.

C. C.
Pully (Switzerland), October 17, 2012

Abbreviations

AMR	*American McAll Record. Devoted to the Interests of the McAll Mission in France* 1 (1883)—51 (1933)
APEQS	Association protestante pour l'étude pratique des questions sociales
BSHPF	*Bulletin de la Société de l'histoire du protestantisme français* 1 (1852)-present
CR	*Cahiers de la Réconciliation*, 1926-present
ÉM	*L'Écho de la Montagne* 1 (1909)-40 (1948)
ET	English translation
ETR	*Études théologiques et religieuses* 1 (1926)-present
IFoR	International Fellowship of Reconciliation
FoR	Fellowship of Reconciliation
RCS	*Revue du Christianisme social* (original title, in 1887: *Revue de théologie pratique et d'homilétique*; since 1888: *Revue de théologie pratique et d'études sociales* ; since 1889: *Revue du Christianisme pratique*; from 1896 until 1972: *Revue du Christianisme social*)
RHPR	*Revue d'histoire et de philosophie religieuses* 1 (1921)-present
SHPF	Société de l'histoire du protestantisme français (Paris)
WCC	World Council of Churches

Henri Nick and André Trocmé among other pastors and their wives (northern France)

Introduction

THIS BOOK PRESENTS ASPECTS of the lives of Henri Nick (1868–1954) and André Trocmé (1901–1971), two men of faith and courage, two towering figures of 20th-century French Protestantism. This is not a full-blown biography of these two pastors. My purpose is more limited: I will seek to show how seeds which were planted in the late nineteenth century among certain French Protestants led to amazing fruits decades later, in the midst of some of the darkest moments of the 20th century. In other words, this book attempts to trace a sort of genealogy, from the pioneers of the "Christianisme social" (the French equivalent of what anglophones call the "Social Gospel") to some of its leaders in the 20th century.

One does not have to be Aristotelian to be convinced that "virtues" are formed and transmitted through social encounters and relations, through communities with their particular, complex histories. Virtues are fostered in part through practices and become a sort of "habit." It is a banality to state that each of us is shaped by specific people and places, by practices and ideas we encounter.[2] The present study is a case study in how people can inspire and shape the lives of others. The reader will be introduced to people who, despite personal flaws (Christians are justified sinners), embody how Christianity promotes peace and active solidarity with the oppressed.

The name of André Trocmé is familiar to those who have heard about his successful effort, during World War II, along with fellow pastors and many parishioners, in rescuing hundreds—perhaps more than one thousand—of refugees, most of them Jewish, in the area surrounding

---

2. For a good reflection on these questions, from a pragmatist standpoint (influenced by William James and others), see Joas, *Genesis of Values*. As is well-known, the theme of virtue formation within a community around a narrative is central in Stanley Hauerwas' theological ethics. It is not a coincidence that the story of Le Chambon has been studied in relation to Hauerwas' works. See Wells, *Transforming Fate*, 134–40.

Introduction

Le Chambon-sur-Lignon (south of Lyon, France, in the department of Haute-Loire). Henri Nick, on the other hand, is not well known at all, even in France. I will seek to remedy that in the following pages. Henri Nick was one of the most influential figures among French Protestants in the first half of the 20th century. He impacted many theology students and future pastors. André Trocmé was one of them.

Together, Henri Nick and André Trocmé span a hundred years of world history and modern Christianity, from the late 19th century all the way to a not-so-distant past. By paying close attention to them, the historian and theologian is able to discern the ways in which two French Reformed pastors responded to two world wars, to totalitarianisms and antisemitism, to new movements in Christianity such as the Salvation Army and Pentecostalism. One can also discern how the pastoral ministry has evolved, and how that ministry can be a sign, however imperfect and feeble, of the ideals (or the realities) it seeks to proclaim, such as justice, reconciliation, and peace. The reader of these pages might thus be led to conclude—as I do—that in Henri Nick and André Trocmé, despite their personal limitations, we see two witnesses of the prophetic dimensions present at the heart of the Jewish and Christian traditions.

A NOTE ON THE SOURCES

This book relies in part on André Trocmé's memoirs, written in 1966–68 ("Mémoires. Notes autobiographiques"; hereafter abbreviated "Mémoires").[3] This source is not the work of a historian and must be read with care. It has occasioned resentment from some people who are mentioned in it. Trocmé did not worry too much about the kind of reactions his text would provoke. It was written exclusively for his family.

The area of Le Chambon is still very much divided regarding André Trocmé's legacy: some have thought, and still think, that he dishonored their relatives in his "Mémoires." The present work attempts to be a work of history, and not of hagiography. It is a scholarly work, not a book written in the style of a novel.[4] Trocmé's memoirs may not have been the work

3. André and Magda Trocmé's papers can be consulted at the Peace Collection, Swarthmore College (Pennsylvania). For a detailed description of these papers, visit: http://www.swarthmore.edu/library/peace/DG100–150/dg107Trocme.htm.

4. For a "novel-like" account, written with a focus on ethical issues, see the well-known book by Philip Hallie, *Lest Innocent Blood Be Shed: The Story of the Village of Le Chambon and How Goodness Happened There*. Several much more reliable works have been published since 1979. See in particular the works by François Boulet, who

Introduction

of a professional historian, but there is no doubt that it is a legitimate source for the historian, as long as one confirms—whenever possible—what Trocmé writes by using external sources. In the instances where it has been possible to do that, I have been struck by the relative accuracy of Trocmé's memory. That he may not have given as much credit to certain key participants in the events he narrates (especially in the pages on the rescue effort during the Second World war) is quite possible. But one needs to be aware of what Trocmé intended to do when writing this text: "My goal is not to produce something a historian would produce, but to show that one may go through a war while practicing non-violence. 'You distort the truth!,' the historian will clamor! In a certain sense, yes, but I can say that I am honest and that my distorting of the truth is involuntary and unavoidable."[5] Trocmé was sophisticated enough, as an intellectual, to be aware of the "work" of memory, which never simply presents the past as it happened.

Unlike Trocmé, Henri Nick did not write a detailed autobiography. That fact, along with a very thin historical record especially of his contribution to the rescue of Jews during the war, explains to a large extent the asymmetry in what follows with regard to Trocmé and Nick's efforts to rescue refugees.

---

wrote a dissertation related to the topic (*Les montagnes françaises, 1940–1944: des montagnes-refuges aux montagnes-maquis*, Villeneuve d'Ascq, Presses universitaires du Septentrion, 1999, 2 vol.), Gérard Bollon, Pierre Bolle, Philippe Joutard, and Patrick Cabanel, listed in the bibliography. Many have seen the moving documentary on Le Chambon by Pierre Sauvage, *Weapons of the Spirit* (1989).

5. "Mon but n'est pas de faire œuvre d'historien, mais de démontrer que l'on peut traverser une guerre en pratiquant la non-violence. [. . .] 'Vous déformez la réalité,' clamera l'historien! Dans une certaine mesure, oui, mais je puis affirmer que je suis honnête et que ma déformation est involontaire et nécessaire." A. Trocmé, "Mémoires," 371.

xvii

PART ONE

The Meanings of Conversion—Henri Nick

HENRI NICK WAS BORN in Paris on April 16, 1868. His father, Georges-Henri, who had German roots, was a branch manager for the *Société générale*, the French bank, which had been founded just four years before Henri's birth. Henri lost his father when he was ten. His mother, Héléna Roussel, raised him in Paris, where he began his studies in the humanities, including ancient languages, at the "lycée" Jeanson-de-Sailly, completing his degree ("bachelier ès Lettres") in Montpellier. In the last months of 1885, he entered the Faculté de théologie protestante in Montauban, the main seminary training Reformed (Calvinist) pastors in the south of France at the time.[1] There, among seventy students, Henri Nick struck a deep friendship with two fellow students, Élie Gounelle (1865–1950) and Wilfred Monod (1867–1943), inarguably the two most important leaders of the Social Gospel among French Calvinists in the first half of the 20th century.[2] It is fascinating to realize that these three young men, who were to play a prominent role in 20th-century French Protestantism, were closely connected right from their student years. The correspondence be-

---

1. The Faculté de théologie of Montauban, founded in 1808, was transferred to Montpellier in 1919, where it is still in existence.
2. Martin, *Élie Gounelle*. Monod, *Après la journée*. For the number of students in Montauban at the time, see the speech by Auguste Wabnitz in *Faculté de théologie protestante de Montauban. Séance publique de rentrée le 10 novembre 1887*, Montauban, Granié, 1887, 6.

tween Élie Gounelle, Henri Nick, and Wilfred Monod, which was in part preserved, reveals the deep bond between the three young men.[3]

HENRI NICK'S THESIS ON THE NOTION OF CONVERSION

In July of 1890, Henri Nick defended his undergraduate (bachelor) thesis in theology, titled *Notion de la metanoia d'après le Nouveau Testament et l'expérience chrétienne*.[4] Nick's work is quite interesting. Its main objective was to clarify the meaning of the term "metanoia" (Nick translates it as "conversion") in the New Testament. The fact that Nick wrote on that topic is telling. He was, and would remain, very interested in the notion (and even more in the reality) of "conversion."

At the end of the introduction, Nick alludes to his experiences in his last year of studies in Montauban: "If our friends were to find at least in our concluding theses a feeble echo of our religious discussions during the academic year 1889/90—a year which will leave in all our spirits and hearts indelible memories of mutual affection and gratitude toward God—then our labor would find more than its recompense."[5] The concluding theses, indeed, do not merely summarize the overall argument of Nick's work, which mainly defends the importance of the person's will

---

3. Bibliothèque de la Société de l'histoire du protestantisme français (SHPF), Paris, papers of Élie Gounelle, box 5 (018Y5), EG IX/4. An edition of Gounelle and Nick's letters (as well as some by Wilfred Monod and others), from their student years until 1897, is in preparation by Grégoire Humbert and the author.

4. Surprisingly, the original version of Nick's thesis is now preserved in the library of the Harvard Divinity School, where I consulted it. It contains a handwritten dedication, partly cut when the volume was bound: "[. . .] président de soutenance, étudiant qui vous est profondém[ent] reconnaissant de la sollicitu[de] chrétienne que vous n'avez cess[é] de lui témoigner ainsi que Mad[ame] Monod. Puissé-je à l'avenir me montre[r] plus digne de votre chrétienne affection. Dieu me soit en aide. Votre bien dévoué et attaché [en] Jésus-Christ. H. N." On the next page, one finds a list of the "examinateurs" who participated in the public defense: "MM. [Jean] Monod, Président de la soutenance, Wabnitz, Montet, Leenhardt." In July 1891, Wilfred Monod defended his thesis on *Les bases psychologiques du dogme de la rédemption* (Montauban, J. Granié, 1891). Two years before, in 1889, Gounelle had completed his training with a study on *L'agnosticisme de M. Herbert Spencer. Étude critique* (Montauban, Granié, 1889).

5. "Nous nous estimerons trop récompensé de ce travail, si nos amis retrouvent tout au moins dans nos thèses finales l'écho affaibli de nos entretiens religieux durant cette année scolaire 1889–1890, qui laissera dans notre esprit et notre cœur à tous d'ineffaçables souvenirs d'affection mutuelle et de reconnaissance envers Dieu." *Notion de la metanoia*, 7.

and its cooperation in effecting religious conversion.[6] Grace and faith both precede and follow the human will, he carefully notes, but there is a moment when the human will, in its autonomy, is responsible and free to act.[7] And so Nick's thesis is a critique of "quietism," "fatalism," and the inertia that results from them, as if one should expect everything from God in utter passivity.[8] Interestingly, the consequences of this emphasis on human action and responsibility are not developed in the study itself but instead in the concluding theses, which Nick mentions in the introduction. There, one finds some of the themes that Nick and his friends had discussed during the preceding year. It is worth quoting several of these theses, as they reveal insights that help us understand Nick's ideals, and his future ministry: "The return of Jesus Christ is conditioned by our faith and the use we shall make of our freedom. Whether we hasten or delay it depends on us. This glorious advent could already be a past event. When the Son of man returns, will he find faith on earth?" (10th thesis).[9] "Both reason and conscience confirm the notion of eternal punishment. A Christian cannot deny that notion. Jesus allowed this terrible uncertainty to hang over humanity" (13th thesis).[10] "We are saved in order to become

---

6. See for instance: "Dans notre conversion, il y a un instant précis, un moment où nous sommes seuls artisans de notre destinée. [. . .] Voilà ce que nous apprendrons, si nous étudions des récits de conversion, ou si nous assistons à des conversions; c'est toujours à nous qu'il appartient de nous prononcer en dernier ressort." *Notion de la metanoia*, 56. Or: "La conversion est donc avant tout, d'après l'expérience chrétienne, un acte volontaire [. . .]." (62). This leads, unsurprisingly, to a critique of Calvin's rejection of the possibility of a human "cooperation" with God's salvific action (41).

7. "Voilà la conversion: 1° grâce et foi; 2° volonté; 3° foi et grâce" (70).

8. "Nous ne voulons plus assister à ce spectacle lamentable, d'âmes d'ailleurs bien disposées, qui s'éloignent du christianisme et se perdent, parce qu'elles se lassent d'attendre un salut qui n'arrive jamais. Elles se morfondent en prières, alors qu'elles n'ont qu'à agir, au lieu d'attendre béatement du ciel, dans un mol quiétisme ou un sombre fatalisme des sentiments, des dispositions, une détermination qui ne relèvent que de leur propre volonté. En conséquence, au nom de la vérité, nous ne saurions trop protester contre un prédestinationisme calviniste dont nous subissons encore le contre coup, qui pousse les hommes à attendre tout de Dieu, et engourdit dans leur inertie des gens qui ne sont que trop disposés à l'inaction. [. . .] La volonté humaine peut beaucoup, beaucoup plus que nous le soupçonnons et que notre paresse ne se l'avoue." *Notion de la metanoia*, 72.

9. "Le retour de Jésus-Christ est conditionné par notre foi et l'usage que nous ferons de notre liberté. Il dépend de nous de le hâter ou de le retarder. Cet avènement glorieux pourrait être à l'heure actuelle un fait passé. Lorsque le Fils de l'homme viendra, trouvera-t-il de la foi sur la terre?" *Notion*, 75.

10. "Les peines éternelles se légitiment également devant la raison et la conscience. Un chrétien est coupable de les nier. Jésus a voulu laisser planer ce doute terrible sur

3

saviors; our individual salvation is intimately linked to the salvation of our brothers" (18th thesis).[11] "The Church is an association of believers who all work for Christ. The faith which saves implies a continuous act of the will" (20th thesis).[12] "The ecclesiastical spirit is a spirit of solidarity and fraternity, but it can only exist in a Church of people who profess their faith" (21st thesis).[13] "The one who proclaims the truth must above all be its witness" (25th thesis).[14] "The evangelical alliance with all Christians from all denominations is more than an order, it is Jesus Christ's prayer, in other words it is an order which is being carried out. It is an act of faith and the source of great blessings. Perhaps the only means to practice it loyally, without pettiness, would be to plan a work of evangelization to those who are outside" (27th thesis).[15] "The tendency to always postpone the realization of Jesus Christ's promises until another century is fatal" (29th thesis).[16] "God is giving some extraordinary opportunities to the Church in our time. It is time for the Church to respond to God's vision, by taking seriously his promises and his orders, and by advancing for the sake of lost souls onto the path of a conquering Christianity" (30th thesis).[17] And, finally, the 31st—and final—thesis: "The synod will find the kind of popularity to which it is entitled among the Churches only when its essential and only concern will be the evangelization of France and the progress of the Kingdom of God."[18]

---

l'humanité." *Notion*, 75.

11. "Nous sommes sauvés pour devenir sauveurs; notre salut personnel est intimement lié à celui de nos frères." *Notion*, 76–77.

12. "L'Église est une société de croyants qui tous travaillent pour Christ.—La foi qui sauve suppose un acte continu de volonté." Ibid., 77.

13. "L'esprit ecclésiastique est un esprit de solidarité et de fraternité, mais ne se comprend que dans une Église de professants." Ibid.

14. "Un prédicateur de la vérité doit en être avant tout le témoin." Ibid., 78.

15. "L'alliance évangélique avec tous les chrétiens de toute dénomination est plus qu'un ordre, elle est une prière de Jésus-Christ, c'est-à-dire un ordre en voie d'exécution. Elle est un acte de foi et la source de grandes bénédictions. Peut-être le seul moyen de la pratiquer loyalement, sans mesquineries, serait de se concerter pour une œuvre d'évangélisation au dehors." Ibid.

16. "La tendance à toujours renvoyer à un siècle à venir la réalisation des promesses de Jésus-Christ est funeste." Ibid., 29.

17. "Dieu accorde de nos jours à l'Église des facilités extraordinaires. Il serait temps qu'elle répondît aux vues de Dieu, en prenant au sérieux ses promesses, et ses ordres, et en entrant par amour pour les âmes perdues, dans la voie d'un christianisme conquérant." Ibid.

18. "Le synode n'obtiendra dans les Églises toute la popularité à laquelle il a droit, que du jour où sa préoccupation essentielle et unique sera l'évangélisation de la France

The Meanings of Conversion—Henri Nick

From all this, it appears that the notions of conversion and salvation were at the center of Nick's thought, and that he had a very realistic interpretation of it, as salvation from "eternal punishment." Here, Nick's roots in a traditional version of Calvinism are visible. The ecumenical and missionary dimension of his thought cannot be missed either: the Churches are called by Jesus Christ to work together in bringing the Gospel to all people, and thus to contribute actively to Christ's return. The Churches are responsible for the fact that the parousia has not yet taken place. Moreover, Nick had little patience for multitudinous Churches where fervor and sacrifice appeared to be lacking. His ideal, it is clear, resembles that of the "free Churches," but these communities of committed (read: converted) Christians, far from being sectarian and withdrawn from a sinful world, should foster a spirit of "solidarity and fraternity" (21st thesis) and seek "those who are outside" (27th thesis).

Nick had been discussing all of these things with his friends in Montauban. They were a group of eight to ten theology students, and as some of them were graduating, being ordained, and beginning to work in various parishes, a circular letter was organized.[19] On May 27, 1889, Nick sent such a letter to his friends, writing, "As Gounelle notes, it is our understanding of the Christian life which is the foundation for our circular letter and our bond."[20] What was the program of this small group? Very simply, but also amazingly ambitiously: the "revival" of France. They called their circular letters "a circular letter for Revivalism" ("une circulaire de Réveil"). The main objective of their lives was "the transformation of the country."[21]

At a time when theological liberalism and orthodoxy were clashing, these students of theology and young pastors, rather than taking part in the ecclesiastical battles and thus contribute to the divide among French Calvinists, were pursuing a different goal: the regeneration of their country.

The members of the circular letter came mostly from Pietist backgrounds. In a French Reformed Church that, after years of tensions, had finally split up into two branches in the wake of a national synod in 1872

---

et l'avancement du Règne de Dieu." Ibid., 79–80.

19. Those involved in the circular letter were, among others, Nick, Élie Gounelle and Wilfred Monod.

20. "Comme le remarque Gounelle, c'est notre conception de la vie chrétienne intime qui est le fondement de notre circulaire et de notre liaison non pas à 4 ou 5 comme l'insinue malignement Gounelle, mais à 8 ou 10 en comprenant certainement Guex." H. Nick, circular letter from May 27, 1889. Private archives of the Nick family (G. Humbert, Paris).

21. H. Nick, circular letter from May 27, 1889 ("la transformation du pays").

Revivalism and Social Christianity

(the more "liberal" *Union des Églises réformées* now coexisted alongside the *Union des Églises réformées évangéliques*), all of the members of the circular letter belonged to the *Église réformée évangélique*, the more conservative, Pietist and orthodox branch. Their families, in many cases, had been affected by the various revivals in France since the early decades of the 19th century. Élie Gounelle's father, Gédéon (1839–1917), was a Methodist minister. Wilfred Monod's father, Théodore (1836–1921), was the pastor of a prominent independent Reformed Church in Paris, the "chapelle du Nord." Under Wilfred Monod's influence, Nick had what he called a "conversion" experience.[22] Here is how Monod described what happened in November of 1889, at one of the regular prayer meetings he was organizing at the seminary in Montauban in order to "awaken" his fellow students—some of whom were pursuing the ministry for the sake of obtaining a respected position funded by the French government (it was only in 1905 that Church and State were separated in France):

> At the beginning of my second year of theological studies, the event—or the miracle—happened during one of the Saturday prayer meetings, on November 27, 1889; suddenly, in front of his comrades, and to their astonishment, the student [...] solemnly dedicated himself to God. The example of this memorable conversion led two other students to similar commitments. At the prayer meeting of December 8, the movement grew stronger: confessions of sins, tears, prayers of praise. [...] We were beginning to breathe in a Christian atmosphere.[23]

With this experience of conversion came a deepened sense of consecration to God and of commitment to the task of preaching the Gospel. But personal conversion was not their only discovery in those months! Monod and his friends, during the year 1890, were also being swept by the "Christianisme social."[24] Together, these two dimensions, namely personal conversion and social concerns, would be crucial for the rest of their lives.

22. "Grâces à Dieu, depuis que je suis converti, je ne suis pas découragé et veux seulement marcher hardiment en avant." Letter to his mother from November 1889.

23. "Au début de ma seconde année de théologie, l'événement—ou le miracle—se produisit, pendant la réunion de prière du samedi soir, le 27 novembre 1889; tout à coup, devant ses camarades stupéfaits, bouleversés, l'étudiant artiste et aboulique se consacra solennellement à Dieu. L'exemple de cette conversion mémorable poussa deux autres étudiants à s'affirmer dans le même sens. À la réunion de prière du 8 décembre, le mouvement se fortifia: confessions, larmes, prières de louange. [...] On commençait à respirer l'atmosphère chrétienne." *Après la journée*, 83.

24. "Vers 1890, à la Faculté de théologie, nous étions plusieurs étudiants montalbanais que le mouvement saisit, comme une lame de fond emporte au large de paisibles

FIRST ATTEMPTS AT INSPIRING A REVIVAL: MIALET (1890-97)

Before beginning his last year of studies at Montauban, Henri Nick became a pastor-in-training ("suffragant") at the small parish of Saint-Christol-lès-Alès, in the Cévennes region, just outside the town of Alès (Gard department, southern France). This was a historical Huguenot region, where stories abounded on the arrival of the "pure gospel" in the 16th century and on the many persecutions Protestants had endured, all the way until the French Revolution. Besides decades of peace here and there, there had been particularly painful periods in the last quarter of the 17th century and the early years of the 18th century, after the Revocation, in 1685, of the *Edict of Nantes* (1598). That period of "wilderness" ("le Désert," as it is known) was very much present in the collective consciousness of the French Protestant communities. In the first years of the 18th century, a war, the "guerre des camisards," had shaken the region (1702–5). Louis XVI's *Edict of Toleration* (1787) put an end to the long era of persecutions, granting civil rights and religious freedom to the Protestants. And so the Reformed Church had slowly begun to rebuild itself in the 19th century.

On August 25, 1889, Paul Minault, a pastor who was ten years older than Nick, came to preach to Saint-Christol and was subsequently named pastor. He would soon become a friend of Nick, Gounelle, and Monod. His nomination meant that Nick had to search for another parish. His prospects were good: even before the end of his studies, his reputation as a young man with a passion for evangelistic mission and revivalism was made among like-minded pastors, who sought to attract him to their own missionary fields or to strategically significant parishes in the struggle against the theologically liberal party.[25] Nick's evangelistic inclinations were so strong that he was not sure whether he should remain within the

---

baigneurs." Monod, "Que signifie," 867.

25. In December 1889, pastor Guillaume Granier tried to convince Nick to seek a nomination in Ribaute. In March 1890, Louis Molines wrote to Nick urging him to go to Monoblet "in order to win a parish and soon thereafter an entire region ["Consistoire"] to the evangelistic cause." Letter from March 17, 1890. Ten days later, on March 26, 1890, pastor A. Malan suggested that Sommières would be a good parish. On April 1, 1890, Nick's own pastor and mentor from Montpellier, pastor Teule, summoned him to accept a position in Uchaud. On September 25, 1890, Wilfred Monod wrote to Nick asking him if he would be interested to work in Paris as assistant-pastor for Charles-E. Greig, one of the directors of the MacAll Mission in Paris. Towards the end of 1891, Émile Lenoir, an evangelist affiliated with the MacAll Mission in Marseille, wrote hoping that Nick would join him in Marseille.

Reformed Church. Should he embark on an independent ministry, perhaps as part of the growing, evangelistic McAll Mission (soon to be named "Mission populaire évangélique de France"), or in the Salvation Army? Wilfred Monod wrote him a long letter arguing that he should not leave the Reformed Church:

> Let us affirm clearly, strongly, our right to be friendly with Finney, Moody and Booth and to remain Reformed. We should not give the ecclesiastical partisans any joy by leaving as soon as they excommunicate us. [. . .] Stay with us, please. We have a great task ahead of us within our Church. [. . .] If your principles are incompatible with those of the Reformed Church, let the Church show that to you. Let her expel you. Don't be the one starting the fight. Look: you are the one saying that the Reformed Church needs a revival, and you refuse a call from that Church?[26]

Nick decided, for the time being, to remain within the Reformed Church. His first position as a pastor was in the village of Mialet, also in the Cévennes region. It was a large parish in size, but small in numbers, with slightly over 1,000 Protestants. The parish only had one pastor.[27] Mialet was (and still is) such a historic site for French Protestants that in 1910 a museum dedicated to the memory of past persecutions opened in the vicinity ("Le musée du Désert").

Nick began his work in Mialet on September 21, 1890.[28] He had the great fortune of having one of his closest friend nearby: Élie Gounelle was a pastor in Alès, approximately seven miles away, in an urban environment, focusing his energy on the youth and assisting two senior pastors. Nick and Gounelle went to work on their great task: to foster a "revival" of their parishes and of the people in their areas. Nick and Gounelle's letters from their years as pastors in the Cévennes (1890–96) reveal their constant sup-

---

26. "Affirmons *nettement, hautement* notre droit de tendre la main à Finney, à Moody, à Booth et de rester réformés. C'est donner trop beau jeu aux cléricaux que de filer modestement dès qu'ils vous excommunient. [. . .] Reste avec nous, je t'en prie. Nous avons une grande œuvre à accomplir au sein de notre Église. [. . .] Si tes principes sont incompatibles avec ceux de l'Église réformée, laisse l'Église te le montrer. Laisse-la te chasser de son sein. Mais ne commence pas, toi, les hostilités. Comment! Tu déclares que l'Église réformée a besoin d'être réveillée et tu refuses un appel de l'Église réformée!" Letter from W. Monod to H. Nick, Sept. 25, 1890.

27. For the number of Protestants in Mialet, see Edmond Davaine, *Annuaire du protestantisme français*, Paris, Fischbacher, 1894, 85.

28. In his letter to Gounelle from September 21, 1891, Nick writes that it has been exactly one year since he arrived in Mialet.

port of each other's ministry. During Nick's first year in Mialet, Gounelle came to talk or preach four or five times, and at one point spent three days with Nick.[29] Their letters betray a deep friendship, one that would last until Gounelle's death in 1950. As pastors with a special responsibility for the youth in their parishes, the two men were especially fond of recruiting new members for their local branches of the *Union chrétienne de jeunes gens* (UCJG, the French equivalent of the Young Men's Christian Association, or YMCA).

On January 6, 1891, Nick gave his friends from Montauban a summary of his recent activities in his parish:

> [. . .] extremely long travels in the rural areas, almost no time to read or to do intellectual work, every once in a while a burial two and a half hours away from my home. On Tuesdays, *Union chrétienne*—on Thursdays and Fridays, meeting of Christians (one in Mialet, the other in a neighbouring village)—I ask each Christian what he has done for Christ during the preceding week, everyone answers, then we come to the Lord and steep ourselves again in his communion. All of that is done very informally. The new converts are joining these meetings and are the most active elements. Finally I must add neighborhood meetings, which are well attended, on the other days. I can't say that we have a revival in the strict sense of the term: no extraordinary manifestation of *God's Spirit, no absolutely intense* and irresistible *feeling* of God's presence.[30]

Six months later, Nick counted seventy "converts" in the parish, and regretted that someone had written an article about the "revival" in Mialet in a local Protestant journal titled *Le Huguenot*. The author of the article should simply have written that "God has blessed us."[31]

29. Letter from Nick to Gounelle from September 21, 1891.

30. "Voulez-vous maintenant que je vous donne un aperçu de mon Église, des courses énormes à la campagne, presque pas le temps de lire ou de travailler, parfois un ensevelissement à deux heures et demi de mon lieu de résidence. Mardi Union chrétienne—jeudi et vendredi, réunion de chrétiens (une à Mialet, l'autre à un autre village)—je demande à chaque chrétien ce qu'il a fait pour Christ durant la semaine et chacun répond, puis nous approchons du Seigneur et nous nous retrempons dans sa communion; tout cela se fait très simplement. Les nouveaux convertis viennent grossir ces réunions et en sont même l'élément le plus actif, plus des réunions de quartier assez fréquentées les autres jours. Nous n'avons pas précisément de Réveil ici: aucune manifestation extraordinaire de *l'Esprit de Dieu, aucun sentiment absolument intense* et irrésistible de la présence de Dieu." Circular letter, private archive of the Nick family.

31. "Je regrette les exagérations des quelques lignes de Fabre sur Mialet. Dieu nous a bien béni, voilà ce qu'il fallait dire. Le nombre des convertis ne dépasse pas ou guère

Revivalism and Social Christianity

Nick dedicated enormous amounts of energy to his ministry. His letters from that period of his life, and in fact his entire life, reveal his conviction that for him ministering meant giving one's life. The letters that Henri Nick, Élie Gounelle, and Wilfred Monod exchanged in the 1890s contain repeated calls to take care of themselves and to avoid "killing" themselves in their work. This aspect is so recurrent that it becomes a *topos* in their letter exchanges.

Between the regular duties of a parish pastor, the many youth activities, and the evangelistic campaigns in neighboring areas and sometimes in other cities, Nick had plenty of reasons to suffer from exhaustion and to be ordered by his doctor to go to "Les Fumades," the thermal baths near Alès. Both Gounelle and Monod urged him to take some time off. Still, Nick found the time to explore the possibility of marrying a young woman as devoted to the cause of revivalism as he was. On February 28, 1895, Nick married Hélène Lèques, who would take on numerous tasks in the ministry of young women.

Like Nick, Gounelle was working tirelessly for a revival in his parish. And his enthusiasm was beginning to bear some fruits among the youth, in the *Union chrétienne de jeunes gens* (UCJG). Every year, he organized a youth day that gathered hundreds of young people from the entire region, who heard some of the best preachers from the entire country.[32] Gounelle shared Nick's vision of a revival, but he was exploring new ways to understand the meaning of "revival": "I am calling for a *revival*, forcefully, passionately; that is the goal. [...] I mean a *revival in all the senses of the term*. I am not looking for neurotic manifestations, but a general awakening of sinful humanity, asleep in the egoism of social classes, in the churches' formalism, in the suffocating atmosphere of church parties, and above all in the almost general indifference. The revival has to come: and for that to happen, we need, *with God's help, through prayer*, deep *minds* and *enthusiastic* people."[33]

70." Letter from H. Nick to Gounelle, no date, probably around June 1891.

32. On April 15, 1894, for instance, Parisian pastor Charles Wagner talked at Gounelle's "fête de la jeunesse" on the topic: "Be a man!" ("Sois un homme!"). Gounelle describes the program of the day in a letter to H. Nick from March 20, 1894.

33. "[...] je réclame vivement, passionnément *le Réveil*; voilà le but. [...] J'entends *le Réveil en tout sens*. Pas de crises de nerfs: mais un éveil général de l'humanité pécheresse endormie dans l'égoïsme des classes, dans le formalisme des églises, dans l'atmosphère étouffante des partis, et surtout dans l'indifférence presque générale. Il faut que le Réveil arrive: et pour cela, il faut avec *l'aide de Dieu par la prière*, des *intelligences* profondes et des *emballés*." Letter from Gounelle to Nick, April 28, 1891.

Gounelle's letter reveals something very important: he was broadening his understanding of what a "revival" might be. Revivalism was not simply about individual conversion to Christ: it also had to be a social, communal reality. Gounelle called for a renewal of "the era of prophetic ministries from twenty-seven centuries ago."[34] The Hebrew prophets had shown the way, because they never isolated judgment of idolatry from their critique of social injustices.

In another letter, written in 1895, Gounelle reflected on the meaning of conversion, in an attempt to

> deepen the idea of *conversion* from a social perspective. Individual conversion more and more seems to me to always be the conversion of a *living being* who, on the day of its second birth, abandons its egotism, or its pretension to be a self-sufficient, "complete whole," and who reclaims the true understanding of *humanity*, its authentic place in the whole, its role as a worker in society, as a servant of his brothers, as a person who is saved and who in turn becomes savior, as a redeemed person who becomes a redeemer of others. Here individual conversion is essentially a social conversion, since at the end of the day it is only useful to the Species. Converting for oneself is not to convert, for one remains self-centered. There is no turning here, one remains attached to oneself, despite all the purely verbal theology one adopts and utters.[35]

Nick was not insensitive to such reflections. Like Gounelle, and in great part under Gounelle's influence, he wished to pay close attention to the social dimension of the Christian message. Far from being exclusively interested in what Protestant authors had to say on the social implications of the Gospel, the two friends were reading prominent Roman-Catholic

---

34. "Il n'y a plus qu'une suprême ressource, celle des prophétiques ministères dont il faut, après 27 siècles, rouvrir l'ère." Gounelle, "Réforme sociale," 34.

35. "J'ai pu lire, réfléchir pendant ces journées de repos forcé, j'ai un peu creusé l'idée de *conversion* au point de vue social. La conversion individuelle me parait [sic] toujours plus la conversion d'un *organe* qui, le jour de sa seconde naissance, se dépouille de son égoïsme c'est-à-dire de la prétention à être 'un tout complet,' se suffisant à lui-même, et qui reprend la vraie notion de *l'humanité*, sa vraie place dans l'ensemble, la place d'ouvrier social, de serviteur de ses frères, de sauvé qui devient par là-même sauveur, de racheté qui devient rédempteur des autres. . . Cette conversion *individuelle* est essentiellement *une conversion sociale* puisqu'elle n'est en somme utile qu'à l'Espèce. Se convertir pour soi, ce n'est pas se convertir, ce n'est que rester *égoïste*; ce n'est pas se retourner, c'est rester attaché à soi, en dépit de toute la théologie purement verbale que l'on adopte et que l'on débite." Quoted in Martin, *Élie Gounelle*, 33. Gounelle develops these points in "La conversion et la question sociale," 245–67.

authors such as Père Alphonse Gratry (1805–72), Lamennais (1782–1854) and Lacordaire (1802–61).[36] All of these influences led the two men to take part, in July 1890 and in October 1891, in the third and fourth general assemblies of the *Association protestante pour l'étude pratique des questions sociales* (APEQS), in Montbéliard (1890) and Marseille (1891). In 1891 they were among 154 participants.[37]

The APEQS was the first, and the most important, nationwide association of social Christians in French Protestantism. It had been founded in 1887 by pastor Louis Gouth (1853–1920) and was presided over by Tommy Fallot (1844–1904), the pioneer of the "Christianisme social" among French Protestants.[38] Its vice-president was Charles Gide (1847–1932), a well-known professor of political economy at the University of Montpellier. Gide was a leading advocate of new forms of economic cooperation. He had founded a group of social Christians called the "école de Nîmes" and had published several influential works on the concept and reality of "solidarity." He was a regular contributor to the journal of the movement, the *Revue de théologie pratique et d'homilétique*, edited since 1887 in Vals-les-Bains by pastor Gédéon Chastand (the journal was renamed *Revue du Christianisme pratique* in 1889, and became the *Revue du Christianisme social* in 1896).

How did Gounelle and Nick become involved in this movement? We know that Paul Minault urged Gounelle to read the paper Fallot had delivered at the second general assembly of the APEQS in Lyon (November 1889).[39]

The movement Henri Nick and his friend Élie Gounelle joined in 1890 had a history. Before we proceed, it may be useful to retrace some

---

36. Gounelle mentions these thinkers in "Pourquoi sommes-nous chrétiens sociaux?" in *Travaux du congrès de Paris*, 119.

37. Nick and Gounelle are already listed as members in the acts of the third general asembly (Montbéliard, July 14–16, 1890). But they are not yet listed among the "membres actifs" in *Association protestante* (1889), 25–26, and they were not present at the second general assembly, in Lyon (November 11–13, 1889). See *Travaux de la deuxième assemblée générale*, 10; *Travaux de la troisième assemblée*, 196; *Travaux du congrès de Marseille*, 202–3.

38. Gounelle calls Fallot "l'âme, le chef, l'inspirateur du mouvement." Gounelle, "Pourquoi sommes-nous chrétiens sociaux?" In *Travaux du congrès de Paris* (1908), 123.

39. "Je débutais alors à Alais dans le ministère, et c'est le regretté *Paul Minault*—encore un nom que nous devons souligner—qui me fit lire, en l'accompagnant de ses commentaires enthousiastes, le beau rapport de Lyon. Ce style nouveau, humain, débordant de vie, faisait bouillonner nos âmes." Gounelle, "Pourquoi sommes-nous chrétiens sociaux?" In *Travaux du congrès de Paris* (1908), 123–24.

of its key moments, since the French version of the Social Gospel is relatively unknown.

TOMMY FALLOT AND THE ORIGINS OF THE "CHRISTIANISME SOCIAL" IN FRENCH PROTESTANTISM[40]

The roots of the French Protestant movement known as "le Christianisme social" arguably are found in Alsace, in a rural county called Le Ban de la Roche, known for its textile industry and agriculture. This is the county where pastor and manufacturer Jean-Frédéric Oberlin (1740–1826), on the basis of a deep sense of Christian philanthropy, sought to improve the living conditions of the local population, especially the workers. Gounelle called him the "true precursor of social Christianity in France."[41] Oberlin's work was prolonged by his successor Daniel Legrand (1783–1859).[42] The founder of the "Christianisme social," Tommy Fallot, was Daniel Legrand's grandson.[43] He was raised in Le Ban de la Roche, where he later began his pastoral ministry. Shaped by Oberlin and Legrand's legacy as well as by his uncle, pastor Christophe Dieterlen (1818–75), who was a regular visitor of the revival movement led by the German Pietist pastor Johann Christoph Blumhardt (1805–80) in his parish of Möttlingen (southern Germany), Fallot went on to study theology in Strasbourg and to become a vicar in Wildersbach, a small parish in the county of Ban de la Roche.[44]

Fallot's Pietist leanings are unmistakable: he could date his "conversion" (October 22, 1865), which took place during a stay in Elberfeld (Wuppertal), a town with deep Pietist roots. At the time, he was reading

---

40. On the origins of the "Christianisme social," see for instance Baubérot, "Aspects," 605–41.

41. Gounelle, "Pourquoi sommes-nous chrétiens sociaux?" In *Travaux du congrès de Paris*, 114. In these pages Gounelle gives a short but interesting survey of the roots of social Christianity internationally.

42. On Daniel Legrand, who had spent several weeks in the home of Friedrich Schleiermacher in Berlin in 1816 and who knew other important Protestant figures of his time, such as August Tholuck, Alexandre Vinet, and Adolphe Monod, see Monnier, *Daniel Le Grand*; Weiss, *Daniel Le Grand*; more recently: Chalmel, "Jean-Luc et Daniel Legrand."

43. Fallot's father, Louis, had married Legrand's daughter Louise-Émilie.

44. Boegner, *La vie et la pensée de T. Fallot*, vol. 2, 34. For the importance of supernatural events of deliverance in Dieterlen's theology, see Dieterlen, *Étude sur la religion de la Bible* (Paris, 1863).

Johann Christoph Blumhardt's meditations.[45] Almost ten years later, in his parish of Wildersbach, he underwent another "réveil" during the winter of 1874-75. While in Paris in 1872, he had met several times the leader of the Holiness movement, Robert Pearsall Smith (1827-99), and he greatly admired the evangelist Dwight L. Moody (1833-99).[46]

Fallot's Pietism went hand in hand with a deep-seated concern for social matters. On August 2, 1872, he completed his theological studies by defending a bachelor thesis on "Les Pauvres et l'Évangile" ("The Poor and the Gospel") in which he lamented the neglect, by the Church, of the poor and the manual laborer.[47] Soon after his "conversion," on March 7, 1866, he wrote to his friend Gabriel Monod: "Several hundred thousand people live in the region of Wuppertal, where I reside, and there are factories everywhere. The misery which characterizes the proletariat is extreme, and unfortunately—it is sad to say—few among the many Christians who live here understand that there is an immense amount of work, of truly Christian work, to be done."[48] This sensitivity to the plight of the workers was revived in Fallot's next parish, the "Chapelle du Nord" in Paris, an independent Reformed-evangelical parish where Théodore Monod (1836-1921) called him to be his successor (Christophe Dieterlen, Fallot's uncle, had ministered the parish in the last year of his life, starting in 1874). The "Chapelle du Nord" was affiliated with the *Union des Églises évangéliques de France*.

Fallot arrived in Paris in the spring of 1876 to begin his ministry at the "Chapelle du Nord," where he remained until 1889. From October 13 to December 22, 1878, he preached a series of eleven sermons on the "Our

---

45. Boegner, *La vie et la pensée de T. Fallot*, vol. 1, 206-10. The book of meditations is the *Sammlung von Morgen-Andachten, nach Losungen und Lehrtexten der Brüdergemeinde, gehalten zu Bad Boll von Pfarrer Blumhardt* (Stuttgart, 1865).

46. Boegner, *La vie*, vol. 2, 30-31.

47. Boegner, *La vie*, vol. 1, 346. Fallot, *Les pauvres et l'Évangile*. Fallot concludes his study, which thoroughly essentializes and generalizes what "the" poor is like, by writing (42-43): "L'Église [. . .] a singulièrement négligé sa mission à l'égard des pauvres. [. . .] Que ne peut-elle comprendre, quand il en est temps encore, l'œuvre admirable qui lui est proposée! [. . .] Qu'elle se décide enfin à considérer ces multitudes dont l'aspect seul suffisait pour remplir de compassion le cœur du Sauveur! Qu'elle abandonne ces alliances avantageuses selon le monde, stériles quant à la cause de Dieu, pour se donner tout entière à ceux auxquels Jésus-Christ s'est donné sans réserve."

48. "Le Wuppertal, où je demeure, compte quelques centaines de mille âmes, et partout fabriques sur fabriques. La misère qu'engendre le prolétariat y est au comble, et malheureusement,—c'est un triste aveu à faire, parmi tous les nombreux chrétiens qui vivent ici, un petit nombre seulement a compris qu'il y avait là une œuvre immense et complètement chrétienne à entreprendre." Boegner, *La vie*, vol. 1, 225.

Father" that represented "a decisive moment of his ministry" and that, according to his biographer Marc Boegner, "inaugurated the preaching of social Christianity within French Protestantism."[49] Fallot was making the following argument: "Socialism has drawn a good deal of its program from the Gospel. It seeks to build society on the pillars of justice, something the Gospel seeks to do as well. In that regard, a condemnation of socialism would represent a condemnation of the Gospel and the prophets."[50] A storm of indignation followed from people who resented Fallot's way of drawing parallels between socialism and the Jewish–Christian tradition. Fallot was on the verge of submitting his resignation. In the end, rather than resigning, he turned his attention in the following decade to various matters that were not strictly ecclesiastical in nature, particularly women's rights. He became the general secretary of the *Ligue française pour le relèvement de la moralité publique*, an association he founded in July 1883. This pioneering work led him to collaborate with the early feminist Josephine Butler (1828–1906) and to give talks all over France to large audiences on topics such as "la femme esclave" (i.e., women enslaved by prostitution).[51] Toward the end of the 1880s Fallot returned to a more ecclesiastically centered ministry, giving lectures on "the advent of social Christianity," in which he stated: "Social Christianity is Christianity applied to communities of people as well as individuals, it is the Gospel as it becomes a salvation for all and in all realms of life. [. . .] If you wish, call this social Christianity the idea of the Kingdom of God on earth."[52]

Fallot's goal was not to banish individualistic expressions of piety from French Protestantism, but rather to broaden its scope and to make sure Christians did not ignore the practical, social consequences of their

---

49. "[. . .] une série de onze prédications sur l'Oraison dominicale, qui marquent un moment décisif de son ministère et inaugurent la prédication du christianisme social dans le protestantisme français." Boegner, *La vie*, vol. 2, 78.

50. "Le socialisme a emprunté à l'Évangile une bonne partie de son programme. Il veut constituer la société sur les bases de la justice; l'Évangile le veut aussi; à cet égard, blâmer le socialisme serait condamner l'Évangile et les prophètes." Sermon from October 27, 1878, quoted in Boegner, *La vie*, vol. 2, 80.

51. On Fallot's work in defense of the rights of women, see Rochefort, "Abolitionist Struggle," 179–94.

52. "Le christianisme social, c'est le christianisme appliqué aux peuples comme aux individus, c'est l'Évangile devenant un salut pour tous et dans tous les domaines. [. . .] Appelez, si vous voulez, ce christianisme social l'idée du Royaume de Dieu sur terre." Conference from February-March 1888, quoted in Boegner, *La vie*, vol. 2, 161. In January 1902, Fallot wrote to fellow pastor Maurice Hirsch: "[. . .] je me suis précipité d'une façon excessive dans les luttes sociale." Boegner, *La vie*, vol. 2, 365.

faith. At the end of the 19th century, Fallot clarified his understanding of Christianity's future:

> A social Christianity is going to succeed the era of individualistic Christianity, which shaped my generation. It will be filled with toils and struggles, but perhaps also with blessings. [...] When I say that individualistic Christianity belongs to the past, I am only judging a theory. I am in no way condemning *individual* Christianity, for that form of Christianity is a fact, present at all times and all places, and if it were to disappear, Christianity would no longer exist. Individualist Christianity was absolutely correct to emphasize conversion and the personal character of piety. The new creature is the only seed from which the new world can germinate. The excellent men to whom we owe the reawakening of life in our Churches were not wrong in what they did. Their only error was perhaps to think that they had completed the work and that their successors would only have to follow in their footsteps. Such illusions are common among powerful generations. [...] Social Christianity has a better understanding of the role of collectivities; it sheds light, for the first time, on the considerable impact of the surroundings ["le milieu"] on personal development. It gives back its importance—an importance which should never have been lost—to the biblical notion of the kingdom of God. It proclaims, to put it succinctly, the good news of divine and human solidarity, which it unearths from the very depths of saint Paul's doctrine, thus helping to complete the practical and social translation, which had been latent since the Reformation, of justification by faith.[53]

---

53. "À la période du *christianisme individualiste* qui a façonné les hommes de ma génération, va succéder celle du *christianisme social*; elle sera grosse de labeurs et de luttes, mais peut-être aussi de bénédictions. [...] En disant que le christianisme individualiste appartient au passé, je vise une théorie, je n'ai nullement en vue le christianisme *individuel*. Celui-ci est un fait; il est de tous les temps, de tous les lieux, et s'il venait à disparaître, il n'y aurait plus de christianisme du tout. Le christianisme individualiste a eu mille fois raison de mettre l'accent sur la conversion et sur le caractère personnel de la piété. La nouvelle créature est l'unique semence d'où puisse germer le nouveau monde. Les hommes excellents auxquels nous sommes redevables du réveil de la vie dans nos Églises ne se sont pas trompés en faisant ce qu'ils ont fait. Leur seule erreur a peut-être été de croire que l'œuvre était achevée et que leurs successeurs n'auraient plus qu'à marcher sur leurs traces. Chaque génération puissante se fait volontiers de semblables illusions. Le christianisme social ne contredit pas le christianisme individualiste, il implique simplement une conception plus large du plan divin: l'Évangile réglant la vie des sociétés aussi bien que celle des individus. Le christianisme social comprend mieux le rôle des collectivités; il met en lumière, pour la première fois, l'influence considérable du milieu sur le développement des individus; il rend à la notion biblique

That was the program, which would be rehearsed again and again by Fallot's most prominent successors in the movement in the 20th century. The "Christianisme social" was not opposed to individualistic piety, but sought to complement and thoroughly revise it by broadening its scope in order to include concerns about society. These are the ideas Gounelle and Nick were discovering around 1890. Ironically, as Gounelle and Nick were joining the movement, Fallot was withdrawing from many of his responsibilites in it, due to his poor health.[54]

But Fallot had paved the way for a new approach to the pastoral ministry in Protestant Churches. As early as 1878, Tommy Fallot began to host weekly student meetings and to organize several "groupes d'aide fraternelle et d'études sociales" in the industrial neighborhoods ("faubourgs") near the center of Paris.[55] He founded a "Société d'Aide fraternelle et d'études sociales" in 1882.[56] Since his arrival in Paris in April 1876, Fallot was collaborating with Robert Whitaker McAll (1822–93), an English clergyman, a Congregationalist who, in 1872, had moved with his wife to Belleville—a neighborhood he had visited a year earlier—to start an

---

du royaume de Dieu l'importance qu'elle n'eût jamais dû perdre, et proclame, pour tout dire d'un seul mot, la bonne nouvelle de la solidarité divine et humaine, qu'il fait jaillir des profondeurs mêmes de la doctrine de saint Paul, fournissant ainsi à la justification par la foi la traduction pratique et sociale, qu'elle réclamait en vain depuis la Réformation." Fallot, *Pour aider*, 8.

54. There is some mystery surrounding this crisis, which happened in June 1891, and other reasons might have been involved. In 1926, Gounelle wrote: "[. . .] avec Minault, Neel et L. Comte, j'ai toujours pensé que la maladie justifiait la retraite de Fallot, mais qu'il y avait quelque chose de morbide et de prophétique, à la fois dans certaines conceptions catastrophiques qui l'amenaient à rompre partiellement au moins et pour ce qui le concernait, avec les méthodes de la Ligue, et à ne plus croire 'qu'à des possibilités individuelles.' Ce retour à un individualisme mystique et profond par un pessimisme qui semble la rançon de douze ans de campagnes et de luttes forcenées, ne saurait étonner personne aujourd'hui. Mais ceux que Fallot avait entraînés se plaignaient. 'Fallot nous lâche, après nous avoir lancés' disaient Comte, Minault et d'autres. . ." "Le Pasteur Louis Comte," 610. Fallot "crut devoir revenir à une spécialisation plus systématique du pastorat et aux méthodes de l'ancienne Église, sans cesser pourtant d'être très solidariste et très chrétien social [. . .]." (642). But Fallot's close friend and collaborator Louis Comte had a different perspective: in an article from 1904, Comte disagreed with those who thought Fallot betrayed the ideals of the movement after 1893. He writes: "[. . .] on s'est plu à opposer le pasteur d'Aouste au pasteur de la chapelle du Nord; on a eu tort. Je n'ai rien lu de Fallot m'indiquant qu'il ait regretté ce qu'il avait fait et l'esprit dans lequel il l'avait fait." "T. Fallot," *L'Avant-Garde* 6, nr. 94 (Oct. 15, 1904) 93.

55. Boegner, *La vie*, vol. 2, 148.

56. Gounelle, *Le Mouvement des Fraternités*, 91.

evangelistic mission among French workers.[57] The choice of Belleville was not a coincidence: a working class and left-leaning neighborhood, it had been the site, in the spring of 1871, of bloodbaths as government troops crushed the revolutionary socialist administration of the capital at the end of the workers' uprising known as the Paris Commune.

There are numerous parallels between McAll's fast growing mission—thirty-five halls in and around Paris, sixty-five in the rest of the country, by 1885[58]—and Fallot's vision, including an interest in mission among the workers, a deep concern for alcohol abuse, for women enslaved by prostitution. And so, for several years, until the summer of 1881, when he had to withdraw because of poor health, Fallot was the secretary of the McAll committee in Paris and the director of the McAll "hall" in La Villette, a neighborhood adjacent to Belleville.[59]

There was, however, a significant difference between McAll's and Fallot's visions: unlike McAll, Fallot did not necessarily intend to convert the workers away from their socialist views! He believed in a basic compatibility between a certain form of socialism (one that refuses violence and materialism) and Christianity. More and more French pastors agreed with Fallot, and so the burgeoning "Christianisme social" was able to consolidate itself through a new association, the *Association protestante pour l'étude pratique des questions sociales* (APEQS), which held its first congress in Nîmes on October 17–18, 1888. As we saw, a few years later, Gounelle and Nick became members of the Association and were thus in contact with all of the pioneers of the "Christianisme social," who were surely delighted to encounter freshly graduated, enthusiastic seminary students who were supportive of their cause.

---

57. On December 7, 1882, the McAll Mission became the *Mission Populaire Évangélique de France (Mission McAll)*. See Morley, *La Mission Populaire*, 1993 and Roussel, "R. W. McAll," 390.

58. *Evangelistic Mission in France, Known as the McAll Mission. Thirteenth Annual Report, for 1884* (Edinburgh: Lorimer & Gillies, 1885) 14.

59. "Rev. Mr. Newell, in the Twelfth Annual Report of the Mission, says of the station at La Villette, 'It was sadly run down. Pastor Fallot, who had been so signally blessed at this station, was obliged to relinquish it in the summer of 1881. [. . .] The attendance has dwindled. Last March we found but thirty at the Sabbath-evening service. La Villette is the valley which receives the material and moral slums of Belleville and Montmartre, and is one of the worst quarters of Paris." *AMR* 2, nr. 2–3 (April–July 1884) 34–35. Fallot's successor, William W. Newell, Jr., was one of the leaders of the Mission in France. For Fallot's position as secretary, see Elizabeth McAll, *La vie et l'œuvre de Robert-W. Mac-All*, 303. Before working at the hall of La Villette, Fallot directed the hall on the boulevard d'Ornano. He worked at La Villette for four to five years (Mours, *Un siècle d'évangélisation*, vol. 2, 53–54).

FROM THE CÉVENNES TO NORTHERN FRANCE

Henri Nick may have been an early participant in the annual meetings of the APEQS—he may even have become one of the trustees ("assesseurs") of the Association around 1902—but it would be a mistake to think that his interest in social questions overshadowed his revivalist tendencies.[60] During his years in Mialet (1890–97), and indeed until the end of his life, Nick was first and foremost an evangelist. But in his view there necessarily was a correlation, never an incompatibility, between his evangelistic ministry and the ideals of the "Christianisme social." His lasting friendship with Élie Gounelle, as well as Gounelle's deep admiration for Nick's ministry, are a testament to the fact that Nick was not simply a traditional evangelist. He belonged to the "Christianisme social," a multifaceted movement in which concerns for evangelization were far from marginal, as can be seen from the subtitle of one of the movement's most prominent journals: *L'Avant-Garde. Journal exclusivement consacré aux questions d'évangélisation.*[61] There is good reason to think, as I have already

---

60. Nick is listed as one of the "assesseurs" for the first time in *Travaux du congrès de Roubaix* (Paris: 1902) 202. He is listed in the subsequent years as well. There was a total of about 30 "assesseurs" or trustees, who probably assisted the "comité directeur," which consisted of Tommy Fallot (honorary president), Édouard de Boyve (president), Charles Gide and Louis Comte (vice-presidents).

61. This original subtitle, used since the very first issue (October 15, 1899), was modified several times: with the 19th issue (October 15, 1902) it became "Organe des chrétiens sociaux de langue française." With the 22nd issue (March 15, 1903) it was changed one last time to: "Journal d'évangélisation, organe des chrétiens sociaux de langue française." *L'Avant-Garde* ceased to be published in 1911. Jean Baubérot is probably right to think that the choice of the word "exclusivement," in the original subtitle, was meant to signal to the readers that the journal would not take part in ecclesiastical (partisan) debates. Cf. Baubérot, *Un christianisme profane?*, 38–40 and 141, where he writes: "Dès qu'elle commence à paraître, *l'Avant-Garde* se donne comme raison d'être 'l'évangélisation des masses ouvrières.'" In 1931, Gounelle wrote about the beginnings of the "Fraternités": "Or nous ne concevions pas une action sociale protestante en dehors de l'évangélisation. . ." *RCS* 44 (1931) 117. See also his call in *RCS* 46 (1933) 6: "*Pas de Réveil religieux sans Christianisme social. Pas de Christianisme social sans Réveil religieux.*" In 1911, Gounelle declared: "Pour un chrétien social, la question de l'Évangélisation n'est pas seulement une question sociale, c'est le fond même de la question sociale." Gounelle, *Le Mouvement des Fraternités*, 9. Baubérot sees five trends within the "Christianisme social": a moralist one (represented by Édouard de Boyve), a social-reformist one (Charles Gide), a socializing one ("socialisant"; Gounelle), an idealist-socialist one (Paul Passy), and an anarchist-communist one (Henri Tricot). Nick belonged to the first and the third trends, it seems to me, with a sensitivity for the fourth. But perhaps a sixth trend is missing from Baubérot's list, especially given the subtitle of *L'Avant-Garde*: the evangelistic trend. "Le christianisme social français de 1882 à 1940," 61.

Revivalism and Social Christianity

suggested, that Gounelle was instrumental in broadening Nick's views on conversion and revivalism. Gounelle was thinking and writing about the meaning of "conversion" not just in a Pietistic and individual sense, but in a social sense as well.

Nick himself wrote, in an undated letter to Gounelle, that their friendship was "one of the greatest joys, one of the greatest privileges in my life."[62] Gounelle sent similar expressions of deep friendship to Nick. And because they both believed that friendship not only allows but requires honesty, at times Gounelle wrote fairly harsh things to Nick:

> In your case, change is good and even, allow a friend to say it to you, *necessary*. You are profound where your soul gives itself; but it can easily be *narrow* and without adequate *breadth*. When one has such tendencies, the passion for salvation risks degenerating into views like those of the Salvation Army. Similarly, if the passion for social salvation gripped you, it would lead you to socialism, perhaps even to anarchy! Your conscience and your reason have often saved you from excesses, but it could be that a change of environment would bring a salutary regeneration... or, at least, it would complement your views. Forgive me for writing that to you. The one criticizing you, without having the right to do so, is a pitiless friend full of awful flaws![63]

Gounelle was urging Nick to consider a change of scenery. It would help Nick overcome his somewhat narrow revivalist tendencies. Gounelle was not disinterested when writing his letter. His ministry among the youth of Alès had borne fruit, but, perhaps because of his success, his relations with his senior colleagues were difficult. And so when an opportunity came

---

62. "Quoi qu'il en soit, je crois qu'en bon ami il vaut mieux constater les petites fissures d'une amitié que je considère comme une des plus grandes joies, et des plus grands privilèges de ma vie, pour y porter aussitôt remède." Nick regularly left his letters undated (in one of his letters to Nick, Wilfred Monod congratulates him for dating a letter). This one seems to have been written in 1895.

63. "Pour toi, le changement est bon et même, permets à un ami de te le dire, *nécessaire*. Tu es profond là où ton âme se donne; mais elle est facilement *étroite* et *sans étendue* suffisante. La passion du salut dégénère en salutisme, quand on a cette disposition d'esprit; de même que, si elle te prenait, la passion du salut social aboutirait chez toi au socialisme, voire à l'anarchie! Ta conscience et ta raison t'ont souvent sauvé des excès, mais peut-être un changement de milieu amènera-t-il une salutaire régénération... ou, du moins complètera-t-il tes conceptions. Excuse-moi de te dire cela. C'est un ami impitoyable et plein d'affreux défauts qui te critique sans en avoir le droit!" Letter to Nick, March 7, 1897. Three days later, Nick thanked Gounelle for his "criticisms, which are always so friendly and true" ("Merci de tes bons conseils d'ami que je trouve toujours si justes, et de tes critiques si amicales et vraies.")

to relocate, he seized it. In 1896, Gounelle moved to the city of Roubaix, in the northern department of Pas-de-Calais, next to the Belgian border. Paul Minault, who had declined the offer to work there, had suggested the names of Wilfred Monod and Élie Gounelle.[64] Gounelle accepted the call and, very quickly, began to work on bringing Nick to northern France. The parish of Lille, only six miles away from Roubaix, was looking for a pastor. Gounelle did everything he could to convince Aquilas Quiévreux, one of the pastors in Lille, to contact Henri Nick. On December 31, 1896, Gounelle wrote to Nick:

> One day or another, you will have to come next to me, as a collaborator. I have said many things about you to *Quiévreux*, who is looking for an *auxiliary pastor*; the position is for a fighter, for an evangelist, it is a modest position but it can become more important because of the immensity of the task. Minault was contacted, and we are urging him to come, to *make this act of decision and dedication*! If he does not accept, it is *you* who will be called. Quiévreux is almost set on this, and I have kept pushing for it.[65]

Nick may have had a certain narrowness about him, but his dedication to the work of evangelization and his interest in moral and social issues were exactly what was needed in Lille, according to Gounelle. After months of hesitation, convinced that he needed to first find a successor for his parish of Mialet before accepting Quiévreux's call, Nick finally accepted, in early May 1897. Gounelle and Quiévreux were ecstatic.[66] The two friends, who had studied together in Montauban and then worked in

---

64. Letters from Paul Minault to Gounelle, November 28, 1895 and December 23, 1895. On Dec. 23, 1895, Minault wrote: "En donnant à M. Ernest Monod mon refus définitif, je lui ai dit 'Permettez-moi de vous indiquer comme hommes qui pourraient, à mon avis, convenir à Roubaix, MM. Wilfred Monod et *Élie Gounelle*, celui-ci [est] un de mes meilleurs amis [. . .]—puis un petit éloge court mais bien senti, si je me souviens bien. J'ai tout de suite eu la conviction que c'était vous ou Wilfred Monod qu'il faudrait là-bas. Mais je vous croyais *enraciné* à Alais et je vous indiquais à M. Ernest Monod sans grand espoir qu'un appel à Roubaix puisse vous déraciner."

65. "Il faudra que tu viennes un jour ou l'autre auprès de moi, comme collaborateur. J'ai beaucoup causé de toi à *Quiévreux* qui cherche *un pasteur auxiliaire pour Lille*; c'est un poste de combat, d'évangéliste, poste modeste mais qui peut devenir à cause du champ immense un poste d'honneur. On a pensé à Minault, et nous le pressons de venir, de *faire cet acte de décision et de dévouement*! S'il n'accepte pas, c'est *toi* que l'on appellera. Quiévreux y est à peu près décidé, et j'ai beaucoup poussé à la roue pour cela."

66. "Je suis très heureux, plus que je ne *sais* l'exprimer. Un bon ami comme toi près de nous!" Letter to Nick, May 11, 1895.

neighboring parishes in the Cévennes, were once again about to collaborate, this time in a very different context, and in a new type of ministry, the legitimacy of which would quickly be much debated within French Protestantism.

Fallot was observing all of that attentively. He sensed that Gounelle and Nick would or could prolong his work. On March 12, 1893, after visiting Gounelle in Alès, Fallot wrote to his friend Paul Minault: "For the time being, I count on you, Gounelle and Nick. Let us not enlarge the circle too quickly."[67] Three days earlier, Nick replied to a letter from Gounelle: "I am very happy to find out that you have received a visit from the great Fallot, who is one of our two or three apostles. I rejoice in your joy, and I will be very happy, believe me, to meet with him and the social-Christians in Crest. Really, he has the heart of a Christian socialist. You can rest assured that I will take advantage of the invitation, which by the way he himself has forwarded to me."[68] Fallot was placing high hope in Gounelle and Nick. These hopes were about to be fulfilled.

THE "FOYER DU PEUPLE" IN FIVES

Henri Nick joined Aquilas Quiévreux in Lille at the end of September 1897. One of his responsibilities was evangelistic work in the workers' neighborhood of Fives, in Lille.[69] From the small rural hamlet of Mialet, and its largely Protestant population of one thousand, to the urban neighborhood of Fives, with its 25,000 inhabitants, most of them Catholics, the change in scenery was impressive.[70] It was the beginning of a long "battle," as Gounelle put it several days before Nick's inaugural sermon in Lille:

---

67. "Pour le moment je compte sur vous, Gounelle et Nick. N'augmentons pas le cercle trop vite." Boegner, *La vie*, vol. 2, 240.

68. "Je suis très heureux d'apprendre que tu as reçu la visite du grand Fallot, qui est un de nos deux ou trois apôtres. Je me réjouis de ta joie et serai te peux le croire bien heureux de me rencontrer avec lui, et les amis socialo-chrétiens à Crest. Décidément il a un cœur de socialiste chrétien. Tu peux bien penser que je profiterai de l'invitation qu'il m'a d'ailleurs lui-même transmise." The letter in which Gounelle wrote to Nick about Fallot's visit appears to be lost.

69. "À Fives l'œuvre populaire, malgré quelques bons éléments, est comme entièrement à réorganiser. Du fait, Henry a le travail d'évangélisation de Fives en sus de tous les services de Lille qu'il se partage régulièrement avec ces messieurs, sauf les catéchumènes réservés à M. Ollier." Letter from Hélène Nick to her friends in Le Vigan, October 2, 1897.

70. The number of inhabitants in Fives is mentioned in Nusslé, "In Northern France," 22.

The Meanings of Conversion—Henri Nick

"We have embarked on a holy war, unfortunately with weak means. But God uses foolish and vile things in order to confound the strong ones! I ask the *divine Power* for you, so that you may communicate it to the souls, the many souls who will surely come to hear you."[71]

Henri Nick did not waste any time. In October of 1897, with the support of the McAll Mission, he opened a small hall that he called "Bonne Nouvelle," in Fives, right next to a very noisy bar, which later compelled him to find a new location. On May 4, 1898, he founded with Gounelle a local "Société amicale d'études morales et sociales," which soon comprised sixty members. The members of the "Société" heard lectures by experts such as Charles Gide and other scholars.[72] As the ministry was growing, through many personal visits, the distribution of Bibles, tracts and leaflets ("colportage"[73]), and regular meetings of various kinds, a barrack was built in Fives. Inaugurated on June 9, 1901, it was named "Foyer du Peuple" ("the People's Home"). A much bigger and sturdier building, again with funding from the McAll Mission, was inaugurated on November 29, 1903.[74] Its main hall could accommodate six hundred people, and at major events and celebrations more than one thousand people could (and did) attend.[75] At the inauguration, Élie Gounelle and other "chrétiens sociaux" delivered speeches in front of a packed hall.[76] With the "Solidarités" Quiévreux and Gounelle had founded, respectively in Lille (June 19, 1898) and Roubaix (November 6, 1898), they had provided the blueprint for Nick's "Foyer du Peuple": a building in which people of all ages could attend religious meetings, talks on religious, moral, and social questions, training sessions, etc.[77]

71. "Nous avons entrepris une guerre sainte, hélas! avec de faibles moyens. Mais Dieu se sert de choses folles et viles pour confondre les fortes! Je demande la *Puissance divine* pour toi, afin que tu la communique aux âmes, certainement nombreuses, qui viendront t'entendre." Letter to Henri Nick, November 19, 1897.

72. Gounelle, "Une Mission chrétienne-sociale," 203–4.

73. In 1911, Gounelle wrote: "Notre ami Nick, à Fives, est encore plus colporteur que pasteur, ce qui n'est pas peu dire." *Le Mouvement des Fraternités*, 31 n. 1.

74. See the booklet Henri Roser began to write, and which was completed and published by several of Nick's collaborators and friends: *Monsieur Nick*, 2.

75. Report by Henri Nick, quoted in Mours, *Un siècle d'évangélisation*, vol. 2, 168.

76. "On Sunday, the twenty-ninth of November, at four o'clock, this hall was crowded. Friends from Roubaix had come over to show their sympathy. Hearty and appropriate addresses were given by Messrs. Quiévreux, Gounelle, Boissonnas, and others, and the singing was excellent, several pieces being sung by choirs of young people and children." Louis Sautter, "Lille-Fives. Inauguration of the 'Foyer du Peuple,'" *AMR* 22, nr. 1 (Feb. 1904) 23.

77. For the dates of these foundations, see "Rapport de M. Quiévreux sur les

Revivalism and Social Christianity

The task at hand, in Roubaix and Fives-Lille, was overwhelming. The workers had to endure exhausting work hours (up to 14 hours a day, for children too), seven days a week. Other major problems included unsanitary living quarters, rampant alcoholism, and prostitution. One of the steps Gounelle took was the creation, with Quiévreux, of a "Ligue contre l'immoralité publique et privée," also known as "l'Étoile blanche." Its first congress, which stands out from other similar events because of its inclusion of women, was held in Roubaix in July of 1899.[78] In addition, as early as 1903, Nick and Gounelle were organizing holiday camps ("colonies de vacances") so that children could get a break from the urban environment and breathe fresh air during several weeks.[79]

What was a typical week like at the "Foyer du Peuple"? In a report from 1900, Henri Nick gives a detailed description, worth quoting at length:

> If we compare the present with the past we cannot but thank God for His goodness to us. Two years ago the work dragged out its miserable existence in a low and damp room, only separated from a public-house by a badly-made wooden partition. The noise of conversation, of drinking songs, and of dancing, was a source of endless annoyance to both speakers and listeners. These were very few in number, finding neither comfort nor quiet. Today in our large and well-ventilated hall we have often more than 200 people. Formerly we had mostly no men, now we have as many men as women, sometimes more. The number of auditors, however, varies greatly, sometimes from 250 it has fallen to 70, or even 60, but a few visits in the district, a lantern lecture, and they come back again. The year which is just over is noteworthy to us by reason of the help which has come to the Mission here by an increase in the number of workers; by the inauguration of mothers' meetings, of temperance soirees, and by real progress in our schools and temperance work. In July the Mission was able to give us the help of a bible-woman—Mlle Cyboulle. She has started at Fives and at Wazemmes mothers'

Solidarités," *Travaux du congrès de Nîmes*, 43.

78. Gounelle, "Le premier congrès de 'L'Étoile blanche,'" 289–94.

79. "Un petit Comité libre de vacances, fondé par l'Association des souscripteurs en faveur des colonies de vacances, et dirigé actuellement par le Dr. Carrière, professeur à la Faculté de Lille, le Pasteur Nick (61, rue de Bouvines, Fives-Lille), et le Pasteur Gounelle, à Roubaix (39, rue des Arts), fonctionne depuis 1903. Placement familial à Illy, dans les Ardennes et la Thiérache, pendant 20 jours. En 1903, 22 colons; en 1904, 28 colons. Prix de revient: 2 fr 20 par jour et par enfant." Eugène Planet, "Les colonies de vacances pour enfants chétifs et pauvres," *La Réforme sociale* 25 (1905) 156.

meetings. She has given much attention to the sewing meeting for little girls, to the meetings for young women, and has put into order the library, of which she has sole charge. [. . .] Mr Vallée, a student of science, has also helped us. He is in request for temperance work, for the Y.M.C.A., for schools, singing, lantern lectures, meetings, visits, and, in spite of his studies, he finds time for all. [. . .] We have also the help of some of the school mistresses; and even some workmen, who are on night duty, give up an hour of rest to come and help in our Thursday School. At the schools we have a crowd of noisy, untidy children, but so interesting! The numbers have increased, and kept up well ever since Christmas. We have from 150 to 200. We endeavour to make them learn long passages of the Bible, and the visits show us how they profit by our teaching. One child, whose parents are unbelievers, tells his mother "all he hears at school"; he refuses to drink beer "because they say at school that it is better to drink water." He calls the school "my dear school." [. . .] Children who have signed the pledge have refused the beer that is given at the school canteen, and, not knowing exactly how to explain themselves, have preferred being punished by the master to taking some. The temperance meetings give us much pleasure. Besides the temperance meeting of the third Sunday in the month, we have, on the first Sunday, a temperance fête, which is always a great success. A professor at the Medical College helps us regularly. Converted young women see to the musical portion of the entertainment. The other day I was touched when I saw there, surrounded by their families and freed from their besetting sins, so many reformed drunkards. I saw twenty or more such cases, and asked myself where they would be without Dr. Legrain's League and the Croix Bleue—for certain among them the temperance pledge has been the means of drawing them to Christ. The reputation of temperance folk which we obtain is amusing. Catholic or unbelieving women send for us to beg us to cure their husbands. "I should like to join the Protestants," said one, "because I hear that those who join it do not drink any more." Or another, just the contrary: "I like the priests better, because at least they let one drink in their religion." We have catechism twice a-week, and have twenty or so boys and girls attending regularly. Our Monday evangelistic meetings continue. We should like more conversions. "Ah!" certain ones, formerly unbelievers, can reply to the mockeries of their factory companions, "I am saved; I know you would be more happy if you believed; I *know* it, for I was like you." Young men show by their changed life the reality of their faith. But all those who come into our hall should be surrounded by an atmosphere of living faith and Christian love, our prayers should lead them to Christ the Saviour, and the lift of Christ should be shown forth in our life. What we have to fear is that those who do not reach conversion should forsake the Gospel and return to their former sins, and that others should be satisfied with a formal religion without feeling or sacrifice. May God breathe His quickening spirit upon us, and, since He has already blessed us in extending all the branches of our work, may He give us, during our new year of work, many conversions, lasting and sincere, so that our little beginning here may become a truly apostolic and victorious church of the people. [. . .] What we now need is a larger hall, on the ground-floor, in the very centre of Fives. Then our work, upheld by Christ, and well organised, will be able to go ceaselessly forward. May God put into the hearts of His children the determination to raise at Fives a centre of light, of temperance, of morality, of Christian life, a very beacon light of salvation. Servants of God, how long will ye be blind? See ye not that the fields are already white unto the harvest?[80]

Henri Nick's report is interesting in many respects (not just because we find out school children were served beer at the cafeteria and were punished if they refused to drink it!). The importance of the fight against alcoholism and other moral issues is obvious, as is conversion to Christ, the ultimate goal of his ministry in Fives, which compels us to ask the following question: Can this evangelistic ministry really be said to be part of the "Christianisme social"? Judging from the many debates around 1900, even among people affiliated with the McAll mission, concerning the "Solidarités" and their leaders, sometimes known as "les Solidaristes," the newness of the "Solidarités" cannot be mistaken: these new halls were the sites of a number of activities and events unheard of in the McAll stations and in the more traditional evangelistic practices.[81] A different approach, which included a strong social component embedded within the more traditional evangelistic ministry, had given rise to a different kind of ministry among the workers, one that did not hide its sympathies with

---

80. Henri Nick, report in *The McAll Mission in France (Mission Populaire Évangélique de France). Twenty-Eighth Annual Report, 1899–1900*, Paris, Office of the Mission, 1900, 35–37.

81. At the forefront of the wave of criticism of the Solidarités and Foyer du Peuple was the conservative ecclesiastical journal *Le Christianisme au XIXe siècle*. Jean Baubérot refers to G. Roussiez, "Solidarité et Solidarisme," *Le Christianisme au XIXe siècle* (March 30, 1900).

socialist ideals.⁸² The response from the workers had been nothing short of amazing. In many ways, Nick's work in Fives was in perfect continuity with Fallot's insights as well as Élie Gounelle's and the entire social Christian movement's orientation toward private *and* social conversion, private *and* social morality. Gounelle's entire project revolved around the idea that desire for religious awakening of the soul and desire for social reform, far from being incompatible, are correlated and condition each other.⁸³ For him, social reform was not simply a means to an end (individual conversion), but was an end in itself. So was individual conversion. To lose sight either of the more traditional Pietistic dimension or of the social concerns of Fallot, Gounelle, or Nick, is to miss the specificity of their endeavour.⁸⁴

There was in fact no lack of social concern at the "Foyer du Peuple," although at times it may look that way. In a report for the year 1902, Nick mentions the circle of men who meet every other week to study religious, moral, and social matters.⁸⁵ Nick invited Alfred de Meuron (1857–1928), a well-known social Christian from Geneva who, like Fallot, had collaborated with Josephine Butler. De Meuron spoke to the people of Fives on "The Cowardice of the Stronger Sex and the Servitude of Woman."⁸⁶ The

---

82. In his yearly report for 1901, Henri Nick alluded, in a footnote, to his position concerning socialism: "It is not socialism that I would criticise, but atheism falsely called social. The working man is discouraged, one said lately: 'I was a revolutionary atheist. I saw that it was all rubbish, I burnt up all their pamphlets. I want to join you.'" Report about Fives-Lille, in *The McAll Mission in France. Thirtieth Annual Report, 1901–1902*, 34.

83. "Y aurait-il incompatibilité entre ces deux aspirations? Nous ne pouvons, nous ne voulons pas le croire." "La conversion et la question sociale," 248.

84. And yet Jean Baubérot's comments are well-founded: "D'une manière générale, les luttes du mouvement contre l'industrie pornographique, la prostitution, l'alcoolisme et pour les droits de la femme auraient pu constituer une partie du combat socialiste si elles avaient été effectuées par des bases plus globalement politiques. Mais il semble que les chrétiens sociaux n'aient effectué des analyses politiques qu'à partir de motivations morales. [. . .] la lutte antialcoolique n'était pas menée à un niveau suffisamment structurel [. . .]." "Aspects," 639. In Gounelle and Nick's writing, one sees, at times, social concerns described as means to an end (conversion). Elsewhere, however, social concerns as such are treated as an end, not as means. One cannot say that they were consistent on this.

85. "Dans notre local se réunit tous les quinze jours un cercle d'homme [sic] pour l'étude des questions religieuses, morales et sociales. Ce cercle nous donne aussi des encouragements." Nick, report to the Société chrétienne du Nord for the year 1902, 4; SHPF, Société chrétienne du Nord, OO2Y7/XXVIII (file: Fives-Lille).

86. "[. . .] we have lectures for the moral education of the people. Thus, M. de Meuron, the well-known Christian, Deputy to the Grand Council of Geneva, very readily responded to our request to give a lecture to the men on 'The Cowardice of

Revivalism and Social Christianity

inclusion of such issues was making a number of donors uneasy.[87] The general director of the McAll Mission in France, Charles E. Greig, had to reassure some of the supporters of the McAll Mission: the buildings of the "Solidarités" did not belong to the McAll Mission, which only contributed a portion of the ministry in Roubaix and Fives-Lille.[88] Within French

---

the Stronger Sex and the Servitude of Women.' Similar lectures on moral and scientific subjects have been arranged for during the course of the year with great success." Henri Nick's annual report for Fives-Lille, in *The McAll Mission in France. Thirty-third Annual Report for 1904–1905*, 62.

87. See Greig's annual report: "Another form of organisation, of a more modern type, adopted already in several branches of the McAll mission, likes to be known under the name of *Solidarity*, or *People's Palace*. Roubaix and Fives-Lille have realised most completely this type of development; St. Quentin tries to follow suit; Limoges and St. Yrieux have already done the same, on a somewhat smaller scale it is true; [. . .] It is no business of mine here to determine which of these programmes answers best to the task which the McAll Mission has been called to accomplish in France." *The McAll Mission in France. Thirty-second Annual Report for 1903–1904*, 11–2.

88. Charles E. Greig alludes to these debates in several of his annual reports on the McAll Mission's work in France. "Attention has been drawn in former reports to what is known in France as the 'Solidarité' movement, and some criticism has been given of the methods adopted by its promoters. Briefly it may be said that it is an attempt to show the modern workman that Christians take a cordial interest in all that his conscience and his intellect recommend as of value, and that the importance they attach to things spiritual and religious does not preclude them from sharing in his enthusiasm for other ideals." *The McAll Mission in France. Twenty-Ninth Annual Report, 1900–1901*, 16–17. In a previous report, Greig had written: "There has been a great deal said and written this year in the French religious papers about 'Solidarités" and 'Solidaristes.' [. . .] The whole debate turns not even upon the relative value of temperance meetings and Gospel services, but upon the order in which they are to be introduced to the people, and upon the amount of space to be allowed to the one and to the other. The 'Solidaristes' would begin by giving lectures on literary and moral subjects, and by founding leagues against forms of sin universally reprobated, and they think that it is only when the confidence of the public has been gained by a display of sympathy in such directions, that they are likely to listen without prejudice to the preaching of the Gospel. Their critics hold that they exaggerate the difficulty of obtaining the ear of the people to the simple presentation of the Gospel, and that the majority of those who have been won to join a 'Ligue Antialcoolique,' or to listen to a lecture on Molière, without being told that there is something better than either, will never go further, and will not come in to listen to the preaching of the Gospel." *The McAll Mission in France. Twenty-Eighth Annual Report, 1899–1900*, 12. Greig seeks to reassure his readers: "The building does not belong to the McAll Mission, which gave only a small contribution towards its construction, and it houses various forms of activity over which the Mission exercises no control. Its sole concern is the preaching of the Gospel, carried on by means of evangelistic meetings, schools, mothers' meetings, &c., and it is this that justifies the apportioning of a certain annual sum to the work in Fives. Our share in the responsibility of the work carried on in the 'Solidarité' of Roubaix is of the same kind." *The McAll Mission in France. Thirty-second Annual Report*

Protestantism, too, several authoritative voices were critical of this new form of ministry.[89]

For all their interest in social issues, Gounelle and Nick did not view themselves as "Marxists" (as some social Christians did). Their rejection of materialistic atheism was unambiguous. Nick's colleague in Lille, Aquilas Quiévreux, clarified their stance in the *Revue du Christianisme social*: "The social Christians wish to be, first of all, disciples of Jesus Christ in their individual lives as well as in their social action. What separates them from mere socialists—I mean the pure disciples of Marx—is the fact that the ultimate basis of their project of social reform is the person's conversion, the inner transformation through personal contact with Christ and through the direct action of the Spirit."[90] In other words, many of the French social Christians, for all their commitment to social action, were not ready to abandon the call to conversion, in its traditional, individualistic sense. What they sought to do was to *revise* the traditional understanding by paying attention to the social dimension.[91] Their goal was to overcome any

---

for 1903-1904, 19-20. See, finally, Louis Sautter's reassuring words in *AMR* 22, nr. 1 (Feb. 1904), 23: "I was able to assure myself, and I am glad to say this to the readers of the *Quarterly Record*, that while our friends at Lille and at Roubaix are preoccupied with the social and moral questions that present themselves in their work, and that while they seek by all the means at their disposal to gain the confidence of the working people and to interest themselves in all that concerns the daily life of the people, this in no wise means that the first place in their preaching, in their convictions, and in their activity in its many forms, is not given to the presentation of the Gospel of the Lord Jesus, simply and faithfully."

89. See Gounelle, "Réponse à quelques bienveillantes critiques de M. Maury sur l'œuvre des Solidarités du Nord." *L'Avant-Garde* (June 15, 1901). For a critical article, see G. Roussiez, "Solidarité et Solidarisme." *Le Christianisme au XXe siècle* (March 30, 1900). In a letter he sent to *La Vie nouvelle* 15, nr. 14 (April 7, 1900), 109-10, Gounelle responds to various articles published in *Le Christianisme au XIXe siècle*: "[...] nous dédaignons de réfuter des attaques qui tournent à l'insulte. Si notre œuvre est de Dieu—et elle est de Dieu—elle subsistera. Sinon, elle tombera d'elle-même. [...] Ah! la triste besogne que vous faites délibérément, sciemment, après pourparlers dans votre comité,—je suis informé, allez!—dans votre journal!" They were "deliberately trying, having discussed the matter among its principal editors, to discredit the social Christian action." Cf. Baubérot, "L'Évangélisation protestante," 166-68. The entire movement was (gently) critized by the theologian Eugène Ménégoz as forgetting the "good news," i.e., the nearness of God's kingdom: "Un côté faible," 161-78.

90. "Les chrétiens-sociaux veulent être, avant tout, des disciples de Jésus-Christ dans leur vie individuelle comme dans leur action sociale. Ce qui les séparera toujours des simples socialistes, je veux dire des purs disciples de Marx, c'est qu'à la base ultime de leur plan de réformes sociales, ils mettent la conversion individuelle, la transformation intérieure par le contact personnel avec le Christ et par l'action directe de son Esprit." Quiévreux, "Le congrès de Rouen," 488.

91. Gounelle was very clear: "[...] le Christianisme social n'est pas le Christianisme

opposition between religious revival and social reform, for they believed the two should go hand in hand. Just as conversion is necessary for a future social renewal, social evils must be addressed if a genuine revival is to become possible—Fallot was particularly sensitive to that second aspect, which he called "le droit au salut," the "right to salvation," a right that is trampled when one's milieu is unhealthy and oppressive, for one is then unable to dedicate time to one's faith—or to even consider religious matters. These two goals, the reform of social surroundings and the religious revival, must be pursued simultaneously. But ultimately the spiritual dimension is at the root of everything, even for a thinker like Gounelle: "We will truly be *social people* only if we are *spiritual people*. Our socialism is first and foremost *mystical*."[92] Or: "To save the soul, that is the essential aspect, the goal of any economic and social reform worthy of its name."[93] Henri Nick would have emphatically agreed with these claims. In 1952, soon after Gounelle's death, in an article commemorating Gounelle's pioneering efforts in Roubaix, Nick suggested that social Christians—himself included, and probably Gounelle too—tended at times to lose sight of the "new birth," given by God's grace, as the "sole foundation of one's Christian life." Working on changing social conditions was an important and legitimate concern, for the sake of the people living in dire conditions, but also for the sake of making conversion possible.[94]

---

traditionnel, *plus quelque chose*. Il est [. . .] une vraie révolution spirituelle et sociale dans le Christianisme lui-même." Gounelle, "Pourquoi sommes-nous chrétiens sociaux?" *Travaux du congrès de Paris* (1908), 195–96.

92. "Nous ne serons vraiment *des hommes sociaux*, que si nous sommes des *hommes spirituels*. Notre socialisme est d'abord et avant tout *mystique*." "La repentance sociale," 348. See Gounelle, "Réforme sociale et réveil religieux," 22–51.

93. "Sauver l'âme, voilà le point essentiel, le but de toute réforme économique et sociale digne de ce nom." Gounelle, "Une mission chrétienne-sociale," 208. See also: "Il ne faut pas craindre d'affirmer, avec une insistance d'autant plus vive qu'on a parfois essayé de mettre ce fait en doute: l'œuvre spirituelle a été et reste au centre de nos Solidarités. Partout, toujours, absolument. Nos foyers du peuple sont avant tout des foyers de l'âme. [. . .] Telle est pour nous la bonne méthode, celle qui va du spirituel au social." *Le Mouvement des Fraternités*, 26. One could add many more similar quotes. See for instance Gounelle, "Pourquoi sommes-nous chrétiens sociaux?" In *Travaux du congrès de Paris* (1908), 196.

94. "Il [Gounelle] n'a certes pas été suivi jusqu'au bout, mais le christianisme social va-t-il jusqu'au bout dans l'obéissance à Jésus-Christ? [. . .] les œuvres évangéliques ne sont pas assez concentrées autour de la nouvelle naissance, seul fondement de la vie chrétienne individuelle, et de la réunion de prière, source d'énergie pour toute communauté qui veut durer. Certes, Élie Gounelle, méthodiste impénitent, était d'accord avec ces principes, mais qui oserait prétendre ne pas céder un jour ou l'autre à la tentation et au péril mortel de compter sur l'effort humain plus que sur la grâce de Dieu,

That is precisely what Henri Nick was trying to do in Fives-Lille, and he was quickly establishing himself as a leader of the "Solidarité" movement and as one of the most well-known social-evangelists in France.[95] And so Nick's ministry among the workers of northern France was an important part of the movement. In 1909, Gounelle listed Nick as one of the chief collaborators in the "Christianisme social."[96] Together, the leaders of the "Solidarités" and "Foyers du Peuple" were building "the spiritual Church."[97]

---

et alors le déclin commence. [. . .] Élie Gounelle savait bien que les conditions où se débattent bien des créatures humaines sont si effroyables qu'elles leur rendent la conversion presque impossible. Il fallait donc briser ce cercle infernal. De là son action sociale." Nick, "Le pionnier de Roubaix," 115. Nick makes similar claims in *L'Avant-Garde* 10 (June 15, 1908), 592 when answering a questionnaire. For Nick, being a Christian means having a social conscience: "Tout chrétien est social." Unfortunately, he adds, too few "social Christians" are practicing what they say. Amusingly, Gounelle comments on Nick's letter in four footnotes.

95. Pastor Samuel Delattre (1856–1939) writes in *AMR* 28, nr. 1 (Feb. 1910), 24–25: "Our friends, Messrs. Nick and Kaltenbach, are doing a blessed work. It is perhaps the best work of evangelization in France."

96. "Voici la liste—encore ouverte!—des principaux *collaborateurs*: MM. R Allier, Henri Anet, Arrousset, Charles Babut, Henry Babut, Blanche de Beaumont, J. Bianquis, Mlle Bidgrain, Marc Boegner, Prof. Henri Bois, De Boyve, L. Comte, G. Chastand, E. Cerisier, Cordey, E. Durand, F. Dürrleman, Dieterlen, J. Dejarnac, Paul Fargues, Prof. G. Fulliquet, E. et L. Ferrière, Ch. Gide, Paul Gounelle, Edmond Gounelle, Elie Gounelle, Louis Gouth, Ch. Grauss, Aug. Holland, Henri Hollard, Roger Hollard, Jézéquel, G. Kaspar, G. Lauga, L. Lafon, E. Ledermann, Paul Monod, Wilfred Monod, A. de Morsier, A. de Meuron, Prof. Maury, Henri Monnier, Hélène de Mülinen, Elie Neel, Henry Nick, Niels, Paul Passy, Paradon, Mme E. Pieczynska, A. Quiévreux, Myriam Reinhardt, E. Roberty, J. Roth, A. Sauzède, Ad. Sibleyras, L. Tarrou, L. Trial, F. Thomas, C. Vallée, Charles Wagner, etc." Gounelle, *RCS* 22 (1909), 4.

97. The program of the congress of social Christians which was supposed to take place in Alès in the fall of 1904, then in the spring 1905 (it never took place), was, besides the new law on the separation of Church and State (Dec. 9, 1905) and the "separation of believers from the churches," the "slow but robust constitution of the spiritual Church through the 'Solidarités,' 'Foyer du peuple,' 'Fraternités,' 'Sociétés d'activités chrétiennes et sociales' and the many other associations which are emerging right now (the "lente mais ferme constitution de l'Église spirituelle par les Solidarités, Foyer du peuple, Fraternités, Sociétés d'activités chrétiennes et sociales et autres associations multiples en germe dans la fermentation actuelle"). Gounelle, *L'Avant-Garde* (April 15, 1904), quoted by Baubérot, "Les évangéliques et la séparation française des Églises et de l'État," in Fath, *Le protestantisme évangélique*, 241 n. 69.

THE ENGLISH BROTHERHOODS' VISIT TO LILLE (1910)

One of the highlights in the life of the "Foyer du Peuple" before the First World War was an event that took place on Pentecost Sunday (May 15), 1910. On that day, the "Foyer du Peuple" invited Keir Hardie (1856–1915), the well-known leader of England's Labour Party and a member of Parliament (1892–95 and 1900–15), but also a former miner (from the age of 10!), a pacifist, a convert to Christianity (1878), to give a presentation to a packed audience in the "Foyer's" main hall. Hardie was not the only guest: he was accompanied by William Ward, the president of the National Council of English Fraternities, who was leading 260 British delegates from the "Pleasant Sunday Afternoon (P.S.A.) Brotherhood of Workingmen," a non-denominational (but very Protestant) movement founded in 1875 by John Blackham (1835–1923), a deacon in the Congregationalist Church. By 1910 the "P.S.A. Brotherhood" boasted 2,000 societies and over 500,000 members. There were 300 societies and 50,000 members in London alone![98] Besides Keir Hardie, other leading figures in the Labour Party, such as Arthur Henderson (1863–1935), the future Nobel Peace Prize laureate, collaborated with the movement. Gounelle was very impressed by it.[99] He was invited to take part in its tenth congress, held in Cardiff in 1909, and used that opportunity to visit several branches.[100] He wrote a piece about the movement in *L'Avant-Garde* and asked Ward to introduce the Brotherhood movement to the French social Christians in the *Revue du Christianisme social*.[101] In his introduction to Ward's article, Gounelle lamented the situation in France: "While our French movement of the *Solidarités*, *Foyers du Peuple* etc. (inaugurated in its clear social Christian form in Roubaix and Lille in 1898) is still being debated—causing its paralysis—and halted due to a lack of men and resources, on the

---

98. And yet William Ward and that movement of "Brotherhood" is almost completely forgotten today.

99. Gounelle included a short historical survey of the movement in *Le Mouvement des Fraternités*, 1911, 49–54. The social Christians from Switzerland were also paying attention: Gounelle mentions (*Le Mouvement des Fraternités*, 1911, 47 n. 1) an article by Rudolf Pestalozzi in *Neue Wege* (July–August 1911).

100. Gounelle, *Le Mouvement des Fraternités*, 43, 50 (n. 1), 53 (n. 1) and 69.

101. Ward, "Les Fraternités," 157–66. Gounelle, "La Fédération des P.S.A. Brotherhoods."

other side of the Channel we see an extraordinary burst of works, associations, urban and rural missions which is almost prodigious."[102]

In the weeks leading up to the English Brotherhoods' visit to Lille, Gounelle advertised the event with enthusiasm in the *Revue du Christianisme social*: since the English Brotherhoods were coming to Lille, why wouldn't the French social Christians meet them in Lille? He invited readers to contact him personally, as he was planning "a social Christian excursion to Lille [. . .] in order to greet England's '*Fraternités*' and to visit the '*Foyer du Peuple*.' This would give us the means to think about how to overcome the misunderstanding which separates the people from the Church and to bridge the gap between the workers and Christ."[103]

Besides Henri Nick and Élie Gounelle, other important figures in the "Christianisme social" were present in Lille on Pentecost day: Paul Passy, a well-known professor at the École des Hautes Études and a militant socialist as well as a Christian, gave a speech and wrote a report in his monthly journal *L'Espoir du Monde*.[104] Pastor Paul Monod, from Lille, wrote a piece about it for the *Revue du Christianisme social*.[105] Two prominent politicians in Lille, Gustave Delory (1857–1925), who in 1896 became its first socialist mayor, and Henri Ghesquières (1863–1918), a socialist "député," participated in the festivities, which ended with the singing of "the Internationale." The tremendously successful day was reported in

---

102. "Tandis que notre mouvement français des *Solidarités*, *Foyers du Peuple*, etc. (inauguré sous sa forme nettement chrétienne-sociale, à Roubaix et à Lille en 1898) est encore discuté, paralysé par là même et arrêté faute d'hommes et de ressources,— chez nos voisins d'Outre-Manche, on assiste à une extraordinaire éclosion d'œuvres, d'associations et de missions urbaines et rurales qui tient presque du prodige." Gounelle, "Introduction" to Ward, "Les 'Fraternités,'" 157. Elsewhere Gounelle deplored the lack of concrete commmitment in France, despite the fact that "social Christianity is in fashion." *Le Mouvement des Fraternités*, 7 and 35.

103. "Nos amis Nick, Kaltenbach, Moll, Monod, préparent la réception. Pouquoi n'irions-nous pas à Lille en nombre, nous aussi?" Gounelle then invites the reader to write "au soussigné qui organisera une excursion chrétienne sociale à Lille [. . .] afin de saluer les 'Fraternités' d'Angleterre, de visiter 'le Foyer du peuple' de Fives, et d'étudier ainsi pratiquement les moyens de faire cesser le malentendu qui sépare le peuple de l'Église et d'associer le prolétariat et le Christ." Gounelle, "Deux Communications sur les Fraternités anglaises." *RCS* 22 (1909), 187–88.

104. *L'Espoir du Monde*, June 1910. In 1908, Paul Passy, who was becoming frustrated with the moderation of the social Christian movement and its leaders (incl. Gounelle and W. Monod), founded with his friend Raoul Biville the "Union des Socialistes chrétiens," which advocated a collectivist and communist society. See Baubérot, "L'évolution," 81–3.

105. "Visite des 'Fraternités' anglaises."

Revivalism and Social Christianity

several European newspapers.[106] Walter Rauschenbusch read about it and mentioned it in his book *Christianizing the Social Order*.[107] A similar encounter, on a smaller scale, took place during Easter the following year in Paris.[108] Far from declining after the separation of Church and State in France (December 1905), the social Christian movement was expanding and making contact with similar movements abroad.[109]

---

106. See the detailed report, by Louise Seymour Houghton (1838–1920), a member of the New York chapter of Leighton Williams' and Rauschenbusch's "Brotherhood of the Kingdom" (founded in 1892), and a key supporter of the McAll mission in the United States, in *AMR* 28, nr. 3 (October 1910), 24–26. She writes: "And to the stupefaction of the bystanders, the pastors of the Reformed Church of Lille and many of their parishioners were in the procession, which was closed by delegates from the various Socialist Unions of the city. United Socialists, English Christians, French Protestants! What could it all mean? [. . .] A few words from Keir Hardie's address must suffice. They were interpreted by M. Paul Passy, Professor in the Sorbonne and head of the French Christian Socialist body: 'The organization which brings us together is bound to no church... We are here in the quality of ambassadors of social democracy, whose King is Jesus Christ... It is the Gospel of Christ and especially the Sermon on the Mount which made me a socialist.' The frantic applause which punctuated the famous orator's utterances showed how his words went home to the hearts of the French people. To discover that they might continue [to be] socialists and still be Christians appeared to drive them almost wild with joy. Let us hope and pray, as 'our' Pastor Nick assuredly does, that this remarkable meeting in 'our' *Foyer du Peuple* may be the means of bringing many of the workingmen of Lille to a new understanding of 'the true liberty,' 'the true equality,' 'the true fraternity,'—to quote the words of one of Dr. McAll's first French hymns." (26) See also Ward, *Brotherhood and Democracy*, 107–20. Ward includes the translation of a long message of gratitude sent to him by Jacques Kaltenbach. Four photos of the mass meeting are included (131).

107. "In May, 1910, about 260 delegates of the English 'Brotherhoods' visited Lille in France and were received by the French trades-unionists and socialists with parades and public meetings. The crowds on the streets did not know what to make of it when they saw the Englishmen marching with the inscriptions: 'We represent 500,000 workmen;' 'We proclaim the Fatherhood of God and the Brotherhood of Man;' 'Jesus Christ leads and inspires us.' What were these men, Christians or socialists? They could not be both. The Frenchmen lost all their bearings when they heard Keir Hardie, the veteran English labor leader and socialist, repudiating clericalism, but glorifying the Gospel and the spirit of Christ, and declaring that it was Christianity which had made a socialist of him." *Christianizing the Social Order*, 109. On p. 105 n. 1, Rauschenbusch mentions "my friend Élie Gounelle" and recommends his book *Pourquoi sommes-nous chrétiens sociaux?* as "[a] remarkable little book." The correspondance between Gounelle and Rauschenbusch, which unfortunately does not amount to much (Rauschenbusch sends bibliographical references, in one letter), is preserved at the SHPF in Paris.

108. On the 1911 event in Paris (and a previous encounter there, in August 1908, which had been reported in *L'Avant-Garde* of that month, and another one in Belgium in 1909), see Gounelle, *Le Mouvement des Fraternités*, 1911, 54.

109. Somewhat surprisingly, Baubérot sees a decline of the movement after 1905,

THE HINGE—JACQUES KALTENBACH

The organization of the event in Lille had fallen in part on the shoulders of Nick's collaborator, Jacques Kaltenbach. A few months later, in September, Kaltenbach accompanied Henri Nick to London to take part in the 12th congress of the English *Brotherhood*. They both delivered short speeches at the congress, which took place in the Royal Albert Hall.[110]

Kaltenbach is only one of a number of bright young pastors who were influenced by Nick's work among the workers and who decided to assist him in his ministry. Born in 1881, like Nick a graduate of the theological seminary in Montauban, he had spent one year at Harvard University, where he studied with William James. For five consecutive and formative years, from 1907 until 1912, he assisted Nick at the "Foyer du Peuple," before moving on to his own parish, in Saint-Quentin (Picardy, northern France). After five years in Lille, he went on to apply some of Nick's methods in Saint-Quentin. In Fives, Kaltenbach had been appreciated by everyone, Nick wrote in his 1913 report, and on the day of his departure Kaltenbach expressed his "gratitude to God for the signs of his power and love which he had witnessed here."[111] On April 21, 1954, shortly after Henri Nick's death (March 9), he wrote a letter to the director of the "Mission populaire" and expressed his gratitude to the "Mission" for his first experiences as a pastor working with Nick in Fives.[112]

In Saint-Quentin, he was one of the pastors of the Trocmé family, and, as youth pastor, was directly involved in the religious education of André Trocmé. Through pastor Kaltenbach, André Trocmé, without at first having any awareness of it, was in contact with the ideals of Nick, Gounelle and Fallot. But before we turn to André Trocmé, we need to review some developments in the "Christianisme social."

---

in "Aspects," 634.

110. Bois, "La Conférence générale," 724.

111. "'Tous l'aiment' écrit celui-ci [i.e., Henri Nick]. Il [i.e., Jacques Kaltenbach] œuvrera cinq ans à Fives et, au moment de son départ, exprimera sa 'reconnaissance envers Dieu pour les preuves de sa puissance et de son amour dont, dit-il, j'ai été le témoin ici.'" Mours, *Un siècle d'évangélisation*, vol. 2, 169. See also Julia Merle d'Aubigné, "Open-air Work at Fives-Lille," *AMR* 27, nr. 2 (April 1909), 7: "You may like to know some of our band. One of the two pastors generally leads us; tall Mr. Nick, with a curious absent way about him, but with the fiery eloquence of the prophet and the humility of the saint. [. . .] Sometimes it is young pastor Gattenbarb [sic! read: Kaltenbach] who takes the lead; short, precise and methodical, as good as gold and quite up to date, he is respected and loved by all."

112. SHPF (Paris), Mission populaire, Fives, O11Y MPE 13, files 48–49.

DEVELOPMENTS IN THE SOCIAL CHRISTIAN MOVEMENT

The "Christianisme social" was being further institutionalized through a multiplication of events and associations around the time of Keir Hardie's and William Ward's visit to Lille. On June 16, 1910, an international meeting took place in Besançon. Two main delegations were present, from France and Switzerland, and there were a few representants from England, Italy and Belgium. Hermann Kutter (1863-1931) and Leonhard Ragaz (1868-1945), the two leading social Christian thinkers in Switzerland, delivered speeches, and a declaration was adopted.[113]

The city of Saint-Quentin was the site of an important event: the constitutive congress, on June 25-26, 1911, of the "Action chrétienne sociale" (ACS), under the leadership of Charles Gide, who became its president, whereas Élie Gounelle was named general secretary. Gounelle used the opportunity of the congress at Saint-Quentin to present a paper on the "movement of the 'Fraternités.'"[114] Henri Nick addressed the project of a French Federation of the "Fraternités" and was elected secretary of the urban "Fraternités."[115] He was by then the leader in the movement, as both Gounelle and Monod had left the "Solidarités" they had founded. Gounelle had left Roubaix in November 1907 in order to become pastor at the Chapelle du Nord in Paris, following in Fallot's footsteps. Freddy Durrleman (1881-1944) succeeded him in Roubaix. Gounelle accepted the position in Paris only after being assured that he would be able to continue to minister among workers. In addition to his parish ministry, he wished to direct the McAll station at La Villette.[116] Monod too had founded a

---

113. The speeches, as well as a report on "la fameuse journée," can be read in *RCS* 23 (1910), nr. 7. Baubérot, *Un christianisme profane?*, 110-15. The "Déclaration de principe" can be read in the *Bulletin de la Fédération des Fraternités Françaises*, nr. 2 (April 1923), 2-3.

114. *Le Mouvement des Fraternités*, 1911.

115. "Il [i.e., Henri Nick] dira tout à l'heure, avec plus d'autorité que moi, ce qu'il pense d'un Mouvement français des Fraternités." Gounelle, *Le Mouvement des Fraternités*, 35. "Congrès de l'Action chrétienne sociale de Saint-Quentin." *RCS* 24 (1911), 623.

116. Henri Merle d'Aubigné, "Notes from the Work in France," *AMR* 25, nr. 4 (Dec. 1907), 8-9: "At Roubaix the situation is also changed. Pastor Élie Gounelle has been called (as has already been said) to the Église du Nord, in Paris, and is succeeded by M. Alfred Dürrleman [. . .]. The promotion was well deserved, but we regret the loss of this young man to the mission, for he has a peculiar gift of speaking to the masses. His place in our mission is not yet filled. In accepting the call of the Eglise du Nord, M. Gounelle made it a condition that he should be free to work among the people in

"Solidarité," in Rouen on March 20, 1900.[117] But he left Rouen in 1907 for Paris. By 1907, Henri Nick was the only one of the three friends from Montauban still at work in a "Solidarité" or "Foyer du Peuple." Astonishingly, he would remain there until his death, in 1954.

Why did Gounelle leave the work done at the "Solidarité" in Roubaix for a more traditional ministry in Paris? Gounelle alluded to his own sense of shortcoming, and indeed failure, at the congress of French social Christians in Saint Quentin in June 1911: "Why would I conceal it? The fact that I was unable to secure the full success of the first *Solidarité* remains the great shadow in my ministry. . . I humble myself for it. The one who has been the most successful on this path is surely our noble and faithful friend Henri Nick. [. . .] it is he who, thanks to God, embodies in the best way the soul of the urban 'Fraternités' and 'Solidarités' [. . .]."[118] Gounelle

---

the laboring quarters, and suggested a connection with the McAll Mission. It will be remembered that it was this pastor, in the youthful beginning of his ministry, who revived from the dead and gave great vigor to our mission in Roubaix. He is an organizer and a brilliant speaker, and will be a great addition to our metropolitan forces." For the date of Gounelle's installation see this interesting note in *AMR* 26, nr. 1 (Feb. 1908), 17: "Pastor Elie Gounelle, whose remarkable work in Roubaix has made him a notable person in McAll circles, was installed over the *Chapelle du Nord*, Paris, on Sunday, November 17th. His installation sermon was from the texts, 'Follow thou me,' and 'Thy kingdom come.' Like a number of the younger French pastors who are active in our Mission, M. Gounelle is an ardent member of the 'Kingdom' movement—a movement the purpose of which is to bring about, here and now, the reign of Jesus Christ on earth by establishing those social as well as religious conditions which are in accord with his life and teachings, and with the teachings of the Old Testament prophets and reformers. As already recorded, M. Gounelle has undertaken the charge of La Villette hall."

117. For this date, see "Rapport de M. Quiévreux sur les Solidarités," *Travaux du congrès de Nîmes*, 1900, 43.

118. "Pourquoi ne le dirai-je pas? C'est la grande ombre de mon ministère de n'avoir pas pu assurer le succès complet de la première Solidarité. . . Et je m'en humilie profondément. Celui qui a le mieux réussi dans cette voie, c'est bien notre noble et fidèle ami Henri Nick. Il dira tout à l'heure, avec plus d'autorité que moi, ce qu'il pense d'un Mouvement français des Fraternités. Mais ce qu'il ne vous dira pas et ce que je veux, moi, vous dire, c'est que c'est lui qui, grâce à Dieu, incarne le mieux l'âme des Fraternités et Solidarités urbaines, comme le vaillant E. Durand celle des Fraternités rurales." *Le Mouvement des Fraternités*, 35. At another congress of the "christianisme social," in November 1928 in Paris, Gounelle made similar comments about Henri Nick, who was not present: "Nous avons regretté l'absence du président des Fraternités françaises, Henry Nick, l'apôtre du *Foyer du Peuple* de Fives-Lille, qui est certainement la plus remarquable, la plus belle de nos Fraternités missionnaires: cela, parce que notre ami y a consacré toute son âme et toute sa vie, sans compter. Nos Fraternités, quel qu'en soit le type,—ecclésiastique, non-confessionnel, missionnaire, ou purement laïque,—sont certainement l'*une des meilleures, peut-être la meilleure réalisation pratique du Christianisme social*." *RCS* 42 (1929), 509–10. And yet, Gounelle added

and Monod left their "Solidarités" as the movement continued to grow: there were six "Solidarités" in France by 1900, thirteen by 1906, and that trend continued until the war.[119] Any "Solidarité" that adhered "to the principles of social Christianity" and that promoted activities related to four of the following seven fields, could join the "Fédération des Solidarités de France": 1. evangelization, 2. temperance, 3. morality, 4. moral education, 5. works of cooperation and fraternal assistance, 6. healthy physical activities or festivities, and 7. works promoting contacts, connection or even fusion between social classes.[120]

THE PARIS CONGRESS ON EVANGELIZATION

Henri Nick was a speaker at a number of congresses related to the social Christian movement, to the "Solidarités," and to the topic of evangelization. In May 1913, he was invited to give a keynote address in Paris on the evangelization of the workers at a six-day Protestant "Congrès général de l'évangélisation," which gathered many of the leaders of French Protestantism.[121] Jacques Kaltenbach, then pastor in Saint-Quentin, also gave a talk. Participants from England, Switzerland and Canada travelled to the "temple du Saint-Esprit" in Paris. In his address, Nick declared that each worker "should feel at ease among us, should realize that his ideal will be respected if he enters our halls. It must be clear, once and for all, that one

---

(517–8): "Ni le Mouvement des Brotherhoods, si admirable qu'ait été cette poussée mystique, ni notre Mouvement français, n'ont eu *assez de force de pensée sociale*. [. . .] l'expérience des Fraternités reste, sinon totalement satisfaisante, du moins concluante. Elles sont le premier essai d'évangélisation chrétienne sociale vraiment pensée, méthodique et organisée."

119. The list in 1906: Alès, Belleville, Clermont, Fives, Montmartre, Neuillac, Orthez, Lille, Roubaix, Rouen, Saint-Denis, Sainte-Foy, Sauveterre-de-Béarn. *Travaux du congrès de Genève* (1906), 167.

120. The two conditions were: "A. *L'adhésion aux principes du Christianisme social, mais sans aucune formule obligatoire* [. . .]. B. *La preuve que l'œuvre à fédérer possède au moins quatre des sept catégories d'activité suivantes*": 1. évangélisation, 2. tempérance, 3. moralité, 4. éducation morale, 5. œuvres de mutualité, de coopération ou d'aide fraternelle, 6. organisation normale du plaisir (exercices physiques, fêtes populaires, etc.), 7. œuvres de contact et de rapprochement, voire de fusion des classes." *Travaux du congrès de Genève*, 1906, 167.

121. Samuel Mours gives a list of some of these personalities: besides Nick and Gounelle, there were Ruben Saillens and Eugène Réveillaud, two early and faithful collaborators of the McAll Mission, Wilfred Monod, Marc Boegner, Freddy Durrleman and Philémon Vincent. Mours, *Un siècle d'évangélisation*, vol. 2, 150. See the imposing volume of the proceedings from the conference: *Congrès de l'Évangélisation*.

can be a faithful disciple of Jesus Christ and a fervent union member or a supporter of the workers' party."[122] He added: "Until the day when there no longer is social classes, and laboring toward their elimination, on what basis could Christ's disciples oppose the peaceful demands of a class which cries out because it is oppressed and dispossessed?"[123] Nick went on to criticize the Christians who support the armament race.[124] He denounced alcoholism as an epidemic that renders people "unable to sustain not just a family but also any political, social and religious life."[125] In all of this, Nick's identity as an evangelist with social Christian tendencies is unmistakable.

HENRI NICK AND WORLD WAR I

Right from the beginning of the war, Henri Nick started working as a military chaplain. His wife Hélène moved to Marseille with their six children. Tragically, she died there, after a long illness, on January 4, 1917.[126] Their

122. "[. . .] *il est essentiel* que l'ouvrier *se sente à l'aise chez nous*, qu'il se rende compte que *son idéal sera respecté s'il vient dans nos locaux*. Il faut qu'il soit entendu, une fois pour toutes, que l'on *peut être un fidèle disciple* de Jésus-Christ et *un fervent syndicaliste ou membre du parti ouvrier*." Nick, "Difficultés spéciales," 23. Sébastien Fath, it seems to me, does not quite do justice to Henri Nick's social interpretation of the Christian faith when he describes him as "une des figures de proue de la tendance évangélique au sein des Églises réformées." Fath, *Du ghetto au réseau*, 42. This is not so much incorrect as incomplete: it does not render justice to the complex figure Henri Nick was. Still, one wonders why Nick is not better known if Fath is correct (as I think he is) when stating (144, n. 47): "Henri Nick est le pasteur évangéliste réformé le plus fameux du XXe siècle."

123. "En attendant le jour où il n'y aura plus de classes et en travaillant à leur disparition, de quel droit le disciple du Christ s'opposerait-il aux pacifiques revendications d'une classe qui se plaint d'être opprimée et dépouillée?" *Congrès de l'Évangélisation*, 22.

124. "Il est aussi difficile à un ouvrier de comprendre que l'on peut être chrétien et partisan de l'accroissement des armements, qu'il ne l'est à un bourgeois de saisir que l'on est partisan sinon de la haine, du moins de la revendication de classe." *Congrès de l'Évangélisation*, 22.

125. "Nous nous bornons à mentionner les ravages de l'*alcoolisme*, qui abaisse le niveau d'une population et la rend incapable de toute vie familiale, politique, sociale aussi bien que religieuse." *Congrès de l'Evangélisation*, 21–22.

126. See her letter from Marseille, Oct. 14, 1914, in *AMR* 33, nr. 1 (Jan. 1915), 15–17, and especially its final words (17): "Our only consolation in the midst of so many tears and sorrows and blood is that we hope to 'make war on war'—once for all. Oh, that His kingdom would come on this earth! Our hearts long that it may come soon." See also Henri Nick's brief note to the people in Boston who supported the Foyer du Peuple, in *AMR* 32, nr. 4 (Nov. 1914), 25. See also his text "On the Front," in vol. 33, nr. 2 (March 1915), 12–15, and the announcement of her death in a letter from

elder daughter Jeanne became responsible for her siblings, and after the war she became the director of the "Unions chrétiennes de jeunes filles" for northern France. Henri Nick voluntarily served as military chaplain in the Ambulance Corps of the First Army Corps, from August 2, 1914, until November 11, 1918.[127] He spent many weeks in the trenches of some of the worst battles, including Douaumont, Péronne, and Verdun. He was wounded in the Somme in 1916 and received several honorary citations, the "Croix de guerre" and the "Légion d'honneur," for his courage and for taking eight German soldiers—who had surrendered—as prisoners.[128] A fellow chaplain, a Roman Catholic, became his friend: the young abbé Achille Liénart (1884–1973) did not forget Henri Nick when he became

---

January 1917 to the Boston Auxiliary of the McAll Mission, which had been supporting the Foyer du Peuple for many years: *AMR* 35, nr. 2 (March 1917), 5.

127. These two dates are found on the cover page of H. Nick's booklet *Pendant la guerre*, 1920.

128. Henri Nick was cited four times for his bravery on the front, rescuing wounded soldiers, "exposing himself without so much as observing that he was in danger." *AMR* 35, nr. 4 (Nov. 1917), 1. "Pastor Nick has received the honor of being named in Army Orders in the following terms: 'Protestant Chaplain Nick. Has given proof, since the beginning of the war, of an unfailing spirit of devotion and self-sacrifice. Has followed close upon the troops during every action, and has asked leave to remain constantly in proximity to the first line of trenches, which he enters without a thought of the danger, as soon as the bombardment gives evidence that there will be wounded in need of his ministrations." *AMR* 34, nr. 2 (March 1916) 1. Nick was then cited a second time: "Chaplain Nick, Protestant chaplain. During the night of February 29th, 1916, and the day of March 2nd, under a most violent bombardment, disdainful of danger, gave proof of devotion literally without limit in his care of the wounded, in looking after their transportation and comforting them by his example and his words of encouragement." Vol. 34, nr. 4 (Nov. 1916), 20. The officer who sent the notice to H. Nick's family added: "Danger seemed to mean so little to him that I have seen him carry water for the cooks who did not dare to risk their lives to bring it themselves. [. . .] No one in the first Army Corps remained in the thick of it at Verdun so long as he and no one exposed himself so constantly." Vol. 34, nr. 4 (Nov. 1916), 20. For the mention of Verdun see idem, vol. 34, nr. 3 (May 1916), 2; for the mention of the Croix de Guerre and the Légion d'honneur, see vol. 35, nr. 1 (Jan. 1917), 5. In a letter from September 5, 1916, Henri Nick describes his wound and the episode with the eight German soldiers: "A ball from a mitrailleuse has shattered the two bones of my left wrist, and I shall doubtless be laid aside for three months. The day after my wound I realized the danger to which I had been exposed when I found the pocket book I carry over my left breast riddled from end to end by another ball. [. . .] A few days before this, the Legion of Honor was asked for me and was given me because, finding myself face to face with eight Germans, I made them prisoners and utilized them to carry in the wounded from a difficult position. I am not proud of this. I have no reason to be, for now every one does his duty, and those who do it in obscurity have the more merit. It is a little sad to reap honors where others only find suffering, tears, and sorrow! Those who deserve honor are those who fall, giving their lives!" Vol. 35, nr. 1 (Jan. 1917), 9.

bishop of Lille in 1929 (and cardinal a year later).[129] Nick and Liénard's friendship confirms the well-known fact that the inevitable proximity between Roman Catholics and Protestants during the war helped many to overcome some of the stereotypes between Christian Churches and thus contributed to the growth of dialogue across divided Churches.

Nick's faithful collaborator Charles Vallée (1875–1941), a professor of sciences in Lille, replaced him at the head of the "Foyer du Peuple" during his four years of service. Shocked, like so many others, by what he had witnessed (according to some estimates 17 million people died during the war, almost half of them civilians), perhaps confirmed by his late wife's cry for peace, soon after the end of the war, Nick was eager to promote the pamphlets published by his colleague Freddy Durrleman on the theme of peace, including "[h]is second book, 'War and Peace According to the Bible' [. . .]. To those who 'do not believe in war,' who are conscientious objectors 'to shedding blood under whatever circumstances,' these books of our former fellow-worker have a message."[130] This mention of those whose conscience "objects" to the killing of human beings is very telling, as will become clear later.

The beginning of the First World War had made it impossible to create an international federation of social Christians. A congress, planned for 1912 in Basel, had to be postponed until the summer of 1914. In an

---

129. "*Monseigneur Achille Liénart* was recently consecrated Bishop in the Church of St. Christophe, of Tourcoing. Among those who filled the Gothic edifice a place had been reserved for pastor Nick. The new Bishop of Lille had shared with pastor Nick the responsibilities of Chaplain of the First Army Corps. At the banquet which followed the ceremony, at the College of the Sacred Heart, *Mgr. Liénart* expressed his gratitude and we cite herewith the account from the *Croix du Nord*: 'How can one ever forget his old comrades of the 201st, his comrades at arms, so many of them tonight in this hall? They cannot all be named, but the name of M. Nick must be cited, M. Nick, the Protestant Chaplain of the Corps, in which he served as my colleague during the war and with whom so many points of evangelical contact were discovered.' This reference to M. Nick includes the following: 'Pastor Nick recalled the bombardment in the sector of Sapigneul. 'Near us,' he said, 'a shell exploded, followed by a cloud of choking gas. I had forgotten my mask and the *Abbé*, though this might mean death to him, offered his mask to me. Not only do I salute our former comrade at the front, but as a Protestant pastor, I salute in the person of the Bishop of Lille the imitator of St. Martin and even more the imitator of our Saviour, Jesus Christ, whose name is Love." *AMR* 47, nr. 3 (May 1929), 5, quoting the newspaper *La Croix du Nord*. This article is also reprinted in *CR* (Jan. 1929), 16. Cardinal Liénart became an important voice in French Catholicism. He presided over Jules Isaac's (1877–1963) *Amitié judéo-chrétienne* and took part in the Second Vatican Council (1962–65).

130. *AMR* 36, nr. 4 (Nov. 1918), 4. Nick already recommends Durrleman's pamphlets in vol. 35, nr. 2 (March 1917), 8–9.

article written shortly before the 1914 conference, Élie Gounelle summarized the goal of the conference: "We are marching toward a new Christian catholicity whose motto is: *to make Christ the king*, and whose program hinges on the following formidable universal duties: the missionary, the social and the pacifist dimensions. [. . .] We ask those who are satisfied with the present order to stay at home: they do not belong at the congress, and their voices would be dissonant in the massive religious protest we must voice, in Christ's name, to Christendom."[131] The international events of that summer (mobilization began in Germany on July 30, in France on August 1st) led to the cancellation of the congress.

As soon as the war was over, however, attempts were made to internationalize the movement. A "World Brotherhood Federation" was founded in London in September 1919, presided by William Ward.[132] This was an opportunity for the French "Solidarités" or "Fraternités" to finally unite. The first attempts, at congresses of the "Solidarités" already in 1900 and 1901, had failed. At the congress of social Christians in Saint-Quentin, in 1911, Gounelle had expressed his wish to see Nick co-preside a French federation.[133] At that congress Nick was elected secretary for urban "Fraternités." Eleven years later, at a congress of French social Christians in Strasbourg (June 25–28, 1922), Nick addressed the participants as president of the "French Federation of the 'Fraternités.'"[134] Gounelle served as honorary president. Fifty institutions, thirty of them in cities, the rest in rural areas, sought to join the French "Federation."[135] A first congress was

---

131. "Nous marchons vers une nouvelle catholicité chrétienne dont la devise est: *Faire Christ roi*, et dont le programme d'action se précise autour de ces formidables tâches universelles: *le devoir missionnaire, le devoir social, le devoir pacifiste.* [. . .] Nous prions ceux qui sont satisfaits de l'ordre social actuel de rester chez eux: leur place n'est pas au Congrès, et leur voix y serait une fausse note dans la formidable protestation religieuse que nous devons, au nom du Christ, faire entendre à la Chrétienté." "Pourquoi irons-nous à Bâle," *RCS* 27, nr. 3 (March 1914) 161 and 163. "Faire Christ roi" ("to make Christ the king") was an expression used by many in those years, including by the Christian Student Federation and the YMCA.

132. Thonger, "Le premier Congrès," 36–37.

133. "Vous vous joindrez à nous pour prier ces deux hommes [i.e. Nick and Émile Durand, the leaders—respectively—of the urban and rural *Fraternités*] de prendre tout à fait à cœur, dans notre Comité, la direction du Mouvement des Fraternités françaises." *Le Mouvement des Fraternités* (1911), 35.

134. Nick's address is included in Gide, et al. *Le Congrès du Christianisme social, tenu à Strasbourg*, 1923.

135. Chastand, "La Conférence Constituante," *RCS* 35 (1922) 521. Chastand lists the criteria for membership, namely agreement with the Besançon declaration promulgated at the international congress of June 1910; activities which fall under at least

organized in Roubaix, on May 5–8, 1923, with 57 delegates and almost 200 local participants from Lille and Roubaix.[136]

What would be on the agenda of this Federation? In a short piece in the second issue of the *Bulletin de la Fédération des Fraternités Françaises*, Nick made it clear that in his opinion the problem of peace was now the most pressing problem confronting the social Christian movement. He gave voice to "certain Christians" who thought the time had come for civil disobedience and conscientious objection, in the footsteps of Christians in the early Church.[137] In the same issue of the *Bulletin*, a list of the topics presented and discussed in the "Cercle d'Étude" of the "Foyer du Peuple" includes: "War and Peace: the Duty of the Christian."[138]

For the sake of peace, Nick was not afraid of alienating the authorities of his own Church. In April 1923, a letter he had sent to the Council of the French Protestant Federation was reprinted in the *Revue du Christianisme social*. In it he protested against the Council's overly cautious and nationalistic response to a call addressed to Christians from all countries by the bishops of Sweden, including Nathan Söderblom, condemning the

---

four of the following fields (523): "Évangélisation; Moralité; Education morale, sociale, religieuse de la jeunesse; Hygiène et Développement physique; Cercles d'études; Mutualité et Coopération."

136. Gounelle, "Le premier Congrès des Fraternités," *RCS* 36 (1923) 406. On the same page Gounelle praises "[n]otre vaillant ami Henry Nick," "son âme apostolique," "ce détachement spécial aux mystiques de sa trempe."

137. "Le problème de la Paix domine toutes les questions actuelles; comme le devoir de l'établir prime tous les devoirs. A quoi bon labourer les champs, planter des arbres pour des hommes condamnés à mort ou en vue de nouvelles générations qui ne verront jamais le jour! [. . .] Désavouons hautement toute politique inhumaine de violence et de haine même pratiquée contre un ennemi dont la mauvaise foi serait avérée et revenons à une politique chrétienne. Des chrétiens partisans du droit de légitime défense pour la sauvegarde de leur dignité morale ou pour la défense des faibles vont plus loin—se refusant à admettre la contrainte de corps et le recours à la violence pour obtenir le recouvrement d'une créance, ils se demandent si l'heure n'a pas sonné de changer de méthode, puisque celle suivie jusqu'ici s'est montrée inefficace, de reprendre les traditions des chrétiens des premiers siècles, de cesser de rendre à César ce qui ne lui est pas dû; de résister à ses exigences illégitimes puiqu'il n'a pas d'empire sur notre raison et notre conscience, de cesser de compromettre à cause de lui leur salut et celui du monde. En inaugurant cette politique nouvelle, fusse au prix de leur sacrifice ils pensent coopérer autant qu'il est en eux à la reconstitution de l'Europe et surtout proclamer, en face de tous les Césars-Etats, la souveraineté de leur Suzerain légitime: Jésus-Christ." Nick, "Guerre et Fraternité," 3.

138. The five topics listed on p. 8 of the *Bulletin de la Fédération des Fraternités Françaises* are: "Divisions Syndicales—L'Interdépendance des nations et pays—Réglementation de la prostitution—L'islamisme[:] à propos des événements actuels—Guerre et Paix: le devoir du chrétien."

military occupation of the Ruhr by French troops. How could the French Protestant authorities not be sensitive to such calls, Nick wrote, especially since these kinds of military occupation "reduce entire populations to unemployment, bitter cold and famine"? "We remain convinced," he continued, "that the supporting and loving spirit of the Gospel is the best antidote to war and the only seed of peace. [. . .] Throughout the world, disciples of the Master, Protestants and Catholics as well as people of all sympathies, are building, untiringly, impartially, and at great cost, a lasting peace. May they be blessed. They lead us to reconciliation and are preparing a fruitful collaboration between peoples."[139] Nick's protest found the support of a good number of French pastors and lay people.

Henri Nick had been sensitive to pacifist themes before the war. But there is no doubt that his years as a military chaplain deeply impacted him and led him to promote work for peace as *the* most urgent task at hand. Significantly, his pacifist orientation was not opposed to the more radical stance of conscientious objectors, whereas the most well-known social Christians in French Protestantism, such as Wilfred Monod and Élie Gounelle, advocated a different kind of pacifism, one focused on international law and friendship.

It would be too much to say that Henri Nick fully embraced a *principled* form of pacifism, one that inevitably leads to conscientious objection, but after the First World War he would be one of the very few Protestant ministers who publicly supported the first wave of conscientious objectors within French Protestantism.

From Tommy Fallot's pioneering work, both in theory and in acts, to Élie Gounelle's attempt to put these ideas into practice in Roubaix and Henri Nick's duplication of his friend's ministry among workers, we have so far examined several important facets of the "Christianisme social." During the First Wold War, a young man in Saint-Quentin, a parishioner of Jacques Kaltenbach (Nick's former collaborator), was discovering the radical message of the Gospel in his own way. He would eventually become involved in the evangelization of northern France, and, like Nick, would seize any opportunity (and create opportunities when they were

139. "[. . .] nous réprouvons des mesures qui, si habiles soient-elles, [. . .] réduisent des populations entières au chômage, au froid et à la famine. [. . .] Nous restons persuadés que l'esprit de support et d'amour de l'Evangile est le meilleur antidote de la guerre et le seul levain de paix. [. . .] Par le monde, des disciples du Maître, protestants et catholiques, et des hommes de toute opinion poursuivent, d'un effort inlassable, avec impartialité, et au prix de sacrifices, l'établissement d'une paix durable. Qu'ils soient bénis. Ils nous acheminent vers la réconciliation et préparent une collaboration féconde entre les peuples." "Autre son de cloche," 348–49.

not there!) to put into practice what inarguably was the single greatest ideal of the "Christianisme social": the ideal of solidarity.

Henri Nick during World War I

Temple (Protestant church) of Saint-Quentin

Part Two

André Trocmé's First Steps in Spiritual and Social Christianity

JACQUES KALTENBACH, PASTOR OF THE TROCMÉ FAMILY

JACQUES KALTENBACH, ONE OF the pastors at the parish of Saint-Quentin (Picardy), where the Trocmé family lived, played a crucial role in André Trocmé's early life, orienting him toward the pastoral ministry, and helping foster a deeper spiritual life and social awareness among the youth in the parish. Kaltenbach also represents a decisive link with the "Christianisme social": for five years (1907–12), Jacques Kaltenbach had been part of the pastoral team at Fives with Henri Nick. In 1912, he became one of the pastors in the large parish of Saint-Quentin.[1]

Jacques Kaltenbach completed his undergraduate studies with a bachelor in the humanities ("ès Lettres") at the University of Paris in 1899, before studying theology at the "Faculté de théologie" in Montauban. He

---

1. Kaltenbach dedicated his book *Le livre qui chante la gloire de Dieu. Études sur les Psaumes*, Strasbourg, Oberlin, 1949, to the parishes where he had served: Fives-Lille (1907–12), Saint-Quentin (1912–18) and Marseille (1918–48) (p. 4). The author(s) of *Monsieur Nick* inaccurately indicate that J. Kaltenbach worked in Fives-Lille from 1905 until 1910 (2).

spent a year of study abroad at Harvard's Graduate School of Arts and Sciences (1903–4) before returning to France in order to complete his studies in Montauban with a thesis, an *Étude psychologique des plus anciens réveils religieux aux États-Unis*, which he defended in December 1905.[2] Studying with William James at Harvard had not been without fruits! It is safe to suspect that James was instrumental in Kaltenbach's decision to study the American revival following a psychological approach, a rather new way of studying religion.[3]

On the basis of his case study of the First and Second Great Awakenings in New England in the 18th and the 19th centuries, Kaltenbach concludes that a significant "socialization of the faith" results from revivals, as they reveal the "need of religious communion between people." In these events "the spiritual treasures are shared."[4] He also notes that youth is "the most favorable age for conversion," the period of life when the most enduring conversions often take place.[5] These sentences help us understand Kaltenbach's interest in ministering to young people. As can be expected, he paid particular attention to the youth group, the "Union chrétienne de jeunes gens" (or simply the "Union"), in the parish. A small booklet he wrote in 1919 on the parish of Saint-Quentin during the war confirms this interest: several pages are devoted to the "Union." They provide a welcome

---

2. A copy of the thesis was sent by Kaltenbach to William James (W. James taught at Harvard from 1872 until 1910). For Kaltenbach's dates at Harvard: *Harvard Alumni Directory. A Catalogue of Men Now Living who have been Enrolled as Students in the University; Including also Officers of Instruction and Administration*, compiled by a committee of the Harvard Alumni Association (Cambridge: Harvard University Press, 1913) 440 and 1616.

3. Kaltenbach writes: "La psychologie religieuse n'en est pas encore, en effet, à l'ère des vastes généralisations. Elle cueille ici et là quelques épis le long du chemin et les lie en gerbes, mais le gros de la moisson est encore debout." *Étude psychologique*, 4.

4. "Il est donc vrai de dire que le réveil au point de vue social est caractérisé surtout par ce trait: le besoin de communion religieuse entre hommes, et que ce besoin est d'autant plus intense que le réveil est plus spontané; le réveil met en commun les trésors spirituels, il opère la socialisation de la foi." Ibid., 46–7.

5. "[. . .] en temps de réveil [. . .] la jeunesse est l'âge le plus favorable à la conversion. [. . .] L'enfance correspond à l'état liquide: elle prend facilement la forme du moule où elle est placée, mais la perd avec une facilité égale; chercher à lui imprimer au cours d'une réunion spéciale un caractère définitif, c'est risquer fort de n'aboutir à aucun résultat, si un instant après elle est replacée dans un milieu tout différent. La jeunesse correspond à l'état malléable; elle est, comme la cire, assez souple pour recevoir une empreinte et assez résistante pour la conserver. Les impressions religieuses s'y gravent avec une profondeur qui les rend ineffaçables. [. . .] Aussi n'est-il pas étonnant que le réveil agisse tout d'abord sur la jeunesse et que le plus grand nombre des conversions durables s'effectuent à cet âge de la vie." Ibid., 52.

confirmation of Trocmé's "Mémoires," which, unlike Kaltenbach's text, were written four to five decades after the facts.

As soon as the war began, regular prayer meetings were organized for the adults, once a week. Fifty to eighty people would meet to hear a meditation on a biblical passage and to pray. After one of the three pastors left Saint-Quentin, it was decided that these meetings would be led alternatively by a pastor and by a lay person. Paul Trocmé (1845–1941), André's father, was the first layman to do so. Eventually, young people began to lead these prayer meetings, for something happened: the "Union," which had barely survived the mobilization, was revived as an informal youth group in the spring of 1915. On June 10, 1915, four young men gathered and decided to invite other comrades to a meeting two weeks later, on June 24. One of the four young men, Arthur Meunier, approached André Trocmé. Paul Trocmé was reluctant to allow his son to join in: the now disbanded "Union" was not particularly known for its devotional practices. But Arthur Meunier, with some help from pastor Kaltenbach, was able to convince André's father that the new group was quite different: their deepest desire, as Kaltenbach puts it, was "to serve God."[6] In August 1915, the young men decide to formally become a "Union chrétienne de jeunes gens," under the leadership of Arthur Meunier (president) and André Delaporte (vice-président). In the first months of 1916, the new group underwent a religious awakening of sorts, after one influential member dedicated himself fully to serving God. The evangelistic fervor of the group became more and more intense. There were forty members as the youth group celebrated its first year, at Pentecost 1916. Only one third came from Protestant families. The "Union" began circulating a small bulletin, titled "The Link" ("Le Lien"). In January of 1917, they decided that the revival should encompass the entire parish. But at the end of the month several members were commanded to assist the Germans in breaking the ice on the streets, and in February some were ordered to leave the city to work in other locations. Finally, in early March 1917 came the general evacuation of Saint-Quentin. What Trocmé and Kaltenbach described as a kind of "religious revival," or as a "kind of resurrection," was cut short.[7]

6. Kaltenbach, *L'Église réformée*, 38 ("un réel désir de servir Dieu"). In his "Mémoires," Trocmé uses the same expression to describe the spirit of the group: they prayed fervently and "tried to serve God."

7. "Six jeunes gens s'étaient mis à prier pour demander à Dieu la transformation de leur vie. Chose remarquable, l'inspiration de ces jeunes se fondait sur une foi totale dans la possibilité de mettre en pratique les absolus: Pureté, amour, vérité, proclamés plus tard par le Réarmement moral. Dieu, affirmaient-ils, devait répondre à leur prière.

André Trocmé's First Steps in Spiritual and Social Christianity

According to his own testimony, it is at the "Union" that André Trocmé learned to express, on his knees, his innermost fears and desires to God. He entered "the wonderful world of religious experience."[8] He was asked to provide a meditation during one of the meetings. These Sunday afternoon meetings at the parish would be some of his first steps on his path toward the pastoral ministry. Decades later, there was no doubt in his mind that the "'Union' at Saint-Quentin" had been "led by the Holy Spirit."[9]

The members of the "Union" did not just pray. They took up the concerns of the Blue Cross and its fight against alcoholism. They visited cafés and bars and tried to win new members there. André Trocmé's father Paul, however, forbid his son to take part in such missionary activities.[10] The young men also organized a discrete meal delivery to some of the Russian prisoners brought to Saint-Quentin by the Germans to build underground fortifications. These civilian prisoners lived in appalling conditions, in an industrial district known as the "faubourg d'Isle," and those who for any reason were no longer able to work risked being shot to death.[11] They were stationed in a former factory which was under the care of a Protestant couple, the Soyeux, who coordinated the distribution of these meals.[12]

Kaltenbach obviously rejoiced in the religious revival of the parish youth. But he was not fond of mere emotional awakenings. Several passages in his thesis indicate that he was not uncritical of the "mouvements

---

Ils étaient libérés de leurs péchés. Un grand enthousiasme régnait parmi eux. On pouvait parler d'un vrai réveil religieux." "Mémoires," 86. Kaltenbach, *L'Église réformée*, 37 ("une sorte de résurrection") and 39 ("véritable réveil spirituel.")

8. "Il me semblait entrer tout droit dans un paradis sur terre. Entraîné peut-être davantage par l'exemple contagieux de mes camarades que par une foi très personnelle, je pénétrai dans le monde merveilleux de l'expérience religieuse. [. . .] Je rentrai chez moi transfiguré: une lumière brillait maintenant autour de moi, un feu brûlait au dedans de moi; Tout était possible, tout avait un sens." "Mémoires," 88.

9. "Poussée par le Saint-Esprit—je n'ai pas peur d'employer ce mot car je crois à la réalité des inspirations que Dieu donne à ceux qui le prient en commun—l'Union de St-Quentin allait de découverte en découverte: Elle découvrit le salutisme, le communisme, la défense de la Personne humaine, et le Pacifisme chrétien, et cela, en l'espace de quelques mois." Ibid., 91.

10. "L'Union allait visiter les cafés et racoler de nouveaux membres chez les plus désespérés. Je ne fus jamais autorisé par Papa à me joindre à ces équipes de salutisme. J'y aurais fait un apprentissage inoubliable qui m'eût beaucoup servi dans mon ministère." Ibid., 92. The "Croix-Bleue" was founded in 1877 in Geneva by pastor Louis-Lucien Rochat.

11. Ibid., 93–94.

12. Kaltenbach, *L'Église réformée*, 40.

de réveil." He wrote: "[...] nowadays more and more people in the United States are of the opinion that the sweet and strong influence of a good religious education has an incomparably deeper effect on children than the fleeting emotions of a revival meeting."[13] Kaltenbach's critique of a certain emotionalism is repeated in the conclusion of a section on the "moral consequences" of the revivals ("les effets moraux du réveil"; 119–26). He praised what he perceived to be a decrease of emotional outbursts as well as an increase in social—or, as Kaltenbach calls it, "moral"—sensitivity in the more recent revivals of the 19th century, especially in Moody's brand of evangelism, which addressed for instance the problem of alcoholism.[14] And so, in the final words of his thesis, he certainly did not condemn revivals, but he also did not take them to be God's

> only means to bring people to himself. If his kingdom at times seems to come with a burst, at other times and in other places it grows in an unnoticeable way. One should not expect the progress of the Church to be always accompanied by the same phenomena, just as one should not expect everyone to convert in the same way. There is the possibility of regular growth for churches, just as there are gradual conversions for individuals; divine intervention is no less disclosed in them than in abrupt conversions and sudden revivals. What matters is not how slow or how sudden things are, but the moral results obtained by them. One does not judge the tree by its shape, but by its fruits.[15]

13. "[...] c'est de nos jours une opinion de plus en plus répandue aux États-Unis que l'influence douce et forte d'une bonne éducation religieuse a sur les enfants un effet incomparablement plus profond que les émotions passagères d'une réunion de réveil." *Étude psychologique*, 57. See also the fourth and fifth theses on 148: "Il est dangereux d'adresser aux enfants des appels trop émouvants. Aucune réunion spéciale ne vaut pour eux une bonne éducation religieuse. [...] Un réveil religieux n'a de valeur que dans la mesure où il est profondément, passionnément moral. S'il est une simple excitation des sentiments il vaudrait mieux qu'il ne se produisît pas."

14. "En résumé on peut dire que dans les réveils américains postérieurs à 1740, si le côté affectif est toujours plus réduit, le côté moral est beaucoup plus grand. C'est là un incontestable progrès." Ibid., 126; Kaltenbach deplores the lack of moral (or social) dimension to the First Great Awakening around 1740 (144).

15. "Il ne faut donc, croyons-nous, ni condamner les réveils, ni les considérer comme l'unique moyen que Dieu emploie pour attirer les hommes à Lui. Si son règne semble parfois venir avec éclat, il est d'autres moments et d'autres lieux où ils progresse d'une façon insensible. On ne peut exiger que les progrès de l'Eglise se révèlent toujours par des manifestations identiques, de même qu'on ne peut attendre que tous les individus se convertissent de la même façon. Il y a pour les églises des progrès réguliers comme il y a chez les individus des conversions graduelles; l'intervention divine ne s'y révèle ni plus ni moins que dans les conversions brusques et les réveils soudains. Ce

Kaltenbach's views, his critique of emotionalism and his emphasis on the moral dimension that should always accompany religious revivals, would prove to be an excellent match with those of Henri Nick, the pastor of the "Foyer du Peuple" in Lille, during the following five years of their collaboration (1907–12). Saint-Quentin, Kaltenbach's first parish as a pastor, was also one of the numerous cities in the North that had a "station" of the McAll Mission (it had been founded by R. W. McAll himself), and Kaltenbach became its director.[16]

Through Kaltenbach, during his years as a student at the "lycée," Trocmé encountered the movement known as "Christianisme social" long before he could name or identify it. It shaped his life even before he found out about the main figures and ideas of the movement. Henri Nick would eventually become a major influence in Trocmé's life, as we will see, as well as in the lives of several other young pastors, and interestingly Trocmé found out only later that his own pastor in Saint-Quentin, Jacques Kaltenbach, had been Henri Nick's close collaborator during five years.[17] Still a schoolboy, Trocmé was shaped for life—through his lessons of catechism and through the new "Union chrétienne de jeunes gens" fostered by Kaltenbach at the parish of Saint-Quentin—by the social Christian movement within French Protestantism.

A DEVOUT REFORMED FAMILY

André Trocmé was born in Saint-Quentin on April 7, 1901, in a rather austere and bourgeois Reformed family. His mother Paula, his father's second wife, was German, the daugher of Johannes Schwerdtmann, a well-known and powerful "Generalsuperintendent" (bishop) in the Lutheran church in Hannover.[18] His father Paul was a wealthy textile factory owner, the vice-president of the local Chamber of commerce, and a pillar in the relatively large Reformed parish of Saint-Quentin (2,500 members in a

---

n'est pas la lenteur ou la soudaineté qui importe, ce sont les résultats moraux obtenus. On ne juge pas l'arbre à sa forme, on le juge à ses fruits." Ibid., 146.

16. *AMR* 37, nr. 1 (Jan. 1919) 14; vol. 38, nr. 3 (May 1920) 4.

17. Trocmé writes: "Je devais apprendre plus tard qu'il [Kaltenbach] avait été à l'école de M. Nick, le très remarquable évangéliste du Nord de la France, qui lui avait communiqué sa vision prophétique du Royaume de Dieu et de l'évangélisation du monde." "Mémoires," 83.

18. Ernst Schering, "Johannes Schwerdtmann. Ein bedeutender Mann der Kirche und der Diakonie Hannovers zu Beginn des 20. Jahrhunderts," *Hannover Geschichtsblätter* NF 43 (1989) 129–77.

town of 55,000 inhabitants before the First World War).[19] Indeed, he was a well-known figure among social Christians, and among Protestants of northern France: he joined the main association of social Christians, the APEQS, fairly early, between the congresses of Marseille (1891) and Le Havre (1894).[20] Since 1910 he was the president of the "Société chrétienne du Nord," an association founded in 1842, affiliated with the Reformed Church of France, which supported evangelistic work in northern France, especially in the mining area in Pas-de-Calais, where Protestantism was almost nonexistant and virtually unknown.[21] The "Société chrétienne du Nord" had been achieving great results in several small towns, including Sin-le-Noble and Liévin.[22] Paul Trocmé served as one of the vice-presidents in the "Action chrétienne sociale," as it was founded in 1911, with Charles Gide and Élie Gounelle at the helm.[23]

Had Paul Trocmé, as the eldest son, not been called upon as a young man to support his family, he would probably have become a pastor.[24] André Trocmé eventually found out about his father's own pacifist leanings. In November 1870, during the Franco-Prussian War, Paul Trocmé had made the decision that, if mobilized, he would serve as a male nurse in order not to carry a weapon. Much later, he gave a letter from that time to his son André, telling him: "You see, after all, I am not that far from you!"[25]

19. "Le nombre des protestants, qui s'élevait en 1888 à dix-neuf cent soixante-quatre, doit s'élever actuellement à près de deux mille cinq cents. [. . .] L'Église de Saint-Quentin est l'une des plus florissantes du Nord de la France, par le nombre et la piété de ses membres." Monnier, *Édouard Monnier*, 179.

20. Cf. the list of new members in *Travaux du congrès du Havre* (1894), 270.

21. One of its pastors, Roger de Vismes, reported on the missionary work in 1913: "Nous avons des protestants, quelques milliers, là où il n'y en avait pas un il y a 25 ans." De Visme, "Notre méthode," 83.

22. Liévin, Hénin-Liétard, Sin-le-Noble, Bruay, Lens, and Aniche are some of the cities, all of them south of Lille in the coal mining region known as the "Bassin houiller du Pas-de-Calais," 50 km wide and 20 km deep, where the "Société chrétienne du Nord" was especially active and successful (Mours, *Un siècle d'évangélisation*, vol. 2, 11). The Baptist churches of the region had already been active among the miners since the 1850s (Mours, vol. 2, 173–76). On the *Société chrétienne du Nord* and its place within French Protestantism, see Encrevé, *Protestants français*, 148–50. See also Schloesing, *Le centenaire*. For the date of Paul Trocmé's presidency, see Barde, *La Société centrale*, 70.

23. "Congrès de l'Action chrétienne sociale de Saint-Quentin," *RCS* 24 (1911), nr. 7-8 (July–August 1911) 461.

24. "Dans sa jeunesse, il avait renoncé à une vocation pastorale pour aider son père malade et prendre soin de sa famille dont il était l'aîné." A. Trocmé, "Mémoires," 208.

25. Paul Trocmé wrote the following in a letter dated November 21, 1870: "Les

As the patriarch of a large family, he had instituted a rigorous devotional life at home: "Morning service at breakfast; reading from the Bible, reading of a meditation, prayer—always the same one, more or less: 'Teach us to do our Duty,' recitation of the Our Father by one of the children. At lunch and dinner, short prayer before eating. On Sunday, participation in Worship (twice a day for my older brothers!). For the younger children: Sunday school at Church, naturally under the leadership of Father [. . .]."[26] As André Trocmé put it in a paper he later wrote as a theology student at Union Theological Seminary in New York City, his "first experience of God was an experience of submission to his will, which was very hard to accept, and not an experience of his goodness."[27] André was home-schooled until the age of ten. In 1911, three months before starting secondary school (the "lycée"), on a Sunday afternoon in June, Paul Trocmé was driving the entire family in the countryside when they had an accident that killed André's mother.

CHAOS AND DISCOVERIES

The orderly world in which André Trocmé grew up was shattered by the death of his mother, and three years later by the war.[28] Saint-Quentin was

---

devoirs qui s'imposent au chrétien en cas de guerre sont une question bien difficile à résoudre, et que je ne prétends pas avoir éclaircie pour mon compte. [. . .] La guerre en elle-même est un péché, et il est mal d'y prendre part volontairement. [. . .] Donc je chercherai toujours à ne pas tenir un fusil, je serai même infirmier si c'est le cas et courrai autant de danger qu'un soldat armé. De plus je refuserai toute espèce de grade, même celui de caporal, parce que je ne veux porter, en commandant, aucune responsabilité de la chose." It seems that, as an adult, André Trocmé always carried a copy of this letter in his wallet. Despite his early pacifism, Paul Trocmé discouraged his son from becoming a conscientious objector. A copy of this letter can be found in the Trocmé papers, Swarthmore College, series A, box 1.

26. "[. . .] Culte au petit déjeuner; lecture de la Bible, lecture d'une méditation, prière toujours à peu près la même: 'Apprends-nous à faire notre Devoir,' récitation du Notre Père par un des enfants. À midi et le soir, courte prière avant de se mettre à table. Le Dimanche, assistance au Culte (mes frères aînés y allaient deux fois par Dimanche!). Pour les enfants: École du Dimanche au Temple, dirigée naturellement par Papa [. . .]." "Mémoires," 83–84. On 50 and 90, André Trocmé describes himself as a "puritain."

27. Paper titled "Has Curriculum to Lead the Pupil to. . . Education? (Gradual unfoldment of the inherent possibilities) or to. . . Conversion?," 6. It was written for a course taught by professor George Albert Coe (1862-1951). Trocmé papers, Swarthmore College, Series B, box 5 (4th folder).

28. I rely in part for what follows on Kaltenbach, *L'Église réformée*.

occupied by the German army from August 28, 1914, after a terrible battle. They stayed until October 2, 1918. During the first two weeks of March 1917, Saint-Quentin was evacuated by the Germans. One of the largest battles of the war, the battle of the Somme, took place only 35 kilometers away, in the second half of 1916. The entire region known as "Nord-Pas-de-Calais" suffered catastrophic casualties and damage. Three of Trocmé's half-brothers (from Paul Trocmé's first marriage, to Marie Walbaum, who died in 1895) were fighting in the war, and one of them, Robert, barely survived a wound to his chest. The German army controlled everything: the "lycée" had been transformed into a hospital; classes were moved to empty factories. German officers lived in parts of the large Trocmé family house.

It is in this context that André Trocmé recalled meeting a German soldier named Kindler, a telegraph operator, on the staircase of the family home. Kindler belonged to a Protestant sect in Breslau, and he told Trocmé that he was not his enemy, that he would not kill André Trocmé's brothers, who were serving in the French army, or any French soldier for that matter: "God has revealed to us that a Christian cannot kill, can never kill. We do not carry any weapon!"[29] This encounter was decisive in Trocmé's life. Indeed, it led to a lifelong commitment to active, non-violent resistance. "Suddenly," he writes in his "Mémoires," "my nationalism, my militarism, crumbled. I saw the war for what it was: a horrible chaos in which those who take part in it, who are in turn criminals and victims, all disobey God, pretending to exercise justice in his place, by using canons."[30]

Trocmé was so taken by Kindler's non-violent stance that he invited him to attend the next meeting of his parish's youth group, the "Union chrétienne de jeunes gens," at the church on the following Sunday.[31] Trocmé recalls that, after the initial surprise of seeing a German soldier, and once they knew that this soldier was as commited to his Christian faith as he was to non-violence, the young men of the "Union" welcomed him. Trocmé wrote, fourty years later: "We knelt, as we always did, in order to pray: Far away, the roar of war never ceased: men, over there, killed one another. Here, French people and a German were opening their eyes to

29. A. Trocmé, "Mémoires," 96. Trocmé does not date this encounter.

30. "D'un seul coup, mon nationalisme, mon militarisme, s'écroulèrent. Je vis la guerre, telle qu'elle est: un épouvantable chaos où tous les belligérants, criminels et victimes à tour de rôle, désobéissent tous à Dieu, en prétendant faire justice à sa place, à coups de canon." Ibid.

31. The Union at Saint-Quentin had been founded very early on in the movement of the YMCA, by pastor Édouard Monnier, in 1857. Monnier, *Édouard Monnier*, 109.

the tangible reality of the Kingdom of God.—Kindler prayed in German. I believe it was one of the first times I expressed my thoughts, aloud and openly, to God."[32]

Without being able to name what he had encountered, namely an expression of the principled version of Christian pacifism, Trocmé's life was changed. But if he had been able really to hear this German soldier and welcome these ideas, it was probably because of some of his friends in the "Union," especially his closest friend Robert Jospin (1899–1990), who was two years older and who, unlike him, came from a socialist family. Even before Kindler's participation in one of their Sunday meetings at the parish, Robert Jospin, who intended to become a pastor, used to speak to the members of the "Union" about the Christian faith as it relates to questions of peace and justice.[33] As we saw above, it is there, at the "Union" of Saint-Quentin, that André Trocmé experienced a "revival." It is also there that he became, as he put it, "enamored with moral absolutes."[34] Or, as he wrote near the end of his "Mémoires," in 1967: "My first liberation happened, I have said it, at the Union of Saint-Quentin during the war, when I saw, with my own eyes, friends who were repenting, reconciling, supporting one another, sharing everything. This vision never disappeared. My entire life, I remained a pilgrim in search for a 'Union' like that one."[35]

---

32. "Nous nous agenouillâmes, selon la coutume, pour prier: Au loin, le grondement de la bataille ne cessait pas: des hommes là-bas, s'entretuaient. Ici, des Français et un Allemand ouvraient les yeux sur la réalité tangible du règne de Dieu.—Kindler pria en allemand. Je crois bien que ce fut l'une des premières fois que je me mis aussi, à haute voix, à livrer mes pensées intimes sans réticences, à Dieu." A. Trocmé, "Mémoires," 97.

33. Robert Jospin "fit passer devant mes yeux des visions de paix et de justice sociale." "Mémoires," 91. Robert Jospin is the father of the French socialist politician and former prime minister Lionel Jospin. In a conversation with Nicolas Offenstadt on January 29, 1990, Robert Jospin said that soon after Kindler's visit at their youth meeting they found out that he had been executed. If that is true (as it very well may be), how is it that Trocmé did not mention (or remember) that? See Offenstadt, *Les fusillés*, 183–84. Nicolas Offenstadt graciously lent me the audio tape of his interview with Robert Jospin.

34. "Épris d'absolu moral depuis l'Union de St-Quentin, ayant abusé de mes forces physiques et nerveuses, je me demandais constamment si mon état moral que je croyais très bas, me qualifiait pour le ministère pastoral, que je plaçais très haut." A. Trocmé, "Mémoires," 140.

35. "Ma première libération survint, je l'ai dit, à l'Union de St-Quentin pendant la guerre, lorsque je vis, de mes yeux, des camarades se repentir, se réconcilier, s'entraider, tout partager. Cette vision ne s'est jamais effacée. Toute ma vie je suis resté un pèlerin à la recherche d'une 'Union' comme celle-là." Ibid., 518.

Revivalism and Social Christianity

EXILE AND THE "FRATERNITÉ" IN CLAMART

The Trocmé family, a group of nine people that included a few relatives and a missionary friend, was evacuated from Saint-Quentin in March 1917.[36] The destination was unknown. In cattle cars, under the surveillance of German soldiers, the family left its home and its city. After a journey of twenty-four hours, they arrived at their destination, which turned out to be the Belgian countryside. The formerly prominent bourgeois family had to come to terms with the fact that they now were refugees.[37] They were given shelter by local farmers, in the area of Marcq, southwest of Brussels, near Enghien. Paul Trocmé organized and led Sunday worships. His son André soon found out that three of his friends from the "Union" of Saint-Quentin, Arthur Meunier, André and Maurice Delaporte, were in the next village, Saint-Pierre-Cappelle (today Sint-Pieters-Kapelle). They resumed their weekly meetings.[38] Even their pastor, Jacques Kaltenbach, had been evacuated to Charleroi, forty kilometers to the south.[39] Since riding trains was forbidden to them, it took the young men seven hours to reach Charleroi by foot each time they visited their pastor. In August 1917, the entire family moved to Brussels, where they celebrated the end of the war in November 1918, before moving to Paris a month later.

In Paris, André Trocmé became involved in the "Union" at the parish of Plaisance (15th arrondissement), where a revival took place.[40] As he was completing his studies at the Lycée Buffon, he was also recruited by the "groupe Rive gauche" (left bank) of the "Fédé Lycéenne," a group of Protestant high school students. During a Protestant youth summer camp on the island of Oléron, where two of Henri Nick's children were present (André and Pierre), his friend Jacques Diény, the leader of the group for the Parisian region—a young man who, according to Trocmé, was filled with "prophetic visions and grandiose plans"—asked Trocmé to replace

---

36. For the date of the evacuation and further details, see Kaltenbach's report, *AMR* 37, nr. 1 (Jan. 1919) 13–18.

37. "Le mot 'réfugié' nous irrita. Nous n'étions pas des réfugiés, mais des 'évacués' que les Allemands avaient chassés de chez eux." "Mémoires," 102.

38. "[...] l'Union chrétienne de jeunes gens, dont le président et le vice-président, ainsi que plusieurs membres, se trouvaient dans le voisinage, reprit également ses séances." Kaltenbach, *L'Église réformée*, 58.

39. "Mémoires," 107–8.

40. After mentioning the revival at Saint-Quentin, Trocmé writes: "[...] j'ai participé plusieurs fois à des 'Réveils' (à l'Union de Plaisance, à l'Union de Clamart, à Sin-le-Noble, surtout) [...]." Ibid., 86.

him while he was away for his two years of military service.[41] This task also involved leading the seven or eight young men of the "Union" at the parish of Clamart, just south of Paris. Flattered by his friend's trust, he accepted.[42] For the first time in his life, still a high school student, Trocmé was in a position of pastoral leadership. He was beginning to overcome his lack of self-confidence. In the footsteps of Diény, Trocmé led the "Union" in a very ambitious missionary project: the young men decided to create a "Fraternité" that would reach out to the other young men in Clamart, then a suburb of approximately 20,000 inhabitants, in order to bring them to faith.

At the inauguration of the new "Fraternité," in 1920, André Trocmé preached a solemn sermon to the young men and their parents in which he made clear the vast missionary goal of the group:

> [. . .] our ambition goes even farther. We not only dream to spread a few rays of light around us, for we dream to reveal who Christ is to the youth in Clamart. We would like to bring Jesus to them, as he was, as he lived and still lives, without any intermediaries which might block this radiant face. With Jesus, we would like to bring a complete renewal of their entire life: we would like to see horrible vices, debauchery, alcoholism and discord disappear. We would like, to summarize, that Christ becomes king in Clamart, and that this movement be only a part of a great movement of conquest so that France as a whole may be [dedicated] to Jesus Christ.[43]

---

41. "Au Lycée Buffon, j'avais deux amis, un nommé Zuber, et un nommé Dieterlen, qui m'entraînèrent dans un groupe de la 'Fédé Lycéenne,' le groupe 'Rive gauche,' dont Zuber était le Z. (Z voulait dire Président, 'Fédé' voulait dire la branche cadette. Diény était (s'il-vous-plaît!) 'Z' de la Région Parisienne de la Fédé Lycéenne!). C'était un garçon maigre et nerveux, aux yeux fulgurants chaussés de lunettes, animé d'un intarissabe enthousiasme religieux, et dont la tête (il était intellectuellement très brillant) fourmillait de visions prophétiques et de plans grandioses." Ibid., 126. Henri Nick's children are mentioned on 128.

42. Ibid., 126–29 and 137.

43. "Écoutez même, nos ambitions vont plus loin—nous ne rêvons pas seulement de répandre quelques rayons de lumière autour de nous, mais nous rêvons davantage, nous rêvons de révéler à la jeunesse de Clamart ce qu'est le Christ,—nous voudrions leur apporter Jésus tel qu'il est, tel qu'il a vécu et tel qu'il vit encore, sans qu'aucun intermédiaire soit là pour intercepter cette figure rayonnante. Nous voudrions leur apporter avec Jésus, une complète rénovation de toute leur vie: nous voudrions que disparaissent les vices affreux, la débauche, l'alcoolisme, la discorde,—nous voudrions, en un mot, que Christ devienne roi à Clamart, et que tout ce mouvement ne soit qu'une partie d'un grand mouvement de conquête pour [. . .] la France tout entière à Jésus Christ." This inaugural sermon, in Trocmé's handwriting, can be consulted at the

Trocmé continued, saying that the adults in the parish should not smile at such dreams and should support, rather than cool down, these young adults' enthusiasm. The rest of the sermon was a clarification, on the basis of the parable of the leaven, of what constitutes a truly life-giving action. In order to be conformed to Jesus' message, the action of the "Fraternité" would have to fully "blend" into its environment, in the working-class neighborhood, like yeast in the dough. The whole process would develop organically, progressively, from the inside out, reaching deeper, beyond quick, quantitative (but superficial) successes.[44]

The "Fraternité" hoped to attract young men to its location through various activities: at first, following the tradition of the "Unions chrétiennes" and its interest not just for the soul but also for the mind and the body, there would be a sports group, a theater group, and a study group. But they quickly realized that their strengths were limited, and that in the event of major recruiting successes the "Fraternité" might quickly lose its Christian orientation. Fearing the "superficiality" he had talked about in his inauguration speech, Trocmé suggested a more limited range of activities. And even if the offer was smaller, he trusted that "by beginning like this more lads will join us later."[45] Since the "Fraternité" hoped to recruit young workers, it had to make sure to provide attractive, enjoyable activities. One of the projects was to organize a "promenade" to Fontainebleau, and Trocmé urged his friends to prepare themselves spiritually for it in all seriousness, through prayer and meditation. He told them: "I have the absolute conviction that our walk will fail if we do not feel its profound seriousness, its almost solemn gravity. It must be the center of our life during the two weeks which precede it. Our victory or our defeat might depend from the walk. I ask you to think about it."[46] Trocmé uses military

---

Peace Collection (Swarthmore College), Trocmé papers, series B, box 7, 1. I am unable to decipher the verb in the last sentence.

44. "[. . .] l'action du levain est progressive, petit à petit, elle gagne toute la pâte, mais il faut souvent attendre longtemps—[. . .] si notre action est superficielle, extérieure, nous n'obtiendrons rien,—absolument rien.[. . .]." Trocmé's inaugural sermon, 5.

45. "Le but de la Fraternité, nous ne devons pas l'oublier est le suivant: Transformer des hommes, en les arrachant à leur égoïsme et à leurs passions, pour les amener au Christ qui les transformera lui-même à son image—*Nous devons juger de tout en fonction de ce principe*. Or ce principe nous interdit de nous lancer dans une action superficielle et vide, qui résulterait du fait que serions débordés. Conclusion, il faut mieux faire une chose à fond que quatre choses superficiellement, même si nous devons avoir moins de types au début. Pour moi je suis sûr qu'un tel début nous amènera plus de types par la suite." Trocmé's notes for a meeting of the "Fraternité"; Swarthmore College, Trocmé papers, series B, box 7.

46. "J'ai la conviction absolue que notre promenade ratera si nous n'en sentons pas

metaphors in a meditation written for the small group of the "Fraternité" on April 30, 1919: "These last days—evil—We cannot deny its existence. In every moment it stops us and says to us: I am here. Social evil: anti-idealism; moral evil: vice; individual evil: apathy, which ruins morality; inner evil: kills our enthusiasm and leads us to say that nothing can be done [. . .]. The Fraternity is only this: an organization which fights against evil. We are not ambassadors, we are a combat unit. We must be aware of this combat."[47] The fight had to be fought for the sake of the youth around them who were "falling." The fight, however, was delayed: they had problems raising funds and furnishing the hall, and the inauguration had to be postponed several times. At one point, one of the main "evils" described by Trocmé, namely the loss of enthusiasm, was looming over the group that for months had been dreaming of victories.[48]

THEOLOGICAL STUDIES IN PARIS

Trocmé was in essence the youth minister to the small group of friends of the "Fraternité" in Clamart. Even before the evacuation of his family to Belgium in March 1917, he knew he wanted to become a pastor. In

---

le profond sérieux, la gravité presque solennelle. Elle doit être le centre de notre vie pendant les quinze jours qui la précéderont.—D'elle dépend peut-être notre victoire ou notre défaite.—Je vous demande d'y penser tout spécialement." Trocmé's notes for a meeting of the "Fraternité." Peace Collection (Swarthmore College), Trocmé papers, series B, box 7.

47. "Nous ne pouvons nier son existence—à chaque instant il nous arrête et nous dit: je suis là. Mal social—antiidéalisme; mal moral—vice; mal individuel—menfichisme ruine morale; mal intérieur—tue nos enthousiasmes qui nous fait dire, il n'y a rien à faire—[. . .] La Fraternité n'est que celà, une organisation pour lutter contre le mal—nous ne sommes pas des embassadeurs mais sommes une unité de combat. Il faut que nous ayons conscience de ce combat." Trocmé's notes for a meeting of the "Fraternité." Trocmé papers, series B, box 7.

48. "Jusqu'ici nous avons vécu dans la théorie—nous avons construit des Fraternités en rêve, mais nous n'avons pas pris contact avec la réalité. Celà est cause que nous envisageons l'avenir avec un certain malaise.—Nous ne savons pas ce qu'il sera—si oui ou non notre fraternité répond à un besoin, si oui ou non 'cela prendra'—De là notre impatience d'arriver à l'inauguration.—Malheureusement cette inauguration recule, recule toujours.—De nouvelles difficultés se présentent toujours aujourd'hui, c'est encore la question d'argent qui m'inquiète de nouveau. [. . .] Si donc nous voulons commencer quelque chose pour cet été, et je n'exagère pas en disant *pour l'été*, il faut commencer maintenant.—Sans celà, nous risquons d'être menacés d'un découragement profond." Notes concerning the Clamart Fraternité. Trocmé papers, series B, box 7.

Revivalism and Social Christianity

Saint-Quentin he had admired his pastor, Jacques Kaltenbuch, who in turn had seen in him a young man who might be called to the ministry:

> He invited me several times to his home, where, in unforgettable conversations, he enjoined me to give myself to God, by practicing purity, truth, love, self-forgetfulness, by entrusting my entire life and will in the hands of a God who saves lost ones. [. . .] What won me over were Kaltenbach's appeals for a lost world, this lost world I could see everyday during the war. "The family inheritance which you will receive," he said to me, "you must use it to serve others. Won't you become a pastor or a missionary?" [. . .] I would have liked to become a prophet, like Mr. Kaltenbach, but I did not feel I was capable of it [. . .].[49]

These conversations, and all of the experiences at the "Union chrétienne de jeunes gens," led to a vocation, which Trocmé shared with his father. Paul Trocmé welcomed his son's desire with great joy, revealing to him that on the day of his birth, in the morning of April 7, 1901 (Easter Sunday), André had been "dedicated ["consacré"] to God" by his parents "in the hope that [he] would one day become a pastor."[50]

Trocmé began his theological studies in 1919, while finishing his high school degree, with a preparatory year that included courses in biblical languages, Church history, and philosophy. Several of these courses were offered by the École Pratique des Hautes Études, at the Sorbonne. After years of a strict, Puritan upbringing, Trocmé was learning new things: "1. In life there are other values besides one's strict duty. 2. One may read and actually enjoy it. 3. When one is enjoying it, one learns by oneself. 4. There is beauty."[51]

---

49. "Il m'invita plusieurs fois chez lui, où, dans des têtes-à-tête inoubliables, il m'adjurait de me donner à Dieu, en pratiquant la pureté, la vérité, l'amour, l'oubli de soi, en confiant toute ma vie et ma volonté aux mains d'un Dieu qui sauve les hommes perdus. [. . .] Ce qui emporta ma conviction, ce furent les appels de M. Kaltenbach pour le monde perdu, ce monde perdu que pendant la guerre j'avais chaque jour sous les yeux. 'L'héritage familial dont tu es le bénéficiaire,' me disait-il, 'tu dois le mettre au service des autres. Ne deviendrais-tu pas pasteur ou missionnaire?' [. . .] J'aurais bien voulu devenir un prophète comme M. Kaltenbach, mais je ne m'en sentais pas capable [. . .]." "Mémoires," 84. On the preceding page, Trocmé writes about his admiration for his pastor despite Kaltenbach's rather smallish and awkward physical appearance and his lack of oratory skills.

50. Ibid., 85.

51. "1) Il y a, dans la vie, des valeurs à côté du devoir strict. 2) On peut lire pour s'amuser. 3) Quand on s'amuse, on apprend tout seul. 4) Il y a la beauté." Ibid., 50.

André Trocmé's First Steps in Spiritual and Social Christianity

He was not an outstanding student, and his theology courses did not particularly interest him. He was introduced to the modern historical-critical method by Maurice Goguel (1880–1955) and Charles Guignebert (1867–1939), and was particularly disappointed—but not too troubled—by the meager results produced by the modern methods on the life of Jesus.[52] So, in September 1921, he decided to take a leave of absence in order to embark on his two-year military service, a decision that is somewhat surprising when one contrasts it with his friend and fellow theology student Henri Roser (1899–1981) who, in January 1923, decided to become a conscientious objector, whatever may be the cost of that decision (he was sentenced to four years of prison, to be served in Rambouillet).[53] Yet even Roser, like Trocmé a pacifist, had taken part in the war, starting in April 1918, commanding a company of 120 men without fighting on the frontlines, and serving in the army until his demobilization in March 1921.[54] Trocmé swore to himself he would not kill and would not train anyone to kill, even after he reluctantly agreed to be promoted to the rank of corporal.[55] That stance was bound to create problems, and during his months of service in Morocco, from October 1922 until April 1923, Trocmé was fortunate to be part of a group led by a Catholic lieutenant who showed some understanding for it, even as he disapproved of it. Trocmé's lieutenant correctly told him that he should have been consistent, expressing his views openly on the very first day of his military service, and not in the middle of it.[56]

---

52. "Mes études étaient moyennes et je ne m'y passionnais pas." Ibid., 140. "J'aurais voulu exceller soit en sciences, soit en sainteté, et je n'y parvenais pas" (156). "A la Faculté, je passai mes grands examens au printemps de 1925 avec un succès moyen." (207). On Goguel, see 131 and 139.

53. Trocmé writes that a sense of his own lack of maturity, and a desire to experience what ordinary men experience, motivated his decision not to postpone his military service any longer (ibid., 140). On 158 he mentions that his father and his professors advised him against interrupting his studies, and adds: "Au contact des brutalités de la vie, me disais-je, je découvrirai si ma vocation est solide ou non."

54. Kneubühler, *Henri Roser*, 23–24.

55. "Mémoires," 145–46, 151–52 and 160.

56. "'Je suis bon catholique,' me dit-il, 'et je sympathise avec vos scrupules, mais voyez-vous, mon jeune ami, si l'on est décidé de ne pas accepter la règle du jeu avant de monter à bord d'un bateau, il est plus correct de le dire d'avance. C'est au moment de votre incorporation que vous auriez dû déclarer à vos chefs: 'Je ne veux pas tuer,' en acceptant la prison qui aurait été la conséquence de votre refus du service militaire.' Je ne pouvais qu'approuver pleinement les paroles du lieutenant qui définissait aussi justement ce qu'est l'objection de conscience. 'A l'avenir,' pensai-je, 'je refuserai de me laisser incorporer.'" Ibid., 188.

Revivalism and Social Christianity

In a text written in the very first days of the Second World War, Trocmé took a retrospective look at his experience in the army and mentions something that, as far as I can see, he omits in his "Mémoires": he writes that he admired two of the officers above him, a lieutenant and a major ("commandant"). "In Morocco, where I spent six months, I was attracted by the life of dedication of the intelligence officers, to the point where at certain moments, moments which were simultaneously hours of religious doubt, I considered abandoning the pastoral ministry in order to embrace military life."[57] An either/or was presenting itself: either total commitment to the homeland, which to him would mean "renouncing faith in Jesus Christ, the prince of Peace, Son of God, the Non-Violent one," or total commitment to Jesus-Christ. "I chose the second path. I have no merit, here. My calling was compelling me."[58]

Trocmé had difficulties reconciling the "prophetic visions" impressed on him by pastor Jacques Kaltenbach (and others) and the world of the army, but also the bourgeois world of the elite circles of Parisian Protestants.[59] Having returned in the fall of 1923 to the "Faculté de théologie," this time as a student living in the residence hall at boulevard Arago in Paris, Trocmé spent much energy catching up with his studies and immersing himself in his coursework.[60] He also continued to lead the "Fraternité" in Clamart.[61] At school, he was now amid a younger group of

---

57. "Au Maroc où je passai 6 mois je fus attiré par la vie de dévouement des officiers de renseignement, au point que je songeai à certaines heures, qui furent aussi des heures de doute religieux, à abandonner le ministère pastoral pour la vie militaire." "Mise au point concernant mon attitude en temps de guerre," text dated September 5, 1939; Swarthmore College, series B, box 5, 6th folder.

58. "C'est ainsi que se posa pour moi la question de tout ou rien: Ou bien: Tout donner à la Collectivité à laquelle je suis lié [. . .]. Mais alors, renoncer à croire en Jésus-Christ, prince de la Paix, Fils de Dieu, le Non-Violent [. . .]. Ou bien: Tout donner à Jésus-Christ [. . .]. C'est le second chemin que je pris. Je n'ai aucun mérite à cela. Ma vocation était impérieuse." "Mise au point concernant mon attitude en temps de guerre," text dated September 5, 1939; Swarthmore College, series B, box 5, 6th folder.

59. "Je ne parvenais pas alors à concilier l'expérience que j'avais du monde, de la caserne, de la rue, d'une part, avec celle que j'avais de l'Eglise de Jésus-Christ, de l'Union de Clamart et de la Faculté de Théologie d'autre part. [. . .] Mais où étaient donc les visions prophétiques communiquées par M. Kaltenbach? Amener le monde à Jésus-Christ, 'faire Christ Roi.' Cette ancienne devise de l'Union de St-Quentin paraissait bien démodée aujourd'hui." "Mémoires," 171. See 177 for the "H.S.P." ("haute société protestante").

60. "[. . .] [je] me mis d'arrache-pied—enfin—à faire de la théologie, mais je ne parvins jamais à rattraper le retard que deux premières années un peu bâclées m'avaient laissé." Ibid., 202.

61. Ibid., 204.

students, several of whom became his friends, including three young men who shared his principled pacifism: Jacques Vernier, born in 1906, who became a missionary in Madagascar, and whose brother Philippe, or "Philo" (1909–85), a theology student several years later, became a well-known conscientious objector in the 1930s; Jacques Martin (1906–2001), another conscientious objector, who later became a close friend of Élie Gounelle;[62] and Édouard Theis (1899–1984), a man who would eventually work with Trocmé in Le Chambon and play an important role in the rescue effort during the Second World War. Trocmé took his final examinations in the spring of 1925, "with moderate success."[63] One last requirement, a final thesis, stood in the way of the completion of his theological studies.

WILFRED MONOD AND THE THEOLOGY OF THE KINGDOM

Wilfred Monod was one of the professors at the "Faculté de théologie protestante" in Paris. He was the son of Théodore Monod (1836–1921) who, as pastor at the Chapelle du Nord, had called Tommy Fallot to succeed him, and who had been an early collaborator of McAll's work in Paris. Wilfred Monod was born into a prominent Protestant family, filled with pastors, many of whom were interested in evangelistic mission.

In Trocmé's eyes, Wilfred Monod was part of "a beautiful professorial team" characterized by its "honest, clear, objective spirit," a "sense for what is real" and a "sincere faith in the living God, in an inner, prophetic, inspirational Christ."[64] Like his colleagues on the faculty, Monod belonged to the Parisian Protestant establishment, for which Trocmé did not particularly care, but Monod's commitment to peace was unmistakable. In 1903 he edited an entire issue of the *Revue du Christianisme social* on the theme of peace ("Pour la paix"). In his introductory remarks the optimistic idealism of the age is patent: "[. . .] we are at a turning point in history. War is fading away; the dawn of peace is brightening the sky."[65] Monod

62. Ibid., 202. See Cabanel, "Le pasteur Jacques Martin."

63. Ibid., 207 ("avec un succès moyen.")

64. "J'étais donc entré à la Faculté de Théologie de Paris, comme élève de Goguel, Lods, Henri Monnier, Wilfred Monod. Une belle équipe professorale. Tous disparus aujourd'hui. Disparu aussi leur esprit honnête, clair, objectif, leurs sens des réalités, et leur foi sincère en un Dieu vivant, en un Christ intérieur, prophétique, inspirateur." Ibid., 134. Trocmé wrote this on April 16, 1956, in Algiers (134).

65. "[. . .] nous sommes à un tournant de l'histoire. La guerre est un astre qui décline; l'aurore de la paix blanchit le ciel." Monod, "Pourquoi ce numéro?" *RCS* 16

added that "pacifist propaganda," far from being optional, was a necessary consequence of the Christian identity.[66]

Monod was one of the founders, alongside Friedrich Siegmund-Schultze, Leonhard Ragaz, Nathan Söderblom, Gounelle and others, of the *World Alliance for Promoting International Friendship through the Churches*. Its constituting conference, on August 1–2, 1914 in Constance, was made almost impossible by world events.[67] The *World Alliance* was a different approach to peace-meaking—through international laws. Jean Baubérot calls it "juridical pacifism" in order to distinguish it from the "integral" or "absolute" pacifism of those supporting conscientious objections.[68]

In his teaching at the Faculté as well as in his many-sided ecclesial activities, Monod often addressed social issues. He had been raised in a kind of religiosity which omitted these questions, and even in secondary school and later at the Sorbonne he was struck by the absence of social considerations, even though they had been "taken up by Israel" in its prophetic tradition.[69] Modern prophetic voices, such as the influential Oratorian priest and theologian Alphonse Gratry, would soon confirm Monod's sensitivity, nourished by his daily reading of Scripture, for the social dimension.[70] As a "lycéen," Monod had been involved in the McAll

---

(1903), 541.

66. "Je m'étonne et je m'afflige qu'on puisse encore se réclamer du héros des Évangiles sans le lancer, courageusement, dans la propagande pacifique [. . .]." Ibid., 544.

67. Gounelle, "La Conférence constituante de Constance," 638–47.

68. Baubérot, "Pacifismes," 21. For a good expression of this kind of pacifism, see Henry Babut's comments: "Qu'est-ce que le Pacifisme?—C'est avant tout une *idée*: l'idée de l'organisation de la Paix dans et par la justice, de l'établissement entre les nations de relations juridiques stables, ou plus brièvement encore, l'idée *d'arbitrage international*." Henry Babut, "Le congrès international de Rouen–Havre et le pacifisme," *RCS* 16 (1903) 573. A good example of the "juridical" form of pacifism is the association created by young Christians (mostly Protestants) in Nîmes in April 1887: "La paix par le droit."

69. "Dans les cadres de l'enseignement secondaire, ou même à la Sorbonne, quand donc ai-je été sérieusement placé par mes maîtres en face du problème économique, ou plutôt de la 'Question sociale,' niée ou même ignorée par Sennachérib ou Nabuchodonosor, mais affirmée par Israël, et qui domine aujourd'hui les destinées du genre humain? [. . .] À peine si l'on parlait de la morale; combien moins de l'idéal social des prophètes israélites!" Monod, *Après la journée*, 38.

70. "J'allais d'ailleurs subir l'influence décisive des ouvrages d'un prêtre oratorien, Alphonse Gratry, le chrétien-social. Dans *Les Sources* (opuscule qui vaut toute une *Somme*), il déclarait: 'Je ne demande au monde contemporain qu'une seule chose, la volonté déterminée d'abolir la misère.' Il savait qu'un pareil programme exigera une croisade idéologique sans rémission, à la surface du globe; mais, avec la simplicité

mission in Montreuil-sous-Bois, a suburb of Paris. There he met a young woman named Dorina, like him a volunteer at the mission, who would become, four years later, his fiancée, wife, and "collaborator in my life and ministry."[71] His first months as a student in Montauban were difficult: he was shocked by the "mundanity" in the seminary. The separation of the Church and the State (December 1905) had yet to be implemented, and many young men were studying in Montauban for the promise of working as civil servants of the State rather than as the consequence of a calling to the pastoral ministry. Monod had been so impressed by the Salvation Army during visits to England and Edinburgh that for a while he hesitated to follow the traditional path—in the footsteps of his father Théodore, his renowned great-uncle Adolphe (1802–56), and his great-grandfather Jean (1765–1836)—of ministering a parish.

In Montauban, Monod sought to foster a religious revival among his fellow seminarians. That goal became a reality when a student, who had been more interested in playing the violin than applying himself to his studies, "solemnly consecrated himself during the Saturday evening prayer gathering, on November 27, 1889." Other students soon followed.[72]

Wilfred Monod went on to become a pastor for fifteen years, first in Normandy, in the town of Condé-sur-Noireau, and later in Rouen, where he opened a "Solidarité" in March 1900. When, at the social Christian congress of Rouen in 1901, a committee in charge of the "Solidarités" was set up, Monod was entrusted with the sub-committee on evangelization.[73] In 1907, he was called by the parish of the "Oratoire du Louvre," where his father Théodore had been a pastor and a close collaborator of Rev. McAll

---

géniale des prophètes, il s'appuyait sur l'oraison dominicale, cette charte surnaturelle d'un 'totalitarisme' chrétien." Ibid., 44–45. By "totalitarism," Monod means a Christianity which, far from simply focusing on the "spiritual" or the "mystical," addresses reality in its totality.

71. Ibid., 46–50 (quote: 49). Dorina (1868–1963) was the daughter of William Monod (1834–1916), a distant relative of Wilfred Monod (three of Wilfred and Dorina Monod's four grandfathers were brothers; see ibid., 49 n. 1.

72. "Toute ma vie intime, et vibrante, restait dominée par la vision d'un réveil religieux au Séminaire. [. . .] le réveil fit explosion au Séminaire! Au début de ma seconde année de théologie, l'événement—ou le miracle—se produisit, pendant la réunion de prière du samedi soir, le 27 novembre 1889; tout à coup, devant ses camarades stupéfaits, bouleversés, l'étudiant artiste et aboulique se consacra solennellement à Dieu. L'exemple de cette conversion mémorable poussa deux autres étudiants à s'affirmer dans le même sens. A la réunion de prière du 8 décembre, le mouvement se fortifia: confessions, larmes, prières de louange. [. . .] On commençait à respirer l'atmosphère chrétienne." Ibid., 83–84.

73. Quiévreux, "Le Congrès de Rouen," 496.

(his great-uncle Adolphe and his great-grandfather Jean had also ministered the parish).[74] Almost simultaneously, he began lecturing at the "Faculté de théologie protestante," in Paris, with a first course on the "Christianisme social." Two years later, he became a professor of practical theology, without abandoning the pastoral ministry.[75] Monod was a prolific author. He published numerous sermons and pamphlets, as well as a two-volume work on *L'espérance chrétienne* (vol. 1: *Le Roi*, 1899; vol. 2: *Le Royaume*, 1901) in which he defended the centrality of the kingdom for Christian theology and life, and therefore the thesis that "the true Christian cannot separate his feelings of piety and his social aspirations."[76] In the final pages of the first volume, and in the introduction to the second volume, Monod quoted an article published by Élie Gounelle in the *Revue du Christianisme social*: "The Kingdom of God, this Ideal which is more real than all the realities of the world, this Idea which realizes itself throughout the centuries and which, day by day, untiringly, conquers the immense world of each single soul, and then also what surrounds them, the institutions, the laws, and then the churches, the peoples and their governments, and then material nature itself. . . The Kingdom of God is a personal power, a living Thought, a victorious Love: it

---

74. Monod, *Après la journée*, 172. See Henri Merle d'Aubigné's report, "Notes of the Work in France," *AMR* 25, nr. 4 (Dec. 1907) 8: "About seven years ago Pastor Wilfred Monod, of Rouen, established an evangelistic mission in that city. A generous member of his church, M. de Visme, bought an old convent and converted it into a Mission Hall, with classrooms, a temperance restaurant and everything necessary for Mission work. It was carried on conjointly by Pastor Wilfred Monod and the pastor of the Methodist church. Unfortunately, the work was not a success, simply because it was too large an undertaking for the few Protestants of Rouen. The *Solidarité* is in a quarter where clerical power is strong, and there are few men of independent minds among the laboring population. The mission was therefore closed some time ago. Now Pastor Wilfred Monod asks the McAll Mission to take it in hand and provide a salary of an evangelist, the Protestants of Rouen agreeing to provide for all the expenses of the purely social work. After much deliberation, the Board in Paris has decided to provide the salary of the evangelist, which will be $600 a year. Rouen is an important centre, one of the strongholds of intemperance in the world, and the material we have to work upon there is therefore very difficult. M. Vautrin, who was formerly of Roubaix (where he was succeeded by M. Alfred Dürrleman), has good qualities, and with the Lord's help he may succeed. If he fails, there is no shame in retreating where others have failed before us. Since these negotiations were begun, Pastor Wilfred Monod has been called to succeed our long-time friend and supporter, the regretted Pastor Decoppet, in the great Church of the Oratoire, Paris."

75. Monod, *Après la journée*, 186.

76. "Mais quand la doctrine du Royaume aura sa place, [. . .] on comprendra que le chrétien véritable, (car c'est de lui que nous parlons), ne peut pas séparer ses sentiments de piété et ses aspirations sociales [. . .]." *L'espérance chétienne*, vol. 2, 110–11.

is the Holy Spirit ruling the earth."[77] The messianic hope, already announced by the Hebrew prophets, had to be rediscovered by Christianity. Monod was convinced that "[. . .] the Church of the Messiah is unfaithful to the one to whom she claims to belong as soon as it ceases to struggle, explicitly, to set up the Kingdom of God on earth."[78]

Unsurprisingly, Monod wanted to combine the social and the spiritual dimensions: "the notion of the Kingdom will allow a synthesis of the the things which occupy Christ's disciples: religious *revival*, social *reform*. These two commandments are summarized in one single word: to *evangelize*."[79] Besides Gounelle's article, Monod quoted Tommy Fallot's works extensively and praised "the valiant precursor" of the "French social Christianity."[80] Indeed, Monod's work on Christian hope can be seen as an attempt to further develop Fallot's insights.

Two figures loom large in Monod's autobiography, *Après la journée* (1938): the great Swiss liberal theologian of religious experience, Alexandre Vinet (1797-1847), and the leader of the ecumenical movement, Nathan Söderblom (1866-1931). With Vinet, Monod rejected all forms of dry, abstract "doctrinarisme" in favor of a lived faith. At the center of Monod's interpretation of the Christian faith lie the Beatitudes. They were "the creed of Jesus Christ."[81] The Beatitudes remain a central text,

---

77. "Le Royaume de Dieu, cet Idéal plus réel que toutes les réalités de ce monde, cette Idée qui se réalise à travers les siècles, et, jour après jour, infatigable, conquiert le monde immense qu'est chaque âme, puis les milieux, les institutions, les lois, puis les églises, les peuples et leurs gouvernements, puis la nature matérielle elle même. . . Le Royaume de Dieu, c'est une puissance personnelle, une Pensée vivante, un Amour vainqueur: c'est l'Esprit saint se soumettant la terre." *L'espérance chétienne*, vol. 1, 452; vol. 2, 9–10, quoting Gounelle's article (*RCS*, 1898, 316).

78. "[. . .] l'Église du Messie est infidèle à celui dont elle se réclame, dès qu'elle cesse de lutter, expressément, pour l'organisation du Royaume de Dieu sur la terre." *L'espérance chétienne*, vol. 2, 226.

79. "La notion du Royaume permettra la synthèse des préoccupations qui travaillent les disciples du Christ: *réveil* religieux, *réforme* sociale. Ce double mot d'ordre se résume dans une seule formule: *évangéliser*." *L'espérance chétienne*, vol. 2, 236.

80. Fallot is quoted almost without interruption from 240–7 in vol. 2 of *L'espérance chétienne*! "La définition que nous venons de transcrire nous fait battre le cœur; nous bénissons le vaillant précurseur qui l'a formulée. Si le christianisme social en France, durant les vingt dernières années, n'avait produit que cette seule déclaration, il n'aurait point perdu son temps. Car elle contient le germe d'une Réformation nouvelle ou d'une Révolution: *Réforme*, si les églises suivent le mouvement qui se dessine, *Révolution* si elles s'y opposent." Ibid., vol. 2, 244.

81. Monod, *Après la journée*, 314, 322, 329, 338, 341, 362, and esp. 332–36, where Monod writes: "Pourquoi. . . les Béatitudes? Parce qu'on ne discerne point d'autre page, dans toute l'Écriture, qui nous porte aussi radieusement, avec la vitesse et l'impétuosité

Revivalism and Social Christianity

recited every day of the year, by the *Veilleurs*, the spiritual "third order" (*tiers-ordre*) founded by Wilfred Monod and his son Théodore in 1923.[82] Söderblom, whom Monod met for the first time in Sweden as early as 1888, invited him to take an active part in the 1925 conference in Stockholm, an important milestone in the ecumenical movement. That conference would be one of the highlights in Monod's life.[83]

Monod's overarching concern as a practical theologian was the training of pastors with a sound spiritual life and a grasp of the center of Jesus' message.[84] His work in ecumenical circles, with Söderblom and others, and his own contribution to the "Christianisme social," in collaboration with Élie Gounelle, can be interpreted as expressions of his focus on Jesus' message concerning the kingdom. Like Gounelle and Nick, his interest in evangelization never diminished.[85] But it is specifically for his social interpretation of Christianity that Monod was known well beyond the borders of his country, and respected by prominent social Christians such as Leonhard Ragaz and others.[86]

As Trocmé entered the "Faculté de théologie," Wilfred Monod was a towering figure in French Protestantism, and a theologian who was nearing the peak of his career. In many ways, as will become evident, Trocmé's

---

d'une flamme, au sanctuaire de l'Ame immaculée, au Cœur sacré. Là rayonnent une pureté sans tache et la révélation rédemptrice. [. . .] un passage qui est le Credo de Jésus-Christ." (334).

82. Ibid., 323–36. "Veilleurs" may be translated by: "those who keep watch."

83. Ibid., 257–62.

84. This point is repeated in *Après la journée* on 11, 70, 134 and 345.

85. See "A Letter to the American McAll Association," written by Monod on December 10, 1931: "Every Christian who rightly understands himself aspires to act as an evangelist. [. . .] So to evangelize France is a magnificent enterprise." *AMR* 50, nr. 2 (March 1932) 4.

86. See Leonhard Ragaz' comments from 1921: "Ungeteilte Freude habe ich auch während des Krieges, wie nachher, an den französischen Hugenotten gehabt, die sich um die Revue du Christianisme social scharen, besonders an Élie Gounelle und Wilfried Monod. Wollen Sie diesen letzten (den andern werden Sie wohl nicht zu leicht treffen, er ist jetzt in St. Etienne) von uns aufs herzlichste grüßen lassen! Er ist ein außerordentlicher Mensch! Hier ist wirklich Fleisch von unserm Fleisch. Mit *diesen* Menschen treffe ich mich stets unmittelbar, und sogar die leichte Differenz in der Beurteilung des Kirchenproblems vermag diese Gemeinsamkeit kaum zu berühren. Welch ein anderes Leben wäre es, mit diesen Menschen zusammen zu arbeiten, statt sich, wie ich jetzt nur viel zu sehr muß, mit dem Theoretismus herumzuschlagen, der immer wieder von jenseits des Rheins herüber kommt, mit jenem unbiblischen 'Tiefsinn,' der sich lähmend auf alles Denken und Kämpfen legt." Letter from January 25, 1921 to Ernst Merz, in Christine Ragaz, Markus Mattmüller and Arthur Rich, eds., *Leonhard Ragaz in seinen Briefen*, vol. 2. (Zurich: TVZ, 1982) 214.

life parallels Monod's articulation of spiritual and social matters. And yet Trocmé disagreed with his professor on the question of peace. Trocmé took part, as a delegate of the students from the Parisian "Faculté de théologie," in a congress of the *World Alliance for Promoting International Friendship through the Churches* in Lille on January 15–16, 1924. He was disappointed by what he heard. It was "too conservative, too ecclesiastical for my taste," as he wrote in his "Mémoires."[87] The ideals of the *World Alliance* were noble, but insufficient. A gap was becoming visible among social Christians, since, for his part, Monod was critical of the new wave of "réfractaires" or "conscientious objectors" (Monod uses the English expression, a sign that the French expression "objecteurs de conscience" was not yet common), because of its negative impact—a demoralizing effect—on French soldiers.[88]

THE "GROUPE DU NORD"

Right after the First World War, the "Faculté de théologie" was composed of two groups of students: older students whose studies had been interrupted by world events, and a younger generation. All of them had been deeply affected by the war. Several of the younger students formed a group called "groupe du Nord," a "team in which we spoke a lot about evangelizing the workers, in which we professed an advanced social Christianity, a group whose hero was Henri Nick, the 'saint' of Fives-Lille."[89] Through his good friend Jacques Diény, Trocmé joined the group, which comprised

---

87. Monod, "tout en prenant position contre le pacifisme radical de Roser, avait fondé, avec Siegmund Schultze, Soderblom et d'autres, 'L'Amitié Internationale par le Moyen des Eglises,' dont le secrétaire général était le pasteur Jules Jézéquel. J'assistai à Lille à l'un des congrès de ce mouvement [. . .]. Le congrès de Lille fut trop conservateur, trop ecclésiastique à mon gré, et je me tournai complètement vers la 'Réconciliation' dont les principes clairs, fondés sur l'Evangile assouvissaient mon désir d'absolu." A. Trocmé, "Mémoires," 157. Jules Jézéquel (1870–1963) was the main leader for the French branch of the "Alliance universelle pour l'amitié internationale par les Églises" (the official name of the organization, which Trocmé gives in a slightly different version) after the First World War. For the proceedings of the Lille congress, see *RCS* 37 (1924), issue nr. 3 (Trocmé's name is listed on 270).

88. In a letter written during the crisis of the Ruhr, Monod criticizes the conscientious objectors and their supporters: "[. . .] [ils] travaillent à miner l'armée française, la seule force militaire qui soit réellement à la disposition de la Société des Nations." "Extrait d'une lettre de M. Wilfred Monod à The Rév. Hon. Sir Willoughby H. Dickinson," *RCS* 36 (1923) 357.

89. "Avec eux fut constitué le 'groupe du Nord,' une équipe où l'on parlait beaucoup de l'évangélisation des ouvriers, où l'on professait un christianisme social avancé dont le héros était Henri Nick, le 'saint' de Fives-Lille." "Mémoires," 132.

the following students: Samuel Cornier, later pastor in Caudry, who died of natural causes in 1943; Émile Fabre (1898–1974), later pastor at Sin-le-Noble, a pacifist; and Marcel Heuzé (1897–1945), a former parishioner of Aquilas Quiévreux who had visited the "Fraternité" in Rouen as a theology student, and who became involved in the "World Brotherhood Federation," taking part in the Executive Committee meeting in Brussels on October 9–10, 1924 alongside Henri Nick.[90] Heuzé became a pastor in Hénin-Liétard, starting in May 1924, before moving two year later to Lens, and since the fall of 1939 in Marseille. He died in deportation, in April 1945.[91] Pierre Ducros (1900–1982), a pacifist and the son of a social Christian pastor, ministered since 1926 among the workers in Lille, and soon afterwards in Charente, in southwestern France, in order to preserve the health of his children.[92] The group also included Jean-Paul Benoit (1898–1975),[93] Daniel Chéradame (1893–1962), pastor in Hénin-Liétard from 1920 until 1931, then in Roubaix with the McAll Mission-*Mission populaire évangélique*,[94] and his brother Robert, pastor at Bruay (Pas-de-Calais), and Jacques Babut (1901–90), pastor in Saint-Quentin since 1925, after 1932 in Douai. Among the slightly older members was Élie Morel (1891–1978), who assisted Albert Aeschimann (1884–1942) in Liévin since 1926 and who later became senior pastor there until 1933.[95] Several in the group, including Trocmé, Babut, Fabre, Cornier, Ducros, Diény, and Robert Chéradame, were pacifists. Some of them were the sons of evangelistic and social Christian pastors. The group was interested in social issues, and most of its members leaned toward

---

90. *Bulletin de la Fédération des Fraternités Françaises*, nr. 6 (December 1924) 2. A list of all the participants (including the French delegation) is on 3. Marcel Heuzé had been called to the pastoral ministry as a soldier during the First World War (he had volunteered to fight). According to his wife Simone, one day after a battle (possibly at the Chemin des Dames) he heard a voice saying: "You will be my witness for peace." Heuzé papers, SHPF (Paris), letter from Simone Heuzé, dated January 18, 1985.

91. See Joseph Valynseele's notice in Encrevé, *Les Protestants*, 251–52.

92. In 1933 he wrote a letter to *RCS* in defense of conscientious objection, criticizing Wilfred Monod. *RCS* 46 (1933), vol. 2, 388. He was responding to Monod, "L'Église et l'objection au service militaire," *RCS* 46 (1933) 192–210.

93. On Jean-Paul Benoit, who joined Henri Nick in Lille from 1931 until 1934 before working in Paris-Belleville (1937–46) and who later served as President of the Société centrale d'évangélisation, see Pierre Petit's biographical entry in Encrevé, *Les Protestants*, 63.

94. *AMR* 49, nr. 4 (Nov. 1931) 18.

95. Albert Aeschimann was a pastor in Liévin and the area since 1910, where he started a section of the "Croix Bleue" (Roger, *Liévin*, 117). He contributed to the French social Christian journal *L'Avant-Garde*.

socialism or communism.[96] In the spring of 1920, members of the "groupe du Nord," joined by other theology students, sent a message to Élie Gounelle and his collaborator Georges Lauga, the editors of the *Revue du Christianisme social*, to express their full support to them and to the social Christian movement.[97] They also included a message from December 2, 1919, signed by twenty-four theology students, calling for a "radical transformation" of France, both at the individual and the communal levels, through the Gospel, for the formation of a closely knit group of men, indeed a "strong and homogeneous phalanx" of people "working together, united in humility and in consecration to God."[98] Gounelle was of course thrilled to see these future pastors express their full agreement with the ideals of the "Christianisme social."

As Trocmé indicates in his "Mémoires," the "groupe du Nord" had a "hero": Henri Nick, whom people often called "Monsieur Nick." After World War I, missionary work such as Nick's ministry continued to attract some of

---

96. "À la Faculté de théologie de Paris, le Groupe du Nord était nettement orienté vers les questions sociales. J'ai raconté plus haut que beaucoup de mes camarades, au retour du front, étaient 'rouges.'" Trocmé, "Mémoires," 274.

97. "En ce qui nous concerne personnellement, nous sommes de tout cœur avec vous; et, saisissant l'occasion qui nous est offerte, nous vous assurons de notre adhésion 'sans réserve.' [. . .] Le mouvement du Christianisme social nous paraît donc destiné à grouper en une puissante synthèse spirituelle tous les travailleurs chrétiens, de quelque catégorie qu'ils soient, répandus dans les organisations humaines existantes." "Message des étudiants en théologie de Paris," *RCS* 33 (1920), 384. The message was signed, among others, by Louis Dallière (from the earlier generation of students), Jacques Babut, Daniel Chéradame, J.-B. Couve, Jacques Diény, Pierre Ducros, C.-Émile Fabre, Marcel Heuzé, A. Trocmé, Daniel Vernier and Samuel Cornier (384).

98. "Au lendemain de la guerre, il nous apparaît plus clairement que jamais, d'une part que notre France a besoin d'être radicalement transformée, individus et société, par l'Évangile,—de l'autre, que nos Églises protestantes sont encore trop étrangères à l'Évangile fidèlement vécu, à l'esprit moderne, à l'action disciplinée, pour que l'effort puisse y être de quelque efficacité, ou même pour qu'elles réussissent encore à y vivre longtemps. En conséquence, nous nous unissons pour tenter: 1. De préciser et de formuler les conséquences que comporte pour notre ministère et notre pensée, le travail spirituel et intellectuel accompli au cours de nos études, et sous l'austère direction de la guerre; 2. De dépasser le stade de l'individualisme anarchique et d'aboutir sur les problèmes posés par la prière et l'étude en commun, à un rapport d'ensemble, qui sera l'expression non plus seulement de tendances individuelles isolées, mais des tendances d'un groupe d'hommes travaillant en commun et unis dans l'humilité et la consécration à Dieu; 3. De prolonger notre initiative en prenant au sérieux dans l'action la volonté de Jésus, et de créer entre serviteurs du Christ unis sur le même programme de vie et de travail une union étroite, formant au point de vue spirituel une phalange homogène et forte au sein des Églises et du monde.—(Paris, le 2 décembre 1919.)" "Message des étudiants," *RCS* 33 (1920) 383.

the best young graduates from the French Protestant theological seminaries.[99] The fact that he was a "red" pastor (Trocmé's word), a friend of socialist ideals, was certainly important, but as we saw earlier he was primarily—and of course Trocmé knew that—an evangelist in the Pietist tradition.[100]

Trocmé describes the ideals of his group of friends: "What attracted us was the workers' world with its communists, its idealism, its rebellion against the Church. We thought their rebellion was the result of a misunderstanding. Once that misunderstanding was eliminated, once the Gospel of total conversion proclaimed, a great religious revival would come throughout Europe and the world."[101]

That was the program! Just like the incredibly ambitious program of the "Fraternité" in Clamart, it may seem out of bound, coming for a small group of young men, but it would be a mistake, as we will see, to understand the "groupe du Nord" as the result of a youthful, passing idealism.

The bond between its members was very close. The group was well organized. It had its own monthly "bulletin," which consisted of two to eight typed pages meant to keep everyone connected, especially as the group was scattered throughout France—and beyond—during their two years of military service (for a period of time the group was named—or was it a different group, with overlapping members?—"groupe des isolés," and also "groupe des militaires"). As Samuel Cornier wrote in the conclusion of the October 1, 1922 bulletin (issue 17): "We hope above all that the circle of prayer will not be broken but will continue for all to be a source of life and mutual consecration."[102]

---

99. Samuel Mours writes about the "deep impact" ("l'écho profond") of the missionary work in northern France on French Protestantism as a whole, and its power of attraction on the most brilliant young pastors: "[. . .] nous voyons, pour la première fois, une œuvre d'évangélisation attirer à elle l'élite du corps pastoral." *Un siècle d'évangélisation*, vol. 2, 144 (see also 143, where he writes about its "retentissement [. . .] dans tout le protestantisme français"). Paul Barde said the same thing in 1927, decades before Mours: "Aujourd'hui [. . .], on ne passe plus pour un original, ni pour un homme héroïque quand, après de solides études de théologie, on s'en va évangéliser les mineurs, les verriers ou les ouvriers métallurgistes du Nord et du Pas-de-Calais. Il y a 36 ans, c'était assez différent [. . .]." *La Société centrale évangélique*, 59.

100. "[. . .] M. Nick lui-même [. . .], quoique 'rouge,' était avant tout un grand évangéliste piétiste [. . .]." Trocmé, "Mémoires," 275.

101. "Ce qui attirait notre groupe, c'était le monde ouvrier avec ses communistes, son idéalisme, sa révolte contre l'Eglise. Il nous semblait que cette révolte avait pour origine un malentendu. Aussitôt ce malentendu dissipé et l'Evangile de la totale conversion annoncé, un grand réveil religieux traverserait l'Europe et le monde." Ibid., 205.

102. "Nous espérons surtout que le cercle de prière ne se brisera pas mais continuera

André Trocmé's First Steps in Spiritual and Social Christianity

During his military service, Trocmé, like the others, missed "the wonderful life at the Faculté, which gives me much strength and awakens in me an immense trust."[103] As a soldier in the mountains of central Morocco, Trocmé would try to read a Psalm in the evening, "thinking about the Faculté, about all of you, about the bright future and its duties."[104] The circle of friends was a tremendous source of support for an isolated young man surrounded by soldiers who, for the most part, remained strangers. "The bulletins, the letters, here is what is needed, at any cost, in order to keep our vocation alive," he wrote.[105] When his sister Louise died, at the end of his time in Morocco, the members expressed their sympathy through the bulletin.[106]

In the issue from October 1922, the young men tackled the theme of "freedom and immorality in the barracks," or "how to preserve one's sense of responsibility, conscience and moral freedom" in the army (previous topics included "the practice of the inner life in the barracks," "purity in the barracks," "alcoholism in the barracks," "laziness in the barracks.")[107] Trocmé, or "oncle Troc," as Samuel Cornier (nr. 17, p. 7) and other students

---

pour tous à être foyer de vie et de consécration mutuelle." "Groupe des isolés," bulletin n. 17 (October 1, 1922) 7; Swarthmore College, Trocmé papers, series A, box 1.

103. "Cette vie si belle à la Faculté me donne de grandes forces et éveille en moi d'immenses confiances." Bulletin nr. 20, January 1, 1923, 5.

104. "Ma bible est sortie de là vieillie, déchirée et moisie, mais tous les soirs ça a été une jouissance pour moi de dresser, avec une planchette de géomètre une petite table improvisée, et de lire un psaume en pensant à la Fac, à vous tous, à l'avenir souriant et à ses devoirs." Message from February 21, in "Bulletin militaire," nr. 22, April 1923, 3-4.

105. "Les bulletins, les lettres, voilà ce qu'il faut à tout prix pour alimenter notre vocation." "Bulletin des militaires," nr. 25, June 1923, 2.

106. Trocmé writes: "C'est au D. I. M. ["Division d'Infanterie Marocaine," it seems; C.C.] de Casablanca que j'ai appris la mort de ma sœur, au milieu de 100 figures nouvelles. L'impossibilité d'obtenir d'un seul de ces hommes un mot de sympathie créa tout à coup entre eux et moi un abîme infranchissable. Je fis la traversée avec eux en muet, soulagé qu'on me laisse tranquille." "Bulletin des militaires," nr. 25, June 1923, 2. In nr. 22 Samuel Cornier writes: "Notre cher Troc vient de perdre sa sœur. Tu sais toute notre affection. Elle est avec toi et nos prières, dans ta solitude." "Bulletin militaire," April 1923, 3. Louise was his half-sister and was significantly older than him (she was born in 1874). He writes about her in his "Mémoires" (37): "Louise était très pieuse, très prise par les 'Unions Chrétiennes de Jeunes Filles' dont elle s'était toujours occupée. Pendant mon service militaire je lui écrivis souvent. Par lettre notre affection s'exprimait plus facilement. [. . .] Elle mourut d'une maladie du cœur, pendant que j'étais au Maroc [. . .]."

107. Samuel Cornier writes: "Je propose qu'en Décembre nous prenions la série des anciens sujets:—la pratique de la vie intérieure à la caserne; les camarades et la vie intérieure.—la pureté à la caserne.—l'alcoolisme à la caserne.—la paresse à la caserne." Bulletin nr. 18 (Nov. 1, 1922) 5.

at the Faculté called him, reports on his experience, half way through his own service in the army, and as he was preparing to travel to Morocco, citing the examples of two fellow soldiers he had encountered, before concluding: "any male association which is not dominated by a very high ideal, and in which the antidote to all vices, i.e., work, does not exist, will fatally indulge in immorality and will lead all of its members to this immorality. This can be observed in all kinds of male reunions (boarding schools, graduate schools, sporting associations, etc)."[108] How then can one preserve one's moral responsibility, conscience, and moral freedom? The answer lies in education at a young age, and in conversion:

> When the individual arrives to his regiment without already having a certain freedom, *all is lost*, unless we are here, with a great love, with our service clubs, with work, which will allow us to demonstrate to B. [an anonymous person used by Trocmé as an example; CC] that the military environment is abnormal, hideous, and that the environment of our club is the only one worthy of imitation. Our action will always be fragile, fragmentary, superficial, because it is too late, at age 20, to educate a man who is already grown. My conclusion is pessimistic, I realize it, but it is conform to the truth. In that situation there is only one remedy left for B.: religious conversion.[109]

In another contribution to the same issue (nr. 17; October 1, 1922) Trocmé suggests the group reflect on the "upheaval" each has gone through

---

108. "Toute assemblée masculine qui n'est pas dominée par un idéal très élevé et au sein de laquelle le contrepoison de tous les vices, le *travail*, n'existe pas, est fatalement livrée à l'immoralité et livre tous les hommes qui en font partie à cette immoralité. Ceci est observable dans toutes sortes de réunions masculines (internats, grandes écoles, sociétés sportives. . .)." "Groupe des isolés," nr. 17 (Oct. 1, 1922), 2. Samuel Cornier writes about "Trocmé qui se prépare à partir pour le Maroc" (7).

109. "Lorsque l'individu arrive au régiment sans posséder d'avance une certain liberté, *tout est perdu*, à moins que nous ne soyons là, nous avec un grand amour, des foyers, du travail, qui nous permettront de prouver à B. que le milieu du régiment est anormal, monstrueux et que le milieu [du] foyer est celui qui seul est digne d'être imité. Notre action sera toujours précaire, fragmentaire, superficielle, parce qu'il est trop tard à 20 ans pour éduquer un homme déjà fait. Ma conclusion est pessimiste, je le sais, mais elle est conforme à la vérité. Dans cet état de choses il ne reste plus qu'un remède pour B.: la conversion religieuse." "Groupe des isolés," bulletin n. 17 (Oct. 1, 1922), 2. The "foyers" ("clubs") refer to the "Foyers du soldat," the hundreds of service clubs set up by the "Union franco-américaine" under the leadership of Emmanuel Sautter (1862–1933) and the support of John R. Mott (1865–1955), following the model of the YMCA. The "Foyers" were designed to serve the young men during their military service or during a war. There were more than 1,500 Foyers by the end of the First World War, and around 400 in June 1919. See Hélène Trocmé, "Un modèle américain."

during their military service. He notes that for him five "dreams" are now dead: 1. "the hope for the coming of the Kingdom" has been replaced by "conversion, the certainty of the existence, immediate and very near, of an elite which represents the seed of the kingdom." 2. "the goodness of man and optimism" is now replaced by "the possibilities which remain despite everything in man's shame and intemperance." 3. "the belief in the freedom of all human beings" has been reduced to "the certainty that, even if the freedom of most human beings is almost nil, a strong education can create dignified and conscientious people." 4. "the belief in our own goodness (an expression of pride)" is replaced by "humility, the consequence of our miserable downfalls." 5. "the belief in the power of words" has given way to "the certainty that acts alone, the religious acts which constitute the leitmotiv of the gospels, are of value here on earth."[110]

From these five points, it appears that Trocmé's beliefs have been severely tested by his first year in the army: his hopes have been dramatically reduced by these months in the midst of other young men whose moral "downfalls" have been overwhelming to him. But, in a way, his faith remains intact: he continues to be certain of the need for missionary work

---

110. "Le régiment produit en nous un bouleversement dont il faut nous rendre compte. Il serait bon de nous communiquer nos expériences les plus intimes. Brusquement ou lentement certains des soleils qui illuminaient notre vie s'éteignent. [. . .]

Les rêves qui meurent:	Les réalités qui croissent:
L'espérance de la venue du Royaume	La conversion, la certitude de l'existence immédiate et toute proche d'une élite formant le germe du royaume.
La bonté des hommes et l'optimisme	Les possibilités qui subsistent malgré tout dans la honte et le laisser aller des hommes.
La croyance dans la liberté de tous les hommes	La conviction que, si la liberté de la plupart des hommes est quasi nulle, une forte éducation peut faire des hommes dignes et conscients.
La croyance en notre propre bonté (elle est orgueil)	L'humilité, conséquence de nos misérables chutes.
La croyance en la puissance des mots (Nous rêvons d'être des orateurs, des entraîneurs)	La conviction que les actes seuls, les actes religieux dont est tissée la trame des évangiles, ont une valeur quelconque ici bas."

"Groupe des isolés," bulletin n. 17 (Oct. 1, 1922), 6–7.

among people, especially among children and young adults. And he has certainly not abandoned the "high ideals" that already characterized his work at the "Fraternity" in Clamart a few years earlier. Finally, the concern for "purity" remains central to him. Indeed, as he writes in the 20th issue of the bulletin: "the problem of purity, which already was a source of anxiety before the army, has only become more important to me, for my own life as well as for the life of others. [. . .] The problem of our own purity, and the purity of others, is *the* question in my life."[111] Trocmé adds this important remark: "The problem of purity is therefore identical for me with the problem of my life, with the problem of all human lives. That is how we must present it. We cannot present to our comrades on the one hand the problem of purity, and on the other the problem of alcoholism, and then add the social problem. The only way to present things is to talk about life as a whole, for life cannot be compartmentalized."[112]

The concern for purity cannot be separated from social concerns. The members of the "groupe du Nord" were in agreement about that, and those who were not serving in the army took part in a reconciliatory gesture at Christmas 1922 by sending greetings of peace to all theology students throughout Germany.[113] A similar gesture had been made during the previous war, in 1870–71, through the UCJG (YMCA).

Responses from ten German universities were listed in the March 1923 bulletin (nr. 21, 3–4). Most of them expressed gratitude for the Christmas message and sent their friendly greetings, while one message (from Kiel), written ten days after January 11, 1923, and the beginning of the occupation of the Ruhr by the French army, conveyed the German students' "inability" to thank the French students.[114]

---

111. "Le problème de la pureté, qui m'angoissait déjà avant la caserne, n'a cessé de prendre de l'importance pour moi, aussi [bien] pour ma propre vie que pour celle des autres. [. . .] La question de notre pureté, et celle des autres, est toute la question de ma vie." Bulletin of the "groupe des militaires," nr. 20 (Jan. 1, 1923), 1–2.

112. "Le problème de la pureté est donc identique pour moi au problème de ma vie, au problème de toutes les vies humaines. Et c'est comme cela que nous devons le présenter. On ne peut pas présenter à nos camarades d'une part le problème de la pureté, de l'autre celui de l'alcoolisme, et d'un 3eme côté le problème social. Il n'y a qu'une manière parler, c'est de parler de toute la vie, parce que la vie ne se divise pas en compartiments." Bulletin nr. 20, 2.

113. "Nous avons adressé à toutes les fac de Théo d'allemagne un message d'affection pour Noël. 18 d'entre nous l'ont signé. Déjà nous avons reçu une réponse de Marbourg avec 17 signatures." Note by "Sam" (Samuel Cornier) in Bulletin nr. 20, January 1 (1923), 4.

114. In some cases the Christmas message led to heated debates in German universities, and not just among students! In Göttingen, Karl Barth clashed with his

THE FRENCH "RÉCONCILIATION"

Trocmé learned about the "Fellowship of Reconciliation" (FoR) during his theological studies. The idea of a "Fellowship" originated during the short-lived congress of Constance (August 1914), and its founders organized it at the end of the war. A French branch was founded in January 1923, after the general secretary of the "Fellowship," Oliver Dryer, along with Halvard Lange (1902–70), while visiting French Quaker communities, organized an information session at the "Faculté libre de théologie protestante" in Paris.[115] On February 6, a "comité provisoire" of the French "Réconciliation," as it would be called, crafted a declaration stating it welcomed people of all faiths, philosophies, and political orientations who were committed to the ideal of brotherhood.[116]

One of the members of this "comité provisoire" was Henri Roser. Encouraged by Dryer and Lange's visit, at the end of January he decided he would refuse to continue to serve in the army. A descendant of Jean-Frédéric Oberlin, he was then preparing himself for missionary work by studying, since November 1921, at the "Maison des Missions," near the "Faculté de théologie protestante."[117] He had also just spent the summer working with Henri Nick, running a youth camp in Aubengue, near

---

colleague Emanuel Hirsch. In the end, as Hirsch had changed his mind and was now ready to sign the letter, which had been drafted by Barth, the administration of the University of Göttingen objected in principle to a reply. See Karl Barth's circular letter from 23 January 1923, in K. Barth–E. Thurneysen, *Briefwechsel 1921–1930*, edited by Eduard Thurneysen (Zurich: TVZ, 1974) 131.

115. "*La section française de la Fellowship of Reconciliation a adopté la déclaration de principe ci-dessous et adressé à ceux des Allemands qui veulent travailler dans le même sens qu'elle, l'appel suivant*: Frères et Sœurs d'Allemagne, À la suite de la visite en France et de la campagne menée dans la seconde quinzaine de janvier par notre ami Oliver Dryer, assisté de Frü Waegner et d'Halvard Lange, une section française de la Réconciliation vient de se constituer." "Déclaration de principes de la Réconciliation, section française de la Fellowship of Reconciliation," *Voies Nouvelles* 5, nr. 6 (April 1923), 54–55.

116. "*La Réconciliation est une association internationale de gens de bonne volonté qui peuvent professer sur bien des points des credos religieux ou philosophiques très différents, et qui appartiennent à des classes sociales et des partis politiques divers, mais que rapproche leur foi commune en un même idéal: celui de la fraternité humaine qu'il faut s'efforcer de réaliser grâce à la puissance de l'amour se manifestant par des actes.*" Ibid., 54.

117. Oberlin was the grandfather of Roser's great-grandmother. Roser's grandfather was a pastor in Oberlin's parish, Ban de la Roche. See Henri Roser "père" (the father of Trocmé's colleague and friend Henri Roser), "Letter from a Descendant of Oberlin," in *Oberlin Alumni Magazine* 13/7 (April 1917), 197.

Boulogne-sur-Mer.[118] In April 1923, Roser was asked to leave the "Maison des Missions" because of his stance as a conscientious objector. Henri Nick immediately invited him to return to Lille to work at the "Foyer du Peuple."[119] Roser spent a year in Fives. Back in the capital, he opened a evangelistic "hall" in Aubervilliers, a working-class neighborhood northeast of Paris. He returned to Fives in the late 1920s for further missionary campaigns[120] and after the war became the director of the "Mission populaire" for almost a decade.

In 1960, looking back at the beginning of what was soon called the "Réconciliation," Roser wrote this about his first encounter with the leaders of the "Fellowship of Reconciliation":

> André Trocmé was present, as well as Jacques Babut, Jacques Diény and others. I was there too and was wonderfully encouraged when I discovered not only that there were thousands like me in the world who professed this Christian pacifism to which I had myself been called a month earlier, but also that there was a considerable tradition regarding this matter in the Church. One was not simply insane, the victim of mental turmoil or of idealist delirium. One was not an asocial crank advocating, as the proper Church authorities had tried to convince me, 'un-Christian and even inhuman' views.[121]

In those years, because of Roser's courageous stance, French Protestantism was discovering the phenomenon of conscientious objection. As an institution, it unambiguously rejected it. Quickly, Trocmé and Roser became leaders in the French Christian pacifist movement. Roser became the editor of the *Cahiers de la réconciliation* in 1927 and, a year later, secretary of the French branch of the "International Fellowship of Reconciliation" (IFoR), whereas Trocmé became a member of its European Council.

---

118. Kneubühler, *Henri Roser*, 25 and 149.
119. Ibid., 26–28.
120. "Characteristic News from Lille," *AMR* 47, nr. 3 (May 1929), 12.
121. "André Trocmé y assistait et aussi Jacques Babut, Jacques Diény, d'autres encore. J'y étais également et reçus un merveilleux encouragement à découvrir que non seulement ils étaient des milliers dans le monde qui professaient ce pacifisme chrétien auquel j'avais moi-même été appelé un mois auparavant, mais qu'il y avait sur la matière une longue et considérable tradition dans l'Eglise. On n'était pas fou, victime d'effervescence mentale et de délire idéaliste. On n'était pas un illuminé asocial, dont la position n'était, comme de bonnes autorités ecclésiastiques avaient tenté de m'en persuader, 'ni chrétienne, ni même humaine.'" Kneubühler, *Henri Roser*, 149, quoting Roser, "La Réconciliation de 1923 à 1944," 3.

The two men met regularly, and Roser's friendship certainly impacted Trocmé.[122]

EARLY INTERNATIONAL PACIFIST ENCOUNTERS

As leaders in the "Fellowship of Reconciliation," Roser and Trocmé also took part in international meetings. In 1923, André Philip (1902–70), a prominent young member of the "Fédé Étudiante" (the "Fédération des étudiants chrétiens"), and a man whose stature as a Christian and a socialist would grow tremendously during the following decades, had taken part with Samuel Cornier and others in a meeting of the "Fellowship" in Nyborg, Denmark. The following year, at the end of July, Roser, Trocmé and Henri Nick travelled to Bad Boll, a small town in southwestern Germany well-known as a Pietist center since the ministry of Johann Christoph Blumhardt (1805–80) and, with the new century, his son Christoph (1842–1919), an important figure in social Christianity. From July 29 until August 7, 1924, Bad Boll was the site of an international gathering of IFoR.

Eighty participants reflected on the general theme of "following Christ in our time" ("die Nachfolge Christi in unserer Zeit") by addressing four topics: "private property," "violence," "class struggle," and "Christ."[123] In his "Mémoires," after mentioning his disappointment with his theological studies in Paris, Trocmé writes: "Nevertheless I felt called to follow other directions: I spoke German, English, I had taken part in several conferences of the Fellowship of Reconciliation, including one in Bad Boll throuch which I came in contact with H. Roser, M. Nick, Siegmund Schultze and an English Labor deputy, Sir Walter Ayles, which deeply impressed impressed me. I was a Christian pacifist, at least in principle."[124] In Bad

---

122. "Henri Roser, à cette époque, commença de jouer, dans mon existence, un rôle important. [. . .] La 'Fellowship of Reconciliation' avait un jour demandé à Roser de devenir secrétaire pour la France, et Roser accepta [. . .] J'étais devenu, à l'époque, membre du Conseil Européen de la Réconciliation [. . .]" "Mémoires," 204.

123. See Leonhard Ragaz's report in *Neue Wege* (Sept. 1924), 388 and 391. Ragaz was disappointed by the conference (392): "Abschliessend möchte ich sagen, dass diese Konferenz in Boll gewiss nicht so freudig und begeisternd gewesen ist, wie die in Nyborg."

124. "Cependant je me sentais appelé vers d'autres horizons: je parlais l'allemand, l'anglais, j'avais pris part à quelques conférences du Mouvement de la Réconciliation, dont l'une à Bad Boll m'avait mis en contact avec H. Roser, M. Nick, Siegmund Schultze et un député travailliste anglais, Sir Walter Agles [sic], ce qui m'impressionna beaucoup. J'étais pacifiste chrétien, tout au moins en principe." "Mémoires," 156. The name of Sir Walter Ayles is mistyped in the original text of Trocmé's "Mémoires."

Boll, Trocmé was introduced to some of the most significant figures in the international Christian pacifist movement, a movement that understood itself as part of the social Christian movement. Walter Ayles (1879–1953), a conscientious objector during the war, had spent two and a half years in prison. Since 1923 he represented the Independent Labour party at the British parliament.[125] Trocmé also met: Leonhard Ragaz, the leading theologian, alongside Hermann Kutter, of the Swiss religious-social movement; Friedrich Siegmund-Schultze (1885–1969), a pioneer of the social-Christian movement in Germany; Pierre Cérésole (1879–1945), the founder in 1920 of "Service Civil International" (also known as the "International Voluntary Service for Peace"; IVSP); and, presumably for the second time, Oliver Dryer.[126] Ragaz, Siegmund-Schultze, Dryer, and Cérésole had participated in the founding of IFoR in Bilthoven, near Utrecht, in 1919. A few years before his death, Trocmé wrote: "It is in Bad Boll, in the charming scenery of the institution which bears the mark of Christoph Blumhardt and his father, that I had the revelation of the power of these men's faith."[127]

Approximately one hundred participants made the journey to Bad Boll (two hundred or so participants had attended the previous conferences, at Sonntagberg, Austria, in August 1922, and Nyborg in 1923, but it was decided that a smaller gathering would be in better position to discuss the question of the religious basis of the "Fellowship"). Besides tackling topics such as the legitimacy of private property, the Franciscan spirit of poverty, economic laws and the importance of educating children, themes that all appear in the notes André Trocmé took during the conference, the Bad Boll conference was significant for the decision made by the "Fellowship" to "firmly confess its Christian roots, without any ambiguity," against voices that were in favor of minimizing the Christian identity of the

---

125. See Walter Ayles's contribution to the pamphlet *Why I Am a Conscientious Objector: Being Answers to the Tribunal Catechism*, London, No-Conscription Fellowship, 1916. Ragaz mentions Ayles' prison sentence and calls him "ein außerordentlicher Mensch" in a letter to Waldus Nestler, January 29, 1923, in Christine Ragaz et al., *Leonhard Ragaz in seinen Briefen* vol. 2 (Zurich: TVZ, 1982) 270.

126. During the Second World War, Siegmund-Schultze asked several Protestant leaders to support the work done at Le Chambon. Grotefeld, *Friedrich Siegmund-Schultze*, 255.

127. "C'est à Bad Boll, dans le cadre charmant de l'institution laissée par Christoph Blumhardt, Vater und Sohn, que j'eus la révélation de la puissance de la foi de ces hommes." A. Trocmé, "Mémoires," 541. Trocmé mentions F. Siegmund-Schultze, J. Nevin Sayre, Leonhard Ragaz, Pierre Cérésole and others.

movement in order to be more inclusive of the pacifists in India.[128] That decision is not surprising, when one realizes that many of the participants in Bad Boll were Protestant pastors. And so the following statement was sent out at the close of the conference:

> The Kingdom of God must come on earth. It is in the certainty of this faith that we have united with one another not in order to form a new brotherhood but to live in the brotherhood founded on that Love with which the eternal Father loves all His children and which was most gloriously revealed in Jesus Christ. We know that there is a way on which Christ is going before us, and that that way leads to the redemption of the world. If we are faithful we shall find that the Helper is greater than the need. The more serious the decisions that confront us in the life of nations, the more will Christ be revealed, and the more wonderfully will His Spirit manifest its creative power in those willing to be used by Him.[129]

---

128. Roser writes: "Des Français et des Françaises participèrent à tous les congrès régionaux ou internationaux organisés par le Mouvement de la Réconciliation. [. . .] On en vit à Vaumarcus, en 1927, comme déjà à Bad Boll en 1924; André Trocmé et moi y fûmes invités à participer, avec M. Nick, à la session du Comité International où Leonhard Ragaz et Natanaël Beskov firent prévaloir la thèse d'une Réconciliation fermement chrétienne, contre la demande d'un pseudo-élargissement qui eût permis de rallier des Hindous. La pensée prévalut qu'ils pouvaient, bien entendu, se joindre au Mouvement si sa position leur paraissait vraie, mais que le Mouvement comme tel devait s'affirmer chrétien sans ambiguïté, comme on présente une lumière d'ailleurs et non comme on s'entoure d'une barrière." Roser, "La Réconciliation de 1923 à 1944," 5. See also Ragaz's report in *Neue Wege* (Sept. 1924), 391, as well as Stevenson, *Towards a Christian International*, 13–14: "The first large international conference met at Sonntagberg, Austria, in August, 1922. Two hundred from twenty nations were present. [. . .] At Nyborg, in 1923, again some two hundred came together. At this conference social and industrial problems received more consideration than previously. [. . .] At Bad-Boll, in 1924, the conference was deliberately restricted to about one hundred, so that there might be more possibility of reviewing foundations. The question of private property and the nature of the basis were examined with much care, and to this conference we owe a statement on the religious basis of the Fellowship." Trocmé's notes, which are laconic and very difficult to decipher, can be consulted at Swarthmore College (Trocmé papers, series B, box 7). As we will see in part 4, the question of the Christian identity of IFoR resurfaced, with greater force, in the 1960s.

129. "The Religious Basis of the International Fellowship of Reconciliation," quoted in Stevenson, *Towards a Christian International*, 49–50.

UNION THEOLOGICAL SEMINARY AND MAGDA GRILLI

Against his father's wishes, André Trocmé decided to spend a fifth year of theological studies abroad. His first choice was to attend the French Institute in Jerusalem, but another student, more familiar with semitic languages, was awarded the scholarship. A scholarship for Union Theological Seminary in New York City was available. He applied and received it. At the end of the summer of 1925, he left France for the United States.

Trocmé was not enthralled by his courses and thought that his professors in Paris were in several cases superior. Reinhold Niebuhr was still a pastor in Detroit at the time (he arrived at Union in 1928). In a paper written for George Albert Coe's course, he sharply criticized his professor's views on education. In a course on Christian ethics, he quoted Élie Gounelle and wrote, in a language he had yet to master, that "[. . .] Christianity has to retake its place as chief dreamer into the humanity. It has no more to follow, but to lead [. . .]. As Élie Gounelle, the leader of the French Christian socialism, said: We do not know very precisely what we want, but what we want, we will it well."[130]

The teacher who had the greatest impact on Trocmé was Harry F. Ward (1873–1966), an English-born leader in the Social Gospel, a professor of Christian ethics at Union since 1918.[131] Ward was a controversial figure, a fervent advocate of the communist economy practiced by the Soviets. He denounced the "idols of the day" such as prosperity, credit loans, the large conglomerates or "trusts" (Rockefeller, Ford, etc.) and their ties to political power.[132] Trocmé asked Ward to supervise his thesis on Alexandre Vinet, the Swiss francophone religious thinker and author. The title of the thesis, which he completed by the end of 1925, was: "Alexander Vinet. A Champion of Individual Socialism in the Beginnings of the Ninteenth [sic] Century."[133] Trocmé submitted it toward the end of the academic year 1925–26. We need to take a quick look at this thesis.

Trocmé begins by introducing Vinet, a little-known author in the English-speaking world, and yet a man who influenced many prominent thinkers including "de Pressensé, the senator; Gaston Frommel, the

---

130. Swarthmore College, Series B, box 5, 4th folder.

131. On Ward, see Duke, *In the Trenches*.

132. "Mémoires," 213.

133. "Encore présentai-je ma thèse en anglais à la fin de l'année, ce qui me donna beaucoup de peine." "Mémoires," 214. The thesis can be consulted at Swarthmore College: Trocmé papers, series B, box 5, 5th folder. The quotes I am using here are followed by the page numbers.

dogmatician; Tommy Fallot, the first Christian socialist in French speaking countries; and, finally, Ragaz, the well known Swiss Christian socialist" (1). Trocmé examines Vinet's religious individualism, his religion of conscience, admitting that for the Swiss liberal thinker Christianity's goal was not to renew society or to build the Kingdom of God (50–1). Indeed, Vinet was "anti-socialist, and seems politically far from the actual [read: contemporary] tendency" (62) in French Protestantism and elsewhere. But that should not lead one to think that Vinet ignored the social dimension of the Christian message. As Trocmé writes in his fourth chapter, on "the Social Mission of Christianity," Vinet's religious individualism and personalism allowed him to defend the right of conscience when confronted by "immoral laws." Hence the intriguing expression "individual socialism" in the title of the thesis. Trocmé summarizes the findings of that chapter, at times paraphrasing Vinet himself (55–56):

> In this study, our first conclusion, if we are sincere, is that order is nothing, without justice. There are some laws which are not just. Vinet does not speak about laws that violate my interest, but about laws that violate my conscience. Sometimes the human law is opposed to the divine. Immoral laws are those which oblige me to act against my conscience. In such a case we must work for the revocation of the law. And if the majority is against us? If the law cannot be revoked? Then, answers Vinet, we have to violate the law, and not only to violate it, but excite the people to resistance. But this is equivalent to breaking the 'social contract' of the state. For the state, 'yes,' says Vinet, but not for us. Conscience is above laws. And if we are condemned by the tribunals? Then we have to accept all the consequences of our resistance, and the suffering that our attitude carries with it, for testimony is valuable when it is transformed into martyrdom. Acting this way we do not derogate our duties as citizens. We must not use force, anyway. Law is using force, and is not essentially different from the use of force. The right to do our duty is the first right. That is everywhere supposed. We do not ask for this right, we take it.

On the basis of several passages from Vinet's works on the freedom of religious faith and practice, Trocmé has unearthed a prophetic dimension in his religious individualism and concludes, quoting him, that "[t]he principle of resistance, far from subservience, is the principle of the life of societies. It is the fight of good against evil" (56).[134] Trocmé has

---

134. Trocmé is quoting from *La liberté des cultes*, Paris, Marc Ducloux, 1852, 364.

found similar views to his own in Vinet's works, and thus describes the Swiss thinker's vision as one "of a non-violent Christian revolution [...] marching through all the countries, in spite of the darkness of the present hour" (58). Vinet had a "prophetic glimpse of the future," (60) but his "revolutionary and prophetic principles" (61) were lost on some of his most fervent admirers.

The fifth and final chapter of the thesis, which also serves as its conclusion, explores "Vinet's Influence on Protestant Thought" and contrasts his thought with the "French Christian socialist movement," its "founder" (62) Tommy Fallot and other more recent leaders. Certainly, Fallot "was not directly under the influence of Vinet" (62), but the two men do have something important in common: they both focused on "human development" and the social conditions that favor or hinder it (63). In more recent years, according to Trocmé, the "school of Fallot," which "is still strongly alive," has been leaning "ever more toward a practically [sic] individualism in society very close to the ideas of Vinet, himself." (63) And yet, Wilfred Monod, "perhaps the most prominent social Christian in French Protestantism," has paid relatively little attention to Vinet's social thought (64–65).

In his conclusion, Trocmé argues that Alexandre Vinet "has a strong chance to become not only a new leader of French Protestant thought, but really for European thought, also" (66). Why so? Vinet's thought combines a "fundamental pessimism concerning human nature" which will resonate with "the German modern school, which accentuates the personal inability of man to do good in order to promote the kingdom of God on earth." (66–67) It is apparent here that Trocmé had some awareness of Karl Barth's theology. That awareness was not without some misunderstandings: he describes Barth as a "disciple" of Ragaz and as "the most prominent philosopher of pessimism and mysticism in modern Germany" (67).[135] Vinet's pessimism might appeal to the Germans, but his "absolute union between faith and life," between religion and ethics, would appeal to the anglophone world (67). Hence Vinet's promise, as a thinker who might help bridge the rift within Western Protestantism on religious

---

He is using Rivet, "L'individualisme," who already quotes, on 82, the same passage from *La liberté des cultes*).

135. Trocmé's description reveals that, despite his good linguistic skills (his mother was German, he had visited his maternal family numerous times since his childhood), he had not read Barth's works closely. Otherwise he would have noticed Barth's rejection of "mysticism" and his self-identification as a theologian, not a philosopher. He would also have noted the increasing critical stance Barth was taking, especially since the end of World War I, with regard to Ragaz and other leaders of the "religiös-sozial" movement.

matters. And yet his promise will be realized only if Vinet's thought is corrected on several points: first, socialism cannot be rejected as easily as Vinet suggested (on the basis of a superficial knowledge of its tenets). Attention to communal realities, to "economic factors and mass reactions" (68), is required. Certainly, unjust laws must be resisted, but a second step needs to be taken: "we must promote just laws" (69). Second, Vinet, who died in 1847, did not live to see "all the consequences of capitalism." Christians must realize "the full weight of its oppressive mass" (69). Third and final point: "there is no real place in his social teaching for love" (70). In the final sentences, Trocmé writes: "Love is not only a thing reserved to friends and immediate surroundings; the lover [read: "the person who loves"] who saves a friend out of the sea is, indeed, a great lover; but the lover who gathers all the ship-wrecked onto the raft is a clever lover, and his love is more extensive. One way is not exclusive of the other" (70). And so the social dimension had to be taken into consideration, even if Vinet had been right to say that "the only way out is through personal christianization" (69). As we will see, Trocmé put this prescient affirmation about love of the multitude into practice during the next worldwide "shipwreck." But for now, what is clear is that by 1926, Trocmé had already developed a deep sense of the necessity, at times, of civil disobedience in order to challenge unjust laws.

MAGDA GRILLI

The story of André Trocmé and Magda Grilli's encounter is quite interesting. From their accounts in their memoirs, and particularly from Magda Trocmé's "Souvenirs autobiographiques," one notices how well suited they were for each other, especially in that they were everything but conventional people.

Born and raised in Florence, Magda Grilli (1901–96) was the daughter of Oscar Grilli di Cortona, an engineer and a colonel in the Italian army who belonged to Florentine nobility, and Nelly Wissotzky, of Russian descent. Nelly Wissotzky had been married for less than a year when she died, within a month of giving birth to Magda, at the end of November 1901. Magda's grandmother, Varia Wissotzky, née Poggio, had moved to Florence from Siberia, accompanying her father Alexander Poggio (he had participated in the 1825 Decembrist uprising in Saint Petersburg). Magda's grandmother had eventually left the Orthodox Church and embraced Protestantism. She volunteered with the Salvation Army. When her daughter Nelly (Magda's mother) died, it was the founding pastor of the Waldensian congregation in Florence, pastor Paolo Geymonat, who celebrated her funeral. He also baptized Magda, who in her youth attended a Waldensian Church. When placed by her stepmother in a Roman Catholic school, in the convent of the Mantellate Sisters, Magda wished to become Roman Catholic but had great difficulties adjusting to Catholic practices and beliefs. In her early teens she was confirmed by the archbishop of Florence, and later re-baptized by a Catholic priest.[136]

In many ways, while growing up in Florence, Magda had become acquainted with the Protestant world and with recent new movements in its midst, to a large extent because of her grandmother. Two maids in the house were from the Waldensian valleys of Piedmont (northern Italy). As a teenager she had spent two weeks in Torre Pellice, the historical center of the Waldensian Church in Piedmont, living with a family from Switzerland. Through her friend Aimée Jalla, who belonged to a well-known family in Waldensian circles, Magda became familiar with the "Unions Chrétiennes de Jeunes Filles" (UCJF, or YWCA). Jalla was the secretary of the UCJF in Florence, and she invited Magda to become a member of the committee. Soon Magda was teaching French, which she spoke fluently, to women workers on Sunday mornings. She also successfully campaigned in San Frediano, a neglected and poor neighborhood, for the opening of a kindergarten. As a consequence of her success, she was asked to lead a month-long camp for young girls affiliated with the UCJF in Cireglio, near Pistoia (Tuscany). The UCJF offered her a scholarship to study at Woodbrooke College, in Selly Oak, Birmingham (UK), an institution affiliated with the Society of Friends (Quakers), to take courses in Scripture and social work and to become a secretary for the UCJF. She refused the offer, however, as she was aware of her inability to fully adhere to traditional Christian dogmas. But her friend Aimée did not give up on her: sensing that an orientation toward social work would interest her much more than biblical studies, she spoke to her about her recent studies at the New York School of Social Work, in Manhattan. Magda was enthused. She applied and received a scholarship.[137]

Magda Grilli arrived in New York City in August 1925. She moved in the "International House," a residence hall for students built by John D. Rockefeller Jr. a year earlier near Union Theological Seminary, on

---

136. Magda Trocmé, "Souvenirs autobiographiques," 53–56.
137. Ibid., 85–87.

Manhattan's Upper West Side.[138] Marcel Christen, a theology student from Switzerland whose father had been a Protestant pastor in Florence, introduced André Trocmé to her at the cafeteria of the "International House" in the spring of 1926. His feelings for her developed quickly: hearing that she was taking part in a trip to Washington DC and Baltimore organized by the members of the "Cosmopolitan Club" at Easter 1926, he became a member of the club and registered for the trip. Soon they were talking about religious, philosophical, and other matters. Their similar involvements with the UCJG, their discovery of the working class, a world that had been foreign to them in their youth, probably facilitated their conversations. On April 18, 1926, they took a ferryboat across the Hudson river, to the Palisades (New Jersey), as people sometimes did on weekends, and during a long conversation, Trocmé asked Magda to marry him. It was their third conversation, and Magda replied by listing all the potential problems, including her complicated family background and her lack of faith in Christianity's dogmas. Trocmé had responses to every single problem. She wrote in her "Souvenirs autobiographiques": "Back in France, we would work for the evangelization of northern France, among the workers. Social work as much as religious work. Moral misery, financial difficulties, a region devastated by the war. A group of young pastors called 'Groupe du Nord,' was intent on transforming the North, France, the Church, for more justice, more humanity, more peace. What a program! Yes, that is what I wanted. Life, work, a kind of revolution rather than fruitless rantings between four walls [. . .]. And so we considered ourselves engaged to each another. The day was April 18, 1926."[139]

André Trocmé had presented her with the program of his future life as a Protestant minister, and Magda Grilli immediately sensed the promise of a life quite different from any conventional married life. Their involvements among workers had prepared them for each other and for a communal ministry for others beyond the confines of traditional ecclesiastical circles.

---

138. M. Trocmé, "Souvenirs autobiographiques," 110.

139. "Rentrés en France, nous travaillerions pour l'évangélisation du nord de la France au milieu des ouvriers. Travail social autant que religieux. Misère morale, difficultés financières, pays ravagé par la guerre. Un groupe de jeunes pasteurs dit le 'Groupe du Nord,' décidés à transformer le nord, la France, l'Eglise, pour plus de justice, plus d'humanité, plus de paix. Tout un programme! Oui, c'était bien cela que je voulais. La vie, le travail, une espèce de révolution et non pas des élucubrations stériles entre quatre murs [. . .]. Et voilà : nous nous sommes considérés comme fiancés. C'était le 18 avril 1926." M. Trocmé, "Mémoires," 123.

THE ROCKEFELLER CHILDREN—RETURN TO FRANCE

They may have been engaged to each other, but Magda Grilli and André Trocmé did not see each other as often as they wished. She was tutoring individual students most evenings until 10 p.m. There was a tradition, for French students who were studying at Union Theological Seminary with a scholarship, of tutoring the children of John D. Rockefeller Jr. (1874–1960) in French. In exchange of a monthly stipend, Trocmé picked up Rockefeller's youngest sons, Winthrop (Winnie) (1912–73) and David (born in 1915), at the Lincoln School, north of Central Park, and brought them back home by bus to 54th street, then the largest private residence in New York City. When he was free, at 6:30 p.m., Magda was still working. On Fridays, he would accompany them to Kykuit, the 40-room Rockefeller family estate north of Manhattan, near Tarrytown, before returning to the city on Saturdays.[140] At Christmas 1925, he accompanied the Rockefellers' other son Laurance (1910–2004) to the family estate in Ormond Beach, Florida. At the end of his first year as a tutor, he joined the family in a long tour by train throughout the United States, visiting several national parks.[141] Like other fellow French theology students before him (including Édouard Theis in 1922–23[142]), he was discovering the world of American billionaires, indeed working for one of the wealthiest men in history! One wonders whether he heard Harry Ward's criticism of the Rockefeller empire at Union Theological Seminary in the morning, before tutoring the Rockefeller children in the afternoon. . . . But Trocmé was also well aware of John D. Rockefeller's fervent Baptist faith, his generous support of churches and seminaries, and of the influence exercised on his employer by the prominent liberal and social pastor Harry Emerson Fosdick (1878–1969).[143]

---

140. André Trocmé, "Mémoires," 217–18.

141. In the Rockefeller Archives, one can see a photo album containing many pictures of Trocmé with the Rockefeller family, horseback riding, camping, etc. ("LRS [Laurance S. Rockefeller] Photographs," "Photo Album 1924–1926").

142. The Rockefeller Archives, to the best of my knowledge, contain only one trace of Theis's work as a tutor: a letter from "Miss Kelly" concerning Theis's compensation, dated Oct. 16, 1922.

143. "Fervent baptiste, John D. subissait l'excellente influence de Harry Emerson Fosdick, un chrétien social, antimilitariste et merveilleux prédicateur." André Trocmé, "Mémoires," 244. Trocmé too enjoyed Fosdick's preaching, as can be seen in a letter he wrote from his parish of Sin-le-Noble to the Rockefeller family: "I always read with the greatest interest the preachings of Dr. Fosdick. I like their practical and direct style. Although they are written for a cultivated audience, they may be adapted for our

Trocmé was greatly appreciated by the family, to the point where they invited him to prolong his stay in New York and to accept a scholarship, which would allow him to pursue a doctorate at Union Theological Seminary.[144] Trocmé was torn between his desire to accept this offer and his sense of calling to return to France to join his comrades from the "groupe du Nord": "The temptation was very strong, excruciating at times. I used to say to myself: what would happen to your calling to be an evangelist, and to your desire for poverty? If I am called by God, must I not renounce the world, even if this world is a world of services which must be rendered to humanity?"[145]

In a letter to his son, Paul Trocmé, who still presided over the "Société chrétienne du Nord," which funded many of the evangelistic ministries of northern France, made sure to remind him that his return to his homeland was expected. Had his son forgotten his calling to join the missionary effort among the workers?[146]

André Trocmé had several projects on his mind. He had been invited to go to the Ivory Coast as a missionary. Another project, which he had shared with Oliver Dryer in June 1926, was to work with Ragaz in Zurich for three months and later to travel to Germany as a French "ambassador" for IFoR.[147] He was also hoping to travel to India to meet Gandhi (1869–1948) and Tagore (1861–1941). All of these projects, including that last one, which was so dear to him that he had discussed it with Magda during their first conversations in April 1925, were put to rest by Paul Trocmé, who asked that they return and celebrate their marriage with both of their families in Saint-Quentin.

---

working people in France." Letter from Feb. 12, 1930; series B, box 1. Fosdick gave an address at the annual meeting of the "American McAll Association" on April 28, 1932; see *AMR* 50, nr. 2 (March 1932) 3.

144. On Dec. 13, 1971, David Rockefeller wrote to Magda Trocmé who had lost her husband André six months earlier: "I recall so fondly the year my brothers and I spent with your husband." Trocmé papers, Swarthmore College, Series B, box 1.

145. "La tentation était très forte, lancinante parfois. Mais alors, me disai-je, que deviendraient ma vocation d'évangéliste et mon désir de pauvreté? Si je suis appelé par Dieu, ne dois-je pas renoncer au monde, même si ce monde est un monde de services à rendre à l'humanité?" André Trocmé, "Mémoires," 231.

146. "[…] les lettres de Papa, qui me disaient combien on m'attendait dans le Nord, pour fortifier l'action missionnaire parmi les ouvriers, me fixaient un destin plus austère, mais aussi plus conforme à mes convictions intérieures." Ibid. Magda Trocmé, "Souvenirs autobiographiques," 127.

147. Letter from Oliver Dryer to A. Trocmé, July 14, 1926, in series B, box 1.

The young couple left New York City on September 11, 1926.[148] The wedding celebrations, both civil and religious, took place on November 10 and 12, 1926, respectively. Trocmé writes: "I would have liked to have my comrades from the groupe du Nord around me: Fabre, Cornier, Babut. I asked Fabre, who belonged to the Réconciliation, to preside at the religious ceremony. He was the only one who was invited. Father categorically refused to invite the others!"[149] In the end, several of his friends, including Samuel Cornier and Jacques Babut, took part in the festivities.[150]

MAUBEUGE—SOUS-LE-BOIS (1926–28)

The "Société chrétienne du Nord" had begun funding a pastoral position in Maubeuge, less than six miles faway from the Belgian border, in 1860. Its first Protestant church was inaugurated by Edmond de Pressensé on November 1, 1877.[151] Two men from the region, pastors Bretegnier and Poinsot, had began working there in 1857, but their modest worship hall had been shut down by the local authorities. The parish of Maubeuge had seen a breathtaking expansion during the ministry of pastor André Durand, who had arrived there in 1902. His conferences in Maubeuge and the surrounding towns, usually in movie theaters, were followed by thousands of people. Two more pastors were sent by the "Société chrétienne du Nord" in order to assist him in his work. Typically, the "Société" would appoint pastors to certain places, while allowing great freedom to them.[152] In 1906, a "Fraternité" was inaugurated in Sous-le-Bois, a suburb of Maubeuge, and it became a successful place for missionary work. The world war was a massive blow to these efforts, but a Protestant community had been established and continued to flourish. By 1924, there were ap-

148. A. Trocmé, letter to Mr. R. W. Gumbel, Sept. 1, 1926; Rockefeller Archives, Record Group 2; Friends and Services, box 129, folder 958 I.

149. "J'aurais voulu avoir autour de moi mes camarades du groupe du Nord: Fabre, Cornier, Babut. Je demandai à Fabre, qui était de la Réconciliation, de présider le service. Il fut le seul invité. Papa refusa tout net d'inviter les autres!" A. Trocmé, "Mémoires," 248–9.

150. "Au Temple il y avait aussi Cornier et Babut, venus de loin tout exprès pour l'occasion. Je ne pus résister à l'envie de les inviter." Ibid., 249.

151. For the date of 1860: Henri Monnier, *Édouard Monnier*, 203.

152. "Notre direction—la Société Chrétienne du Nord—choisit ses agents, je veux le croire, très consciencieusement, Mais, pour notre méthode de travail, elle nous fait un large crédit: 'Travaillez, faites du bon 'ouvrage'[']: c'est le seul mot d'ordre qui nous soit donné. Telle est la méthode de notre Société, que nous approuvons sans réserve." De Visme, "Notre méthode," 62.

proximately six hundred Protestants in Maubeuge.[153] Pastor Paul Conord (1896–1985) ministered the parish from 1921 until 1926, after being ordained by Henri Nick.[154]

In December 1926, André Trocmé began his work, as assistant minister, in Sous-le-Bois, a workers' neighborhood which resembled a slum in some ways. There were several big steel factories.[155] He was required to spend two years of pastoral training ("proposanat") under Paul Perret, a Swiss pastor born in 1888 whose socialist leanings would hopefully be a good match.[156] Pastoral work was not entirely new to Trocmé: as a student he had worked in Hénin-Liétard under Daniel Chéradame's guidance, and even before that, since 1920, there had been the "Fraternité" in Clamart.[157] But Trocmé was now finally realizing his objective, which he had developed as a student and as a member of the "groupe du Nord," to work in northern France among the miners and the factory workers, surrounded by colleagues engaged in the same effort and ready to fully commit themselves to the task. Everything, his studies and even his military service, had meaning only insofar as it had prepared him for this ministry. On February 21, 1923, in a note to his friends written in the final weeks of this military service, near the end of a 300 kilometer-long expedition in the muddy terrain of the Zerhoun mountain of central Morocco, he added: "Nevertheless I am happy, the training is excellent for the North later. [. . .]

153. Barde, *La Société centrale*, 47, who lists the names of the pastors at Maubeuge, including "Walbaum," probably Ferdinand Walbaum (1813–83), the father of Paul Trocmé's first wife Marie. Ferdinand Walbaum was the president of the "Société chrétienne du Nord" from 1860 until 1882 (ibid., 69–70). Barde writes (47–48): "*Maubeuge est une des œuvres qui se sont le plus développées et une de celles aussi où il a fallu le plus de courage, de persévérance et de foi pour rester debout, parfois malgré une opposition violente. Aujourd'hui Maubeuge–Sous-le-Bois est une église importante, formée de quelques anciens protestants et d'une grande majorité de prosélytes. Le temple inauguré en 1877 est encore là, ainsi que la Fraternité, ils ont souffert de la guerre, mais ont pu être entièrement restaurés. La communauté de Maubeuge–Sous-le-Bois s'est rapidement relevée après la grande tourmente: fin 1924 elle comptait 600 protestants* [. . .]."

154. Pierre Bolle, "Paul Conord," in Encrevé, dir., *Dictionnaire*, 137–8.

155. Magda Trocmé writes: "*Eh bien, ce Sous-le-Bois n'était qu'un infecte faubourg, mais intéressant, très intéressant à cause de sa population; intéressant surtout quand on veut faire du travail religieux ou du travail social. Il y avait là de grandes aciéries avec de grosses usines, un enfer;* [. . .] *c'était le sous-produit de l'humanité, des gens désespérés, des buveurs, vraiment le fond, la lie de la société.*" "Souvenirs autobiographiques," 152.

156. "*Sa théologie et ses idées socialistes se rapprochaient des miennes.*" A. Trocmé, "Mémoires," 253.

157. Ibid., 292.

I bless the harsh life I am living right now which eliminates social conventions and which leads one to fight, pitifully, against nature. This toughens my body, and it will be useful later when dealing with the mud of the Pas-de-Calais region."[158]

Magda was beginning to meet the members of this small group of young men who had big dreams for the world and the Church. Her husband's passion was obvious when he was speaking about his friends, and what he was telling her reassured her: these were not stuffy, traditional pastors.[159] As Magda put it in her "souvenirs autobiographiques": what her husband was describing to her was a group of trailblazers.[160]

The "groupe du Nord" was still very much alive, as can be seen from the bulletin from June 1928. Its topic is "Survey on Religious Education" ("Enquête sur les instructions religieuses"), and various members, including Samuel Cornier, Jacques Babut, Élie Morel, Paul Perret and Trocmé, summarized their own approaches. The bulletin included a letter from Jacques Diény, who had recently moved to the parish of Longwy, a small mining town in Lorraine, close to Belgium and Luxembourg.[161]

Despite his past experiences, Trocmé had much to learn about the pastoral ministry. In a letter from March 1931, he admits that the first

---

158. "Mais je suis quand même content, l'entraînement est excellent pour le Nord plus tard. [. . .] Je bénis la vie rude que je mène en ce moment et qui fait tomber les conventions, et vous livre, misérable, à se battre contre la nature. Cela me fait un corps durci qui me sera utile plus tard pour fendre la boue du P.D.C." "Bulletin militaire," nr. 22, April 1923, 3–4 (notes dated Feb. 21, 1923).

159. "'Tu verras,' disait André, 'tu verras mes camarades les pasteurs du Groupe du Nord, ils sont comme moi, ils ne sont pas comme tu les imagines, des hommes guindés qui parlent avec un ton spécial, qui serrent la main d'une drôle de façon! Non! Non! Tu verras! [. . .] Le Groupe du Nord ne travaillait pas dans de vraies églises officielles; il s'agissait plutôt d'œuvres d'avant-garde. Maubeuge était donc une œuvre d'évangélisation." Magda Trocmé, "Souvenirs autobiographiques," 131. She repeats some of this on 141.

160. "Pauvre André, lui qui voulait devenir pasteur d'avant-garde, qui voulait révolutionner les églises et le monde et qui avait accepté de renoncer aux 'fantaisies,' selon l'expression de son père, par amour pour moi!" Magda Trocmé, "Souvenirs autobiographiques," 129. Emmanuel Chastand described the "Solidarités" and "Fraternités" as "une œuvre d'avant-garde du protestantisme." "Le Mouvement des Fraternités Françaises," 427.

161. In his message Diény writes: "Je me sentirai[s] loin et perdu si je ne possédais l'assurance que n[ou]s restons liés et ardemment unis, par delà les distances, dans la même adoration et dans la même offrande. Cette assurance se fonde sur t[ou]t ce qui a été depuis 2 ans, notre vie commune, nos victoires communes, nos joies et nos humiliations communes." "Bulletin du Groupe du Nord," June 1928, 4.

André Trocmé's First Steps in Spiritual and Social Christianity

years have been difficult.[162] In four years he has not heard a single person tell him that his sermons have been helpful. He adds: "Glory be to God! but it is hard."[163]

Among his initial missteps at Sous-le-Bois was a questionnaire he circulated among both Protestants and Catholics, on behalf of the "Men's Circle" he had founded. In it he asked "intrusive questions about morality and religion." Even though the responses were supposed to remain anonymous, the project was a fiasco.[164] Another, greater disappointment concerned his project to work in a factory for several months before beginning his pastoral ministry. He had been inspired by his friend at the "Faculté de théologie," Arnold Brémond (1900–83), a Swiss who had spent seven months in a factory in Ivry-sur-Seine in 1925–26.[165] Trocmé's project had been approved by the "Société chrétienne du Nord," but as soon as he arrived in Sous-le-Bois everyone, including the factory owner, was opposed to it.[166] Trocmé's desire to experience directly the life of the factory workers did not leave him for several years. In March 1931, Trocmé wrote to a friend about his long hesitation concerning the pastoral ministry: "Would it not be better to plunge into reality, to return to the people, to become a worker, to experience the struggle with the people and to seek the light with them? I am far from having abandoned these tendencies, and I am

---

162. "Les premières années furent pénibles." Letter from March 19, 1931 to a friend editing the "Bulletin des Volontaires." Series B, box 1. The "Volontaires du Christ" was a small group within the Fédération française des associations chrétiennes d'étudiants. Its members were "dedicating their lives to evangelization." Fabre, "L'émergence," 152.

163. "Sécheresse des 'discours religieux' que sont les premiers sermons. Déception d'être incompris, même lorsque l'on se *donne à fond*. Depuis 4 ans je n'ai pas reçu un seul témoignage sur le bien qu'avait pu faire un de mes sermons! Gloire à Dieu!—mais c'est dur." Letter from March 19, 1931 to a friend editing the "Bulletin des Volontaires." Series B, box 1.

164. "Par ailleurs, mes débuts dans le ministère furent difficiles: Sous l'œil goguenard de Perretto [i.e., Paul Perret], j'avais entrepris une enquête (avec formulaires imprimés que je répandis chez les protestants et les catholiques) où je posais des questions indiscrètes sur la morale et la religion. La réponse devait rester anonyme, mais les gens se méfiaient et j'essuyai un échec." A. Trocmé, "Mémoires," 257. A "questionnaire" which originated in the "Cercle d'hommes de Sous-le-Bois" is preserved at Swarthmore College (Series B, box 5). It includes twelve questions, such as: "What is materialism? What is spiritualism? How do science and materialism relate? [...] What is a religious experience? What is an hallucination? Can the existence of God be proven?"

165. Ibid., 202–3. Trocmé calls him "celui qui demeura peut-être, au cours de longues années, mon meilleur ami." See Brémond, "Une explication."

166. Magda Trocmé, "Souvenirs autobiographiques," 162.

grateful to my Church at Sin-le-Noble, a workers' parish, for allowing me to make, in part, the plunge I desired to make."[167]

Paul Perret, the senior pastor who served as his advisor and mentor, was keeping a very close eye on the young couple, to the point were they felt constantly monitored, even on such matters as how to cook! Stories and rumors often landed at the doorstep of André's father, in Saint-Quentin. Even his friends from the "groupe du Nord" were asked to keep him in "the right path": one day, his friend Marcel Heuzé, who was then a pastor sixty miles away in Lens, arrived unexpectedly in Sous-le-Bois with a simple but surprising message, urging Trocmé to preach "the pure gospel." Trocmé immediately suspected that Perret's indiscretions had something to do with Heuzé's visit.[168]

The "Fraternité" at Sous-le-Bois was the object of much attention from the young pastor. It had been founded in May 1922 by Paul Conord, under the name "Association Fraternelle d'Hommes," and had sent delegates to the congresses of the "Fédération des Fraternités Françaises" in Strasbourg (1922) and Roubaix (1923). By the end of 1924, there were 23 active members.[169]

Working with the youth, and trying to prevent the spread of alcoholism using the methods of the "Croix Bleue," were among the areas in which Trocmé was somewhat successful.[170] But there were disappointments. In his "Mémoires," Trocmé recalls several memorable episodes, including the day when the janitor at the "Fraternité," a former drunkard who had been

---

167. "Je suis entré dans la carrière pastorale après de longues hésitations. [. . .] Ne valait-il pas mieux faire un plongeon dans la réalité, retourner au peuple, devenir ouvrier, souffrir les luttes avec le peuple et chercher avec lui la lumière?—Je suis loin, d'ailleurs, d'avoir abandonné ces tendances, et je remercie mon Église de Sin le Noble, qui est ouvrière, de m'avoir fait faire en partie, le 'plongeon' désiré." Letter from March 19, 1931; Swarthmore, series B, box 1.

168. "Un jour, un bon collègue de mon âge, Marcel Heuzé, vint tout exprès me morigéner, pour me reprocher de ne pas annoncer le pur Evangile. Je réalisai que Perret avait eu la langue trop longue et que nos débuts dans le ministère, commentés par lui parmi les pasteurs et les laïques, leur avaient offert l'occasion de se faire du souci pour mon âme et pour celle de Magda, et de prier pour notre salut." André Trocmé, "Mémoires," 257–58. Magda Trocmé writes about Heuzé's unannounced visit in her "Souvenirs autobiographiques" (159).

169. Paul Conord's report in "Nouvelles des Sections," *Bulletin des Fraternités Françaises*, nr. 6 (Dec. 1924) 5–6.

170. "[. . .] mon ministère à Maubeuge n'était pas entièrement stérile. Je m'occupais surtout de Croix-Bleue et de la jeunesse." A. Trocmé, "Mémoires," 259.

"lifted up" ("relevé") from his past addiction, left his wife, disappeared for a full day only to return, drunk and furious, with an axe in his hand.[171]

In the summer of 1927, Trocmé was invited to be one of the speakers at a large gathering organized by the socialist party in Aulnoye, a neighboring town, on the theme of peace. He was beginning to realize that he had a talent for speaking before large audiences. He also took part in a congress organized by IFoR in connection with the Passion Play in Oberammergau, Bavaria.[172] On August 31, 1927, André and Magda's first child, Nelly, named after her maternal grandmother, was born at home in Sin-le-Noble (Magda had planned to give birth at the Ambroise Paré hospital in Lille, an institution founded in 1923 by several Protestant women with the support of Henri Nick).[173] Magda nearly died while giving birth. Before Nelly's birth and during her recovery from it, she was assisted by a young woman, Simone Pévenage, who would later (then known as Simone Mairesse) play an important role in the rescue effort in the region of Le Chambon.[174]

Under Trocmé's leadership, the social issues of the day were discussed in the parish. On August 29, 1928, Trocmé wrote a letter to the secretary of the "Ligue des Droits de l'Homme" in Paris, on behalf of the "Association Fraternelle des Hommes de Sous-le-Bois," the parish's "Men's Circle," of which he was the secretary. In it, he presented the results of two meetings of the "Association Fraternelle" on a survey which had been circulated by the "Ligue." The topic of the survey was female prostitution, and the tenor of Trocmé's letter was a call for compassion rather than punishment, except for the men who profit from prostitution.[175]

---

171. Ibid., 259.

172. Ibid., 258.

173. Jeanne Nick, "Un hôpital-école." Diebolt, "Femmes protestantes," esp. 127–29; Vernier-Escande, *Infirmières et pionnières*. One of the four founders, Eva Durrleman (1881–1993), was the sister of Freddy Durrleman, a well-known member of the "Christianisme social" (Jacques Kaltenbach's sister Elizabeth married Freddy Durrleman in 1909). Nick praised the project of a hospital in *AMR* 41, nr. 1 (January 1923) 2; see also vol. 42, nr. 2 (March 1924) 3.

174. Magda Trocmé, "Souvenirs autobiographiques," 163. A certain "Pévenage" is listed as a delegate (from the "Fraternité" in Maubeuge) to the first Congress of the "Fédération Française des Fraternités" in Roubaix, May 5–8, 1923. *Bulletin de la Fédération des Fraternités Françaises* nr. 3 (July 1923) 12.

175. "La réponse à votre enquête a fait l'objet de deux séances plénières de notre association, au mois d'Août. Le texte ci-après reflète l'opinion de la majorité de nos membres, qui se recrutent principalement parmi les ouvriers métallurgistes du bassin de la Sambre. [. . .] La prostituée est à soigner souvent, à relever parfois, à enfermer rarement, mais elle est toujours à plaindre. Son crime mérite plus de pitié que de rigueur. Le proxénète, au contraire, a l'œil lucide et l'intelligence claire. En lui, point de

Revivalism and Social Christianity

When Trocmé found out that his friend Émile Fabre, from the "groupe du Nord," was leaving the parish of Sin-le-Noble, a town in the same region but closer to Lille and the mining area, he seized the opportunity and applied for the position, even though he had not yet completed the required two years of training. When he received a positive response from the parish of Sin-le-Noble, he announced to Perret that he would be leaving Maubeuge at the end of the 1927–28 school year.[176] Trocmé was experiencing difficulties with his mentor, and he was longing for a parish of his own.

TROCMÉ'S FINAL THESIS

While in Maubeuge, Trocmé had to write a thesis in order to complete his bachelor in theology at the "Faculté de théologie libre" in Paris. He submitted it some time in 1927. He had chosen the following topic: "An Experiment in Social Christianity: The Churches and the Prohibition of Alcohol in the United States."[177] The thesis consists in two parts: a historical presentation, followed by a critical evaluation. In his conclusion, Trocmé expresses his admiration "for the perseverance and charity with which the American Church is working on eradicating social injustice," and wishes that French Protestants would learn from that example. But he also denounces what he sees as the "warrior mentality" of the "Anti-Saloon League."[178] Whether the Prohibition would be successful was impossible to say. Ultimately, everything would depend on "those who will apply and

---

passion, c'est pour de l'argent qu'il 'travaille.' C'est, sous des dehors parfois honorables, un homme d'affaires, un homme sale d'affaires louches. Nous assimilons au proxénète tout complice de la prostitution ou de la traite des blanches, tout homme qui tire un profit quelconque de la prostitution [. . .]. Des hommes ont sur leurs mains le sang des martyrs de notre société. Pour eux la loi ne sera jamais assez dure." Swarthmore College, Series B, box 1; 1 and 3.

176. Magda Trocmé, "Souvenirs autobiographiques," 162. André Trocmé, "Mémoires," 263.

177. "Une expérience de Christianisme social: Les Églises et la prohibition de l'alcool aux États-Unis. Thèse présentée pour l'obtention du Grade de Bachelier en Théologie, devant la Faculté libre de Théologie Protestante de Paris. 1927." Swarthmore College, Trocmé papers, series B, box 5, 6th folder.

178. "Nous admirons sans réserve la persévérance et la charité avec laquelle l'Église américaine s'efforce de faire cesser l'injustice sociale. Nous voudrions voir notre Église Française souscrire à un tel programme de réforme. Mais nous regrettons que la lutte antialcoolique ait souvent fait baisser l'esprit de charité dans l'Église américaine, et que l'activité de l'Anti-Saloon League soit si guerrière." (177).

André Trocmé's First Steps in Spiritual and Social Christianity

support the law. Everything will depend on their spiritual life and their charity."[179] If the Church succeeds in eliminating evil from itself, as it tries to do the same for society, then "perhaps, having escaped the greatest temptations which Christ himself faced, it will have done more than any other for the coming of God's kingdom, on earth as it is in heaven."[180] Trocmé's hope for the coming of God's kingdom, which had been challenged during his military service, seems to have been restored.

SIN-LE-NOBLE (1928–34)

In the 1920s, Sin-le-Noble was a small town of approximately 10,000 inhabitants located on the outskirts of the bigger city of Douai, in the mining region south of Lille.[181] As with the entire region of northern France, it was predominantly Roman-Catholic, with a very small Protestant presence (less than 4%). Starting in 1881, the "Société chrétienne du Nord" had begun sending evangelists in the region. First, there was Pierre Bion, from Rouen, who worked in Liévin among the miners. Two years later, he had one hundred and thirty parishioners, and forty children were attending Sunday school. A second evangelist, named Boyer, came to help in 1885, first in Hersin-Coupigny, a small town west of Liévin, and three years later in Hénin-Liétard (since 1971: Hénin-Beaumont), six miles away from Sin-le-Noble. Soon thereafter, Georges Boissonnas (1865–1942), who became a well-known evangelist, began working in the area.[182] He arrived in the small town of Hénin-Liétard in October 1889, where he found more than five hundred bars ("estaminets"), some owned by the local mining company, and eleven Protestant families.[183] Due to the mining industry, Hénin-Liétard's population increased rapidly, from 6,000 in 1875 to 20,000 in 1913.[184] At the time, answering the Protestant evan-

---

179. "Tout dépend de ceux qui appliqueront et soutiendront la loi. Tout dépend de leur vie spirituelle et de leur charité." (177).

180. "[. . .] si elle sait chasser le mal de son cœur, comme elle s'efforce de le chasser de la société, alors, peut-être, ayant échappé aux plus grandes tentations qui se soient présentées au Christ lui-même, aura-t-elle fait plus que toute autre pour que le règne de Dieu vienne, sur la terre comme au ciel." (177).

181. For some of what follows, I am indebted to Mours, *Un siècle d'évangélisation*, vol. 2, 150–175; Barde, *La Société centrale*, 56–66; Barde, *Sin-le-Noble*.

182. Madame Georges Boissonnas, *Expériences d'un évangéliste*. Henri Nick said of Boissonnas: "Il a été l'apôtre du Nord" (5 and 14).

183. Madame Georges Boissonnas, *Expériences d'un évangéliste*, 27, 31 and 36.

184. Pfender, "Le Bassin Houiller," 48. The neighboring town of Liévin saw a

gelists' call to conversion potentially meant losing one's job, one's rental home—generally owned by the mining company—in the miner's rows of houses (the "corons"), and enduring the mockery of people, including one's own relatives.

Roman Catholic priests had no intention to let the Protestant missionaries establish parishes in the area. But at the end of 1891, Boissonnas was asked to celebrate the burial of a young man who had committed suicide. The local Catholic priest had refused to do it. Boissonas celebrated it, made a strong impression and was invited to return by the mourning family. He eventually turned his attention to the city of Sin-le-Noble, which had no Protestant community.[185] He was so successful that the town's first Protestant church building was dedicated, in August 1892, and he asked his colleague Paul Barde (1866–1927) to replace him in Hénin. In 1896, Boissonnas returned to Hénin, and Barde took over in Sin-le-Noble. Over the years, despite all the difficulties, the parish grew to include three hundred people and became one of the success stories of the "Société chrétienne du Nord."[186] In 1904, Barde and Boissonnas moved to Paris to lead the "Société centrale évangélique." As a second generation of pastors and evangelists was arriving in the region in the first decade of the 20th century, most of them with a social Christian agenda, several "Fraternités" were created: there was a "Fraternité du Nouveau monde" in Bruay-en-Artois (1909), and another "Fraternité" in Liévin (1913). Émile Fabre, Trocmé's friend and predecessor, founded one in Sin-le-Noble in the spring of 1924.[187]

His studies and training now completed, Sin-le-Noble was Trocmé's first parish as senior pastor. His position was funded by the "Société chrétienne du Nord," not by the French Reformed Church.[188] In addition to Sin-le-Noble, he was in charge of several neighboring villages, including Aniche and Marquette (now Marquette-en-Ostrevant). Sin-le-Noble comprised approximately fifty Protestant families, many of whom had

---

similar surge after the discovery of coal in 1858, from 2,075 inhabitants in 1870 to 25,698 in 1914. By 1914 there were 700 bars ("estaminets"). Roger, *Liévin*, 75 and 91.

185. Madame Georges Boissonnas, *Expériences d'un évangéliste*, 212. Barde, *Sin-le-Noble*, 1–3.

186. "[. . .] l'œuvre de Sin-le-Noble, qui est devenue 'le plus beau fleuron' de la Société du Nord, a été son [i.e., George Boissonnas'] œuvre personnelle." Monnier, *Édouard Monnier*, 205.

187. See "Adhésions nouvelles," in *Bulletin de la Fédération des Fraternités Françaises*, nr. 5 (May 1924) 7.

188. A. Trocmé, "Mémoires," 303.

André Trocmé's First Steps in Spiritual and Social Christianity

abandoned Roman Catholicism within the previous four decades, as a result of the Protestant missions.[189]

In Sin-le-Noble, Magda and André Trocmé, who already had a daugther, Nelly, became the parents of three sons: Jean-Pierre (1930), Jacques (1931) and Daniel (1933).[190] Magda was very active in the parish. She was responsible for the weekly meetings of the "Unions chrétiennes de jeunes filles," and at one point she gave parenting classes to some of the wives of the Italian workers in the area.[191]

André Trocmé felt at home in this town of miners and factory workers. His pacifism and socialism led to tensions, now and then, but these six years were among the happiest in his life. "Despite everything, in Sin-le-Noble, for the first time, I felt I was ready for the task, and I became more assured toward and against others."[192] How did that happen? In part through the influence and the presence of one man: "I was helped by this great prophet and great believer, Henri Nick, pastor in Fives (Lille), the last survivor of the generation of social Christian evangelists such as Boissonnas, Gounelle, Dürrleman, Aeschimann. [. . .] this potential genius had left everything in order to become a disciple of Christ."[193]

Just as Fabre, his predecessor, had done, Trocmé called on Nick for assistance on several occasions: first in Aniche, where the communist mayor, having recently returned from the Soviet Union, organized a large political meeting to which Christians were invited for a contradictory debate.[194] A well-known communist leader, Florimond Bonte (1890–1977),

---

189. Ibid., 277.

190. Daniel's birth was very difficult. Magda Trocmé writes: "Je ne devais pas recevoir de visites, sauf celles d'André. Mais ne voilà-t-il pas qu'un jour, la porte s'est ouverte à peine, doucement, et j'ai vu la tête de Monsieur Nick, le 'pasteur-prophète,' qui s'est avancé tout doucement, qui m'a fait signe de ne pas parler. Puis il est entré tout entier. Il est arrivé à côté du lit, et il m'a dit: 'Je me sauve, je me sauve! Si ces demoiselles me voient, elles vont me gronder!' Il m'a embrassée sur le front et il est parti. C'était la plus jolie visite pastorale que j'aie jamais eue de ma vie." "Souvenirs autobiographiques," 192–93.

191. Magda Trocmé, "Souvenirs autobiographiques," 184.

192. "C'est à Sin-le-Noble malgré tout, que, pour la première fois, je me sentis en possession de mes moyens et je pris de l'assurance envers et contre tous." A. Trocmé, "Mémoires," 269.

193. "J'y fut aidé par ce grand prophète et grand croyant qu'était M. Nick, pasteur à Fives (Lille), le dernier survivant de la génération des évangélistes chrétiens sociaux qui avaient noms: Boissonnas, Gounelle, Dürrlemann, Aeschimann. [. . .] ce génie en puissance avait tout abandonné pour être un disciple du Christ." Ibid., 269.

194. Henri Nick reports on a recent visit to Sin-le-Noble in "Pastor Nick Tells," 19–20: "Last Sunday a large crowd of men gathered in the town hall of Sin-le-Noble,

the editor in chief since 1929 of the French newspaper *L'Humanité*, was the guest speaker. The two pastors did their best to convince the audience in the crowded and smoky municipal hall that it was a mistake to think, with Aniche's mayor, that communism in Russia had succeeded in overcoming all of man's "evil instincts."[195] Trocmé writes in his "Mémoires": "M. Nick then spoke, and I have a pretty clear memory of what he said. He described Jesus as the first socialist, the friend of the poor. He contradicted the mayor and gave examples (alcoholism, adultery) which are not the consequence of economic competition. He then gave examples of people who had been lifted up through the power of Jesus Christ."[196] But the main speaker, Bonte, won the crowd with his denunciation of non-violence and forgiveness, showing how it had been abused to defend tyrants and to maintain oppression. Trocmé's attempt at answering these criticism fell on deaf ears, as the audience was already leaving the hall while the Internationale was playing.[197] Trocmé claims that, following that evening in Aniche, he began to realize that individual conversion cannot be the sole answer to injustice and war. "Institutions must change."[198]

Trocmé called on Henri Nick a second time when the socialist municipal council in the town of Aniche, following a dispute with the local Roman Catholic priest, suddenly decided to forbid the celebration of the mass! The priest had left town, and now the municipal council was offering

---

near Douai. Pastor Fabre of Sin-le-Noble presided. The subject of the discussion was, 'Peace and the Means of Attaining It.' The mayor and different orators spoke. Six hundred men were present and not another could have crowded into the hall. [...] I went to speak of peace in the name of the Prince of Peace."

195. "Le grand soir arriva. La salle communale d'Aniche était remplie d'une foule d'hommes en casquette, et noyée dans la fumée des cigarettes. Je me rappelle distinctement ce que dirent le maire d'Aniche et Florimond Boute [sic]. Le premier affirma avoir observé en Russie que le communisme, en abolissant la concurrence à tous les niveaux, avait non seulement supprimé l'inégalité entre les classes, mais encore fait disparaître les mauvais instincts de l'homme." A. Trocmé, "Mémoires," 271.

196. "M. Nick parla ensuite, et j'ai gardé un souvenir assez net de ses propos. Il décrivit Jésus comme le premier des socialistes, l'ami des pauvres. Il contredit le maire, et donna des exemples de péché (alcoolisme, adultère) qui ne sont pas la conséquence de la concurrence économique. Il donna ensuite des exemples de relèvements accomplis par la puissance de Jésus Christ." Ibid.

197. "Hélas, les quelques paroles maladroites que je prononçai en dernier pour défendre la non-violence, n'atteignirent pas la foule qui déjà, grondante, aux sons de l'Internationale, quittait la salle." Ibid., 272.

198. "Je n'ai jamais oublié cette réunion. Pour la première fois je comprenais que la conversion individuelle ne suffit pas pour résoudre le problème de la justice et de la paix. Les institutions doivent changer." Ibid.

the use of the church and the presbytery to the Protestant minister, that is to Trocmé! Nick came to Aniche to lead the negotiations, which did not go very far, since both buildings, since the separation of Church and State in 1905, belonged to the Catholic Church.[199]

Trocmé suffered some setbacks. Since 1931, a Baptist evangelist, Edmond Evrard (1890–1981), was in charge of Aniche and Marquette, and with Trocmé he was publishing a small journal, *La bonne semance*, whose purpose was to present "the social and international implications of the Christian faith." The journal had to be discontinued when Evrard, in an article, bluntly called for people to support the Socialist party.[200] The committee of the "Société chrétienne du Nord" warned Trocmé not to mix partisan politics with the Christian message.

DEVELOPMENTS IN THE "GROUPE DU NORD"

By the mid- to late 1920s, most of the members of the "groupe du Nord" were working as pastors in the same region of northern France. Trocmé mentions some of their activities: they met once a month to conduct "fervent prayer meetings" and travelled to whatever parish wished to welcome them for a "mission." Invitations were coming mostly from northern France, but at times members of the group travelled further south, all the way to Marseille.[201] The parishes hosting a "mission" were asked to prepare themselves spiritually a month ahead of the visit. The pastors stayed there between four and seven days. Converts could, if they wished, sign special cards as a record of their commitment.[202]

---

199. A. Trocmé, "Mémoires," 272–3.

200. Ibid., 267, where he writes: "J'avais fondé un petit journal mensuel, la 'Bonne Semence,' où je tâchais, au milieu des nouvelles paroissiales, de montrer la portée sociale et internationale de la foi chrétienne." According to Céline Marrot-Fellag Ariouet, Edmond Evrard, then pastor in Nice, preached on the book of Amos in the presence of Trocmé and Theis in Le Chambon in 1943. See http://lamaisondesevres.org/cel/cel5.html (accessed October 10, 2011).

201. André Vermeil mentions how pastor Jean-Baptiste Couve invited his friends from the "Groupe du Nord" J. Babut, R. Chéradame, A. Trocmé and M. Heuzé to speak in Aouste and Blacons (Drôme) for a series of meetings. "Entreprises communes," 109.

202. "Le 'Groupe du Nord' [. . .] rassemblait ses membres en ferventes réunions de prière et commença à parcourir les Églises qui lui demandaient des 'missions.' [. . .] La 'mission' durait quatre jours, une semaine parfois. Nous allions jusqu'à Aouste, près de Valence, et Marseille. Mais les Églises du Nord nous appelaient de préférence. On exigeait d'elles une préparation spirituelle d'un mois. Des cartes d'engagement étaient proposées à la signature des 'convertis.'" A. Trocmé, "Mémoires," 275.

Revivalism and Social Christianity

Trocmé was one of the younger members of the group and did not have a say on whether he would take part in a mission trip. Babut and the two Chéradame brothers decided who would go where.[203] Here is Trocmé's description of these years of collaboration with the "groupe du Nord": "I must say that these years of ministry were, without a doubt, among the most fruitful of my life. Humbled by the sincerity, the total consecration, the profound faith of my comrades as I listened in wonderment to their powerful message, I was in touch once again with the fervor of my beginnings in Saint-Quentin in 1915–17. There was the same openness, the same absence of defensiveness, the same honesty before God. My shyness [. . .] was finally gone. In those years, God's grace made me into a man."[204]

Returning from a mission trip in Bruay, in Robert Chéradame's car, Trocmé had a significant religious experience. One could describe it theologically as an expression of theological realism, in which the reality of God, independently of any human standpoint, is seen as the all-important truth. Trocmé wrote about this realization in his "Mémoires": "It was an illumination: Whatever your inner state, depressed or filled with pride, dry or sentimental, whether you feel close to or distant from God, the *fact* of God's sacrifice for you, in Jesus Christ, is irrevocable. It remains outside of you, despite you, as a greater reality than yourself. Therefore, be filled with trust!"[205]

---

203. "Étant le plus jeune de la bande, je ne fus pas toujours invité à prendre la parole. Une sorte de triumvirat: J. Babut et les frères Chéradame, organisait les missions. On en était ou on n'en était pas." Ibid.

204. "Je dois reconnaître que cette période de mon ministère fut, à coup sûr, une des plus fécondes de ma vie. Humilité par la sincérité, la consécration totale, la foi profonde de mes camarades dont j'écoutais, émerveillé, le message percutant, je retrouvai la ferveur de mes débuts à St-Quentin en 1915–1917. C'était la même ouverture, la même absence d'auto-défense, la même droiture devant Dieu qu'autrefois. Ma timidité [. . .] fut enfin balayée. C'est à cette époque-là que la grâce de Dieu fit de moi un homme." Ibid., 276.

205. "Ce fut une illumination: Quel que soit ton état intérieur, dépressif ou vaniteux, sec ou sentimental, que tu te sentes près de Dieu ou loin de Dieu, le *fait* du sacrifice de Dieu pour toi, en Jésus-Christ, ne peut être aboli. Il subsiste hors de toi, malgré toi, comme une réalité plus grande que toi. Donc, aie confiance!" Ibid. The tenor of these sentences is quite Barthian, and so it makes sense to read, in Trocmé's "Mémoires," that the Chéradame brothers were moving closer to Barth's theology at the time.

REVIVAL

One evening during the winter of 1930–31, during a reunion of the small "Men's Circle," a revival began in Trocmé's parish of Sin-le-Noble. In a letter to Samuel Cornier from January 7, 1931, Robert Chéradame mentions his recent visit to Trocmé's (or, as he calls him: "Troc") parish and writes that in Sin-le-Noble "everything is wonderful; Troc's calm, strength, humility, his prayer life and his joy are graces which he has received abundantly. How will this revival spread to the region? God knows it, and He wants us to surrender to him, on our knees, in complete dependence, that much is certain."[206] On that evening, Trocmé was presenting a book published in 1924 by Paul-Louis Couchoud titled *The Mystery of Jesus*. In it, Couchoud defended the idea that Jesus was a mythical being who never existed. Remembering what his professor Maurice Goguel had taught him, Trocmé carefully refuted Couchoud's thesis and concluded that if Jesus's existence is not mythical, then his teachings are not mythical either and can be taken seriously. Indeed, they are relevant for this world.[207]

> I had said these words, very calmly, to the ten men who were present. I had not planned or wished anything in particular, but we suddenly found ourselves on our knees, and each one of us, one after the other, we made an unforgettable confession to God. An hour later, we stood up again and we looked at one another with new eyes. A weight of secrecy, defensiveness, pride had been lifted. The Spirit of God was there and we decided right away to share that very evening this extraordinary news with our wives. That was the beginning of the "revival at Sin-le-Noble," which was to last three to four months.[208]

206. "J'ai été lundi dernier à Sin: tout est merveilleux; le calme, la force, l'humilité, la vie de prière, la joie de Troc sont des grâces qui lui sont données en abondance. Comment ce réveil s'étendra-t-il à la région? Dieu le sait et Il nous veut livré à Lui, à genoux, dans une entière dépendance, c'est sûr." Samuel Cornier papers (Cornier family, Paris). This revival only grew in the following weeks. On February 18, 1931, Chéradame wrote to Cornier: "Nous avons jusqu'à ce matin vécu et prié dans l'inconnu, ignorant tout du mouvement spirituel de Sin... [...] Nous sommes depuis ce matin dans la joie des bonnes et merveilleuses nouvelles reçues, par toi et puis par M. Deransart, au sujet de Sin. [...] Oui, il faut louer Dieu, humblement et joyeusement pour une action aussi directe du Saint Esprit. Je pense que les Trocmé doivent être bouleversés... et nous sommes les uns et les autres rivés à nos Églises. [...] Perret naturellement ne sait rien de Sin, c'est dommage. M. Nick, vu lundi, en sait quelque chose par Benoit et l'un et l'autre prient avec nous."

207. A. Trocmé, "Mémoires," 278.

208. "Je dis cela, très calmement, aux dix hommes présents. Je n'avais rien prévu, rien voulu, mais nous nous retrouvâmes soudain tous à genoux, et chacun, l'un après

Revivalism and Social Christianity

The news spread throughout the parish and even to the mines, where Trocmé and others were distributing leaflets, etc. Several men who had resisted these missionary efforts converted and gave testimonies to their colleagues and friends. The revival in Sin-le-Noble, with its obvious Pietist characteristics, was not devoid of a social dimension. Under Trocmé's guidance, the "Men's Circle" organized annual "Men's Congresses" ("Congrès d'Hommes"), which took place in Fives-Lille, Lens, and Hénin-Liétard, three towns in the region known as "Nord–Pas-de-Calais." The speakers were mostly the pastors from these towns, Henri Nick (Lille), Marcel Heuzé (Lens), and Daniel Chéradame (Hénin-Liétard, from 1920 until 1931[209]), as well as Henri Roser and the former worker-pastor Arnold Brémond. One of these congresses attracted four hundred men, who heard Roser talk about Christian pacifism.[210] Nick was very impressed by these events and praised Trocmé's organizational skills as well as his "deep faith," even if Trocmé did not follow his suggestions when it came to which speakers to invite.[211]

---

l'autre, fit à Dieu une confession inoubliable. Une heure après, nous nous levâmes, et nous nous regardions les uns les autres avec des yeux nouveaux. Un poids de secret, d'autodéfense, d'orgueil avait été levé. L'Esprit de Dieu était là et nous décidâmes séance tenante de partager ce soir-même cette nouvelle avec nos épouses. Ce fut le début du 'Réveil de Sin-le-Noble' qui dura trois ou quatre mois." Ibid.

209. In 1931, Daniel Chéradame and his wife began working for the Mission populaire évangélique (McAll Mission) in Roubaix. *AMR* 49, nr. 4 (Nov. 1931) 18.

210. "Le 'Cercle d'Hommes,' ce petit groupe d'ouvriers remué par le Saint-Esprit avait déployé son activité dans une autre direction: S'adressant tout d'abord à Monsieur Nick, à Fives-Lille, puis à Marcel Heuzé, à Lens, puis à Daniel Chéradame, pasteur d'Hénin-Liétard, [. . .], le Cercle avait entrepris d'organiser des congrès d'hommes annuels qui se réunirent dans les trois villes ci-dessus, avec un succès croissant. À Hénin, quatre cents hommes remplissaient la grande salle pour écouter Henri Roser parler de pacifisme chrétien. À Lens, Arnold Brémond nous avait parlé de ses expériences de 'pasteur-ouvrier' dans la banlieue parisienne." André Trocmé, "Mémoires," 292. The Trocmé papers at Swarthmore College contain notes for a "Congrès d'hommes" to take place in 1934 in Hénin-Liétard on Easter Sunday and Monday. Series B, box 5, 7th folder. A text by Philippe Vernier (SHPF in Paris) gives a report on the 1933 congress, which took place in Fives; *Bulletin de la Fédération des Fraternité françaises*, n° 20 (May 1933), 5–6. The *Bulletin* at that time was no longer printed: it consisted of a typed text. The "Rédaction" (in fact: R. Le Goff) explains that support for the publication, which used to come from "frère Thonger" (William Thonger, a Methodist pastor) in Brussels, had to be discontinued. In a letter from April 29, 1933 presumably to Charles Greig, Henri Nick writes about the great success of the congress, which gathered 150 men in Fives (SHPF, Paris; Mission populaire, Fives; O11Y MPE 13, folders 48–49).

211. In a letter to Charles Greig dated February 2, 1934, Nick writes about the upcoming congress in Hénin-Liétard: "Il y aura là à Hénin *un Congrès* d'hommes le dimanche et le lundi de Pâques. C'est André Trocmé de Sin qui en a l'initiative, et c'est

DOUGLAS SCOTT AND THE PENTECOSTAL WAVE

Soon after the revival at Sin-le-Noble, the British Pentecostal evangelist Douglas R. Scott (1900–67) arrived in the region.[212] Scott, who had been influenced by the aftershocks of the Welsh Revival (1904–5), had first come to Le Havre for a brief period of time in 1927 in order to learn French, since he was planning to embark on a missionary trip to the Belgian Congo.[213] Three years later, in January 1930, having postponed his journey to Africa, Douglas Scott returned with his wife Clarice to Le Havre "for a rest," but instead embarked on a mission: "as we saw the city given over to idolatry our rest has been turned into a campaign for the salvation of souls and bodies. [. . .] To briefly summarise, over seventy-five have found Jesus as their Saviour. [. . .] Nearly every conversion has followed a healing, which seems to be the Lord's way of dealing with these people. [. . .] Several deaf people now hear."[214] By 1932, Scott had established the first Assembly of God on French territory, in Le Havre. He spent the decade in France, leaving for Africa at the end of 1939.[215]

Douglas Scott accepted Trocmé's invitation to visit him in Sin-le-Noble. He spent three days with the Trocmé family. The visit was a success, even if the sick people on whom Scott had laid hands were not healed: "[. . .] he was unpretentious, fraternal, showing no signs of exaltation."[216]

---

lui seul qui choisit les orateurs, il n'accepte pas ceux que je lui propose. Je dois dire que c'est organisé vraiment bien, car c'est un homme de grande foi." SHPF, Paris; MPE 13, folders 48–49.

212. As far as I can see, the most thorough work on Scott is Stott, "The History," ch. 3–4. Yet Stott's work, while useful, is not without problems: it has some large gaps and tends to be hagiographic. This is unfortunate, given the significance of Douglas Scott's work: everything indicates that he single-handedly exported Pentecostalism to France. Laurent Amiotte-Suchet confirms this impression in "'Mettre Dieu dans sa vie.' L'apprentissage de la confiance en soi en milieu pentecôtiste français." In Fath, *Le protestantisme évangélique*, 195.

213. Scott, "Saved for Service. Testimony to the Glory of God and the Saving Power of the Lord Jesus." *Redemption Tidings* 10, nr. 2 (Jan. 15, 1934) 5.

214. Douglas and Clarice Scott, "Mr. and Mrs. Scott (Associate Missionaries) See Great Blessings En Route for Mission Field." *Redemption Tidings* 6, nr. 6 (July 1930), 8. For another report on Scott's missionary work (and a photograph of Scott), see: "Pentecostal Revival in France and Belgium. Splendid Report from Mr. Donald Gee." *Redemption Tidings* 8, nr. 3 (March 1932) 17–18; Scott, "The Pentecostal Movement in France. How the Revival Began and Spread." *Redemption Tidings* 11, nr. 2 (Jan. 15, 1935) 3–4; 11, nr. 3 (Feb. 1, 1935) 3–4.

215. "Reinforcements for the Congo Field. Mr. & Mrs. Douglas Scott Leave for Kalembe-Lembe." *Redemption Tidings* 15, nr. 32 (Nov. 3, 1939) 12.

216. "Il y passa trois jours et se montra simple, fraternel, sans aucun signe

Revivalism and Social Christianity

Magda Trocmé, however, warned her husband about the Pentecostal evangelist. She had looked upon the recent revival at the parish with favor, but Scott worried her, and she wondered whether her husband was on the verge of losing his senses.[217] Listening to her, André Trocmé decided not to invite Scott to return to Sin-le-Noble to lead further revival meetings.[218]

Douglas Scott's Pentecostal revivalism impacted several of the parishes under the care of members of the "groupe du Nord," with different effects: a revival was underway in Samuel Cornier's parish in Caudry (near Cambrai), and Cornier was among those who had "received the Holy Spirit."[219] Similar things were happening in Jacques Babut's parish, in Douai. But other members of the group had not been touched by Scott's message, so Cornier organized a reunion in Douai for the "groupe du Nord" and their mentor, Henri Nick. It was a prayer meeting with Douglas Scott, who enjoined each pastor to kneel and surrender completely to the Holy Spirit.[220] Trocmé was deeply moved by Scott's message and willing to surrender, but he did not "spit a kind of black mucus," the signal, according to the Pentecostal evangelist (as reported by Trocmé) that someone had completely surrendered. He left the prayer meeting with a deep sense of loneliness. Jacques Babut, Samuel Cornier, and Marcel Heuzé had accepted Scott's message.[221] Henri Nick was not opposed to it, but he was unable to speak in tongues, and thus remained

---

d'exaltation." A. Trocmé, "Mémoires," 294.

217. Magda writes: "J'avais vraiment marché en plein dans ce réveil de la paroisse qui semblait normal, quelque chose de bien, quelque chose de français, quelque chose de protestant." Magda Trocmé, "Souvenirs autobiographiques," 187. On the same page she adds that she was very much afraid of Douglas Scott's Pentecostalism ("J'avais très peur de cela. [. . .] quand il prêchait, quand il faisait ses réunions, cela m'effrayait beaucoup. Je me disais: 'Pourvu qu'André ne tombe pas dans le filet!'").

218. "Toutefois, une dernière hésitation me retint: Ne risqué-je pas de tomber dans l'exaltation religieuse si je suivais Scott jusqu'au bout? D'ailleurs au milieu même du réveil de Sin-le-Noble, j'avais éprouvé soudain le vertige d'un abîme mystique, sur les bords duquel je me retins. Disons-le très franchement: mon épouse Magda, qui craignait que je ne perde le contrôle de mon bon sens, me retint. Je ne fis donc jamais venir Scott à Sin-le-Noble pour des réunions [. . .]." A. Trocmé, "Mémoires," 294.

219. Samuel Cornier can be seen on a photograph taken at a Pentecostal Convention in Le Havre in 1934; *Redemption Tidings* 11, nr. 1 (Jan. 1, 1935) 1.

220. In her "Souvenirs autobiographiques," Magda Trocmé describes the reunion in Douai as a "pastorale" for all of the Protestant pastors from the region, not just the "groupe du Nord." Magda Trocmé, "Souvenirs autobiographiques," 188.

221. Samuel Cornier's papers (Cornier family, Paris) contain a letter from Douglas Scott dated September 23, 1933 in which Scott rejoices about Cornier's enthusiasm: "Cela fait que le pont est établi entre nous et vous."

somewhat on the margins (for Scott, receiving the "gift of tongues" meant one had received the Holy Spirit in plenitude).²²² Nevertheless, in September 1934, Nick took part in the fourth convention of the "Assemblées de Dieu" in Le Havre.²²³ Daniel and Robert Chéradame, for their part, rejected Scott's Pentecostalism and were moving closer to Barthian ideas. Trocmé now felt isolated, the lone member of the group for whom the "Réconciliation" was a crucial concern. There was no animosity among the members of the group but, according to Trocmé, their bond, based on mutual understanding, had been broken.²²⁴

REVIVALISM OR SOCIAL CHRISTIANITY?

Trocmé's interest in personal conversion and revivalism is quite striking. He followed in the footsteps of both Henri Nick and Jacques Kaltenbach,

---

222. On glossolalia and Scott, see Hébert Roux's testimony: "Sur ce point j'ai eu des discussions nombreuses avec Scott, déjà dans la Drôme, à Bordeaux plus tard. [...] ['] si l'on n'a pas le signe du don des langues, c'est qu'on n'a pas reçu la plénitude de l'Esprit.' Il liait les deux étroitement." Roux in Bolle et al., *La vie des Églises protestantes*, 172.

223. Samuel Cornier's papers (Cornier family, Paris).

224. "Samuel Cornier [...] avait convoqué très solennellement le 'Groupe du Nord.' Nous y étions tous, plus Monsieur Nick. Scott aussi était là, vedette de la réunion. Il nous parla très simplement d'une façon très pressante: 'Vous allez vous agenouiller,' dit-il soudain, 'et demander à Dieu son Esprit. Il le donnera à ceux d'entre vous qui lâcheront toute résistance intérieure. Ceux qui ne recevront pas l'Esprit, cachent en eux un obstacle, un interdit. Ils refusent de se livrer entièrement au Saint-Esprit.' J'étais très impressionné et désireux de 'lâcher toute résistance' moi aussi. Nous nous agenouillâmes et la réunion dura longtemps: Prières, soupirs, supplications, parler-en-langues de Scott et de Cornier. Puis Scott se mit à nous imposer les mains. Il pétrissait littéralement la tête de chaque 'patient,' affirmait 'sentir' l'obstacle spirituel. 'Quand vous vous serez abandonné,' nous disait-il, 'quelque chose remontera de vos poumons. Vous cracherez une sorte de glaire noire: le mal vous aura quittés. Alors vous parlerez, vous parlerez en langues. Ce sera l'Esprit Saint venant sur vous.'—Sous les mains de Scott, plusieurs de mes collègues parlèrent en langues. C'est du moins ce que Scott affirma au milieu des Alléluias! (En fait, ce n'étaient que quelques soupirs assez incohérents. [...].) [...] Pour ma part, je n'osais lever les yeux pour regarder ce spectacle, mais quand Scott vint à moi, je sentis tout de suite que j'étais 'en dehors' de l'exaltation commune. Certes tout ce que Scott disait sur les résistances intérieures qu'il faut abandonner pour se livrer à Dieu, était vrai. Mais que dire de l'histoire du crachat noir qu'il fallait expectorer? La chose me répugnait, et le 'parler en langues' me paraissait très différent de la soif de Dieu qui me remplissait. Scott perçut les questions que je me posais comme une 'résistance.' Il n'insista pas et, comme la réunion se terminait, je me retirai. J'étais seul, très loin de mes camarades. De ce jour, le 'Groupe du Nord' fut scindé en deux clans, ou plutôt en trois. On s'aimait bien, mais on ne se comprenait plus." A. Trocmé, "Mémoires," 296.

in this regard. It is quite certain that, to some, it must have looked as if he had abandoned the social Christian movement. In a letter to a friend from the "groupe du Nord" from March 19, 1931, he takes a look back at his first years of pastoral ministry and addresses this potential criticism: "How are souls converted? How is God's work done? [...] Certain students will say: Here we go again, one of ours has given in, his horizon is slowly narrowing itself, he is abandoning social Christianity and its broad inspirations for the most narrow revivalism."

To this possible critique, Trocmé immediately replies:

> No, we are not abandoning anything, the horizon is not getting narrower: it is in fact deepening. Behind the social issues in the foreground, I glimpse souls immobilized in sin, and behind these souls, God. As a student, I believed that the kingdom of God would stretch all across the world; as a pastor, I am learning that it takes root in people's lives. [...] There are periods of uselessness and emptiness [in my ministry], but then suddenly God reveals himself, building on rock, building the true Society, I find myself surrounded by people on their way, I am on my way too in their midst, we are walking by faith, toward Heaven.[225]

Just as Nick and Gounelle did not view evangelization as being opposed to the ideals of the social Gospel, Trocmé was convinced that awakenings among Christian communities had something to do with "the true Society" envisioned by Jesus of Nazareth.

BUILDING PEACE

Trocmé may have been in the midst of a revival in Sin-le-Noble, but these events did not lead him to forget his calling to work for peace. Indeed, we see a flurry of activity centered on peace, starting in 1931. Did the rise of fascism in Western Europe give him a renewed sense of

---

225. "Comment se convertissent les âmes? Comment se fait le travail de Dieu? [...] Des étudiants penseront: Ça y est, encore un des nôtres qui succombe, dont l'horizon, peu à peu, se rétrécit, et qui lâche le christianisme social et ses larges inspirations, pour le revivalisme le plus étroit. Non, nous ne lâchons rien, l'horizon ne se rétrécit pas, il s'approfondit. Derrière le gros premier plan des problèmes sociaux, j'aperçois des âmes immobilisées dans le péché, derrière ces âmes encore, Dieu. Étudiant j'ai cru que le Royaume de Dieu s'étendrait à travers le monde; pasteur j'apprends qu'il se creuse dans des vies. [...] Il y a des périodes inutiles, vides [...] puis, soudain, Dieu se révèle, il bâtit sur le roc, bâtit la Société véritable, je me trouve au milieu d'hommes en marche, je marche moi aussi au milieu d'eux, nous marchons par la foi, vers le Ciel." Swarthmore College, Series B, box 1.

urgency? That is quite likely. Now was the time to awaken consciences which would rebel against war and counter the rearmament efforts across Europe and beyond.

He created a "Comité d'Action pour la Paix," which held its first meeting in the city hall of Sin-le-Noble on February 21, 1931. The meeting must have energized him: on the following day, he wrote the draft of a letter he meant to send to the Rockefeller family about his project of a "peace campaign" in northern France. He wrote this message, in English, to his former employer:

> We want to protest strongly, as disciples of Christ, against every preparation of a new war, urge disarmament as the only way out of present difficulties. But how? You know how like [sic] of small influence are our protestant Churches in France—and how. . . let us say 'narrow minded'—[. . .] we want to manage this summer a peace Campaign in northern France, showing the horrors of a new war. How realize this scheme? I. a Peace exhibition [. . .] 2. Means for transporting that exhibition every Sunday in a new town or village. A light truck (camionnette) arranged for the purpose 35.000-40.000 frs. 3. a 'Peace Center' allowing for permanent Christian peace action in northern France [. . .] Why not raise funds in France? 1. Because as French churches missionary society are in constant deficit since the war we are engaged as protestant ministers *not to raise funds* in France *for non properly ecclesiastical aims*. 2. Because French Protestantism is not interested in its majority in such a campaign *although it would not be disapproved if managed by a private committee*.[226]

Starting in February 1932, and culminating in Geneva on April 3, 1932, IFoR organized a "European Youth Crusade for Disarmament and World Peace," with meetings in Belgium, France, Germany and Switzerland.[227] During two weeks, Trocmé travelled to Germany with an international group which included Muriel Lester (1883–1968), Lilian Stevenson (1870–1960), both from England, and John Nevin Sayre (1884–1977) from the United States. They spoke to large audiences in Frankfurt, Offenbach, Heidelberg, and Reutlingen, meeting young socialists but also people who were fascinated by the "Führer."[228] Before leaving for Germany, Trocmé

---

226. Letter from February 22, 1931; Swarthmore College, series B, box 1. I do not know how the Rockefeller family responded to Trocmé's call, but the answer was probably negative. The campaign did not happen.

227. Stevenson, *Towards a Christian International*, 19–20.

228. A. Trocmé, "Mémoires," 289–91.

organized a "Conférence pour la paix et la Désarmement" at Sin-le-Noble. The event was reported, albeit incompletely, by a local paper in Douai (*La Scarpe*, February 21, 1932) which prompted him to write a letter clarifying the intention behind the conference. In his letter, he emphasized the following four points: his stance against war is a consequence of the "Christian conscience." Awakening that conscience will be the only way to put an end to war. The French people should lead the world in that endeavour. The person who, during the conference, talked about Hitler's pacifism was, admittedly, a source of embarrassment.[229]

Around the same time, Trocmé was contacted by Gerhard Halle (1893–1966), a German who had served as an engineering officer during the First World War, had been wounded near Soissons in 1915, and who, since 1919, had been in contact with the Quakers in Berlin. Halle wished to return to France to denounce violence and to ask for forgiveness.[230] During the war, Halle had taken part in the destruction of several villages in the area near Cambrai. He had been severly wounded at Douaumont and in two other battles. In May 1932, after joining IFoR, he decided to embark on a speaking tour in northern France at the end of that same month. There were three evenings, organized by Trocmé, in Sin-le-Noble, Douai, and Fives-Lille, on May 20–22. At Sin-le-Noble, Halle's talk was a success: the packed audience was captivated by his speech, and Trocmé's "Men's Circle" was galvanized by what they heard.[231] But the talk in Douai's city hall turned out differently: a man who had been wounded during the war shouted that Halle's visit, in a region "drenched with the blood of martyrs," was a scandal. Many Protestants in Douai and elsewhere in the region shared that opinion, and Trocmé's pastoral career was in jeopardy.[232] One of his cousins, who lived in Douai, sent him a harsh letter

---

229. "Mon attitude personnelle est celle de la *conscience chrétienne* en révolte contre la guerre. [. . .] Je crois que la révolte des *consciences individuelles contre la guerre est le seul moyen de mettre fin à la guerre*. [. . .] Je crois que les Français, sur ce point comme sur tant d'autres, doivent frayer la route, et être vaillants pionners d'une nouvelle morale internationale. Ce sera là, pour notre peuple, non pas une honte, mais un honneur. [. . .] J'ai été froissé, comme les 'quelques auditeurs,' par les 'gaffes' que Mme Alken a commises, en parlant d'un Hitler 'pacifiste' et de la 'bagatelle' du non paiement de l'Allemagne." Letter from February 23, 1932 to the "Rédacteur en Chef de 'La Scarpe' Douai." Series B, box 1.

230. On Gerhard Halle see Hartmann, *Kriegsdienstverweigerung*, 36-40 (photograph on 111); Bredemeier, *Kriegsdienstverweigerung*, 136–50.

231. For an excerpt from Halle's talk, see Halle, "Confession."

232. A. Trocmé, "Mémoires," 288–89.

criticizing "the young pastors of the new school and their views, which are so un-French."²³³

THE PROTESTANT CONSCIENTIOUS OBJECTORS: NICK'S "CHILDREN"?

His cousin was right about one thing: some in the new generation of pastors were raising questions that had not often been raised in French Protestantism. The *Bulletin de la Fédération des Fraternités Françaises* raised the issue of conscientious objections in 1931 by circulating ten questions on the topic. It published its findings in March 1931. Some of the responses pointed out that the ten questions had obviously been written by a conscientious objector himself, and were themselves advocating for the legitimacy of that stance.²³⁴

The year 1932 was a turning point in that regard. The problem of conscientious objection became acute with the trial, in May 1932, of Camille Rombaut, a teacher who was about to travel to Africa for missionary work. Henri Nick, who knew him since Rombaut was a child, and André Trocmé, testified in his defense during the trial. The political economy professor and social Christian André Philip was his lawyer.²³⁵ Rombaut was sentenced to four months of prison. Later that year, on October 9, another trial occurred, this time for Jacques Martin, who had refused to serve a twenty-one day period in the reserve forces. Besides Nick and Trocmé, prominent figures such as André Philip, the writer Jean Guéhenno, the Catholic social Christian Marc Sangnier, and the leader of French Protestants Marc Boegner, were heard.²³⁶ Martin, a secretary for the "Fédé"

---

233. His cousin deplores "[. . .] les manifestations si peu françaises des jeunes pasteurs de la nouvelle école." Letter from March 24, 1932; Swarthmore College, series B, box 1. The author's last name is "Harmegnies." It could be Jacques Harmegnies, the son of Marguerite Trocmé and Jean Harmegnies.

234. *Bulletin de la Fédération des Fraternités Françaises*, nr. 18 (March 1931) 3–10 (the Bulletin printed only three responses to the questionnaire).

235. See *CR* (June 1932), which is titled: *Le procès de Camille Rombaut*, with Nick and Trocmé's testimonies (9–10). Trocmé concludes his speech with: "L'acte de Rombaut est le signe d'un réveil religieux" (10). The trial took place at Lille on May 26, 1932. Gounelle's report can be found in *RCS* 45 (1932) 558–59. See also Cabanel, "Les courants pacifistes," 168.

236. See "Le procès de Jacques Martin, objecteur de conscience." *CR* (Nov. 1932), 7–24. Jean Guéhenno, "Notes d'un témoin." *Europe* (Nov. 1932) 459–63. Guéhenno spoke on the basis of his humanist worldview. Boegner, who was Tommy Fallot's nephew (Boegner's mother was Jenny Fallot, Tommy Fallot's sister) and who assisted

(the French branch of the "World Student Christian Associations"), was sentenced to one year of prison and was released after six months, but his renewed refusals to serve as a reservist led to further—shorter—imprisonments in 1937, 1938, and 1939.[237] On August 24, 1933, finally, Philippe Vernier's trial took place, and he too was condemned to one year of imprisonment. A second trial took place a year later, and he was condemned to two more years of prison.[238] These events, especially the last two, were publicized on the national stage. André Philip was the defense lawyer at all of these trials.

Amazingly, it appears that many (and perhaps all!) of the Protestant conscientious objectors in France who appealed to religious convictions in the 1920s and early 1930s were associated in one way or another with Henri Nick: Henri Roser was a collaborator of Nick at the "Foyer du Peuple" around the time of his refusal to serve in the army (1923) and in the years that followed; Nick knew and supported Rombaut since his childhood; Jacques Vernier collaborated with Roser in Aubervilliers, where the "Foyer" of Fives was used as a model; Philippe Vernier had participated in Nick's ministry in Fives. Nick had been a close friend of their father, Frédéric Vernier (1868-1951), at the "Faculté de théologie" in Montauban. When one adds Trocmé's own story, and how he too was influenced by Nick, one can only be amazed at the many links between Henri Nick and these young pacifists who were challenging "the system" (not just the State, but also their Church institutions!) and paying the price for it. Why these links? Because, of all the Protestant pastors in France, despite his

---

Fallot in the final months of his ministry in Aouste, became one the most important figures in 20th century French Protestantism. He presided both the "Fédération protestante de France" (1929–61) and the "Conseil national de l'Église réformée" (1938–61). See Mehl, *Le pasteur*: "Que Fallot ait été pour Boegner à la fois un maître à penser et un guide spirituel, c'est, croyons-nous, l'évidence même." (22). Boegner disagreed with the French "Réconciliation" and its principled pacifism: "Si l'on appliquait aux relations entre les peuples le principe de la non-résistance aux méchants, la porte serait ouverte aux pires brigandages et c'en serait fait de la sécurité dans le monde!" Boegner's personal notes from October 17, 1917, quoted in Mehl, 58. For a brief account of Marc Sangnier's pacifist engagement, see Farrugia, "French Religious Opposition."

237. See "IIe procès de Jacques Martin." *CR* (March-April 1935), which includes a long letter of support by Wilfred Monod (24–31) and, on Martin, Patrick Cabanel, "Le pasteur."

238. See the Sept.–Oct. 1934 issue of *CR* (27 pages) titled: "IIe procès de Philippe Vernier." There is a short narrative which introduces Vernier and gives some context (1): as soon as he was freed, in April 1934, Vernier was commanded to join his "régiment." Refusing to do that, he was arrested again. His second trial took place on August 1, 1934.

André Trocmé's First Steps in Spiritual and Social Christianity

own criticisms of principled forms of pacifism, Nick was perhaps the most supportive of the young men who thought the "Sermon on the Mount" had to be read and practiced literally.[239]

As these trials were taking place, Trocmé continued to participate in events which fostered collaboration and reconciliation between Germany and France. At the annual meeting of the German section of FoR, on August 27–30, 1932, a "French-German encounter" took place, in Bad Herrenalb near Karlsruhe in southwestern Germany. André Philip, Henri Roser, and André Trocmé were part of the French delegation, which met thirty Germans.[240]

In August–September 1932, a summer school for children aged six to fifteen, "open to all regardless of their religion, political inclination or country of origin," which Trocmé had set up four years earlier, was given a "specific character": "we will found a true children association: 'Children of Peace,' which will operate during six weeks, from Tuesday, August 23 until Sunday, September 25." The purpose of the camp will be "to teach children to love children from other countries, and to detest war. Politics will be absent," as well as "religious pressure." Each of the five weeks of the summer school will be dedicated to a particular region of the world and to a particular "race" (native Americans, Asians, Africans, Indians, etc.), ending with France, a country "in the midst of other Nations and other races."[241] Trocmé was using the model designed by Emmanuel Chastand,

---

239. In his "Mémoires" (204), Trocmé mentions the "grand homme, [le] seul homme qui ouvrit les bras aux objecteurs de consciences, Henri Nick, le génial pasteur de Fives-Lille." Henri Nick's closest collaborator, Charles Vallée, was one of the first members of the French "Fellowship of Réconciliation," alongside Trocmé and Roser. See Roser, "La réconciliation," 3: "Cependant le Mouvement s'était étendu par la dispersion de ses premiers adhérents. Jean Bresch en Alsace, Charles Vallée dans le Nord, Jacques Martin à Paris se portaient responsables."

240. *CR* (July-August 1932) 23 and 25. There are several parallels between André Philip and André Trocmé: Philip had received a grant from the Rockefeller Foundation, which allowed him to spend some time in the United States in 1924–25. In 1928–29 he visited India for four months and met Gandhi. Dolléans, "La vocation."

241. "Notre 'école de vacances' va s'ouvrir pour la quatrième fois. Mais nous avons resolu, cette année, de lui donner un caractère particulier: [. . .] Cet été, nous fonderons une véritable société d'enfants: 'les enfants de la paix' [. . .]. Art. 2.—But de la Société: Apprendre aux enfants à aimer les enfants des autres pays, leur apprendre à détester la guerre. Il ne sera pas fait de politique. [. . .] Cette Société est ouverte à tous les enfants de 6 à 15 ans, sans distinction de religion, de parti, ou de pays [. . .]. Il ne sera pas exercé de pression religieuse. [. . .] Du 19 au 24 Septembre.—Semaine de la France au milieu des autres Nations et des autres races." Peace Collection, Series B, box 1.

Revivalism and Social Christianity

the very dynamic director, since 1907, of the "Solidarité" in Nantes, who had founded a "Société des enfants de la paix" in 1924.[242]

On October 4, 1933, Trocmé sent a detailed report of recent developments in France to IFoR's associate secretary, John Nevin Sayre. Thanks to excellent coverage by the press both locally and nationally, he writes, the problem of conscientious objection is no longer "considered theoretically":[243] "there is presently no Frenchman ignoring conscientious objection[244] and many of them know the names of Rombaut, Martin or Vernier. In religious, philosophical or political papers, the question has been passionately discussed." Interestingly, Trocmé then addresses the response to these trials among two groups: the Protestant Church and "the working people." He notes that the Protestant Church officials, "living in Paris, under the influence of big protestant capitalists and the more nationalistic attitude of the Capital since the Hitler Revolution[,] are *fearing* conscientious objection in the church" for the following three reasons: they see the possibility of the Church being dragged into politics, they fear a split within the Church, and they are afraid that Protestantism might come to be seen as anti-French and thus lose whatever influence it has. For all these reasons, Trocmé adds, the official stance has been harsh: Henri Roser's application for consecration to the pastoral ministry was denied; Jacques Martin was not allowed to minister a parish; Robert Chéradame was called to meet with the Church authorities in Paris as a result of his participation in Philippe Vernier's trial; and Trocmé himself was "threatened with exclusion and asked not to speak any more in public meetings."

---

242. In May 1924, Chastand reported that he had recently created a "society of the 'Children of Peace' ("Les Enfants de la Paix")." He adds: "I am hoping that many groups of this society will be organized in France. I am enclosing a leaflet showing what I am aiming at in this organization. We are asking the children to abandon their war toys and games and we have received from them a quantity of play guns, spears, etc. These they have brought spontaneously. When our annual peace festival comes we shall have a bonfire of joy in the court." *AMR* 42, nr. 3 (May 1924) 8. In 1927, after twenty successful years at the Solidarité in Nantes, Emmanuel Chastand, a nephew of Gédéon Chastand, became the director of the McAll Mission/Mission populaire évangélique; *AMR* 45, nr. 4 (Nov. 1927).

243. What follows is based on Trocmé's letter to Nevin Sayre, October 4, 1933; Swarthmore College, Peace Collection, Series B, box 1. Trocmé's report to Sayre confirms Norman Ingram's conclusion: "It was only in January 1933 [. . .] that the French government suddenly perceived that it had a 'conscientious objection problem.'" "The Circulaire Chautemps," *French Historical Studies* 17 (1991) 390. Yet, as Ingram notes, there were prior instances of conscientious objection. See the story of Gontaudier (who is not mentioned by Ingram), below.

244. Trocmé writes: "C. O."

A general synod of the French Reformed Church, gathered in Auteuil on June 20–23, 1933, had affirmed that "propaganda in favor of conscientious objection was incompatible with the pastoral ministry." But there was hope: the Protestant people viewed the conscientious objectors in a much more positive light: "Our churches belong to the socialistic majority and are entirely sympathetic to conscientious objection[,] although many of their members have not yet made a personal decision. In my church in Sin, there is not one member against objection." Moreover, the pastors from the post-war generation also disagree with the official stance. Trocmé had seen it from his own eyes at a second annual gathering of young ministers organized by the "Groupe du Nord" in La Michaudy (Jura), in early September 1933. All of the pastors who had begun their ministry after the war had been invited. Among the thirty-six pastors at the retreat, only two opposed conscientious objection. The Barthian Pierre Maury (1890–1956), who presided over the gathering, sided with the majority. Maury himself had been denied a position in a prominent parish of Paris because of his leniency on conscientious objection.[245] Trocmé added that "we cannot be very severe against the officials who really do not know what to do."[246] The French workers, at least those he knew in northern France, supported the conscientious objectors. Trocmé had seen their respect for Philippe Vernier and the other Protestant objectors in his parish at Sin-le-Noble.

DEBATING CONSCIENTIOUS OBJECTION

For a while, the trials of Rombaut, Martin, and Vernier put the question of conscientious objection squarely at the center of the debates within French Protestantism. The "Christianisme social" had itself grappled with the question at the congress in Rouen, in 1901, in connection with the case of Gontaudier, a Roman Catholic who had become a Quaker while living in the United States. He returned to France in order to serve in the army,

---

245. "Pierre Maury, secretary of the Student movement and a very influential man, although not objector, will very soon express the sorrow of the younger generation about the lack of Inspiration in the Commmittee decisions. Pierre Maury has been refused as pastor in one of the important churches of Paris because he did not accept to take position against objs." Letter to Sayre, October 4, 1933. On Pierre Maury, see Smyth-Florentin, *Pierre Maury*, who briefly evokes the gathering at La Michaudy (65). See Jacques Babut and Roger Casalis' reports, "Camp pastoral de la Michaudy, du 5 au 8 septembre 1933," *La Confiance. Correspondance fraternelle et privée de l'Association des Pasteurs de France* 17, nr. 6 (Oct. 1933) 79–81.

246. Letter to Sayre, Oct. 4, 1933.

Revivalism and Social Christianity

but in 1895, shortly after his conscription, he refused to carry a gun and asked to serve in a different capacity, for instance in a military hospital. His request was rejected, and he was condemned to two years of imprisonment. After his release, he was again conscripted and commanded to carry a gun. For a second time, he refused, and he was jailed for another two years. The army then suddenly discovered that he had a parent in his care, and thus that his service in the army was no longer warranted.[247] As a report by Aquilas Quiévreux on the 1901 social Christian congress in Rouen reveals, a number of young Protestants had been moved by Gontaudier's trials—in all the senses of the term—and wrote to the leaders in charge of planning the congress in Rouen, asking them what should be done. These young men never received a reply from the organizers, for the leaders themselves did not know how to respond: they were torn between "national solidarity, i.e., the necessity of loving one's country, and Christ's command to love and not to kill." Quiévreux added: "All we could agree on was the duty to work on changing the kind of mindset which leads to war and armed peace."[248]

In 1927, Élie Gounelle took a position on the question, in a short text following a report on IFoR. His stance must have been disappointing to the members of the "Réconciliation":

> We will follow carefully and with a respectful feeling of friendship the Movement known as the "*Réconciliation*," as well as the one of the Resistants or "conscientious objectors," despite irreducible and essential reservations which we will have to present in the Revue. Our pacifism, which is associated with "La Paix par le droit" and the "Alliance Universelle pour l'Amitié internationale," follows a narrow ridge in its ascension toward perpetual peace. This ridge overlooks two cliffs: on the right, nationalism and militarism, which unfailingly lead to war, and

247. See Polydore Fabreguettes, *Traité des délits politiques et des infractions par la parole, l'écriture et la presse*, vol. 2. Paris: Chevalier-Marescq, 1901, 271–72; "The French Conscience Cases," in *Friends' Intelligencer* 59 (1902) 175; "Consciences of Another Sort," *Liberty* 14, nr. 5 (1903) 6.

248. "Une autre question tragique a été soulevée: c'est la question de la guerre, ou plutôt, car nous sommes tous d'accord contre la guerre, la question de l'armée et du service militaire. Quelques jeunes gens émus par l'exemple de Gontaudier l'avaient écrit à l'un d'entre nous pour lui demander ce qu'ils devaient faire. Nous n'avons point répondu à leur question. Nous nous sentions nous-mêmes profondément troublés entre les devoirs de la solidarité nationale, les nécessités de l'amour de la patrie, et l'ordre du Christ qui prescrit d'aimer et défend de tuer. Nous n'avons été d'accord que sur le devoir de travailler à changer l'état d'esprit qui produit la guerre et la paix armée." Quiévreux, "Le congrès de Rouen," 494.

on the left, the more or less sheep-like pacifists and the individualists who absolutize things, who do not see the obstacles, and who are ready to sacrifice themselves and their homeland on the altar of the Ideal. *In medio stat virtus. . . et vera pax!* [*Virtue stands in the middle. . . as does true peace!*]²⁴⁹

Such comments, which Gounelle repeated in the following years, certainly complicated the picture for the young members of the "Réconciliation." It appeared that, despite its leaders' "friendliness," the "Christianisme social" rejected the principled pacifism advocated by FoR. Still, the *Revue du Christianisme social* published reports on the Fellowship's congresses, and at a conference in Prag in 1928 Gounelle described the "Réconciliation" as one of the many "forces for peace."²⁵⁰ In 1934, in a text that is actually quite prophetic itself, he cautioned that "the sacred right of prophetism must be maintained at all cost [. . .]. If the churches decide to cast away the group of conscientious objectors, it would be deprived of an elite group of people who have beautiful consciences. It is our conviction that the experiences and the tragic ordeals of the war which is coming could very well transform them, suddenly, into heroic defenders of what is right. For there will be many different ways, some bloody, others spiritual, to be engaged in the total war which is looming. . ."²⁵¹ Gounelle may have had hesitations concerning conscientious objection (and they appear in that last quote too, since he writes about a sudden transformation of these young men

---

249. "Nous suivrons attentivement et avec une respectueuse sympathie le Mouvement dit de '*Réconciliation*,' et aussi celui des Réfractaires ou 'Objecteurs de conscience,' malgré d'irréductibles et essentielles réserves qu'il faudra bien que nous exposions dans la Revue. Notre pacifisme, qui est celui de La Paix par le droit et de l'Alliance Universelle pour l'Amitié internationale, suit dans son ascension vers la paix perpétuelle un chemin de crête qui surplombe deux précipices: celui, à droite, des nationalismes et des militarismes, qui mène infailliblement à la guerre, et celui, à gauche, des pacifistes plus ou moins bêlants et des individualistes qui poussent les choses jusqu'à l'absolu, ne voient pas les obstacles, et se déclarent prêts à immoler sur l'autel de l'Idéal, et eux-mêmes, et leur patrie. *In medio stat virtus. . . et vera pax!*" *RCS* 39 (1926) 1060.

250. See for instance Roser, "Le Congrès du Mouvement," 955–8. For Gounelle's comment ("forces de paix"): see *RCS* 41 (1928) 955. Gounelle returned to more negative comments in *RCS* 43 (1930) 309–11, while calling for the creation of a civil service in France, following the examples of Denmark (1917), Sweden (1920), Norway (1921) and Holland (1923) (311). See also *RCS* 45, vol. 2 (1932) 272.

251. "Il faut maintenir à tout prix le droit sacré au prophétisme [. . .]. En chassant de nos Églises le groupe des réfractaires, nous nous priverions d'une élite de belles consciences que les expériences et que les épreuves tragiques de la guerre qui vient pourraient bien transformer soudainement, c'est notre conviction, en défenseurs héroïques du droit, car il va y avoir bien des manières, les unes sanglantes, les autres spirituelles, de mener la guerre totale de demain. . ." *RCS* 47, vol. 1 (1934) 485.

into defenders of justice, as if they were not already imbued by that ideal!), but he knew there was something prophetic too about their stance, insofar as their criticism of flawed human institutions was made in the name of a higher, transcendent authority. It was a grave mistake, he thought, for the Protestant churches to prohibit conscientious objectors to serve as pastors or missionaries.[252] But the French Protestant churches did precisely that, after having set up a committee, presided over by Marc Boegner, to study the question.[253] As we will see, at least with regard to André Trocmé (but the same would be true of others), Gounelle's prediction about the war and the potential role of these young men was fulfilled: when the time came, the conscientious objectors did not act in a cowardly or purely passive fashion, as some people thought they would.

SEARCH FOR A NEW PARISH

The living conditions of the Trocmé family in Sin-le-Noble were even more rudimentary than in Maubeuge–Sous-le-Bois. The sanitary conditions in the town itself were not good, and many inhabitants suffered from tuberculosis. Indeed, according to Magda and André Trocmé's memoirs, in the entire parish there was only one family—from Belgium—in which no one suffered from tuberculosis.[254] Their four children were constantly sick. Nelly, their eldest, was suffering from fever, to the point where she had to be sent away to the Swiss Alps to recover.[255] The three boys had

252. *RCS* 47 (1934) 486.

253. See Gounelle, "Une Consultation théologique." Boegner headed a "Comité d'Études des Intérêts généraux du Protestantisme." Among its members were Henri Monnier, the dean of the Faculté libre de théologie in Paris, Jean Cadier, the Neo-Calvinist theologian Auguste Lecerf, Marc Boegner and Pierre Maury (all of them Reformed), Adolphe Lods (Lutheran), Th. Roux (Methodist), André Aeschimann and Georges Grosjean (free Churches) and Georges Rousseau (Baptist). They produced a text condemning conscientious objection: "En conséquence, il paraît à la Commission que, dans l'état actuel des choses, l'Église, se fondant sur l'Écriture et s'appuyant sur une tradition suffisamment constante en cette matière, notamment sur le consensus des réformateurs, doit recommander à ses enfants d'accepter les obligations du service militaire. Elle y voit à la fois une forme de la soumission aux autorités et une acceptation des solidarités humaines voulues de Dieu.'" Gounelle, "Une Consultation," 218.

254. "Car à Sin-le-Noble, il y avait beaucoup de maladies, beaucoup de tuberculose. Nous avions calculé que dans toutes notre paroisse, il n'y avait qu'une famille, et encore c'étaient des Belges, qui n'avait pas la tuberculose." Magda Trocmé, "Souvenirs autobiographiques," 181. André Trocmé, "Mémoires," 302.

255. André Trocmé mentions a duration of "deux ans" in a letter to Roger Casalis from Sin-le-Noble, May 3, 1934; Swarthmore College, series B, box 1.

similar problems.²⁵⁶ Without any cure, at the time, for tuberculosis, the family doctor was advising them to leave the region, and they decided to move to a different region.

Henri Nick could not understand their decision: applying the same (very high) standard he was using for his own life, he viewed it as a form of disobedience.²⁵⁷ André and Magda Trocmé then contacted two women who were Nick's "spiritual advisors," Mlle Guex and Mlle Gonin. They were both wives of pastors, and both collaborated with the "Mission populaire évangélique"-McAll Mission. They opined that, since God had allowed their children to become sick, it was probably a sign that God wanted them to work somewhere else.²⁵⁸

Trocmé spent the first half of 1934 considering several options. He received calls from three parishes: Clamart (Paris), Thonon-les-Bains (Haute-Savoie, near Switzerland), and Die, in the Drôme valley south of Lyon.

CLAMART

Trocmé was contacted in the first months of 1934 by the parish of Montrouge–Malakoff–Clamart. The parish, which comprised these three towns, was looking for a second pastor. In Clamart, Trocmé had several old friends from the "Fraternité" that he had helped create right after World War I. Several of these friends were now serving as "elders" in the Reformed congregation. André Trocmé preached a trial sermon on February 25, 1934. The first pastor in Clamart, Albert Finet, wrote to him saying that the parish council had been very impressed by it. They viewed him

---

256. "[...] les enfants faisaient encore de la température et avaient des grippes sans arrêt." Magda Trocmé, "Souvenirs autobiographiques," 199. "[...] nos enfants étaient toujours malades." A. Trocmé, "Mémoires," 302.

257. "Nous consultâmes donc notre maître à penser, Monsieur Nick, qui en fut très assombri: 'Vous avez pris l'engagement de consacrer toute votre vie au Nord. C'est une désobéissance.'" A. Trocmé, "Mémoires," 302–3.

258. "Nous consultâmes les conseillères spirituelles de Monsieur Nick, les demoiselles Guex et Gonin, qui habitaient Genève: 'Si Dieu permet que vos enfants soient malades,' nous dirent-elles, c'est qu'il vous veut ailleurs.'—Et nous nous mîmes à chercher cet 'ailleurs.'" Ibid., 303. Trocmé does not give their first names, but it is likely that Mlle Guex was related to Henri Guex, the director of the Mission populaire évangélique/McAll Mission in France from 1913 until 1927; *AMR* 45, nr. 3 (May 1927) 3–5. Mme Gonin was probably related to pastor Louis Gonin (in Reims from 1905 until 1934; he resurrected the McAll station in 1923, calling it "Foyer Bon Accueil"). *AMR* 35, nr. 4 (Nov. 1917) 14 and *AMR*. 41, nr. 3 (May 1923) 24–6.

as "the man they are looking for to attempt an evangelization campaign." Finet urged him to accept the position.²⁵⁹

On March 1, 1934, eleven members of the "Fraternité" signed a short message "to their former President, Mr. Pastor André Trocmé," in which they expressed their affection and urged him to accept the call from the parish. They added that "they were solemnly committing themselves to place all of their energy and enthusiasm at his disposal."²⁶⁰ On the following day, March 2, 1934, Albert Jospin (1886–1976), a plumber, wrote to him on behalf of the "Union," following a suggestion by André Coutris, the president of the "Fraternité," to inform him that they were "anxiously awaiting" his decision, for "you have conquered our hearts. In order to demonstrate that there is nothing platonic in all this, we have decided to create as of now a section of the Croix-Bleue, so that we may obey the call you forcefully expressed on Sunday, and we are seeking to intensify our spiritual life. I hope, Dear Pastor and Friend, that this wish and this letter will touch your heart, that they will contribute to help you make the decision we wait for, and that from that communion great hopes will arise for the evangelization of this corner of the Parisian suburbs."²⁶¹

---

259. "Tous les conseillers ont été très impressionnés par ta prédication du 25 février dernier[,] ils pensent que tu es l'homme qu'il faut pour tenter une campagne d'évangélisation, et ils sont pleinement résolus à t'appuyer de toutes leurs forces." Letter from March 4, 1934. Series B, box 1.

260. "Clamart le 1er Mars 1934. Les Soussignés, réunis à la Fraternité à l'occasion de la séance de l'U.C.J.G., envoient à leur ancien Président, Monsieur le Pasteur André Trocmé, leurs messages affectueux. Après l'avoir entendu Dimanche dernier ils souhaitent ardemment le voir accepter l'appel de l'Eglise de Montrouge Clamart et s'engagent solennellement à mettre à sa disposition toutes leurs forces et tout leur enthousiasme. Ils demandent à Dieu d'exaucer ce vœu et d'en permettre la réalisation totale." Among the people who signed are Paul Weisser, Simone Henry, D. Jospin, H. Jospin, A[lbert] Jospin, Jean Coutris.

261. The entire letter is worth quoting: "Le 2. Mars 1934. Cher Monsieur Trocmé, C'était hier soir réunion d'Union, les membres présents, sur l'initiative d'André Coutris, et en communion intime avec tous les membres de la Fraternité et de l'Eglise, vibrant à l'unisson, ont décidé de vous envoyer ce vœu qui est l'expression de leur affection, de leur consécration renouvelée, et de leur attente quelque peu angoissée de la décision que vous allez prendre. Attente angoissée, croyez le bien, exprime exactement notre état d'esprit—vous avez conquis nos cœurs. Pour vous prouver que tout cela n'était pas un vœu platonique nous avons décidé de créer dès maintenant une 'Section de Croix Bleue' afin de nous montrer obéissant à l'appel que vous avez fait retentir Dimanche, et à intensifier notre vie spirituelle. Je veux espérer Cher Pasteur et Ami que ce vœu et ce mot iront à votre cœur, qu'ils contribueront à favoriser la décision que nous attendons et que de cette communion naîtront de grands espoirs pour l'Evangélisation [de ce] coin de banlieue parisienne. Dans cette attente je vous prie de croire à nos sentiments fraternels. Pour la Fraternité de Clamart et par ordre, A. Jospin."

On March 24–25, 1934, Trocmé returned to Clamart for a second visit. He met with the parish council and received an unanimous vote. A nomination seemed likely until, a few days later, Finet informed him that he had received a letter, dated March 22, from Pierre Durand-Gasselin, a Church official in Paris, the president of the "executive commission" of the Reformed Church.[262] In it, Durand-Gosselin warned the parish not to pursue the candidacy of Trocmé, a well-known advocate of conscientious objection. On April 11, Trocmé decided to go to Paris to clarify the situation with the Church authorities. He seems to have forced his way into a session of the "commission exécutive," where he was heard. On the following day, Durand-Gasselin sent another letter to Finet with a simple message: the parish must not hire Trocmé. On April 23, Trocmé received a letter from the "commission exécutive" to the effect that his nomination was being blocked. A week later, the parish of Montrouge–Malakoff–Clamart announced to the president and members of the "commission exécutive" its decision: "the parish council has decided not to call pastor Trocmé. This decision was made with profound sadness and only out of a sense of obedience. For the sake of truth, the council must emphasize the fact that this decision goes against its sentiment and against the almost unanimous vote of the parish under its care."[263] It is thus an authoritarian decision by the central authorities of the French Reformed Church that led Trocmé to keep searching for a parish.

FIRST VISIT TO LE CHAMBON-SUR-LIGNON

Then came a call from the parish of Thonon-les-Bains, in Haute-Savoie. As in Clamart, the Church council nominated him. But one member voted against him, because of Trocmé's pacifism, and the whole process collapsed.[264] Trocmé had just finished exploring the possibility of working in Thonon when Roger Casalis, a friend from the "Faculté de théologie" in Paris, wrote to him on April 29, 1934, from his parish of Le Chambon-sur-Lignon (Haute-Loire), in the mountains not too far south of Saint-

262. Pierre Durand-Gasselin had become a member of the Paris Committee of the McAll Mission in 1928; *AMR* 46, nr. 2 (March 1928) 1.

263. "[...] le Conseil presbytéral renonce à adresser un appel à Monsieur le pasteur Trocmé. C'est avec une profonde tristesse qu'il a pris cette décision et uniquement par esprit de discipline. Il se doit, par respect pour la vérité, de souligner qu'il agit ainsi contre son sentiment et celui de la presque unanimité de l'église dont il a la charge." Letter from April 30, 1934; Swarthmore College, series B, box 1.

264. A. Trocmé, "Mémoires," 306.

Revivalism and Social Christianity

Étienne. Casalis had been a member of the "groupe des isolés," the group of theology students who shared their thoughts during their years of military service in the early 1920s. After his studies, he had tried to implement a group based on the model of the "groupe du Nord," but one dedicated to France's rural areas.[265] His first parish was Le Chambon-sur-Lignon, where he arrived in August 1927, succeeding Charles Guillon (1883–1965), a social Christian who (as we will see) would play at decisive role during the war.[266] After seven years, he was moving to a different location, which turned out to be Sainte-Foy-la-Grande, near Bordeaux (Gironde), and he wondered if Trocmé would like to succeed him in Le Chambon.[267] The two friends had renewed their friendship not long before at the gathering of young pastors organized by the "groupe du Nord" in La Michaudy (Jura), in the summer of 1933. Trocmé wrote back to Casalis:

> At first glance there are several reasons in favor of accepting to come to Le Chambon:
> 1. It would be good, for the church and for the pastor who is leaving, if the new pastor could continue the work already begun in the same direction, that is, as you indicate, in the direction of a Revival. It would be encouraging for me to find a place which has seen preparatory work. Our time at La Michaudy has shown us the extent to which the ministry has brought us closer, through similar experiences. I think there is a sign here.
> 2. My children indeed need a stimulating climate. This is the only reason why I am thinking about leaving the North.[268]

Le Chambon seemed to be a most welcoming parish. A good number of the pastors in the region, and several prominent members of the

---

265. "[. . .] il avait essayé de mettre en œuvre un groupe rural semblable à notre 'Groupe du Nord.'" Ibid., 307.

266. *L'Écho de la Montagne* 19, nr. 9 (September 1927) 3.

267. In his message to his parishioners, besides health concerns, Casalis indicates his desire to pursue further theological studies in order to become a professor. He prays that God will call "un homme inspiré" to Le Chambon. *ÉM* 26, nr. 5 (May 1934) 3.

268. "À première vue, il y a plusieurs raisons pour j'accepte de venir au Chambon: Il serait bon, pour l'église et pour le pasteur sortant, que le nouvel ouvrier continue le travail entrepris dans la même direction, c'est à dire, tu l'indiques toi-même, dans le sens du Réveil. Pour moi, ce serait encourageant de trouver un terrain déjà préparé. Les heures de la Michaudy nous ont assez prouvé combien le ministère nous avait rapprochés dans des expériences analogues. Il y a là, je crois, une indication. [. . .] Mes enfants ont effectivement besoin d'un climat tonique. C'est la seule raison pour laquelle je songe à quitter le Nord." Letter to Roger Casalis from Sin-le-Noble, May 3, 1934; Swarthmore College, series B, box 1.

parish, were in favor of pacifism and conscientious objection. A female parishioner, Ms Matile, a pacifist, led a small group of women, the "Mothers and Educators for Peace" ("Mères et Educatrices pour la Paix"). But there were also two major problems: first, Le Chambon was a "regular" or traditional parish under the care of the French Reformed Church. This would be a new experience for Trocmé. He was not sure whether he was ready for it (his recent troubles with the "commission exécutive" in Paris had only confirmed his sentiment). He preferred the less established evangelizing posts of northern France, which had been planted by the "Société chrétienne du Nord." He wrote to Casalis:

> 1. I feel called by God toward evangelization rather than toward a ministry seeking to maintain an old parish. While remaining faithful to God's direction, I could only consider a ministry such as the one I would have in Le Chambon to be provisional, for the sake of my children's health. May the parish council not be afraid by this term "provisional"! I wish to be absolutely honest. "Provisional" does not mean that I would not dedicate all of my energies to God's work.
>
> 2. My oldest is seven years old. We have just spent two years without her because of her health. We are not ready to consider another separation when she will be old enough to go to secondary school. I therefore cannot commit myself to a longterm ministry in Le Chambon. I can envision five years at the most, i.e., until my eldest reaches the age of twelve years.[269]

This last concern was a familiar one among the parishioners of le Chambon: they had lost a beloved pastor, Louis Bertrand (1867–1941),

---

269. "À côté de ces raisons pour mon acceptation, il y a aussi des raisons *contre*. Les voici:

Je me sens appelé par Dieu vers l'évangélisation plus que vers un ministère de conservation dans une ancienne église. Tout en étant fidèle aux directions de Dieu, je considérerais un ministère comme celui que je pourrais avoir au Chambon comme un ministère provisoire, accepté en raison de la santé de mes enfants. Que ce mot 'provisoire' n'effraye cependant pas le Conseil Presbytéral. Je veux être absolument franc avec lui. Provisoire ne veut pas dire que je ne me donnerais pas de toutes mes forces au travail de Dieu.

Mon aînée a 7 ans. Nous venons de nous en séparer pendant 2 ans pour raisons de santé. Nous ne sommes pas disposés à envisager une nouvelle séparation lorsqu'elle aura l'âge d'entrer au lycée. Je ne puis donc m'engager pour un ministère de longue durée au Chambon. Je pourrais, au maximum, m'engager pour 5 ans, jusqu'au moment où mon aînée atteindrait 12 ans." Letter to Roger Casalis from Sin-le-Noble, May 3, 1934; Swarthmore College, series B, box 1.

when, after sixteen years of ministry in the parish, he had to leave in order to live closer to a "lycée."[270]

On May 27, 1934, Trocmé visited Le Chambon and preached a sermon. Everything must have gone well, for on June 6 he wrote to the parish council accepting their call. His letter reveals that a sort of "revival" would be among his goals in the parish. It also contains a prescient sentence:

> I do not have any experience working in rural areas, I do not have much physical strength or the kind of spiritual power needed to lead your large flock on the path to revival, but I do believe in God, I count on Him, and since I have met brothers among you who trust in Him, there is no reason why we would not see great things being accomplished.[271]

The following chapters are going to show how these final words became reality in the ensuing years.

André Trocmé, arrival in Le Chambon (1934)

270. *ÉM* 2, nr. 13 (Oct. 1910) 3 and nr. 14 (Dec. 1910) 3.

271. "Je n'ai ni l'expérience des milieux ruraux, ni beaucoup de forces physiques, ni suffisamment de puissances spirituelles pour conduire votre grand troupeau vers le réveil, mais je crois en Dieu, je compte sur Lui, et puisque j'ai rencontré parmi vous des frères qui se confient en Lui, il n'y a aucune raison pour que nous ne voyions pas de grandes choses s'accomplir." Letter to the parish council at Le Chambon from June 6, 1934; series B, box 1.

PART THREE

The "Conspiracy of Good" in Le Chambon-sur-Lignon

"We will *never* find such a place anywhere else, a place imprinted to such an extent by our ideas."

ANDRÉ TROCMÉ to MAGDA TROCMÉ,
Letter written while in hiding, November 19, 1943.[1]

LE CHAMBON BEFORE THE WAR[2]

FAR FROM BEING AN unknown parish on the Protestant "map" of France, Le Chambon-sur-Lignon—or, as it was often called from 1893 until 1923, Le Chambon-de-Tence—was a well-known Protestant town.

---

1. "Nous ne retrouverons *jamais* ailleurs un endroit pareil, ayant à ce point accepté l'empreinte de nos idées avec tant d'amis sérieux et fidèles." Trocmé papers, Swarthmore College, Series B, box 1.

2. Many books and articles have been published on the rescue effort which took place in the area of Le Chambon-sur-Lignon during World War II. In the following pages, the main resources on which I draw, besides some of the documents preserved at the Trocmé papers at Swarthmore College (Pennsylvania), are: Bolle, *Le Plateau Vivarais-Lignon*; Boulet, *Histoire de la Montagne-refuge*; Maillebouis, *La Montagne protestante*. Boismorand has a very useful chronology in *Magda et André Trocmé*, 355–72.

Revivalism and Social Christianity

The whole region had a much higher percentage of Protestants than the national average (10 percent of Protestants in nearby Ardèche, compared to approximately 2 percent of Protestants in France).[3]

In Aquilas Quiévreux's view, it was there that the first "real" congress of social Christians had taken place, in August 1899.[4] The theme of the congress had been the evangelization of the workers. Among the most important outcomes of the congress was the creation of the social Christian journal *L'Avant-Garde*. A national synod of the French Reformed Church had taken place in Le Chambon in June 1913.[5]

Starting in 1893, Louis Comte, one of the leaders of the "Christianisme social" among French Protestants, had set up summer camps for children in the area of Le Chambon and the neighboring villages. Eventually, each summer some 2,500 children, many of them abandoned by their parents, would leave their cities to breathe fresh air and recover their health.[6]

Only one year or so before the Trocmé family's arrival, a second major congress of the social Christian movement was held there (September 17–21, 1933), gathering 260 delegates, including Élie Gounelle and André Philip, a professor of political economy and a soon-to-be major political force on the national scene. The participants at worship and at the keynote addresses amounted to 1,200 people, a significant number since Le Chambon had about 2,500 inhabitants (including the surrounding farms).[7] Among the questions which were discussed in smaller sessions was how to support conscientious objectors. A manifesto calling the Reformed

---

3. Or 26,000 for a population of 272,000 inhabitants in Ardèche, according to Mours, *Le Vivarais et le Velay*, quoted in Encrevé, *Les protestants français*, 390 n. 3.

4. Quiévreux, "Le congrès de Rouen," 485–86. Quiévreux distinguishes between the many congresses of the "Association protestante pour l'étude pratique des questions sociales" (APEQS), which gathered "scholars," and the social Christian movement, which is a "fédération d'œuvres."

5. *ÉM* 5 (March 1913) 2; (June 1913) 2.

6. On this "Œuvre des enfants à la montagne," see Maillebouis, *La Montagne protestante*, 106–9. In 1904, Louis Comte recalled how he had heard Tommy Fallot give his conference on "La femme esclave" in Geneva, where Comte was studying theology, and how he was won over to the "Christianisme social," in *L'Avant-Garde* 6 (Oct. 15, 1904) 92–93.

7. See de Félice's demographic indications about Le Chambon: "Sur 2,543 habitants recensés en 1931, l'Église réformée évangélique compte 1,397 membres ou enfants, plus une cinquantaine de non-rattachés; les catholiques sont environ 150, en 45 familles; le reste ressortit au darbysme, à l'exception de quelques salutistes et libristes." "Essai démographique," 38. There is a detailed report on the congress of Le Chambon in *RCS* 46 (1933).

churches to further study the question of conscientious objection was signed by many participants, including several lay people from the parish of Le Chambon.[8]

At three thousand feet of altitude, the area surrounding Le Chambon-sur-Lignon is sometimes called "La Montagne" and "Le Plateau." Protestants influenced by Jean Calvin's Reformation lived in the region since the 16th century, and the memory of the Wars of Religion, of the "dragonnades" (the persecution at the hands of Louis XIV's troops), was still very much alive. In the first decades of the 20th century, Le Chambon was one of seven parishes in the consistory of Saint-Voy. A local journal, *L'Écho de la Montagne*, was published, starting in October 1909, to bring announcements and news and to serve as a bond to the 2,000 families affiliated with the Reformed Church and scattered in various villages and farms of the region.[9]

The parishes of the region were inclined toward revivals. The revivalist and social Christian pastor Frank Thomas (1862–1928), from Geneva, had preached and lectured on the theme of revivals in Le Mazet Saint-Voy in 1911, and in Le Chambon one year later. He returned in 1924.[10] A

---

8. "Pour que les Églises étudient à fond le problème de l'objection de conscience et celui des rapports de l'Église avec l'État," in *RCS* 46 (1933) vol. 2, 386–88. This text, which was later circulated under the title "Appel à la Conscience Protestante," was published in various journals including *L'Avant-Garde* of Jan. 1934. This "appeal" was endorsed by 372 people, 22 of whom lived in the area of Le Mazet–Saint–Voy and Le Chambon. It urged for a deeper reflection on the issue of conscientious objection and "on Church–Sate relations (God and Caesar)." Among those who signed it were many pastors and lay people, including A. Trocmé (Sin-le-Noble), Jacques Babut (Douai), Mlle L. Bollon (Le Chambon), Roger Casalis (Le Chambon), Chéradame (Walincourt), Paul Conord (Albi), M. et Mme Darcissac (Le Chambon), Delanno (Fives-Lille), Pierre Ducros (pastor in Cercoux), Émile Fabre (pastor in Ponzauges), Marcel Jeannet (Mazet–Saint–Voy), Jospin (pastor in Vitré), Mme G. Jouve (Chambon), Jean Lasserre (pastor, Bruay), Mlle A. Matile (Chambon), Pierre Maury (Paris), Mme L. Pélissier (Chambon), André Philip, Mme Riou-Bollon (Chambon), Henri Roser (pastor in Aubervilliers), Camille Rombaut (Hellemmes–Lille), Mlle Sogne (Chambon), Édouard Theis (missionary, Madagascar), Toureille (pastor in Congénies), Charles Vallée (Hellemmes–Lille), Mlle Marguerite Vallée, Arnold Brémond (pastor in Divonne-les-Bains), and many others. See *RCS* 46 (1933) vol. 2, 586–88. Jacques Martin was the first person to receive financial support from the "Caisse de Solidarité pour les Objecteurs de Conscience Chrétiens," a solidarity fund which was set up at the 1933 congress in Le Chambon; *RCS* 47 (1934) vol. 1, 322.

9. For the number of 2,000 families, see *ÉM* 1, nr. 1 (Oct. 1909) 1. Thanks to the effort of the Société d'histoire de la Montagne, *L'Écho de la Montagne* is available for consultation on the website of the Société: http://shm43.free.fr/d2_5.htm The journal ceased to exist in May 1948 when it was fused with another journal, *Labour*.

10. *ÉM* 3, nr. 22 (July 1911) 1 and 3; *ÉM* 4, nr. 34 (July 1912) 3; *ÉM* 16, nr. 6-7

Revivalism and Social Christianity

series of regional revival meetings were organized in 1921.[11] Missionary work was also a familiar topic, as can be seen from the many reports from missionaries in Africa (Madagascar), Asia (Korea, Japan) and elsewhere in *L'Écho de la Montagne*, which also reported the successes of the inner mission among the workers in Pas-de-Calais.[12] The Pentecostal evangelist Douglas Scott had come to the region in February 1933, when he visited the parish of Le Riou for two weeks for a "mission de réveil."[13]

BEGINNINGS

Trocmé began his ministry in Le Chambon in early October 1934.[14] The parish was much larger than anything he had experienced in nothern France, and everyone was expecting a visit from the new pastor, which led to some feelings of impatience. André and Magda Trocmé tried to assuage these by communicating with their parishioners in "brief letters from the pastor to his parishioners" in *L'Écho de la Montagne*.[15] The fact that these

---

(June–July 1924). The name of Henri Nick was also not necessarily foreign to the readers, as can be seen in *ÉM* 11, nr. 2 (Feb. 1919) 3: a text by Henri Nick, titled "Pour les Régions libérées," was reprinted.

11. *ÉM* 13, nr. 12 (Dec. 1921) 3.

12. *ÉM* 3, nr. 25 (Oct. 1911) 2–3. Under the heading "Société Centrale Évangélique," the 1913 conference on evangelization in Paris was announced in *ÉM* 5, nr. 4 (April 1913) 6.

13. *ÉM* 24 (Feb. 1933) 2.

14. *ÉM* 26, nr. 10 (Oct. 1934) 3: "Bienvenue," and 4 (short message signed: "A. et M. Trocmé"): "Chers amis, votre nouveau pasteur et sa femme se mettront au travail à partir du dimanche 7 octobre. Ils ont été touchés par les marques de confiance que leurs nouveaux paroissiens leur ont déjà témoignées. Ils se réjouissent de pouvoir bientôt travailler avec vous dans le service du même Dieu."

15. "*Petite lettre du pasteur à ses paroissiens.* Chers amis, depuis un mois déjà, j'ai fait pas mal de chemin pour aller vous voir, et Mme Trocmé avec moi. Mais vous êtes très, trop nombreux, et nous vous demandons patiemment d'attendre votre tour. Si toutefois vous êtes impatients (ce qui est bon signe), il y a plusieurs moyens rapides de faire connaissance avec le pasteur: 1° Aller au culte et lui toucher la main à la sortie, en lui expliquant qui vous êtes; 2° Aller aux réunions de quartier et rester cinq minutes après la réunion pour lui parler; 3° Venir chez le pasteur un matin dans la semaine (sauf lundi et jeudi) pour lui faire une visite. Le samedi matin, ceux qui sont fatigués peuvent venir se reposer au presbytère et prier avec le pasteur pour préparer avec lui la journée du dimanche. En agissant avec nous sans façons, vous nous aiderez dans notre travail et nous ferez plaisir. A. et M. Trocmé." *ÉM* 26, nr. 12 (Dec. 1934) 3. See also the issue from Oct. 1935, 2: "Vous comptez que je viendrai vous voir. Je m'efforcerai de le faire. Rappelez-vous qu'une visite *demandée* par vous sera toujours rendue le plus vite possible." See also Nov. 1935, 3, on the eventuality of reducing the number of pastors

messages were signed by both André and Magda Trocmé indicates their close collaboration in the ministry.

One of Trocmé's first decisions was to consult the entire parish concerning Sunday worship, asking people to answer a series of questions about it. The responses were overwhelmingly positive: people wrote about worship as spiritual nourishment, as a source of joy etc. Still, Trocmé was dissatisfied with the number of people who came to worship and addressed the situation in several messages.[16]

Trocmé created a "Fraternité" of men on November 3, 1935. Its purpose was clear: "The goal of the Association, as its names indicates, will be to realize between its members the ideal of brotherhood taught by Jesus-Christ toward any human being, without distinction of class, of wealth, of political affiliation or of religion."[17] The "Fraternité" will "dedicate itself to the intensive and impartial study of the problems of our time, and will support any fraternal initiative which seeks to banish from the earth the old politics in which people are at each other's throat."[18] Last but not least: "The *Fraternité* will not be satisfied with a theoretical fraternity. It will commit its members to a practical action with an eye toward more fraternity in our local area."[19] There would be weekly meetings. One of its members remarked that this ideal of brotherhood "might lead us far." Trocmé liked that comment so much that he included it in one of his short letters to his parishioners.[20] Indeed, the entire parish would go very far with its new pastor.

---

on the Plateau: "Votre pasteur, qui vous visite déjà si peu, verrait encore son travail augmenter."

16. *ÉM* 27, nr. 8 (Aug. 1935) 2, and nr. 10 (Oct. 1935) 2.

17. "Le but de l'Association, comme son nom l'indique, sera de réaliser entre ses membres, et à l'égard de tout homme, sans distinction de classe, de fortune, de parti ou de religion, l'idéal de fraternité enseigné par Jésus-Christ." The entire document is preserved at Swarthmore College, Series B, box 1.

18. "Cependant, en face des grandes injustices du monde contemporain, et, en particulier, en face de la guerre, la *Fraternité* ne saurait rester neutre. Elle se livrera à l'étude intensive et impartiale des problèmes de notre époque, et se prononcera en faveur de toutes les initiatives fraternelles qui veulent bannir de la terre la vieille politique des loups." Swarthmore College, Series B, box 1.

19. "La *Fraternité* ne se contentera pas d'une fraternité théorique. Elle engagera ses membres dans une action pratique en vue de plus de fraternité dans notre commune. Chaque membre sera donc prié de s'inscrire dans l'un des *Comités d'Action* suivants: Comité de propagande, de réception, de visites, d'entr'aide, d'excursions, de tempérance, de débats et études, de délassement, etc., etc." Trocmé papers, Swarthmore College, Series B, box 1.

20. "*Petite lettre du Pasteur à ses Paroissiens.* Chers amis, depuis quelques

Revivalism and Social Christianity

André Trocmé and Magda Trocmé's messages to their parishioners in *L'Écho de la Montagne* reveal their efforts to revive the parish. When they arrived, there were only seven or eight young women and three to four young men involved in the parish, about forty families, and as many widows or older women came to worship. Soon enough, young people from the surrounding countryside were gathering in larger numbers for prayer meetings and a "movement of repentance" began, with several "conversions."[21] As in his previous parishes, Trocmé was seeking to move as much as possible beyond a multitudinist church toward a church in which people are committed to the Gospel not just in words, but also in acts.[22]

SPANISH REFUGEES

One of these acts was to welcome refugees from the Spanish Civil War (1936–39). Already in 1936, Trocmé and other local leaders, including Charles Guillon, published an "Appeal to the population of Le Chambon," asking the local population to welcome thirty to forty Spanish children.[23] The department of Haute-Loire welcomed almost two thousand refugees, in three waves, from October 1936 until the spring of 1939.[24] Soon, Spanish children and their mothers arrived in Le Chambon and nearby villages. A parishioner, Marguerite de Félice, dedicated some of her resources to

---

semaines, Le Chambon a sa 'Fraternité.' Les hommes qui font partie de ce groupement s'efforceront de vivre entre eux fraternellement. L'un de nous disait: 'Cela peut nous mener loin, cette idée de fraternité.' Il avait raison. L'amour des frères peut nous conduire parfois très loin, mais sur ce chemin-là, Dieu nous accompagne et nous garde." *ÉM* 27, nr. 12 (Dec. 1935) 3.

21. A. Trocmé, "Mémoires," 320–21.

22. *ÉM* 27, nr. 5 (May 1935) 3: "Petite lettre du pasteur à ses paroissiens. Chers Amis, Mme Trocmé, accaparée par les soins du ménage et des enfants, ne peut plus courir la campagne comme pendant les premiers mois de son séjour ici. Elle en est peinée. Vous lui ferez plaisir en venant la voir. Songez aussi aux jeunes gens et jeunes filles qui ont terminé depuis Pâques leur instruction religieuse, et auxquels se posent la question: 'Veux-tu entrer dans l'Eglise de Jésus-Christ?' L'Eglise de Jésus-Christ (la vraie, et non celle que l'on voit), ne se compose pas de ceux qui déclarent: 'Je me suis donné à Dieu,' et qui ne lui appartiennent pas en réalité. Elle n'est pas, non plus, constituée par ceux qui, se sentant trop faibles pour tenir des engagements, préfèrent garder leur liberté et rester dehors. Elle se compose de ceux qui, se sentant trop faibles pour rester fidèles, *se repentent* de cette faiblesse, ne regardent plus à eux-mêmes *et croient* que Christ les affranchit de tout péché. Où en êtes-vous? A. et M. Trocmé."

23. On this "Appel à la population chambonnaise," see Boulet, "Étrangers et Juifs," 302–21, and Maillebois, *La Montagne protestante*, 97.

24. Boulet, *Histoire de la Montagne-refuge*, 137.

welcoming these refugees. In January 1939, another group of 72 Spanish children and adults arrived in the region.[25] Most of these refugees left the area by the end of 1939.

A SPIRITUAL RETREAT

In 1937, André Trocmé created a retreat center in Le Chambon which he called "Retraite spirituelle du Chambon-sur-Lignon." He advertised this project in the *Revue du Christianisme social*. A house one kilometer away from Le Chambon (at a place called Bois-du-Genest) had been readied for people who would want to go there for a retreat between July 1st and October 1st. It was open to people "of any religion, believers as well as nonbelievers." Three common prayers, all of them optional, would take place every day, following the model of the retreats in Saint-Germain-en-Laye (near Paris), and in Provence at Pomeyrol.[26] This project was repeated the following year, but it seems to have been short-lived because of the war. Nevertheless, it is proof that Trocmé was not oblivious to the new movements of spiritual retreats which were then burgeoning within French Protestantism, and which would play a decisive role in the rebirth of monasticism among Reformed churches (Pomeyrol, Grandchamp, Taizé).[27] He was in contact with Antoinette Butte (1898–1986), who was then the leader of retreats at Saint-Germain-en-Laye and who a year later would be in charge of what became the community of Pomeyrol.

THE "ÉCOLE NOUVELLE CÉVENOLE"

In 1938, Trocmé was joined in Le Chambon by Édouard Theis, who shared his pacifist views and who like him had studied at Union Theological

---

25. Maillebouis, *La Montagne protestante*, 99–100.

26. "Sur appel de M. le pasteur A. Trocmé, l'équipe de la Retraite spirituelle de Saint-Germain-en-Laye ouvre cet été, au Chambon-sur-Lignon, une nouvelle maison. Celle-ci est située au Bois-du-Genest, à 950 mètres du Chambon, en pleine forêt de sapins, avec vue étendue sur un vallon solitaire et les monts Mezenc et Gerbier-des-Joncs [sic]. Ouverte du 1er juillet au 1er octobre, la maison s'adresse à tous ceux qui veulent vivre quelque temps de retraite disciplinée dans la solitude, la prière, la méditation. [. . .] Des chambres seront à la disposition des retraitants de toutes religions, croyants ou incroyants. Trois cultes en commun auront lieu chaque jour, comme aux Retraites de Saint-Germain et de Pomeyrol." *RCS* 50 (1937) 461. There are more details on the daily schedule on 462.

27. De Vries, *Vers une gratuité*.

Seminary and tutored John D. Rockefeller's children (Theis had also been a missionary in Cameroon and Madagascar). Theis's arrival was linked to the creation of the "École nouvelle cévenole" that same year. The former pastor of Le Chambon (1921–27), now its mayor (1931–40), Charles Guillon, had envisioned a secondary school since 1936. Trocmé was fully supportive of the project, which was in part an attempt to reduce the flood of young men and women who left the region for the cities in order to go to school and to work ("exode rural," or rural depopulation, was a significant concern).[28] The Trocmé family too, would be able to remain in Le Chambon much longer because of that school. To that pragmatic motivation, Trocmé and Theis of course added their own vision to the project: a student-centered pedagogy oriented toward internationalism and peace-building.[29] The school started on a small scale, with four professors, of which only one, Theis, who worked part-time, was paid, and eighteen students during the first academic year, 1938–39.[30] Theis's colleagues were his wife Mildred, who was American and taught English, Magda Trocmé, who taught Italian, and a German teacher named Mrs. Hoefert, an Austrian who was half Jewish and had left her country after the "Anschluss."[31]

THE FIRST MONTHS OF WAR AND THE BEGINNING OF THE RESCUE EFFORT

On September 7, 1939, Trocmé sent a letter to Marc Boegner, the president of the National Council of the French Reformed Church, to inform him that he would refuse to be part of the armed forces, but that he would gladly serve in a civil capacity. Boegner replied on October 4, 1939: "Your letter has deeply touched me. I hope you will understand if I do not discuss with you what I, like a great many of your colleagues, consider to be a major error in the interpretation of Holy Scripture and Christian doctrine. I will limit myself to assuring you, as I do with your friends, whom I am seeing here, that I will do whatever I can so that those who share

---

28. Boulet, *Histoire de la Montagne-refuge*, 144.

29. "J'insistais sur l'enseignement du pacifisme." A. Trocmé, "Mémoires," 326.

30. Olivier Hatzfeld, *Le Collège Cévenol a cinquante ans. Petite histoire d'une grande aventure*. Le Chambon-sur-Lignon: Collège Cévenol, 1989. There were 40 students in 1939, 150 students in 1940 because of the refugees, 250 in 1941, 300 in 1942, 350 in 1943. There were so few classrooms that Magda one year had to teach a class in a bathroom throughout winter. . . . A. Trocmé, "Mémoires," 345–46.

31. Ibid., 328.

your conviction may be able to show that they are not afraid of danger."[32] Trocmé expressed his disappointment with Boegner's stance on October 16, 1939: "Mister President, I am pained and surprised by the content of your October 4 letter. In it you write that you consider me to be in error (error in the interpretation of Scripture, error in Christian doctrine). And yet the Oxford ecumenical Conference, where you served as one of the vice-presidents, abstained from such a judgment. It considered the three attitudes of the Christian toward the war as equally possible and worthy of respect."[33] It was obvious that the highest authorities of the French Reformed Church were not supportive of conscientious objectors, which they perhaps suspected of cowardice.

Trocmé expected to be mobilized in the French army, as had been the case of his pacifist friends "Philo" Vernier and his brother Pierre, as well as Jacques Martin and Henri Roser. But because Trocmé had four children, he was among those who would be mobilized last. Refusing to serve, his friends went to jail, whereas he continued his ministry in Le Chambon.[34] They were freed in the wake of France's sudden defeat, in June 1940. Roser, the Vernier brothers, all headed as quickly as they could to Le Chambon.[35] Not wanting to give the impression that pacifists are fearful of violence,

32. "Votre lettre m'a vivement touché. Vous comprendrez que je n'entre pas en discussion avec vous sur ce que, comme un très grand nombre de vos collègues, je considère comme une grande erreur d'interprétation de l'Écriture Sainte et de doctrine chrétienne. Comme à vos amis, que je vois ici, je veux me borner à vous donner l'assurance que je fais mon possible pour que ceux qui ont votre conviction soient mis en mesure de montrer qu'ils n'ont pas peur du danger." Swarthmore College, Series B, box 1.

33. "Monsieur le Président, Je suis douloureusement étonné par le contenu de votre lettre du 4 octobre. Vous y déclarez que vous me considérez comme étant dans l'erreur (Erreur d'interprétation de l'Écriture, erreur de doctrine chrétienne). Cependant la Conférence œcuménique d'Oxford, dont vous étiez l'un des vices-présidents, s'est abstenue de porter un tel jugement. Elle a considéré comme également possibles et dignes de respect, les trois attitudes du chrétien devant la guerre." Swarthmore College, Series B, box 1.

34. In his notebook, Marc Boegner wrote on Christmas Day 1939, three days after Roser was sentenced to four years of prison: "The conscientious objectors are constantly on my mind." ("La pensée des objecteurs de conscience m'obsède.") Ph. Boegner, *Carnets*, 15.

35. A. Trocmé, "Mémoires," 331 and 340. In 1940, Trocmé was 39 years old, but because of his large family he was considered by the army to be among the men who were 47 years old. Roser, who also had four children, was called to serve because his children had not been officially declared. On Sept. 29, 1940, Marc Boegner preached in Le Chambon (he spent two nights with the Trocmé family) and noted during his visit the presence of "a small group of conscientious objectors" ("Il y a ici en ce moment un petit groupe d'objecteurs [. . .].") Ph. Boegner, *Carnets*, 51.

Trocmé travelled to Paris with Theis to see if the Red Cross would accept them as ambulancemen, which meant they would likely be placed in the most dangerous areas. A letter Trocmé wrote to the American Red Cross on May 22, 1940, confirms what he writes in his "Mémoires." He explicitly inquired whether it would be possible to work "as a nurse or as a chauffeur, in order to help especially the civilian population in the war zone and at a dangerous place, of course with no salary [. . .]."[36] Trocmé's application was rejected.[37]

In the first months of the war, hearing of the masses of people on the road to safety, Trocmé probably thought of his own experiences in 1917. His own father, Paul Trocmé, now 95 years old, was among the many people who were fleeing northern of France. He reached La Rochelle.[38]

As we have seen, Le Chambon had a tradition of welcoming large number of people, children and adults. The town actually usually thrived economically during the summer season, when hundreds of people from other areas of France, including a large number of Protestants from Paris, came to spend some time on the "plateau," many of them renting summer homes. It was common for the population to be multiplied by five or six, sometimes more, for several months.[39]

As the war began, in September 1939, there were about 300,000 Jews in France, of which 110,000 were French since generations, 70,000 had become French citizens, and 120,000 were foreigners or stateless. In May 1940, 40,000 Jewish refugees from Belgium, Holland and Luxembourg fled to France.[40]

The first refugees who arrived in Le Chambon and nearby villages were for the most part French, coming especially from Paris and northern France. Something remarkable happened in those months: the Protestant network of Trocmé's friends and acquaintances led to a number of them coming to Le Chambon. In September 1940, three months after France's traumatic defeat, Pierre Nick, a son of Henri Nick, who was a medical doctor in Inchy (Pas-de-Calais), arrived in Le Chambon with his family for a temporary stay. He continued to practice as a medical doctor, and

---

36. Swarthmore College, Series B, box 1.

37. A. Trocmé, "Mémoires," 337. One of the conditions was that one no longer was susceptible of being called by the army. Trocmé did not satisfy that condition.

38. Ibid., 336.

39. Boulet, *Histoire de la Montagne-refuge*, 147.

40. Lazare, *Dictionnaire des Justes*, 24.

his children enrolled in the local elementary school.[41] Two of Trocmé's colleagues from the "groupe du Nord," Jacques Diény, then pastor in Saint-Amand-les-Eaux, and Jacques Babut, pastor in Douai, arrived in Le Chambon not long after the defeat of June 1940.[42] At the end of 1940, André Philip, a socialist "député" who, as a very young professor of political economy, had become a well-known speaker at social Christian congresses already in the 1920s, moved to Le Chambon with his wife Mireille and their children (Trocmé did not know him well). Closely monitored by the Vichy regime for his socialist affiliation and his involvement in the "Résistance," at the end of July 1942 Philip travelled from the southern coast of France to join general de Gaulle in London. His arrival was announced on the BBC, and a few days later, on July 30, he was heard declaring his allegiance to general de Gaulle, who had named him "Commissaire national à l'Intérieur": Philip was in charge of all actions on French territory. On November 20, during a visit to the United States, as a special envoy of de Gaulle, he met for one hour with president Roosevelt at the White House.[43]

In a Declaration from June 23, 1940, the day after the armistice was signed by Marshal Pétain and Hitler in Compiègne, Trocmé and Theis described the kind of resistance he thought is conform to the Gospel: "The duty of Christians is to counter the violence that will be applied on their conscience by using the weapons of the Spirit. [. . .] We shall resist, when our adversaries demand submission to orders which run counter to those of the Gospel. We shall do that without fear, but also without pride or hate."[44] [see Appendix] This message was deeply offensive to some of his

41. Pierre Nick returned to northern France in the first weeks of 1941. Besin, *Pierre Nick*, 20–21.

42. Boulet, *Histoire de la Montagne-refuge*, 148. Both wrote about their impressions as they arrived to the peaceful region of Le Chambon, far from the bombs, after a harrowing journey: J. Diény, "Le Plateau 'terre d'asile,'" *ÉM* 32, nr. 7 (July 1940) 1; Babut, "À ceux qui sont partis: À ceux qui sont revenus: À ceux qui sont troublés: Message d'un Pasteur Aumônier-Militaire," *ÉM* 32, nr. 8 (Aug.–Sept. 1940) 3.

43. Poujol, "André Philip," 195–97, 208–13. Philip was in contact with Simone Weil, Léon Blum, Emmanuel Mounier, Hubert Beuve-Méry, Gabriel Marcel, and many other prominent intellectuals and politicians. Whereas André Trocmé is a good example of one way in which the social Christian ideal of "solidarity" was practiced, Philip is arguably the best example, in France, of the ways in which one could embody the social Christian call to change the very structures of society for the sake of greater justice for all. In 1944 Philip wrote "Les Réformes des structures," a text which was partly put into effect in France starting in 1945 (social security, rights of each person, participation of the workers in the management of factories etc.). Philip gave this important document to de Gaulle in July 1944. Ibid., 234–35.

44. "Le devoir des chrétiens est d'opposer à la violence exercée sur leur conscience,

parishioners, who could only see in it a lack of patriotism. Wasn't he supporting France's enemy with his radically non-violent message? Weren't his German roots (Trocmé's mother was German) obvious behind such views? And what about his Italian wife? That same month of June 1940, after Mussolini had declared war on France (June 10, 1940), Magda and André Trocmé found these words written in chalk on their front door: "Go back to Italy with your Italian, Boche, and leave us in peace!"[45] In fact, Trocmé had nothing but contempt for fascist tendencies and was deeply worried by the fact that the Vichy regime was modelling itself after Mussolini's Italy. Trocmé and Theis were lonely figures in the parish, as they maintained a radical pacifist stance in the face of Nazism. After the defeat, their isolation increased as they expressed their criticism of the Vichy regime, which in these first months enjoyed widespread support throughout France.[46]

Le Chambon was located in the southern zone of France, which for the most part remained free of the German occupant ("zone libre"). It was also quite remote from the valleys and the cities. Refugees could do worse than seeking refuge there. In his "Mémoires," André Trocmé describes how, one day, in the midst of France's defeat (May–June 1940), a Jewish woman from Germany knocked on his door seeking refuge. Magda and André Trocmé hoped some of the French Jewish families who were then staying in Le Chambon would help, but that was not the case: in their eyes welcoming foreign Jews would endanger French Jews.[47] Charles Guillon, too, seems to have opposed her staying. Guillon soon left Le Chambon and went to Geneva, where, as it turns out, he was able to contribute decisively to the rescue of Jewish refugees who had found temporary shelter in the area of Le Chambon. Despite Magda's efforts, the Jewish woman from Germany, after spending the night in the Trocmé family's home, was asked to continue her journey.[48]

les armes de l'Esprit. [. . .] Nous résisterons, lorsque nos adversaires voudront exiger de nous des soumissions contraires aux ordres de l'Évangile. Nous le ferons sans crainte, comme aussi sans orgueil et sans haine." Boismorand, *André et Magda Trocmé*, 128. The expression "weapons of the spirit" was used by Bédarida, *Témoignage*, and by Pierre Sauvage for the title of his remarkable documentary on Le Chambon, *Weapons of the Spirit* (1989).

45. "Retourne en Italie avec ton Italienne, Boche, et fous-nous la paix!" A. Trocmé, "Mémoires," 330. "Boche" is a French curse word for "German."

46. Ibid., 338.

47. "On nous répondit qu'en protégeant des Juifs allemands, nous mettions en danger les Juifs français qui, à l'époque, n'avaient encore rien à craindre." Ibid., 351.

48. Ibid., 350–51. Trocmé is sometimes said by his detractors (including people in

It appears that the first people who came to the rescue of foreign Jews seeking refuge were not mainline Protestants of Le Chambon, that is members of the local Reformed (or Calvinist) Church, but farmers who belonged to the "darbystes," a small Protestant movement founded in France by John Nelson Darby (1800–82).[49]

As the number of refugees was growing, the parish of Le Chambon set up several large houses to welcome them. During a trip to Marseille to explore the possibility of visiting some of the refugee camps in southern France, as a new organization, the Cimade (the "Comité Inter–Mouvements auprès des Évacués"), was already doing, Trocmé met Burns Chalmers, who worked for the Quakers. Chalmers convinced him to give up his project and to do something else: help welcome children, adolescents and adults in his remote and peaceful parish. The parish council voted and agreed to do that. Shortly before the war, French Protestants had been unambiguously urged by their authorities, the Fédération Protestante de France, and especially by Marc Boegner, to welcome refugees.[50]

Support for this effort would come from the Quakers, from the Fellowship of Reconciliation and from the Congregationalist Church in the United States. Information and funds would be channelled through people like Charles Guillon. Guillon was closely involved in the nascent World Council of Churches, in Geneva, as one of the vice-presidents of its provisional committee ("Comité provisoire").[51]

Le Chambon) to have taken all of the credit for the rescue effort, which was regional and involved many people. One may see in this page of his "Mémoires" an honest account of a decision Magda and André Trocmé must have regretted for a long time. He writes: "[. . .] la Juive disparut, en nous laissant sur la conscience le souvenir de notre naïveté et de notre sottise. Nous n'entendîmes plus jamais parler d'elle, mais nous prîmes la résolution de ne plus raconter désormais nos secrets aux autorités." (351).

49. Ibid., 349.

50. See, for instance, Marc Boegner's call, in 1939: "Vous vous arrêterez donc et, à l'exemple du bon Samaritain, vous vous pencherez sur les malheureux dont je viens de vous entretenir. Si surchargée de préoccupations, si trépidante que soit l'existence d'un grand nombre d'entre vous, vous prendrez le temps de réfléchir à cette grande misère humaine, de vous informer de ses causes, de rechercher si et dans quelle mesure vous pouvez concourir à la soulager. Ne dites pas que vous ne pouvez rien accomplir d'efficace, parce que le temps ou les capacités vous manquent. D'autres, non moins occupés que vous, offrent leur bonne volonté. Vous ferez comme eux." Boegner, *L'Évangile et le racisme*, 37–38. Bolle, "Les réfugiés d'Europe centrale," 61–65.

51. See Bolle, "Charles Guillon." Guillon played an important role in hosting the national congress of the movement in Le Chambon in September 1933. He worked since 1927 at the world headquarters of the YMCA in Geneva and kept that position even as he became mayor of Le Chambon. He had been a keynote speaker at the Congress of the "Fédération du Christianisme social" in Bergerac, June 6–9, 1926; *RCS*

By the end of 1941, there were several houses available for refugees in and near Le Chambon.⁵² Eventually, more homes would be opened. Here is a list of the main ones:

"La Guespy": it opened on May 16, 1941, housed approximately twenty children. It was funded by the "Secours Suisse aux Enfants" and the American Quakers. It was run by Juliette Usach, who had herself come to Le Chambon with her father, a Spanish pastor, as a refugee from the Spanish civil war.

"L'Abric" welcomed refugees since November 12, 1941. It was operated by the "Secours Suisse aux Enfants" and could house thirty-five people.

"Faïdoli," up and running before the end of 1941, was under the care of "Service civil international."⁵³ It could welcome 30 to 40 children. The person in charge was August Bohny, a Swiss who worked for "Service civil international" and who oversaw the "Secours Suisse aux Enfants" in Le Chambon.

"Les Grillons" could house twenty to twenty-five children, with funding from the United States (FoR, the Quakers). André Trocmé asked his thirty year old cousin Daniel Trocmé, a teacher, to supervise this house. Daniel Trocmé began his work on October 1, 1942. On December 15, 1942, there were nine girls and eleven boys: eleven Catholics, eight Jews and one Protestant.⁵⁴

---

39 (1926) 324. Guillon travelled extensively and took part in the 1937 conference of "Life and Work" at Oxford, replacing Élie Gounelle. He remained a member of the municipal council of Le Chambon even after he resigned from his position as mayor on June 23, 1940. Trocmé, who does not seem to have had much sympathies for him, not quite accurately writes in his "Mémoires" that Guillon left Le Chambon immediately after the armistice of June 1940 ("Mémoires," 351; Trocmé does acknowledge Guillon's involvement in the rescue effort on 353). In fact Guillon was in Switzerland at the end of July 1940, but returned regularly to Le Chambon, where he presided the municipal council meetings until February 19, 1941, and three more times after that (May 25 and August 30, 1941, June 5, 1943). He served as mayor after the war, from 1945 until 1959.

52. A. Trocmé mentions seven of them in his "Mémoires" and adds that they existed by the end of 1941 (355). I count only six such houses (Trocmé includes perhaps "Les Genêts," another house, run by pastor Henri Braemer, in his list), and some of them opened after 1941. I rely here in part on Boulet, *Histoire de la Montagne-refuge*, 203.

53. Founded by Pierre Cérésole, whom Trocmé had met in Bad Boll in 1924, the secretary of this movement, from 1935 until 1941, was Rodolfo Olgiati, who in 1942 led the Swiss Red Cross' "Secours aux enfants." He visited Le Chambon in these months and was convinced it could become an important area for refugees.

54. See Daniel Trocmé's cards to his brothers, quoted in Bollon, "Contribution," 394.

"Le Coteau fleuri," since the Spring of 1942, was operated by the Cimade, the "Comité Inter-Mouvements auprès des Évacués" founded by Madeleine Barot and other young Protestants in 1939.[55] Among the people in charge were Françoise Perrotte, an evangelist the Trocmé family had known in northern France, Hubert Meyer, and a pastor, Marc Donadille. It could house eighty people.[56] At the end of July 1942, it housed seventy refugees, from newborn to elderly, all of them foreigners freed from French camps.[57]

"La Maison des Roches," or "Les Roches," a former hotel about two kilometers from the town of Le Chambon, was transformed into a boarding house and opened its doors to refugees in February 1942. It had a capacity of about thirty rooms and was funded by the "Fonds européen de secours aux étudiants" and the prefecture.[58] In March 1943, André Trocmé asked Daniel Trocmé to supervise "Les Roches" in addition to "Les Grillons." Daniel Trocmé renamed the house "Foyer universitaire des Roches." Most of the young men were foreigners, with a majority of German refugees. In his "Mémoires," André Trocmé writes that few of them were Jews, but in reality, as Gérard Bollon has shown, there was a majority of Jews. Of the 90 students or so who lived there between February 14, 1942 and June 29, 1943, 46 were Jewish, 11 were Catholic (there was a contingent from Spain, who had fled the Civil War), 10 were Protestant, and 3 were Orthodox Christians (no religious affiliation was indicated on the files of 19 others).[59] Many of them had been interned in camps in southern France (Gurs, Recébédou, Rivesaltes, Agdes, Les Milles etc.). Some had been sent by pastors who were actively involved in rescuing refugees, such as pastor Pierre Toureille, in Lunel.[60] Among the people who gave lectures to the students of "Les Roches" was André Philip, who had a home in Le Chambon.[61]

---

55. The best recent resource on the Cimade is Gerdes, *Ökumenische Solidarität*. See also Barot, "La Cimade," 217-26.

56. Bollon, "Contribution," 392.

57. See the letter from Claire Julien to Hubert Meyer, April 28, 1942, quoted in Gilles Charreyron, "La Cimade sur le Plateau Vivarais-Lignon et dans le Puy-de-Dôme dans les années quarante." In Patrick Cabanel et al., *La Deuxième Guerre mondiale*, 138-39.

58. Boulet, *Histoire de la Montagne-refuge*, 198.

59. A. Trocmé, "Mémoires," 394. Bollon, "Contribution," 395-96. Bollon includes a detailed list of all the young men who lived in Les Roches (415-19).

60. On Toureille's extraordinary life and work, see Zasloff, *A Rescuer's Story*.

61. Poujol, "André Philip," 192.

Revivalism and Social Christianity

Eventually, there would be twelve such children houses and thirty-nine boarding houses in Le Chambon alone.[62] In addition, other refugees were living in private homes as well as in farms in the surrounding area. The Trocmé family had two guests: "Monsieur Colin" and "Madame Berthe."[63] Their real names were Mr. Kohn, a 35 year old cabinetmaker from Berlin, and Bertha Grünhut, a 50 year old woman from Karlsruhe, whose son Egon lived in "Les Roches." They were Jewish.

The Vichy regime adopted the Nazi regime's antisemitic Nuremberg Laws on October 3, 1940.[64] On October 4, 1940, a law was promulgated on the immediate internment of foreign Jews in various camps in southern France.[65] Very quickly, the young Protestants who had formed the Cimade were visiting these camps in order to provide assistance. Prominent people, such as Willem Visser't Hooft, the leader of the World Council of Churches, and Marc Boegner, visited the camp of Gurs and were shocked by what they saw.[66]

The situation for the refugees became even more difficult in the spring and summer of 1942. The first deportation of Jews took place on March 27, 1942. Their destination was kept secret. Since June 13, 1942, Jews aged six and older who lived in the "Occupied Zone" were ordered to wear the Star of David. In June 1942, Eichmann decided that France had to roundup 100,000 Jews to be handed over to the German army. Hence the subsequent roundups in the summer of 1942, both in the northern "Occupied Zone" and in the "Unoccupied Zone" to the south. An agreement had been reached between Vichy and the Nazi regime that 22,000 foreign Jews from the "Occupied Zone," and 10,000 from the southern zone, would be handed over.[67] On July 16 and 17, 1942, over 13,000 Jews were arrested in Paris. This major roundup took place in part at the Vélodrome d'Hiver (Vél' d'Hiv).

62. Bollon, "Contribution," 392.

63. A. Trocmé, "Mémoires," 362.

64. With the 1935 Nuremberg Laws, German Jews, or anyone descending of three or four Jewish grandparents, lost their citizenship and became "state subjects" ("Staatsangehörige"), could no longer marry other Germans, and were banned from many professions.

65. François Delpech, "Les Églises et la persécution raciale." In De Montclos, *Églises et chrétiens dans la IIe guerre mondiale*, vol. 2: *La France*, 262. On these camps see Grynberg, *Les camps de la honte*, and Peschanski, *La France des camps*.

66. Barot, "La Cimade," 221. Boegner visited Gurs with Madeleine Barot on April 2, 1941. Ph. Boegner, *Carnets*, 95–96.

67. Delpech, "Les Églises," 269.

The "Conspiracy of Good" in Le Chambon-sur-Lignon

Less than a month later, in the middle of August 1942, Vichy' State secretary for the youth, Georges Lamirand (1899–1994), visited the region of Le Chambon and paid a visit to the town, since it was well-known for its work with the youth. Far from finding a town in celebratory mood for the "distinguished" visitor, Lamirand was surprised to find a rather austere atmosphere. After a worship service in the church, he was handed a document in which some of the upper-level students at the "Collège cévenol" (or "École nouvelle cévenole"), including some future theology students, protested against the recent roundup at the "Vél' d'Hiv" and made it clear that if such things were to be planned in the "Unoccupied Zone" of southern France, where they lived, they would encourage their Jewish friends to disobey any orders to be deported or even to take a census. Not just that: they would help their friends hide from the authorities. For, they wrote, "we do not make any difference between Jews and non-Jews. This contradicts the teachings of the gospel."[68] Lamirand was livid and seems to have left precipitously. According to Trocmé, the prefect of Haute-Loire, Robert Bach, was equally furious.[69] That could well be, but recent studies indicate that Bach was actually communicating with the people of Le Chambon and the surrounding towns about upcoming roundups. He had also supported the creation of "Faïdoli," one of the homes for children, and was relieved of his functions by the Vichy regime on October 16, 1943.[70] And so it could well be that Marc Boegner's letter to Robert Bach, dated August 20, 1942, in which he protested the attempts at rounding up the children of "Coteau fleuri," did not fall on deaf ears.[71]

---

68. Some twenty-five years after the facts, André Trocmé gives his recollection of this text, which he probably wrote, in his "Mémoires," 360: "Monsieur le Ministre, Nous avons appris les scènes d'épouvante qui se sont déroulées, il y a trois semaines, à Paris [. . .]. Nous tenons à vous faire savoir qu'il y a parmi nous un certain nombre de Juifs. Or nous ne faisons pas de différence entre Juifs et non-Juifs. Cela est contraire à l'enseignement évangélique. Si nos camarades dont la seule faute est d'être nés dans un[e] autre religion, recevaient l'ordre de se laisser déporter ou même seulement recenser, nous les encouragerions à désobéir aux ordres reçus, et nous nous efforcerions de les cacher de notre mieux."

69. Ibid., 360–61.

70. Boulet, *Histoire de la Montagne-refuge*, 189.

71. An excerpt of the letter, which Madeleine Barot urged Boegner to write, is quoted in Gerdes, *Ökumenische Solidarität*, 201. Bach did not favor a "politique de répression en force," according to Jean-Pierre Azéma, "Les protestants sous l'occupation." In Encrevé, *Les protestants français pendant la seconde guerre mondiale*, 315.

On August 25, 1942 at dawn, a roundup took place at the "Maison des Roches."[72] Trocmé immediately informed Boegner about it.[73] Similar operations took place, on that day and the following one, throughout the "Unoccupied Zone." The sixteen refugees, all of them Jewish, knew something was coming when policemen had checked their identities a few days earlier. They had even been informed of the precise day and time of the upcoming roundup, and had gone into hiding, first into the woods (they later left Le Chambon). Eleven of the young men were arrested in September 1942 near the Swiss border and sent to the camp of Rivesaltes.[74]

A system had been put into place: every refugee would disappear into the forest at a signal. A day after the roundup at "Les Roches," the twenty-six Jews from the "Coteau fleuri" had disappeared as well before the French police arrived. Two more roundups, in the middle of September and in early October, were loosely conducted. The result of 35 similar operations in the region between August 19 and September 13, 1942 was more than thin: one person was arrested, a man named Paul Straube, who was released not long afterwards.[75] The two or three big buses used by the police returned as empty as they had arrived. On October 20, 1942, Robert Bach reported to the Interior Ministry that "the Israelites, in all likelihood, had left the region. [. . .] Therefore I have taken the decision to eliminate the temporary police station of Le Chambon-sur-Lignon."[76] Such words would probably not have come easily from an avidly antisemitic political leader.

How many Jewish refugees were in the area of Le Chambon in the summer of 1942? The number, according to Trocmé, was "not that high: 100 to 150 perhaps, not more. All of them were known to us."[77] For now,

72. Bollon, "Contribution," 403.
73. Ph. Boegner, *Carnets*, 195.
74. Bollon, "Contribution," 404.
75. Boulet, *Histoire de la Montagne-refuge*, 194 and 350.
76. "L'échec de tous les efforts et les renseignements recueillis de différents côtés donnent lieu à penser que les israélites ont quitté la région. [. . .] Dans ces conditions j'ai jugé opportun de supprimer le poste temporaire de gendarmerie du Chambon-sur-Lignon." Quoted in Boulet, *Histoire de la Montagne-refuge*, 191. Between August 30 and September 18, 1942 there were 625 home visits, and the identity of 1,350 people was checked. The temporary police station was designed to keep an eye on the touristic summer population, which was suspected of sympathies with de Gaulle. Boulet, *Histoire*, 195; Bollon, "Contribution," 404.
77. "Combien y avait-il de Juifs au Chambon en l'été 1942? Pas tellement: 100 à 150 peut-être, au maximum. Ils nous étaient tous connus." "Mémoires," 362. I read such sentences as further confirmation that Trocmé did not write his "Mémoires" in order

The "Conspiracy of Good" in Le Chambon-sur-Lignon

they were safe. No one had been arrested. But on November 11, 1942, the German army began to occupy southern France. The "Unoccupied Zone" no longer existed.

WHY SUCH SOLIDARITY?

We need to take a step back from our narration and ask the important question: how is it that the population in Le Chambon and the surrounding area almost unanimously embraced the rescue effort? Some have argued that there was money to be made, but that answer does not carry much weight, since the risk which accompanied the whole enterprise far outweighed any potential or actual economic profit.[78] A better answer will have to take into consideration several factors, including the various "affinities" between Jews and Protestants.[79] This, of course, does not mean that all French Protestants fought antisemitism![80] But the Jewish refugees who were given shelter were almost always respected for who they were, and it seems that no attempts at converting them were made. So, why such a broad solidarity in the area known as "la Montagne"?

First, historically, French Protestants had experienced persecution and could relate to the fate of the Jews. Their collective memory of the

---

to boast about his prowess. Léon Poliakov wrote in 1946 about his arrival in Le Chambon three years earlier with a small group of Jewish children: "Le soir, j'assistai à l'hôtel May à un spectacle bien chambonnais: une assistante sociale venait d'amener un petit groupe d'enfants dont les parents avaient été déportés ou se cachaient à Marseille ou à Lyon. Apeurés, ils se tenaient dans un coin de la salle. Entre un premier couple de paysans: 'Nous aurions pris une petite fille de huit à douze ans,' explique la femme. On appelle la petite Myriam: 'Veux-tu partir avec l'oncle et la tante?' Intimidée, Myriam ne répond pas. On l'emmitoufle de couvertures, on la porte dans le traîneau; la voici partie vers la ferme où, jusqu'à la fin de la guerre, elle vivra la vie simple et saine de ses provisoires parents... En un tour de main, tous les enfants furent casés de la sorte, sous l'œil bienveillant du pasteur Trocmé." *L'Auberge des musiciens. Mémoires.* Paris: Mazarine, 1981, 109. Poliakov describes Trocmé as the "doyen des pasteurs de la région" (108).

78. On this aspect of the rescue see Boulet, "Juifs et Protestants." In Encrevé, *Les protestants français pendant la seconde guerre mondiale*, 358–59. A refugee, Elizabeth Kaufmann, has testified that in Le Chambon no one was asking about people's religious affiliations, and no one was rescuing others simply because money could be made. Flaud, *Paroles de Réfugiés*, 122. For a reflection on the very small minority of people, in Europe, who were paid for helping Jews, see Nechama Tec's contribution in Andrieu, *Resisting Genocide*.

79. See Cabanel, *Juifs et protestants*.

80. On the right-wing Protestants who professed antijudaic sentiments, and their leader, pastor Noël Vesper (his real name was Noël Nougat, 1882–1944), see Freychet, "Sully."

era of the "Désert" ("wilderness"), in the 17th–18th centuries, when they were persecuted for their faith, was a crucial, never forgotten part of their identity as "Huguenots."

There are also certain theological aspects. Far from simply being (or remaining) an abstract discourse, theology often shapes lives, for better or for worse. To the Protestants of Le Chambon, the Jews who were seeking refuge in their region were the chosen people of God. The election of Israel had in no way been cancelled by the "new covenant" in Jesus. In addition, Jews and Protestants were people of the Book. In a striking conflation, some of those involved in the rescue of Jews sometimes referred, using coded terms, to a particular refugee as an "Old Testament" or a "book" in their correspondence ("An Old Testament has arrived from Marseille," or: "I am sending you a book next week").[81] It did not matter that the Protestants, as Christians, had a larger collection of normative texts than the Jews, for they shared an extensive corpus. Jean Calvin, much more than Martin Luther, had a deep conviction about the substantive continuity between the two covenants in Scripture: the new covenant in Jesus Christ, far from adding any new "content" or "substance" to the covenant between God and the people of Israel, only differs from the older covenant in the "mode of dispensation," or in the way God relates to his people and to the world. What Calvin strongly emphasized was the "similarity—or rather, unity" between the two covenants. His very high regard for the Hebrew Scriptures clashed with other Protestants of his time who, in Calvin's own words, "regard the Israelites as nothing but a herd of swine."[82] The Calvinists, or Reformed Christians, were thus encouraged to read and love the Hebrew Scriptures. Their choice of Hebrew names for their children (Élie, Samuel, Abraham, Sarah, Gédéon etc.) is a sign of their respect for the people of the first covenant. Their decision to name their sanctuaries "temples," rather than "churches," was not just an example of

---

81. See the testimony of pastor Daniel Curtet, who quotes a letter he wrote on February 5, 1943 about this use of the word "book" in Bolle, *Le Plateau Vivarais-Lignon*, 57.

82. Calvin, *Institutes of the Christian Religion*. Book 2, ch. 10, section 1, trans. Ford Lewis Battles. Philadelphia: Westminster Press, 1960, vol. 1, 429. After having stressed the unity of the two testaments, Calvin goes on to list five differences (in the mode of dispensation, not in substance): the New Testament reveals the grace of eternal life "more plainly and clearly" (450), the "figures," "foretaste" of the Hebrew Scriptures have become "substances" (453–54), the New Testament is "spiritual" and not "literal" (456), it is a covenant of "freedom" (458), universal in scope (460). But, as Calvin wishes to make clear again and again, God has "taught the same doctrine to all ages" (463).

The "Conspiracy of Good" in Le Chambon-sur-Lignon

anti-Catholicism (although it was that too): it was a testimony of their love for God's covenant with Abraham and Moses.

Third, the area of Le Chambon, as we have seen, had been shaped in the decades before the war by the "Christianisme social" and its ideal of solidarity. Louis Comte and Charles Guillon, to name only two of the most prominent people, had made significant contributions to the life of the area (Guillon continued to do so during the war, mainly from Geneva). In fact, all of the pastors in the area were unanimous in supporting the rescue effort.[83] Trocmé had continued in the footsteps of Comte and Guillon, in many ways, for instance by creating, as we have seen, a "Fraternité d'hommes" which sought to embody the ideal of brotherhood in very concrete ways (in 1943, he wrote a series of guidelines for another group of men, the "Order of the Servants"—"Ordre des Serviteurs")[84]. The social Christians had been very clear in their rejection of antisemitism, through several publications. Jacques Martin published these astonishing sentences about death camps in the *Revue du Christianisme social* in August 1939:

> Only a few months ago, for instance, five thousand Polish Jews were put in a special train and disembarked in a small Polish village where they have been kept since then, trying to survive, unable to enter Poland or to return to Germany. It appears that other groups of Jews, similarly deported, are enduring the same fate at the doors of other countries, on strips of land which are in a way neutral, by the German border [. . .]. And so these refugees are still waiting for a hypothetical visa, many wander across Europe and the world, others are cooped up on strips of land between two borders, in 'no man's land' areas were a few barns house thousands of people. The only outcome is death.[85]

---

83. For a list of the local parishes and their pastors in those years, see Boulet, *Histoire de la Montagne-refuge*, 152–53. It is clear that Trocmé did not adequately underline the breadth of the rescue effort in his "Mémoires." But he did not write this autobiographical text in order to give a comprehensive historical account of what happened in the area of Le Chambon during the war: he wrote it to tell his story for a small group of readers, namely his descendants.

84. Trocmé papers, Swarthmore College, Series B, box 5, 8th folder. See Boulet's article in Bolle, *Le Plateau Vivarais-Lignon*, 411.

85. "Il y a quelque mois, par exemple, cinq mille Juifs polonais ont été mis dans un train spécial et débarqués dans un petit village polonais où ils sont parqués depuis lors, vivant comme ils peuvent, ne pouvant ni entrer en Pologne ni revenir en Allemagne. On compte que d'autres groupes de Juifs ainsi expulsés vivent de la sorte aux portes de divers pays, sur des bandes de territoires en quelque sorte neutres, aux frontières de l'Allemagne [. . .]. Ainsi, les réfugiés en sont-ils toujours à attendre quelque visa hypothétique, beaucoup errant à travers l'Europe et le monde, d'autres

Fourth, André Trocmé had organized a very efficient method in order to disseminate his message: since Le Chambon was not just a town, but an area too large to be supervised by one pastor, he set up thirteen Bible and prayer groups in various places within the parish. Every other week, the leaders of these groups, who were lay people, would gather in the "temple" with Trocmé: "we would discuss the two questionnaires for these two weeks, which were meant to provoke from the group itself a valid interpretation of the selected biblical text."[86] Then these group leaders would go to their own group and bring these insights to them. These groups became very popular, more and more people, including young adults, participated in them. Trocmé writes in his "Mémoires": "It is there, nowhere else, that answers came from God to the very complex problems we had to solve in order to provide shelter and to hide the Jews in the months that followed. There, we conceived of non-violent resistance, which is not a theory one projects onto reality, but a journey one explores day after day in common prayer and obedience to the Spirit's instructions."[87] Trocmé was of course already committed to non-violent resistance, but these reunions of Bible studies and common prayer were, if one takes him at his word, an important place where the concrete ways of practicing this form of resistance were discovered and discussed.

But all of this would soon end. Starting in February 1943, Trocmé's ministry began to be disrupted, to the point where much of the rescue effort which took place from then on happened without him. But he, along with others who shared his commitment to peace and solidarity with the persecuted, had planted the seeds. He had shaped his parish in very specific ways, in particular through his sermons and his interpretation of Scripture.[88]

---

parqués sur des bandes de terre entre deux frontières, ces 'no man's land' où quelques étables abritent des milliers de malheureux. La seule issue est la mort." Jacques Martin, "L'antisémitisme païen... et chrétien," *RCS* 52 (1939) 121 and 123. Quoted in Joutard et al., *Cévennes, terre de refuge*, 218.

86. "[. . .] on y discutait les deux questionnaires de la quinzaine, destinés à faire jaillir de l'auditoire lui-même une explication valable du texte biblique choisi." "Mémoires," 357.

87. "C'est là, et non pas ailleurs, que furent reçues de Dieu des réponses aux problèmes très complexes que nous avions à résoudre pour héberger et cacher les Juifs dans les mois qui suivirent. La résistance non-violente, c'est là que nous l'avons conçue. La non-violence n'est pas une théorie surimprimée à la réalité, c'est un itinéraire, que l'on explore jour après jour dans la prière commune et l'obéissance aux directives de l'Esprit." A. Trocmé, "Mémoires," 357.

88. See Batten, "Reading the Bible."

ARREST AND INTERNMENT

On Februry 13, 1943, as Trocmé was returning home at the end of the day, his wife Magda told him that two policemen were inside waiting for him.[89] He knew right away what was happening. Magda had prepared a suitcase for her husband precisely for this kind of event. With great reluctance, which he communicated to the Trocmé family, Sébastien Silvani, a commandant in the police forces of Haute-Loire, accompanied by a lieutenant, placed André Trocmé under arrest. In a very telling and typical gesture, Magda Trocmé served them dinner. She also sent someone to inform the town. Soon enough, to the astonishment of the policemen, parishioners were ringing the church bell to say goodbye to their pastor, coming to the Trocmé home, the "presbytère," with little bags of food, warm socks and so forth.[90] Then Trocmé said goodbye to his family and those who had come. He wrote in his "Mémoires" of this very emotional moment, since no one could foresee whether they would meet again. And yet, he added: "Inside I was calm, almost joyful: It was the hour I had awaited since a long time, the hour when I would witness to my deepest convictions."[91]

Two other leaders in Le Chambon were arrested that evening besides Trocmé: Édouard Theis, his friend and colleague in the pastoral ministry, and the school director Roger Darcissac (1898–1982), who forged false documents. The three men were taken to Le Puy for the night, and at dawn, by train and police wagon, to the camp of Saint-Paul-d'Eyjeaux, near Limoges (Haute-Vienne). The camp looked like any other concentration camp, surrounded by barbed wire and watchtowers mounted with machine guns. There were five hundred inmates at the time, and many of them did not look very healthy. For the most part, they were communists. There were some socialists and some Catholics as well. The purpose of the camp was "reeducation," not forced labor. Despite the difficult conditions, inmates were cheerful.[92] Theis and Trocmé organized a Sunday worship. The nine people who attended it enjoyed so much that they asked for daily

---

89. For the date, see Boulet, *Histoire de la Montagne-refuge*, 222. Ph. Boegner, *Carnets*, 233.What Boulet writes on 252 indicates that the arrest might have taken place on February 12, 1942. According to Gérard Bollon, the arrest took place on February 18, 1943. Bollon, "Contribution," 395.

90. "Mémoires," 376.

91. "Intérieurement j'étais calme, presque joyeux: C'était l'heure que j'attendais depuis longtemps; l'heure du témoignage que je devais rendre à mes convictions profondes." Ibid., 377.

92. Ibid., 379–80.

services... The pastors were allowed to lead services three times a week. Soon, there were forty participants, half of them unable to fit in the small barrack assigned by the administration of the camp.

On March 16, 1943, three weeks or so after their internment, the three men were suddenly, inexplicably freed.[93] Who had intervened? A number of people, including Marc Boegner, the president of the "Fédération Protestante de France," who later told Trocmé that he had written to Vichy. A letter he sent to Magda Trocmé on March 18, 1943 confirms this: Boegner wrote twice to René Bousquet, who was in charge of the Vichy police. Boegner travelled to Vichy to meet with him on February 19.[94] Robert Bach, the prefect of Haute-Loire, claimed he protested in favor of Trocmé in a conversation with Pierre Laval, Vichy's Prime Minister.[95] Daniel Trocmé went to the Interior Ministry at Vichy right after visiting André Trocmé at the camp of Saint-Paul-d'Eyjeaux.[96] August Bohny also traveled to Vichy. It is not clear which of these interventions was, or were, decisive, even though it appears that Boegner's letters were crucial.

In order to be released, the three men had to sign an oath of allegiance to Pétain.[97] The two pastors were unwilling, or unable, to comply and were sent back to their barrack, realizing they had just committed a sort of suicide (after a moment of hesitation, Darcissac agreed to sign

93. When they asked why they were being released, they were told by the director of the camp that it was as unclear as the reason for their internment. "Et comme nous nous étonnions, il nous répondit: 'Je ne sais rien, ni la cause de votre arrestation, ni celle de votre libération.'" Ibid., 387.

94. "Je venais de vous écrire lorsque j'ai reçu une lettre de M. Bousquet, retour de Nîmes, m'informant des instructions qu'il venait de donner en vue de la libération immédiate des trois internés, puis une lettre de M. Chaudier me racontant à la suite de quelles circonstances mes collègues n'avaient pas été autorisés à sortir. J'ai immédiatement écrit à M. Bousquet pour lui expliquer les raisons religieuses du refus opposé par votre mari et Édouard Theis à la demande qui leur était faite et l'ai prié de maintenir sa première décision. J'espère vivement qu'avec la même bonne volonté qu'il a mise à répondre à ma première demande il voudra bien donner satisfaction à la seconde." Quoted in Bolle, *Le Plateau Vivarais-Lignon*, 396 n. 2. For Boegner's visit to Bousquet, see Ph. Boegner, *Carnets*, 233.

95. A. Trocmé, "Mémoires," 390. Trocmé adds: "Tout ceci est probablement vrai [...]" (391), before adding that the mention of their arrest on the BBC might have contributed to the decision to free them: the Vichy authorities were very sensitive when the media spoke of the similarities between them and the Nazi regime.

96. See his card from March 11, 1943, quoted in Bollon, "Contribution," 395.

97. Here is Trocmé's recollection of the oath: "Je soussigné . . . jure fidélité à la personne du Maréchal de France, chef de l'Etat. J'obéirai sans les discuter aux ordres qui me seront donnés par les autorités gouvernementales, en vue du salut de la Patrie, etc... Signature..." A. Trocmé, "Mémoires," 387.

and was freed.) But in fact the following day, after an intervention from the authorities in Vichy, they were released without being required to sign the oath.[98]

The three men returned to Le Chambon, to the relief and joy of the town. The twenty-three year old police inspector Léopold Praly, who had been hand-picked by prefect Robert Bach, was keeping a close eye on them, as well as on all the foreigners who resided in Le Chambon. He wrote the following report to the prefecture on April 1, 1943: "The majority of the population of Le Chambon-sur-Lignon, which is for the most past Protestant, welcomed the liberation of pastors Trocmé and Theis with an immense, undisguised joy, for they are unanimously known and esteemed here and enjoy a great popularity."[99] On August 6, 1943, Praly was assassinated by members of the "maquis."[100]

Several roundups had taken place while they were interned, including one, led by policemen from Le Puy, on February 24, 1943. Nine young Jewish teenagers and young adults, who lived in various houses ("Coteau fleuri," "Maison des Roches" and "Grillons") were arrested and taken to Le Puy.[101] Someone had paid attention to the detailed, regularly updated lists of foreigners currently living in Le Chambon which police inspector Praly was sending to the chief commissioner of the intelligence services ("Services des Renseignements Généraux") in Le Puy. Praly's lists included the religious affiliation of all foreigners.[102]

At the same time, refugees were arriving in large numbers in the region. According to a document preserved in the departmental archives of

---

98. The letter from Marc Boegner to Magda Trocmé, quoted above, confirms many aspects of this episode.

99. "La majorité de la population de Chambon sur Lignon, essentiellement protestante, a accueilli avec une joie immense et non déguisée la libération des pasteurs Trocmé et Theis en effet ceux-ci unanimement connus et estimés dans la localité jouissent ici d'une grande popularité." Quoted in Boulet, *Histoire de la Montagne-refuge*, 223.

100. Boulet, *Histoire de la Montagne-refuge*, 257. It was the first assassination on the part of the "maquis" (armed resistance groups) in Haute-Loire.

101. According to Boulet, who lists some of their names (Wolfradts, from Coteau fleuri; Winitzer, from Les Roches; Schiebel, from Les Grillons), their fate is not clear. Boulet, *Histoire de la Montagne-refuge*, 187. In a card from March 11, 1943, Daniel Trocmé writes that he went to Le Puy and was able to bring a young man, a 16 year old who was under his care, back to Le Chambon. Bollon, "Contribution," 395.

102. On Praly's lists, see Bollon, "Contribution," 401.

Haute-Loire, 286 foreign adults arrived in Le Chambon and were placed in various homes and boarding-houses between March and August 1943.[103]

ROUNDUP AT THE "MAISON DES ROCHES"

Since December 1942, some German officers and soldiers were convalescing in one of Le Chambon's hotels. Were they the ones who alerted the Gestapo about the presence of Jewish refugees in the area? What is certain is that on Tuesday, June 29, 1943, at 6.30am, the Gestapo circled the "Maison des Roches," rounded up the students and arrested the director of the house, Daniel Trocmé, André Trocmé's young cousin.[104] André Trocmé was not in Le Chambon on that day—he was vacationing near Pomeyrol, in Provence—and it is possible that the Gestapo mistook Daniel Trocmé for his older cousin. Neither the French police, nor prefect Robert Bach, had been informed about the roundup. One of the students, a Spaniard who was not a Jew, and who had saved the life of a German soldier who was drowning in the river Lignon, was freed thanks to Magda Trocmé's efforts: as the roundup was taking place that morning, she pleaded in his favor with an officer of the German army who, with great reluctance, agreed to talk with the members of the Gestapo in "Les Roches." Nineteen others, including Daniel Trocmé, were placed in a military truck and taken to various jails or camps. Daniel Trocmé was taken to Moulins, in a prison of the "Wehrmacht," then to Compiègne, before being sent to Buchenwald and Dora. He died in Majdanek in the first days of April 1944. On May 13, 1944, Daniel Trocmé's family was informed of his death.[105] At least five of the students left Paris–Bobigny for Auschwitz on July 18, 1943. It seems that only three of the nineteen young men returned from the camps.[106] The roundup of June 29, 1943 remains the greatest tragedy in the history of Le Chambon during the war.

---

103. Ibid., 392 n. 6.

104. Ibid., 407–11. Robert Bach protested about the roundup. He sent another letter on July 20, 1943, asking for informations concerning Daniel Trocmé. In both cases, he does not seem to have received any answer.

105. Ibid., 411.

106. Jean-Marie Schoen survived the camps of Buchenwald and Dora. André Guyonnaud returned from Compiègne and Dora and became a pastor. Ibid., 410. According to Boismorand, ten of the nineteen young men died in the camps (nine of them survived). *André et Magda Trocmé*, 364.

IN HIDING

A month later, at the end of July 1943, one of the young "maquisard" in the region, that is, one of the people who had chosen armed resistance and who, for the most part, lived in hiding, came down to Le Chambon to warn Trocmé and Theis: their lives were in danger. He said he had overheard a conversation in Valence: the Gestapo was paying French criminals to execute "undesirables." That way no one was blaming the Germans. Other people, including two fellow pastors, Noël Poivre and Maurice Rohr, advised Trocmé to go into hiding.

What were the two pastors of Le Chambon supposed to do? Trocmé thought he had to stay in his parish and continue his work. But everyone, from the parish council to his friends, including Daniel Trocmé's father, Henri, who did not want any more arrests, was urging him to go into hiding.[107] By staying in Le Chambon, André Trocmé was told, he was endangering not just himself but his entire family. And if he were to be assassinated, the parish would perhaps abandon its non-violent stance. Trocmé relented and left Le Chambon at the end of July (Theis did the same thing a few days later; he returned after the liberation of France). Some twenty-five years later, as he was writing his "Mémoires," Trocmé was still unsure whether he had made the right decision.[108] One could say that the rhetoric of self-sacrifice, which Trocmé shared with Henri Nick and his colleagues from the "groupe du Nord," did not prepare him to handle the sense of guilt and shame which accompanied him throughout these long months in hiding and even long after the end of the war.

Trocmé first stayed in the pastor's house in Lamastre (Ardèche), not too far from Le Chambon, with a new identity card provided by Darcissac. His new name was "Mr. Béguet," and his moustache was gone. Then he moved to a nearby farm, where a family welcomed him. Pastor Estoppey, from Intres, a small town in the region, south of Le Chambon and Saint-Agrève, received a visit from the Gestapo: Trocmé was suspected to be hiding there.[109] He was thus compelled to move again,

---

107. On May 30, 1943, Roland de Pury, the well-known pastor of Lyon, an active member of the "Résistance" who also helped bring Jewish refugees to safety in Switzerland, was arrested as he was preparing to lead Sunday worship. He was freed from the Gestapo prison of Fort Montluc (Lyon) on October 20, 1943.

108. "Je me laissai convaincre, mais je ne suis pas encore sûr aujourd'hui d'avoir eu raison. [. . .] Encore aujourd'hui, ces questions m'agitent, et je me demande ce que je dirai à Dieu, quand je comparaîtrai devant Lui, et ce que Lui me répondra." A. Trocmé, "Mémoires," 402.

109. Ibid., 403.

Revivalism and Social Christianity

to another house in the region, near Chalancon, between Lamastre and Vernoux (Ardèche). Finally, Trocmé relocated to the "castle of Perdyer," in the Drôme valley, near Châtillon-en-Diois. A Jewish man, Mr. Tamar, was hiding there as well.

Among the few documents from the war which are preserved in the Trocmé papers at Swarthmore College are André Trocmé's letters to his wife Magda from these long months in hiding, from the end of July 1943 until his return to Le Chambon on June 14, 1944.[110] Since these documents are basically unknown, I will quote them at length.

In several undated letters which seem to go back to the first months in hiding, Trocmé wonders if he has made the right decision.[111] "Here I no longer have the impression of being part of what God wants, I feel like a coward who mistook vague rumors for facts."[112] The first dated letter, from September 8, 1943, is very short. In it, he gives some indications to his wife on how to preserve his anonymity: she should place the stamps upside-down, use different handwritings, send the letter to Mr. Bosc in Lamastre and add a small dot on the left side of the envelope to indicate to Mr. Bosc that the letter is to be forwarded to him. Trocmé inquires about the parish and his son Jean-Pierre's progress in school. On October 20, 1943, he writes that a young girl recognized Magda when she recently came to visit: "I have to leave. [. . .] Lots of rumors, down at the factory. Everyone knows I am here. [. . .] Let me know if I can return to Le Chambon."[113] On October 28, he writes that he was hoping for a letter: "My life, for now, is very monotonous, I do not go out. [. . .] I have the impression that in the great turmoil of Le Chambon I have already been forgotten."[114] On October 29: "I am *begging* for news."[115] His mood becomes worse a week later, and he writes on November 3: "Still no news! My isolation is complete since five

---

110. Trocmé papers, Swarthmore College, Series B, box 1.

111. "D'ici, le danger paraît illusoire. Je me demande si je n'ai pas eu tort, quand même. L'unanimité de mes conseillers et amis m'y a poussé." In another letter: "J'ai l'impression que j'ai eu tort de partir. J'ai fait une idiotie."

112. "Ici je n'ai plus l'impression d'être dans la volonté de Dieu, mais d'être un trouillard qui a pris de vagues bruits pour des réalités."

113. "*Mais* il faut que je parte. Une jeune fille t'a reconnue—Gros bavardage, à l'usine du bas. Tout le monde sait déjà que je suis là. [. . .] Dis-moi si je peux rentrer au Chambon."

114. "Ma grande chérie Magda, [. . .] J'espère tant voir une lettre tout à l'heure. [. . .] Et Jacquot? Je ne sais encore rien. Cependant je voudrais savoir. Hier lettre de Chabut, mais rien de toi.—J'ai l'impression que dans le grand tumulte du Chambon je suis oublié, déjà."

115. "Envoie-moi des nouvelles, je *pleure* après des nouvelles."

days, as if I had been forgotten, as if I were lost."[116] Finally, on November 5, a bundle of letters has arrived. On November 19, he describes his "Trappist life": not a sound around him, in the landscape covered with snow. He writes to Magda of his attachment to his parish: "We need to think carefully before we make any move about leaving it. We will *never* find such a place anywhere else, a place imprinted to such an extent by our ideas, a place with so many earnest and faithful friends. [. . .] Why struggle so much, why endure all of these blows? But I know that as soon as the war is over, we will move on, like Don Quixote against his windmills. Without many expectations, humanly speaking, but with a great, ultimate hope."[117] On November 26, he rejoices again about the mail he has just received: "My darling, At last some news! I live again! I exist again! I no longer am a pale small retired man who splits wood while waiting for death. [. . .] I feel like I am far away, forgotten, filed away! Four months, that's a long time, when the leadership slowly but surely goes into other peoples' hands."[118]

Trocmé was using some of his free time to write a book, a sort of introduction to the Christian faith which could also serve as a catechism. The working title was "Oser croire" ("Dare to Believe"). But Trocmé was not happy with what he was producing: "I would like my book to be a masterpiece, but I do not feel that I am capable of it."[119] During the winter months, his solitude was relieved by visits from his sons Jean-Pierre and, a bit later, Jacques, who was experiencing difficulties in school and who

116. "Toujours pas de nouvelles! Mon isolement est total depuis 5 jours, comme si j'étais oublié, perdu."

117. "Enfin, tout cela me détache un peu de ce pays, et me rattache au Chambon. Il faut bien réfléchir avant de faire un geste pour le quitter. Nous ne retrouverons *jamais* ailleurs un endroit pareil, ayant à ce point accepté l'empreinte de nos idées avec tant d'amis sérieux et fidèles. [. . .] Pourquoi tant lutter et récolter tant d'horions? Cependant je sais que sitôt la guerre finie, nous repartirons, comme Don Quichote contre les moulins. Sans espoirs humains beaucoup, mais avec une grande espérance finale." In another letter, undated, but from his stay in or near Lamastre, Trocmé wrote: "Belle vie calme à Lamastre. Il ne vient pas un chat au presbytère. Ce que le pasteur n'entreprend pas n'existe pas. Ce n'est pas un église, c'est un pasteur qui travaille et qui entraîne quelques personnes quand il est là. Le Chambon est une Église, où tout vit et fuse par tous les bouts. Comment s'en détacher jamais?"

118. "Ma chérie, Enfin des nouvelles! Je revis! J'existe de nouveau! Je ne suis plus un pâle petit monsieur retraité qui casse du bois en attendant la mort! [. . .] Comme je me sens loin, oublié, classé! 4 mois, c'est long, quand la direction, peu à peu passe entre les mains des autres." This letter confirms that Trocmé went into hiding at the end of July.

119. "Voudrais faire de mon bouquin un chef d'œuvre, et ne me sens pas capable." Letter to Magda, November 23, 1943. The manuscript of the book is preserved at Swarthmore College. Its content is, indeed, disappointing.

stayed with his father for a longer period. While picking Jacques up one day at the Lyon train station, he was nearly arrested during a roundup but managed to find a way out.[120]

Magda, for her part, was hard at work. Since the winter of 1942, she had a helper by her side: Alice Reynier (1894–1989) had been sent to them by Antoinette Butte, the leader of the retreat community of Pomeyrol in Provence. "Jispa," as Alice Reynier preferred to be called, was supposed to spend one winter with the Trocmé family.[121] She stayed with them until her death.

THE CONTINUING RESCUE EFFORT

Much happened during Trocmé's long absence—ten months, from the end of July 1943 until early June 1944. The parish was under the care of Marcel Jeannet, a Swiss pastor in charge of the nearby parish of Le Mazet. The rescue continued, with many people taking risks. More roundups took place in August 1943, but, like previous ones led by the local French police, they did not produce any results.[122]

The success of the rescue effort depended on the discretion and solidarity of an entire town and region, and on the absence of denunciations (hence Pierre Sauvage's fortunate expression, a "conspiracy of good"). But there were leaders too, of course, particular people who took on greater responsibilities, with corresponding risks for their safety. Among these people were Mireille Philip, the wife of André Philip. Simone Mairesse, née Pévenage, whom Magda and André Trocmé knew since Maubeuge, now lived in Le Mazet-Saint-Voy and was placing many refugees in various farms of the region. Interestingly, she also took part in certain aspects of the armed Résistance.[123] In Le Chambon as in many other places in France, the Résistance and the "maquis" operated more and more boldly as the

---

120. Trocmé gives a detailed and lively account of this harrowing event in "Mémoires," 406–11.

121. "Jispa" stands for "Joie du service dans la paix et l'amour" ("joy of service in peace and love"). In September 1941 and 1942, Pomeyrol was the site of two important gatherings of pastors who, following the model of the famous Barmen Declaration (1934), produced two texts on the world situation, including a clear condemnation of antisemitism. Bolle, "Les thèses de Pomeyrol."

122. Bollon, "Contribution," 414.

123. For a personal testimony about Simone Mairesse's work, see Spiero, *Innocents et pourchassés*, 67–72. Claude Spiero became a leader in Joseph Bass' "Résistance" group in the region of Le Chambon.

The "Conspiracy of Good" in Le Chambon-sur-Lignon

end of the war was nearing.[124] Oscar Rosowsky, also known as "Plunne," produced illegal documents. August Bohny, pastors Daniel Curtet (with his wife Suzanne), André Bettex and others, from Le Chambon but also from the region, were assisting refugees. Édouard Theis was near the Swiss border, were he worked with the Cimade. Each of the thirteen pastors in the area (six of whom were Swiss), and many of their parishioners, participated in the rescue effort.[125] Beyond the "Plateau," a whole underground network of people, Protestants and Catholics, were working on bringing people to safety, using presbyteries, priests' homes and monasteries.[126] As long as the names of the refugees were on lists which could be given to the Swiss authorities (Charles Guillon submitted some of these lists), they would be allowed on Swiss territory. From Le Chambon, some of the refugees entered Switzerland in remote, mountainous areas.[127] Many of these people had been guided to Le Chambon from various French cities, especially Marseille, Saint-Étienne and Grenoble, by an underground network called "Service André," directed by Joseph Bass (code name: "Monsieur André"), with the assistance of Denise Siekerski, née Caraco ("Colibri"), Hermine Orsi and Émilie (Hélène) Guth, among others.[128] Toward the end of the war, Bass was also in charge of a maquis, in the region of Le Chambon, which recruited Jewish men. Bass had perhaps heard of Le Chambon from Marcel Heuzé, pastor in Marseille, Trocmé's friend from the "groupe du Nord."[129]

---

124. Fayol, *Le Chambon-sur-Lignon*.

125. I am only counting the pastors who ministered a parish. According to Gérard Bollon there were no less than 23 pastors in total on the "Plateau." Bollon, "Contribution," 393.

126. The Trappists monks of Tamié (Haute-Savoie) were involved in this network, as well as pastor Paul Chapal and his wife Odette (Annecy), Pierre Galland, Pierre Piton, abbé Folliet, abbé Marius Jolivet (Collonges-sous-Salève, a French village very close to the Swiss border), Catholic priest Jean Rosay (Douvaine) and Joseph Lançon (Douvaine). Fayol, *Le Chambon-sur-Lignon*, 55–58. Neury, "La banalité du bien." Fivaz–Silbermann, "Le sauvetage" (171) writes that about ten thousand Jews crossed the Swiss border in the canton of Geneva during the war. See also the recent publications by Limore Yagil (bibliography).

127. Munos-du Peloux, *Passer en Suisse*.

128. See Denise Siekerski's testimony in Joutard et al., *Cévennes, terre de refuge*, 175–82.

129. Boulet makes this suggestion, which is plausible, in Bolle, *Le Plateau Vivarais-Lignon*, 405.

Among the many children and teenagers who were rescued were Hanne Hirsch and her future husband Max Liebmann, and Rudy Appel.[130] The three of them were born around 1924 in the south of Germany (Karlsruhe, in the case of Hanne Hirsch; Rudy Appel and Max Liebmann were from Mannheim). In the fall of 1940, Hanne Hirsch and Max Liebmann were deported to the internment camp of Gurs, in southwestern France (Basses-Pyrénées), where the Cimade and other organizations were working to improve the appalling living conditions and to negotiate with Vichy in order to free as many people as possible, especially children. In early September 1941, thanks to these efforts, Hanne Hirsch, with six other children, was transferred to Le Chambon.[131] She had to say goodbye to her relatives, who could not accompany her. She stayed in the house called "La Guespy," in Le Chambon. In the first days of August 1942, hearing that her mother was very ill, she returned to Gurs to see her. The only moment she could spend with her was an hour or so, near the freight train which was about to take her mother and many other people. Her mother sensed this would be her final journey and said so to her seventeen year old daughter. Hanne Hirsch went back to Le Chambon, unable to think about anything but her mother's words to her. It was the last time she saw her mother. The destination of the train which took her and around one thousand prisoners away from Gurs was Auschwitz.

In August 1942, Max Liebmann reached Le Chambon. He and Hanne Hirsch met in Gurs and had grown fond of each other. Since roundups were occuring in those weeks, Hanne Hirsch left "La Guespy" and stayed for a night in the home of August Bohny, with ten other children, and later, for four weeks, in two different farms, which were both visited—but not searched—by the French police (hidden upstairs, she could hear the conversation taking place in the kitchen). Max Liebmann went into hiding, and only a month after his arrival the network of rescuers managed to bring him to Switzerland. First pastor André Morel (1914–96), and later a young boy, escorted him and, after many hours of walk, he finally entered Switzerland in a mountainous area. Hanne Hirsch entered Switzerland on March 1, 1943, with the help of August Bohny and her Swiss aunt who helped her get a visa. After a journey through Saint-Étienne, Lyon, a

---

130. Rudy Appel has narrated his story in "A Journey to Escape." See also Flaud, *Paroles de Réfugiés*, 42-50 (Rudy Appel) and 55-59 (Hanne and Max Liebmann). Thanks to Nelly Trocmé, I have had the privilege of meeting (and interviewing) Hanne Liebmann and her husband Max, as well Rudy Appel, several times in New York City.

131. She was not "freed" but "transferred." She had to sign forms, and her new place of residence (Le Chambon) was known to the French authorities.

Catholic school in Annecy, and Annemasse, she crossed the border only after having to lie to a policeman who asked her if she was Jewish. Both parents of Max Liebmann were deported to Auschwitz, where they died. Hanne Hirsch and Max Liebmann married in Geneva in April 1945 and moved to New York in 1948.

The situation in Germany was so bad in the late 1930s that Rudy Appel (born in 1925) was sent to Holland, where he continued his schooling. His mother was not able to find a smuggler who would help her go to Holland, but she made it to Belgium. His father had been arrested during "Kristallnacht" (November 9–10, 1938) and sent to the camp of Dachau. He later obtained a visitor's visa and moved to the United States. He was released from the camp and joined Rudy Appel's brother, who had emigrated to America a few years earlier. After the invasion of Holland, on May 10, 1940, Rudy Appel obtained a visa and joined his mother, in Antwerpen and Brussels. They were arrested by the French police just as they entered the "Unoccupied Zone," near Angoulême, as they were trying to go to Marseille to board a ship headed to Cuba (his father had obtained visas). They were sent to the camp of Riversaltes. A few months later, around July 1942, he was separated from his mother and transferred to Les Milles, near Aix-en-Provence. He had the good fortune of not being on the lists of people selected for deportation. When Les Milles was shut down, he was sent back to Riversaltes. His mother wrote to him urging him to lose his identity documents and pretend to be fifteen years old. That way, because of a rule promulgated not long before, he would be considered a child and would not be deported if a parent is not with him.[132] Two weeks after his return to Riversaltes, in September 1942, he was transferred to Le Chambon. He lived first in "L'Abric," later in "La Guespy," and remembers attending many Jewish ceremonies on holy days, in a classroom of the "École cévenole," where he studied, and in a room in the church of Le Chambon. A professor of classics from Paris led these prayer services. After the war, he was reunited with his mother, and in 1946 with the rest of his family in the United States.

---

132. Boegner too had heard of this exemption, along with others, directly from René Bousquet, the general secretary of the Vichy police. During a conversation on September 10, 1942, Boegner also heard from Bousquet that Jews who had arrived in France since 1933 would be rounded up. He asked Bousquet: "Qu'allez-vous faire à leur égard?—Nous les chercherons.—Alors ce sera la chasse à l'homme avec chiens policiers et le reste?—Nous les prendrons là où ils sont.—Vous allez braquer l'opinion publique partout où il y a des Juifs cachés.—Nous devons les chercher. Les Allemands savent tout ce qui se passe de ce côté." Ph. Boegner, *Carnets*, 203.

Revivalism and Social Christianity

RETURN TO LE CHAMBON

As soon as André Trocmé heard about D–Day (June 6, 1944), he tried to return to Le Chambon, with his son Jacques who was with him. Sensing that the wind was turning, and under increasingly bold attacks from the "maquis" and various groups of the "Résistance," the German troops and the French "Milice" (Vichy's paramilitary force) did not hesitate to shoot at civilian cars, and so extreme caution was in order, but after a few days Trocmé was back in Le Chambon, ten months after having left the parish. Some of what he saw horrified him: "Le Chambon had changed, in ten months. The 'maquis' was no longer in hiding. The young men strutted around in the streets, displaying their submachine guns [. . .]. There were more refugees than ever."[133] By then, most people were "Gaullists" and members (or partisans) of the "Résistance."[134] Those who had collaborated with the occupant feared for, and sometimes lost, their lives. Trocmé was disappointed with his colleagues who had led the parish in his absence: non-violence had faded away, many young people, including those who

---

133. "Je retrouvai certes un Chambon très changé depuis dix mois. Le maquis ne se cachait plus. Les jeunes paradaient dans les rues, en arborant des mitraillettes [. . .]. Il y avait plus de réfugiés que jamais." A. Trocmé, "Mémoires," 415.

134. Even the great leader of the French Protestants, Marc Boegner, who unceasingly denounced the antisemitic aspects of the Vichy government, did not mention the fact, in his detailed 1945 report on the war (*Les Églises protestantes*), that he had been Vichy's "conseiller national" and that he had called for support of Pétain as late as September 1941. Casalis, "La jeunesse protestante," 103. Trocmé, for his part, took offense that Le Chambon and the surrounding area were not mentioned at all by Boegner in his detailed report from 1945. A. Trocmé, "Mémoires," 394. And yet, Madeleine Barot, who was in contact with Boegner throughout these years as general secretary of the Cimade, far from criticizing Boegner, praises him for his clear-sightedness: "Marc Boegner, dès son premier voyage à Vichy, avait exprimé son inquiétude." Barot, "La Cimade," 225. Marc Boegner's notes confirm his constant concern for Jews. Ph. Boegner, *Carnets*. And so: "Accuser Boegner de pétainisme nous paraît [. . .] tout à fait excessif. Le seul reproche sérieux qu'on puisse lui adresser, c'est qu'il a donné à travers toute la France non occupée des conférences qui apportaient le soutien manifeste de son autorité à l'idée de Révolution nationale." Mehl, *Le pasteur Marc Boegner*, 139. "Cet engagement en faveur de l'idéologie du Maréchal ne signifie en aucune façon—il faut le souligner avec force—un engagement dans la voie de la collaboration avec l'hitlérisme alors triomphant." (140.) Boegner wrote this very telling sentence in his notebook, during his stay in Le Chambon on September 29, 1940 (51): "Intéressant entretien avec conseil presbytéral. Il y a ici des éléments très 'laïques' qui n'ont aucune confiance dans le gouvernement actuel, qui sont déçus, tentés de se tenir à l'écart." Boegner was surprised by some of the lay people of Le Chambon, who placed no trust in Pétain's government. He did not share that sentiment, at that time.

had come to Le Chambon with the intent of becoming pastors, had joined or were joining armed groups.

TWO TRAGEDIES

Some of these young armed men led to the death of an important figure in Le Chambon: on August 4, 1944, Roger Le Forestier, a medical doctor who had worked with Albert Schweitzer in Africa, and a good friend of the Trocmé family, was arrested by the Gestapo in Le Puy, where he had gone with two "maquisards" to try to help free two young men from Le Chambon who had been arrested for their involvement in the "Résistance." The Gestapo had found a loaded weapon hidden in the car Le Forestier and the two men had driven to Le Puy! The two men had not listened to Le Forestier who, as a practicioner of non-violence, had commanded them not to bring any weapon.[135] What happened in the weeks following the arrest is not entirely clear, but on August 20, 1944 Roger Le Forestier was executed at the Fort de Côte Lorette (Saint-Genis-Laval, near Lyon).[136] Only a few weeks later, on September 3, 1944, Le Chambon was freed by general de Lattre de Tassigny's army.[137]

The month of August 1944 saw another tragedy in Le Chambon, one from which André and Magda Trocmé (and their children) never fully recovered: their son Jean-Pierre accidentally killed himself, in their home, on August 13, while replaying François Villon's "Ballade des pendus," of which the family had seen a performance not long before by actor Jean Deschamps. That day, André Trocmé writes in his "Mémoires," he "lost faith in the God of his youth," a providential God who guards those who obey him.[138] Far from being a omnipotent "guardian," God is "totally immersed in the suffering of creation."[139]

---

135. A. Trocmé, "Mémoires," 426–29. Trocmé thought the idea of going to Le Puy was foolish. He had urged Le Forestier not to go.

136. Le Forestier, "Roger Le Forestier," 116–35.

137. Boulet, *Histoire de la Montagne-refuge*, 284. A. Trocmé, "Mémoires," 460.

138. A. Trocmé, "Mémoires," 434–39. Quote on 438.

139. "Non plus un Dieu gardien, ou un Dieu tout-puissant, mais un Dieu totalement immergé dans les souffrances de la création, un Dieu dont on ne sait ni d'où il vient, ni où il va, mais qui s'identifie pleinement avec mon néant et mes espérances." Ibid., 440.

THE END OF THE WAR

As France was being freed from the German occupant, Trocmé's work was not quite finished: the lives of German prisoners of war were now at risk! The old suspicion concerning Trocmé's pro-German sentiments (since he was not ready to fight Hitler, and since he did not like Pétain very much, he must have been pro-German, some Chambonnais had thought early in the war) was resurfacing as he did everything he could to ensure these German prisoners were not being mistreated.[140] The last German soldiers from Le Puy, 120 of them, were imprisoned in Pont-de-Mars, a site where a fortified building used to stand, on the territory of Le Chambon, which means that in Trocmé's mind he was their chaplain. He went there, along with Hans-Ruedi Weber, a young theology student from Switzerland who was working for the Red Cross in Le Chambon, and August Bohny, to bring supplies and lead worship services on Sundays.

But the war was over, and soon Le Chambon emptied itself: the refugees who were still there, adults and children, left. The various children's homes shut their doors, and the Collège cévenol's student population was reduced by half (among its professors was a young philosopher who, influenced by André Philip, had been a participant in the "Christianisme social": Paul Ricœur had just arrived at Le Chambon at the end of 1944 from a prisoners' camp in Germany, and taught philosophy at the "Collège cévenol" for three years).[141]

RETROSPECT

Looking back at these years of war, and his life until the "libération," Trocmé wrote the following on September 5, 1967:

> In 1944, I was only forty-three years old, and yet I had lived the most important years of my life. Whatever came later was only the consequence, a commentary on the discoveries made

---

140. Ibid., 451.

141. Ricœur wrote on July 1, 2002: "[. . .] je répondais alors, au retour de ma captivité comme prisonnier de guerre en Allemagne, à l'appel des directeurs du Collège Cévenol, les pasteurs Theis et Trocmé et Madame Lavondès, à venir enseigner au Collège. Les trois années que j'y passai sont quelques-unes des plus heureuses de ma vie. C'est là que j'écrivis mes premiers livres, tout à la joie de la famille et de l'enseignement. Ces travaux portent la marque de l'expérience partagée autour du Collège, du village et des communautés diverses du Plateau." "Préface" to Cabanel et al., *La Deuxième Guerre mondiale*, 7. See also Ricœur, "André Philip."

through two World Wars. To practice, through faith, the Gospel of Jesus-Christ is not only possible for an individual, it is also a collective possibility, for a group of believers committed to do it. The Church of Jesus-Christ, the face of which we often look for in vain in our traditional parishes, is nothing but such groups of men and women who dare to take the risk to act through faith, in obedience to Jesus Christ, day after day, in an adventure always renewed and whose fruits no one can foretell, an adventure which is made possible by the daily directives God gives to those who listen to him and who attempt to obey him.[142]

Trocmé goes on to write: "I have known, certainly, a small number of exceptional human beings, born to become saints or leaders. These human beings, when they are disciples of Jesus-Christ, lead the crowd of those who are more hesitant. They form disciples, they create a school. Personally, I never had their charisma. I have never thought of myself as a leader, because I have always doubted, not of God, but of myself, and this lack of confidence in myself has always paralyzed me at the moment when I could have exercised the kind of influence leaders have."[143]

One may beg to differ with Trocmé, who, during the war, did lead his parish of Le Chambon, just as other pastors led their parishioners in the surrounding area, in a massive effort to protect the lives of those who were persecuted. But, if Trocmé did not consider himself a "leader," who then are these "leaders" and "saints" he had in mind in this text? I would be surprised if Trocmé did not think, among others, of his mentor Henri

---

142. "En 1944, je n'avais que quarante-trois ans, et cependant j'avais vécu les années essentielles de ma vie. Tout ce qui va suivre n'a été que la conséquence, le commentaire des découvertes faites à travers deux guerres mondiales: Pratiquer, par la foi, l'Évangile de Jésus Christ, ce n'est pas seulement une possibilité individuelle, c'est aussi pour un groupe de croyants décidés à le faire, une possibilité collective. L'Église de Jésus Christ, dont nous cherchons souvent en vain le visage dans nos paroisses traditionnelles, n'est autre chose que ce groupe d'hommes et de femmes qui prennent le risque d'agir par la foi, en obéissance à Jésus Christ, jour après jour, dans une aventure toujours renouvelée, dont on ne sait jamais d'avance ce qu'elle donnera, mais qui est rendue possible par les directives journalières que Dieu donne à ceux qui l'écoutent et s'efforcent de lui obéir." A. Trocmé, "Mémoires," 463.

143. "J'ai connu, certes, un petit nombre d'hommes exceptionnels, nés pour être des saints ou des chefs. Ces hommes, quand ils sont disciples de Jésus Christ, entraînent derrière eux la foule des hésitants. Ils forment des disciples, ils font école. Personnellement, je n'ai jamais possédé leur magnétisme. Je n'ai pas conscience d'avoir été un chef de file, car j'ai toujours douté, non pas de Dieu, mais de moi-même, et ce manque de confiance en moi m'a toujours paralysé au moment où j'aurais pu exercer l'influence majeure que possèdent les chefs." Ibid., 463–64.

Nick, who, like him, had not remained inactive during the war, as we will now see.¹⁴⁴

HENRI NICK DURING THE WAR

Trocmé is well-known for his extraordinary work during the war. With his colleagues and the people of the entire "Montagne," Jews were rescued, in Le Chambon, in neighboring villages such as Le Mazet-Saint-Voy, by Protestants, to be sure, but also by Catholics and non-believers. Hundreds of refugees, including many Jews, were saved. How many? No one really knows. Some say 2,500 or 3,000, others think 500 to 900 Jews were rescued.¹⁴⁵ It is very hard to say, but the truth seems to be closer to the second range of figures.

In northern France too, in very difficult circumstances, since the German occupant was present right from the defeat of June 1940, attempts at saving lives were made. There were several thousand foreign Jews in the department of Pas-de-Calais, most of whom had moved there from central and eastern Europe between the two world wars. The city of Lens had a large community of Jews who had recently emigrated from Poland. That community was decimated during the war: 1311 Polish Jews from the Pas-de-Calais region died in death camps. Lille had a somewhat smaller, but very lively, Jewish community.¹⁴⁶ In retrospect, it

---

144. Trocmé gives a list of people he admires for their pacifism in his "Mémoires": "Ce que je vais raconter laisse intacte l'admiration que j'éprouve pour les grands hommes de la Réconciliation: Henry Hodgkin, son fondateur, Mathilda Wrede, Leonhard Ragaz, Henri Roser, Muriel Lester, A. J. Muste, Nevin Sayre, resteront dans l'histoire de la foi religieuse au XXe siècle comme des personnalités d'une taille exceptionnelle, dominant leur époque par leur courage, leur fidélité, leur capacité de pardonner. Les petits défauts, parfois comiques, de chacune de ces personnalités n'ôtent rien à leur valeur exceptionnelle et prophétique." Ibid., 518.

145. The *Dictionnaire des Justes* claims that one of the homes in Le Chambon, Faïdoli, which was under the responsibility of August Bohny, helped rescue "at least eight hundred children." "Bohny, Auguste," in Lazare, *Dictionnaire des Justes*, 103. This figure seems very high. Boulet guesses 500 to 900 Jews came through Le Chambon and the surrounding area between 1940 and 1944. If these figures are correct, it means that through these years the Jewish refugees amounted to 10% of the local population, a figure significantly higher than in another somewhat remote region of France where Protestants were a majority of the population, namely the Cévennes region, where the Jews who were rescued amounted to only 3% of the population. Boulet, *Histoire de la Montagne-refuge*, 209.

146. Delmaire and Hilaire, "Chrétiens et Juifs," 451–52.

is clear that those who were French since generations had a much higher chance of avoiding deportation.

Henri Nick took part, on February 8, 1939, in an ecumenical gathering of more than one thousand people in Lille who protested in the wake of "Kristallnacht" (November 9–10, 1938).[147] During the war, he used his ecumenical contacts, and his own network within French Protestantism, to save lives. The clinic Ambroise Paré quickly became an important place for various groups affiliated with the "Résistance."[148] People who were in danger (British soldiers, communists, young men who refused obligatory work, and of course Jews) could be brought to safer places through the clinic and Nick's "Foyer du Peuple."

The first major roundups took place around September 12, 1942: foreign and recently naturalized Jews were arrested. The train which took them away departed from Fives. The railroad workers managed to free between twenty and thirty children, who were placed by several people, including Henri Nick, in various families in the region.[149] In most cases, the rescue took place through placement in families willing to take the risk of hiding Jews. Pierre Nick, a son of Henri Nick, was a medical doctor in the village of Inchy, near Cambrai. With his wife Odile, he assisted his father in finding such families. In January 1943, Avraham Lipszyc (or "Lif"), a teenager, the son of the rabbi of Lille's immigrant (mostly Polish) Jewish community, arrived in the home of Pierre and Odile Nick and stayed with them for a year.[150] The rabbi, his wife, and two younger children were deported to Auschwitz. They did not return.[151] But Abraham and two of his sisters, Perla and Haya, survived the war, first in the region of Lille thanks to Henri Nick and the people working at the Ambroise Paré hospital, and then in Trélon, at a Catholic institution for children called the "Préventorium," where an extraordinary woman, Jeanne Rousselle, provided shelter to over fifty Jewish children during the war.

---

147. Delmaire and Hilaire, "Chrétiens et Juifs," 452. Léon Berman ("Grand Rabbin" of Lille), the mayor of Lille, the prefect of northern France, a representative of Cardinal Liénart, participated in that event, which was organized by Abbé Paul Catrice, a Roman-Catholic priest. Among the speakers was pastor Chéradame, of the "groupe du Nord" (whether it was Robert or Daniel is not clear to me). Besin, *Pierre Nick*, 19.

148. Besin, *Pierre Nick*, 21.

149. Delmaire and Hilaire, "Chrétiens et Juifs," 454.

150. Lazare, *Dictionnaire des Justes*, 429–30. Besin, *Pierre Nick*, 39. Yagil, *Chrétiens et Juifs*, 613. Yagil, *La France, terre de refuge*, vol. 1, 160, 417 and 443; vol. 3, 213 and 217–8.

151. Besin, *Pierre Nick*, 42.

Revivalism and Social Christianity

Henri Nick helped rescue a prominent member of the Jewish community in Lille, Mr. Leser and his family.[152] Mr. Leser informed the family of David Bugajski that Henri Nick gave shelter to Jews. As massive roundups were under way in Lille and the region, David Bugajski stayed for three or four days in Nick's home, rue des Bouvines, a place "through which many Jewish children passed," according to his testimony. From there he was sent to a Roman-Catholic priest, abbé Stahl, a confirmation that ecumenical contacts were efficient.[153] Another person, Guy Treister, born in 1933, was hidden in Le Cateau, in the home of Mr. and Mrs. Lamotte, while a shelter was provided for his mother and brother in a large farm owned by Jean Crombez, a Catholic, in Inchy.[154] His testimony is worth quoting at length, especially since sources about Henri Nick and his son Pierre are sparse:

> Right from the beginning of the anti-Jewish persecutions, my mother received precious assistance from the Protestants. First of all, in Lille, where we lived (228, rue Pierre Legrand), I was welcomed by the Protestant community during the school year and during the vacations. [. . .] This situation could not last: the roundups were increasing in frequency and the Gestapo came to our apartment and placed seals on the door. My mother had to resign herself to separating herself from her children: my sister was placed under the care of Mr. et Mrs. Aymard, 33bis rue de Lens in Lille. My brother went to a Protestant family in Croix, near Lille. Thanks to the efforts of the Protestants, and especially pastor Nick, I was placed with a Catholic family in the town of Le Cateau in Cambrésis, but stayed in close contact with the Protestants of Le Cateau: I used to go to the Protestant church on Sundays and Thursdays, there I was taught the Torah and of course also the Gospels; the Pastor asked me to memorize entire verses of the Torah, but—and this is still very clear in my mind—never a single line from the Gospels. [. . .] And so it is in

---

152. Letter from Suzanne Besin to Lucien Lazare, April 30, 1992. Files of the Nick family, Yad Vashem (Jerusalem).

153. "Le 11 septembre les rafles commencent. . . L'affolement saisit les familles. Ma mère apprend par M. Leser que certains curés sauvent des enfants juifs. Par des contacts difficiles à reconstituer, je suis placé trois ou quatre jours dès le 12 septembre chez un pasteur protestant, le pasteur Nick, rue des Bouvines à Lille, chez qui transitent de nombreux enfants. Il n'est pas possible de rester éternellement chez lui, et par ses contacts avec l'évêché, il nous envoie chez l'abbé Stahl [. . .]." Quoted in Delmaire and Hilaire, "Chrétiens et Juifs," 454.

154. Letter from Suzanne Besin to Lucien Lazare, December 9, 1991. Files of the Nick family, Yad Vashem (Jerusalem). Besin, *Pierre Nick*, 37.

Inchy that my Mother and myself came to know Doctor Nick, the son of pastor Nick, and his family. He practiced his profession with such enthusiasm: his father, a Protestant pastor, must have shown him what it means to live in the service of others, selflessly. Several times I was invited by Doctor Nick for a small mid-afternoon meal with his children, and what impressed me deeply was that, each time, there were different people, which were systematically introduced to me as their uncles, aunts, or cousins. [...] After the war, I found out that in fact M. and Mrs. Nick often provided shelter for Jewish families passing through, and that Doctor Nick used his many connections to try to find a place for them.[155]

Despite efforts by people such as Henri and Pierre Nick, the deportations were devastating in northern France. Only a very small percentage escaped deportation and death. Antisemitism was widespread in the local population. In Lens some applauded as the trains headed east were passing before their eyes.[156]

Nick was 77 years old by the time the war ended. He had lost his wife Hélène in January 1917, and three of his six children (not counting Pierre, the doctor, who died in 1950.)[157] The "Foyer du peuple" had experienced several crises in the 1930s, first with the fundraising issues following the worldwide economic crisis, which severely impacted the

155. Guy Treister wrote to Lucien Lazare on March 24, 1992: "Dès le début des persécutions antijuives, les protestants apportèrent à ma mère une aide précieuse. [...] Moi-même, je fus confié, grâce aux recherches effectuées par les protestants et notamment le pasteur Nick, à une famille catholique de la ville de Le Cateau en Cambrésis, tout en restant en étroit contact avec les protestants de la ville du Cateau: je fréquentais le temple protestant le dimanche et le jeudi, où l'on m'enseigna la Thora et aussi bien sûr les Évangiles; le Pasteur m'obligea à apprendre par cœur des versets complets de la Thora, mais, et cela est encore très net dans mon esprit, jamais une seule ligne des Évangiles. [...] C'est donc à Inchy que ma Mère et moi-même avons connu le fils du pasteur Nick, le Docteur Nick et sa famille. Il exerçait son métier de médecin avec un enthousiasme peu commun: son père, pasteur protestant, lui avait sans doute montré la voie du dévouement et du don de soi. Il m'est arrivé d'être invité chez le Docteur Nick à plusieurs reprises à un goûter avec ses enfants et ce qui m'a terriblement marqué, c'est qu'à chaque invitation, j'ai vu des gens différents qu'on me présentait toujours comme des oncles, ou des tantes sinon des cousins. [...] Après la guerre, j'appris qu'en fait, M. et Mme Nick hébergeaient très souvent des familles juives de passage et que le Docteur Nick s'efforçait de leur trouver un point de chute en utilisant ses très nombreuses relations." Files of the Nick family, Yad Vashem (Jerusalem).

156. Delmaire and Hilaire, "Chrétiens et Juifs," 452.

157. His six children are: Paul (1896–1933), born in Mialet, Jeanne (1897–1944), Pierre (1900–1950), who became a doctor, André, who died in 1927. His daughters Héléna and Madeleine survived him.

fundraising capacities of the "Mission populaire" (many of its donors were from the United States), and then with a crisis in the leadership of the "Foyer" around 1937.[158] Nick had retired from his position as director of the "Foyer du peuple," but he remained very involved in many of its activities.[159]

The "groupe du Nord" was not left untouched by the war. Two of its members, both of whom had been impacted by Douglas Scott's Pentecostalism, died: Samuel Cornier died of natural causes in his parish of Caudry, in 1943, leaving his wife and eight children behind. Marcel Heuzé, pastor in Marseille, where he was in charge of the neighborhood known as "République–Vieux-Port," was outspoken in his sermons against the Nazis and their collaborators. At the end of December 1942, he expressed such strong views against Hitler's regime that some of his parishioners worried for his safety. Heuzé knew of Le Chambon, of course, and advised a young man who wished to study theology to go there. That young man, Jacques Balter, lived in "Les Roches" and was among those who were deported and killed in Auschwitz.[160] Despite his denunciations of the Nazis from the pulpit, Heuzé's arrest, on February 27, 1943, was, it seems, the consequence of a private conversation he had had a week earlier, on February 16, during the funeral service of an eighty year old woman. In the course of a conversation with the two adult children of the defunct, he talked about the legitimate sorrow the children were experiencing but then contrasted their loss with the recent events in Marseille, as the Vieux-Port had been

---

158. Philippe Blanc (1906-1993), a young pastor whom Nick fully trusted—and the son of Maurice Blanc (1866-1945), a very close friend of Nick, even before their theological studies in Montauban—clashed with the direction of the Mission populaire over the question of the adequate methods for evangelization. It is likely that Blanc's Pentecostal leanings—in 1935, Nick had sent him to Charmes, pastor Dallière's parish, *the* hotbed of Pentecostalism within the Reformed Church—had something to do with these tensions as well. On May 19, 1937, leaders of the Mission populaire (the unsigned letter seems to have been penned by Emmanuel Chastand) wrote to Nick to inform him that Blanc's contract would not be renewed, and that pastor Blanc should leave the "Foyer du peuple." SHPF (Paris), Mission populaire, Fives. On July 19, 1937, another letter was sent to Nick in an attempt to convince him that Philippe Blanc should leave Fives. Blanc had begun his work in Fives in 1932. He stayed there until 1972.

159. A leaflet at the SHPF (Paris), Mission populaire (Fives), indicates his retirement date: January 1, 1940. That date is followed by these words: "Mais il reste à son poste, occupe toujours le presbytère du 61 rue de Bouvines et consacre toutes ses forces au Foyer qui a été, pourrait-on dire, toute sa vie." Nick still wrote a report for the Mission populaire in July 1952, at the age of 82.

160. Bollon, "Contribution," 410 n. 23.

emptied of its residents (some of them, who were Jewish, were taken to the camp of Drancy and later deported) and then completely destroyed by the German army, at the end of January and during the first seventeen days of February.[161] Heuzé's comments seem to have led to his denunciation and arrest: the mourners were German sympathizers, they had gone to the Gestapo. He was arrested ten days later and taken to the jail of "Saint-Pierre" in Marseille, where he remained for three months. He then spent four and a half months (early June until September 15, 1943) in the camp of Compiègne, where he met Daniel Trocmé. He was then sent to the camp of Buchenwald and later Dora, a labor camp for political prisoners well-known for its hellish conditions. Heuzé left Dora on April 4, 1945, in cattle wagons, first to Oslerode (Thuringia), then, during nine days without any food or water, to Ravensbrück, where he died on or around April 26, 1945, only days before the liberation of the camp (April 30).[162] Marcel Heuzé was one of six French Protestant pastors who died in deportation.[163]

Trocmé and Nick were both affected by these deaths: in the late 1930s, Samuel Cornier had been asked, for a while, to succeed Nick as director of the "Foyer du Peuple" in Fives. Nick and Trocmé both comment on Heuzé's deportation and death in their writings.[164] Now a man of 77

161. Ryan, "Vichy and the Jews," 358.

162. Marcel Heuzé's widow, Simone, wrote a text on March 27, 1973 about these events. It is preserved at the SHPF in Paris. Ch. Bury, "Dernier témoignage...," a text written on January 3, 1946 recounting Marcel Heuzé's final weeks, published in the *Bulletin de l'église réformée évangélique de Marseille* 63 (February 1, 1946) 2. Ch. Bury writes: "Monsieur Heuzé est devenu pour beaucoup de camarades, la force morale, la force spirituelle, l'incarnation d'un courage calme et de la foi vivante en Dieu. À Compiègne il a créé l'Église protestante du camp, il a dirigé les études bibliques fréquentées de tous nos camarades. Mais c'est surtout à Dora, dans l'enfer, dans ce tunnel noir, où il était pour nous tous l'exemple de la foi et du courage. [. . .] c'est Monsieur Heuzé qui m'a donné la force de tenir jusqu'au bout." Someone else wrote the following in the same parish journal, under the title "Marcel Heuzé": "Il était anti-nazi avec une résolution intraitable. Sous l'occupation, il dénonçait publiquement les crimes de l'Allemagne Hitlérienne et nombreux sont ceux qui se souviendront de cette prédication de fin décembre 1942, après laquelle on se demandait s'il n'allait pas être arrêté."

163. Seventeen pastors and three theology students were deported. Six of the pastors, two of the students, died, according to Aimé Bonifas in Encrevé et al., *Les protestants français pendant la seconde guerre*, 578.

164. Trocmé's account is not based on accurate informations, but his sentences are worth quoting: "Au moment de leur retraite, si bien ordonnée, du Midi, les Allemands décidèrent d'emmener avec eux les prisonniers politiques. Ils les chargèrent dans plusieurs trains. La plupart arrivèrent à destination, en Allemagne, entre autres celui qui transportait mon ami Marcel Heuzé, pasteur à Marseille, trop ami des Juifs lui aussi. Il mourut en 1945, lorsque son camp de concentration fut libéré par les Américains, de s'être réalimenté trop brusquement." A. Trocmé, "Mémoires," 456–57.

year, Henri Nick began one of his yearly report to the Mission populaire (written in the first half of 1946) by mentioning three people he knew who had not survived the war. He began with Marcel Heuzé: "Someone asked a Frenchman who lived during the French Revolution what he had done in those years. He answered: 'I lived.' It is of course something to survive catastrophes which have claimed so many lives. I think about several people, the old pastor of Lens, M. Heuzé, who, after being tortured, died in one of those hellish camps for political prisoners."[165]

Lille, and the entire region of northern France, suffered tremendously throughout the war, but particularly during the defeat of May–June 1940 and the final weeks of the war, before its liberation on September 3. In a report written in the last days of 1944, Nick describes the long lines of refugees fleeing south, and how German planes were strafing them. The "Foyer du Peuple" opened its doors to refugees who had come from further north, from Dunkirk and other places, as well as from Belgium. But many who had fled south by foot returned to their homes when the German army, which was progressing very quickly, blocked roads. Nick recalls leading a funeral service in the neighborhood of Hellemmes, near Fives, for twenty-four air force soldiers who had been shot down. Eventually, half of the buildings in Fives and Hellemmes were flattened. His own house, as well as the "Foyer," remained intact, except for the stained glass. He describes walking around ruins and piles of bricks. The houses on France's northern coast of France which had been used for summer holiday camps (400 children spent vacations there with their families every summer, before the war) were destroyed.[166]

---

165. "L'on demandait à un français au temps de la révolution française ce qu'il avait fait. Il répondit: 'J'ai vécu.' C'est évidemment quelque chose d'échapper à des catastrophes où ont sombré tant d'existences. Je pense à plusieurs, à un ancien pasteur de Lens, M. Heuzé, qui, après avoir été torturé, a péri dans un de ces camps infernaux des déportés politiques." Henri Nick, Report for the year 1946 to the Mission populaire, SHPF (Paris), Mission populaire (Fives). Nick goes on to mention Marcel Heuzé's successor, Mr. Olivès, who died, along with his wife and child, during a bombardment of Lens in August 1944.

166. Henri Nick, Report written in the first half of 1946 to the Mission populaire, SHPF (Paris), Mission populaire (Fives).

Part Four

After the War

NEW RESPONSIBILITIES

How does one live after such personal, but also national and worldwide tragedies? Nick continued his ministry at the "Foyer du peuple." The reports he sent to the "Mission populaire," like the ones he sent before the war, contain narratives of conversions, of (re)discovery of faith, give indications about the various groups at the "Foyer" ("Unions chrétiennes," Sunday school etc.).

Magda and André Trocmé, for their part, travelled extensively. André's pastoral position in Le Chambon was reduced by half, the rest of his time he served as European secretary for the "International Fellowship of Reconciliation" (IFoR), which involved a lot of travelling. These "travels were, after our great mourning, the healing medicine I needed."[1] Starting in 1945, Magda and André regularly visited the United States, giving lectures in many different places, in order to raise awareness about non-violence. After André Trocmé began working full-time for IFoR, in 1949, they also travelled east, to Poland, Russia and Japan, among others countries.[2] Magda went to India to represent France at the World Pacifist

---

1. "[. . .] les voyages furent, après notre grand deuil, la médecine guérissante dont j'avais besoin." A. Trocmé, "Mémoires," 529. Trocmé is alluding to the accidental death of his son Jean-Pierre in August 1944.

2. Reports and letters from these journeys are preserved at Swarthmore College, Series B, box 2.

Meeting.³ In the 1950's she was in contact with the Civil Rights movement in the United States and met Martin Luther King, Jr. in Montgomery, Alabama.⁴

In France too, André Trocmé often gave talks: there was a talk at his old parish of Maubeuge, another one organized by Robert Jospin, his old friend from Saint-Quentin, yet another one in Saint-Étienne on February 27, 1949, presided by Élie Gounelle, with George Lasserre, a partisan of cooperation in economic matters, and André Philip.⁵

Starting in 1946, when the *Revue du Christianisme social* resumed after a long interruption due to world events (March 1940–March 1946), Trocmé was a member of the "comité de direction" (his friend Jacques Martin was secretary and "rédacteur.")⁶ From then on, he became a regular contributor to the *Revue*. The following year, he was one of the speakers at the Congress of the movement in Lyon (February 16–18, 1947), where he talked about the quest for justice and the necessity to "evangelize the world." The quest for peace should be subordinated to the proclamation of the Gospel, he claimed, sounding more Barthian than ever. No one should dream of building up the kingdom of God.⁷ Apparently, the shock of World War II did to Trocmé what World War I had done to many others: it had destroyed (at least for the time being) any illusion of a linear, irreversible progress of civilization. "Human nature," he said in Lyon, "is corrupt and incapable of peace. Since it cannot be realized in the individual, peace will remain an impossible and disappointing collective dream."⁸ But Trocmé

---

3. Boismorand, *André et Magda Trocmé*, 214–24.

4. Ibid., 235–47.

5. The flyers for these public conferences are preserved at Swarthmore College, Series B, box 2.

6. Cf. *RCS* 54 (1946), flip side of the front cover. Here is the list: "rédacteur: Jacques Martin; comité de rédaction: Élie Gounelle (Président), J. Martin (Secrétaire), Th. Gounelle, Maurice Albaric, Élie Lauriol, Georges Lasserre, Georges Lauga, Roger Mehl, Henri Roser, André Trocmé, Maurice Voge, André Monnier, Poujol, J. Bois, Ducros."

7. "La lutte pour la paix est tellement absorbante et enthousiasmante que nous risquons de confondre la cause de la paix avec celle du Royaume de Dieu. [. . .]. La tâche n° 1 de l'Église c'est l'évangélisation du monde et c'est d'annoncer Jésus-Christ et non la paix. [. . .] Tentation suprême: Croire que la Justice de l'homme établit le règne de Dieu, penser que l'homme pourra élever un jour jusqu'au ciel un monument à sa propre gloire." Trocmé, "Les tâches," 262–3. André Philip had already made similar claims, expressing a mild criticism of Gounelle's views, in 1928. Baubérot, "Le christianisme social français de 1882 à 1940," 158.

8. "Or, la nature humain corrompue est incapable de paix. La paix irréalisable dans l'individu est, et restera un rêve collectif impossible et décevant." Trocmé, "Les tâches,"

in fact had not given up his dreams. They still lay with what he called "the totalitarians of the left" (the word "totalitarian" had not yet become a pejorative term, for Trocmé in February 1947!), who hold "a good measure of the truth of the gospel, a truth which is forgotten and rejected by our capitalist individualism."⁹

A HOUSE FOR RECONCILIATION (VERSAILLES)

Magda and André Trocmé left Le Chambon in 1950 to live near Paris, in Versailles, were they rented a large property in need of renovations. They baptized the house "Maison de la Réconciliation" (they also called it: "Moulin de la Paix," or "Mill of Peace") and transformed it into an international meeting place for peace. The house could welcome up to forty people. People came from various countries, including Germany and the United States. André Trocmé hoped to use this place "to test a new approach to evangelization."¹⁰ He hoped to offer something to the visitors rather than ask something of them. What Magda and André Trocmé had to offer was, of course, their vision of non-violence and brotherhood.

THE NUCLEAR THREAT

From 1945 until his death in June 1971, André Trocmé, now a well-known figure in ecclesial and pacifist circles in France and beyond, never ceased to continue his work for peace. On certain occasions, he sought the support of well-known churchmen, intellectuals and politicians: his archive at Swarthmore contains letters, written in the late 1950's by

---

270. Trocmé mentions Auschwitz, Buchenwald, Dora, Ravensbrück, Mauthausen, Dachau and Belsen (275).

9. "[...] (et je ne cache pas ici ma sympathie pour les totalitaires de gauche porteurs d'une bonne portion de vérité évangélique oubliée et rejetée par notre individualisme capitaliste) [...]." Trocmé, "Les tâches," 265. Ricœur too could write in those years, in the conclusion of a lecture: "La Révolution d'octobre reste, à travers bien des crimes, une promesse pour nous tous; tout ce qui s'efface et trahit cette promesse est pour nous un motif de deuil." Ricœur, "Le Yogi," 54.

10. "Il y avait longtemps que je rêvais de mettre à la disposition de la Réconciliation un centre de ce genre, et de mettre à l'épreuve un nouveau système d'évangélisation!" A. Trocmé, "Mémoires," 507.

Martin Niemöller,[11] Pierre Mendès France,[12] Gustav Heinemann,[13] François Mauriac,[14] abbé Pierre[15] and even Charles de Gaulle, to whom he had appealed on July 14, 1959 concerning tests for the nuclear bomb in the Sahara desert.[16] Trocmé was then seeking support for the "Fédération française contre l'armement atomique," which he founded with Alfred Kastler in April 1959.[17] Their manifesto calling France to abandon its experiments with the atomic bomb was signed by 350 prominent personalities. In 1958, thirteen years after the catastrophe, André Trocmé participated in a congress in Nagasaki and Hiroshima against the nuclear bomb.

ALGERIA AND "EIRENE"

At a meeting of the Continuation Committee of the Historical Peace Churches–IFoR in Geneva on February 18–20, 1957, Willem Visser't Hooft challenged the delegates to set up an organization dedicated to peace in North Africa. He had been impressed by the situation in Algeria

---

11. Martin Niemöller (1892–1984), a well-known Lutheran pastor and—since the WCC's 1954 conference in Evanston—a pacifist, played a crucial role in the formation of the Confessing Church (*die bekennende Kirche*) and its opposition to the nazification of German Lutheranism. He was arrested in 1937, sent to Sachsenhausen in 1938, transferred in 1941 to Dachau, before being freed in 1945.

12. Pierre Mendès France (1907–82) was a French politician who opposed French colonialism. He had been arrested by the Vichy government but managed to escape and join de Gaulle in London. After the war he was named Minister for National Economy by de Gaulle, a position from which he soon resigned. He remains a major political figure in France's Third and Fourth Republics.

13. Gustav Heinemann (1899–1976), a prominent politician, was affiliated with the Confessing Church in the 1930's. A member of the Social Democratic Party, he was president of the German Republic from 1969 until 1974.

14. François Mauriac (1885–1970) was a French author who won the Nobel Prize in Literature (1952). He became a member of the *Académie française* in 1933.

15. On November 6, 1958, abbé Pierre wrote a card to Magda Trocmé and another one to André Trocmé to express his condolences on the death of their son Daniel, who committed suicide in Colorado, where he lived.

16. Letter to Alfred Kastler and André Trocmé from July 31, 1959. Trocmé papers (Swarthmore College), Series B, box 1. Alfred Kastler (1902–84) was a physicist who received the Nobel prize in physics in 1966. As part of his commitment to pacifism, he opposed nuclear weapons. De Gaulle's letter is a (brief) response to Kastler and Trocmé's manifesto. Among the other intellectuals who wrote to Trocmé are Georges Duhamel and Jean Rostand.

17. A folder on the Fédération française contre l'armement atomique can be found at the Trocmé papers, Swarthmore College, Series B, box 2. For a selection of texts, see Boismorand, *André et Magda Trocmé*, 259–86.

during a visit soon after the war. Visser't Hooft's call was taken up by André Trocmé and other pacifist Christians, especially the "Brethren" from Germany. Together they founded "Eirene" ("peace" in Greek) in August 1957. The name was adopted at a meeting in Karlsruhe (Germany) on August 12. Another meeting took place on November 11, 1957 in Bienenberg, near Basel.[18] This organization, which is similar to what Pierre Cérésole had envisioned with his "Service civil international," would soon send volunteers, many of them conscientious objectors, to Morocco, Algeria and other countries, to foster peace through humanitarian efforts and volunteer work with local populations. Trocmé had become sceptical of endless talks on peace and pacifism. Now was the time to send young men and women to different regions of the world to work for justice and to create bonds of friendship.[19]

The beginning of André Trocmé's involvement in Algeria after the war began in 1955. That first visit was followed by many others. Magda and André were there on May 13, 1958, on the day when the rebellion against France's colonial rule began.[20] André Trocmé was interviewed about these events for the newspaper *Le Monde*. When Hubert Beuve-Méry, the founder and director of the newspaper, decided not to publish certain parts of the interview, Trocmé complained.[21]

Even after the end of the war in 1962, Algeria was still one of Trocmé's main concerns. On April 25, 1966, he sent a letter from Algeria to his friends. He had met the new president, Houari Boumédiène (1932–78) at the Presidential Palace, but was not fooled by the big receptions: he knew that "behind the sumptuous dinners [. . .] there is unemployment, a harvest which does not look good, the slowing down of exports, a terrible chaos, a tragic administrative inefficiency, muted fights between political

18. A "Memorandum. The Development, Purpose, and Organizational Structure of Eirene. International Christian Service for Peace," penned by Milton J. Harder, a Mennonite pastor, and dated February 4, 1958, can be read at Swarthmore College (Trocmé papers, Series B, box 1).

19. Trocmé concluded a conference at the national Congress of the French Protestant social Christians (Lyon, April 1955) with the following question: "Peut-on formuler le désir de voir nos Églises employer moins de temps à des discussions théoriques sur la paix universelle et consacrer beaucoup plus de ressources matérielles et morales à envoyer des hommes et des femmes là où d'autres hommes, et d'autres femmes ont soif d'estime, d'encouragement et de justice?" Trocmé, "Un pont de bonne volonté," 507.

20. Magda's note in A. Trocmé, "Mémoires," 546.

21. Trocmé papers (Swarthmore College), Series B, box 1. Beuve-Méry replied saying the decision had been based on certain inaccuracies in the content of the interview.

clans, rivalries between minorities! Only four things remain: 1. The *beauty* of the land. 2. The *goodness* of people. 3. The revolutionary vision of certain devoted civil servants. 4. The incredible patience of malnourished masses (four days of French strikes have led to the deaths of hundreds of babies who had no milk; Algeria does not produce any milk, it is imported from France!)."[22]

SAINT-GERVAIS (GENEVA)

After a decade of activism for peace, based in the "Maison de la Réconciliation" in Versailles, André Trocmé returned to the pastoral ministry, when he was elected, with a huge majority, by the parish of Saint-Gervais in Geneva.[23] And so 1960 was a year of major transitions for him and Magda. Together with Jispa they organized for the last time the annual congress of the "Réconciliation," held in Versailles (February 27–March 1, 1960.)[24]

André Trocmé began his ministry on May 1, 1960, succeeding Max Dominicé, at one of the main parishes in Geneva. A year later, he published his first book of theology: *Jésus-Christ et la révolution non-violente* (Geneva, Labor et Fides, 1961).[25] The great New Testament scholar Oscar Cullmann wrote appreciatively of this study of the synoptic gospels and the non-violent dimension of Jesus' message, even though, "as a specialist," he had reservations.[26] Trocmé inquired with Abingdon Press about a possible translation in English, but he received a letter which hurt his feelings:

22. "Derrière l'écran des dîners somptueux [. . .] dans les restos de luxe des familles riches pieds noir, il y a le chômage, une récolte qui s'annonce mauvaise, le ralentissement des exportations, une terrible gabegie, une inefficacité administrative tragique, des luttes sourdes entre clans politiques, des rivalités entre minorités! Seules subsistent 4 choses: 1) la *beauté* du pays 2) la *bonté* des gens 3) la vision révolutionnaire de quelques fonctionnaires dévoués 4) la patience incroyable des foules sous alimentées (4 jours de grèves françaises ont fait mourir des centaines de bébés privés de lait, car l'Algérie ne produit pas de lait—tout vient de France!)." For a selection of texts by Magda and André Trocmé on Algeria, see Boismorand, *André et Magda Trocmé*, 287–310. André Trocmé published a number of short articles on Algeria in *CR* in the 1950's.

23. 188 votes in favor, 8 opposed, 8 abstentions. Letter from Annette Lasserre, October 19, 1959. Trocmé papers (Swarthmore College), Series B, box 1. These figures match those printed in *CR* (Feb. 1963) 34.

24. *CR* (July–August 1960) 2 and *CR* (Nov. 1960) 1–3.

25. A first English translation was published by Herald Press in 1973. A new edition, edited by Charles E. Moore, was published by Orbis Books in 2004. Trocmé had already published several children's books. He was a gifted storyteller.

26. Cullmann added that the argument "looks very interesting, anyhow, it should be discussed." Trocmé papers (Swarthmore College), Series B, box 1.

"it [is] very clear that biblical scholarship would be exceedingly critical of the book, and since the premise of your argument is very much related to biblical authority, we feel that results of publication would be exceedingly disappointing."[27]

Trocmé did not give up his hopes to make a contribution to theology. In 1966, he asked André Chouraqui, who had been rescued in the area of Le Chambon during the war, with the help of pastor Roland Leenhardt, and who went on to publish a well-known translation of the Bible, to support his request for a grant, which would enable him to spend a sabbatical of three to four months at the Hebrew University of Jerusalem. The topic of his research would be "the biblical Jubilee," a topic he had already explored in *Jésus-Christ et la révolution non-violente*. Trocmé received the grant but was not able to travel to Israel.[28]

Trocmé's return to the ministry in no way ended his work for peace and justice. On May 30, 1963, he founded the "Protestant Association of Technical Assistance Saint-Gervais-Philippeville," or in short "Saint-Gervais–Philippeville."[29] The parish of Saint-Gervais provided support for a program in the northeastern Algerian town of Philippeville (Skikda), where people were taught how to repair diesel machinery.

That same year, France finally adopted a law on conscientious objection, with the implementation of a civil service whose duration, in order to limit the numbers of candidates to it, would be twice longer than the regular military service. All of the conscientious objectors who were in jail at the time were freed.

---

27. Letter from Emory Stevens Bucke from December 19, 1962. Trocmé's reply, which expresses his disappointment, can be read at the Peace Collection (Swarthmore College).

28. Letter from André Chouraqui to the ambassador of Israel in Bern (Switzerland) and to the "Municipalité de Jérusalem," December 13, 1966. Trocmé received a positive letter from Eliyahu Honig, Deputy of the Hebrew University, on May 7, 1969. Trocmé had written to him (undated letter): "My concern is to do research work about the biblical Jubilee, and to do it in Jerusalem, where the restoration of the Jewish State poses the problem of the application of Old Testament institutions to our modern times." Trocmé wrote another letter on March 22, 1971, alluding to the "Medal of the Righteous" (Righteous among the Nations) he had received a few months earlier, in January: "This is refreshing my wish to spend some months in Israel, in order to complete my knowledge of rabbinic literature in the days of Jesus Christ." Trocmé inquired about the courses which would be offered in English during the academic year 1971–72.

29. "Association Protestante d'aide technique St-Gervais–Philippeville." A large folder concerning this Association is preserved in the Trocmé papers at Swarthmore College. For a selection of texts, see Boismorand, *André et Magda Trocmé*, 303–10.

Trocmé's extraordinary work in Le Chambon was celebrated here and there in the last decades of his life. In February 1964, he was invited to attend a commemoration, planned for May 3, 1964, in honor of Jules Isaac, the founder of the "Amitié judéo–chrétienne" (Jules Isaac's son Daniel had lived in Le Chambon during the war, where he worked as a teacher). Trocmé accepted the invitation and spoke at the event, held in the Palazzio Vecchio in Florence.[30] In his address, he said: "To erect tombs for the prophets without picking up the mantle they have just dropped is a hypocrisy, said a Jew: Jesus of Nazareth. And so if we speak, this morning, of Jules Isaac, it is in order to commit ourselves to continue the struggles he embarked on. For Jules Isaac was a prophet. I still remember the rigour of his exhortations when, in 1943, he came to my parish in Haute-Loire, asking me to read the manuscript he handed to me (the first draft of his book *Jesus and Israel*), urging me to exculpate with him the Jews of the crime of deicide, a crime which they are being accused of committing since nineteen centuries."[31]

THE "INTERNATIONAL FELLOWSHIP OF RECONCILIATION" AND ITS IDENTITY CRISIS

A major crisis shook the "International Fellowship of Reconciliation" (IFoR) in 1968, when a decision was made, at a Council meeting in Oslo, to omit from then on any mention of the Christian roots of IFoR. Debates on this matter had been raging for several years. As vice-president of IFoR, André Trocmé contacted Henri Roser, Jacques Martin, Philippe Vernier, Édouard Theis and twelve others, asking them to come to Lausanne on November 22, 1968, in order to discuss "concerns regarding the future of

---

30. Letter from Giorgio La Pira, February 11, 1964. On May 15, 1966, Claire Huchet Bishop, a children novelist who worked at the New York City Public Library, wrote to Trocmé: "[. . .] mon grand et vénéré ami Jules Isaac m'avait beaucoup parlé de vous. Je vous savais aussi présent à Florence, d'où seule la maladie m'avait tenue éloignée."

31. "Bâtir les tombeaux des prophètes sans relever le manteau qu'ils viennent de laisser tomber, c'est une hypocrisie, a dit un Juif: Jésus de Nazareth. Si donc nous parlons, ce matin, de Jules Isaac, c'est pour prendre l'engagement de continuer les combats qu'il a menés. Car Jules Isaac fut prophète. Je me rappelle encore la rigueur de ses exhortations lorsqu'il vint en 1943, dans ma paroisse de Haute Loire, me prier de prendre connaissance du manuscrit qu'il me remit: la première rédaction de l'ouvrage *Jésus et Israël* et m'adjura de disculper avec lui les juifs du crime de déicide dont on les accuse depuis dix-neuf siècles." Swarthmore College, Series B, box 2.

IFoR."³² A document was signed and sent to Hannes de Graaf, the chairman of the Council, that same month. It expressed

Consternation

This is why we feel at once free and compelled, as we consider the full implications of the Oslo decision, to express to you our consternation at having to abandon the Christian character and basis of the I.F.O.R. although such a change had been rejected for the past ten years [. . .].

Fragmentation

Even if the different national F.o.R.s are to be left free to declare themselves christian [sic], we must acknowledge that our common universal position will suffer by being fragmented into diverse national positions.

Effectiveness weakened

Furthermore, many members of different national F.o.R.s have not concealed the fact that they felt personally affected and weakened by this uncertainty, since their christian convictions make it difficult for them to accept that one can just as effectively work for peace with or without Christ.

Is it possible to re-open the question? [. . .]

A clear Christian affirmation attracts more than it repels

We have given only a few brief suggestions, whose originality, if they have any, can only spring from a motivation that is clearly, joyfully and explicitly christian. The motivation must be such that, so far from being a barrier, it would be a brotherly invitation to men of good will, who hold other concepts or belong to other religious or ideological traditions and who are also seeking justice.

We therefore propose that the Oslo decision be reconsidered

Therefore, dear friend, we strongly express the wish that the disturbing Oslo decision be reconsidered. We reserve the right to make known our point of view among the national F.o.R.s without long delay, unless, in response to our request, you circulate our text through the international Secretariat within, say, three weeks. [. . .]³³

32. "[. . .] l'avenir préoccupant de la IFoR." André Trocmé's invitation to gather in Lausanne is found at Swarthmore in Series B, box 2.

33. Trocmé papers (Swarthmore College), Series B, box 1.

Revivalism and Social Christianity

It is very interesting to see André and Magda Trocmé fighting to preserve the Christian roots of the "International Fellowship of Reconciliation" at a time when many thought what mattered was to eliminate explicit Christian references so that others who do not share these convictions may join the movement. We see here two radically different approaches, which are still battling each other in our time in the field of ecumenical and interreligious dialogues: on the one hand, some argue that one's identity needs to be revised or "toned down" in order to facilitate dialogue and cooperation, whereas others think dialogue and cooperation, far from being enriched, are impoverished when religious convictions are reduced or suppressed. It should go without saying that Magda and André Trocmé's desire to explicitly maintain the Christian roots of the movement in no way meant that they were not interested in cooperating with members of other religious traditions in the work of peace.[34] But they thought abandoning Christian references would "weaken the authority of I.F.o.R. among the Christian Churches and would paralyze the proclamation of the Gospel of non-violence to the world." Trocmé concluded: "By putting into question the very basis of its inspiration and faith, I.F.o.R. has thrown down its best weapons on the eve of the battle."[35]

At a Council meeting at the headquarters of IFoR in Nyack (New York) on August 20–23, 1969, the following text was adopted as a response to the deep concern expressed by several prominent members of IFoR: "The Fellowship began as a witness against war, motivated by loyalty to Jesus Christ. Most national Fellowships have a basis formulated in traditional Christian terms, while some include other traditions and insights as well. All the members feel obliged to act on the ground of conscience for the good of mankind." André Trocmé and Henri Roser were present at that meeting (they are listed as vice-presidents, alongside John Nevin Sayre) and took part in the vote, which resulted in 15 votes in favor of the

---

34. It is not clear whether André Trocmé accepted Thich Nhat Hanh's invitation to attend a conference in Paris, on June 8–10, 1969, on the war in Vietnam, but there would of course have been no principled reason why Trocmé would have refused such an invitation. A Buddhist monk born in 1926, Thich Nhat Hanh was a major figure in those year in the anti-Vietnam war movement. In 1966, he had urged (and convinced) Martin Luther King, Jr. to publicly take a stance. The following year King nominated him for the Nobel Peace Prize.

35. "Cette décision risque [. . .] d'affaiblir l'autorité de l'IFoR auprès des Églises chrétiennes et de paralyser la proclamation face au monde, de l'Évangile de la non-violence. [. . .] En remettant en question la base même de son inspiration et de sa foi, la IFoR a jeté ses meilleures armes à la veille du combat." Trocmé papers, Swarthmore College, Series B, box 2.

text, 1 opposed, and 6 abstentions. Trocmé was probably not among those who accepted the text. The minutes of the meeting include his questions: "'Is this text the new basis of IFOR or is it a description of a situation? Do we believe the International FOR needs a basis or not?'" He asked that a study be made of "'what IFOR really believes and to whom and what she really belongs.'"[36]

JUBILEE OF THE "FRATERNITÉ" IN CLAMART

In 1970, the year of André Trocmé's retirement, it had been fifty years since a small group of young men, with Trocmé as one of their leaders, had founded the "Fraternité" of Clamart, near Paris. A jubilee celebration was planned. On November 15, 1970, there would be a worship service, followed by a meal and a "fraternal gathering." A handwritten note from René Gauthier was added to the printed flyer sent to Trocmé: "A message from you would be welcome. Resuscitate the heroic times! Warm greetings. We think Jacques Diény will be there."[37] On the printed invitation, one reads: "50 years ago. A small band of young people who dreamed of proclaiming Jesus Christ to people their age created the 'Fraternité' of Clamart. Troubled by the madness of the world, eager to create a new city, swept up by the enthusiasm of their youth, they wanted to put up *Jesus Christ* in their city."[38] The text of the invitation then turns to the present and future: are the means used to reach that end "still suitable? Haven't they begun to dull? [. . .] Should they be modified?"[39] But the goal, i.e., evangelization, has not changed, and remains an immense task.[40] Trocmé still was very fond of what he called the "Frat." He sent the following text for the celebration:

---

36. Minutes of the Council meeting of IFoR, August 20–23, 1969. Trocmé papers, Swarthmore College, Series B, box. 1.

37. "Ton message serait le bienvenu. Faire revivre les temps héroïques. Bien affectueux messages. Nous pensons avoir Jacques D.[iény]."

38. "*Il y a 50 ans*. Une poignée de jeunes gens qui rêvaient d'annoncer Jésus Christ à ceux de leur génération créaient la *fraternité* de Clamart. Troublés par la folie du monde, soucieux de faire une cité nouvelle[,] emportés par l'enthousiasme de leurs 20 ans[,] ils voulaient établir *Jésus Christ* dans leur cité."

39. "Le cinquantenaire nous invite à regarder l'outil et le travail. Est-il encore adapté? Ne commence-t-il pas à s'émousser? [. . .] Faut-il le modifier?"

40. "Quand au travail, il est le même dans ce sens qu'à vue d'homme, il est immense et déconcertant."

Adolescence is a time for dreaming, the same is true of old age. If the dream of the adolescent is cut off from the real world (anarchy, religion or drug), then the world will make sure to destroy that dream, and to transform the adolescent into a failed adult. But now that, in my seventieth year, without the burden of heavy responsibilities, I begin to dream anew, I realize why the 'Frat' at Clamart has been an exceptional event for many of us, dead or alive. The 'Frat' was a dream seeking to be realized in the world as it really was, in the wake of World War I. The dream? A small group of young men who believed that Jesus Christ was capable of transforming the world. The world? A typical room in a café, across from Clamart's train station. [...] The world did not convert to Jesus Christ. A second world war came on top of the first one, like a layer of silt and blood. [...] What can we do to heal this world? Go backwards? Call into question the methods from the old days? No. We can run toward the One who is ahead of everything that happens in America, Russia or China. It is up to us to catch up with him, to ask him in prayer to reveal to us where he is to be found and which earthly path to take, in order to find him again, where he is, not in Heaven but on earth, among human beings of good will. Could the 'Frat' be a new starting point, for a new generation of believers who yearn for this adventure? Why not? There is only one way to celebrate its Jubilee: by putting God to the test. He is ready to grant things beyond all hopes to those who run forward, toward Christ, with all their faith."[41]

41. It is worth quoting this text in full: "L'adolescence est l'époque du rêve, et la vieillesse aussi. Si le rêve de l'adolescent se détache du monde tel qu'il est (anarchisme, religion ou drogue), le monde se chargera de détruire le rêve, et de faire de l'adolescent un adulte raté. Mais maintenant que, dans ma soixante-dixième année, déchargé de responsabilités trop lourdes, je me reprends à rêver, je réalise pourquoi la Frat de Clamart a été un événement exceptionnel pour beaucoup d'entre nous, morts ou vivants. La Frat, c'était un rêve cherchant à se réaliser dans le monde, tel qu'il était au lendemain de la première guerre. Le rêve? Une poignée de jeunes gens qui croyaient que Jésus-Christ était capable de transformer le monde. Le monde? Une salle banale d'un café, face à la gare de Clamart. Le monde? Des portes qui se claquaient à notre nez lorsque nous annoncions Jésus-Christ de porte en porte dans la petite ville provinciale qu'était Clamart en 1920. Le monde? L'étranglement de notre pauvreté, et le scepticisme de nos aînés, qui ne croyaient pas à notre réussite. Le monde encore? Nous voulions un local, donc un terrain. Le terrain fut prêté, le local, une baraque Vilgrain en planches, transplantés: que de sueurs, que d'erreurs, que de joies, quelle foi, retrouvée dans la prière, permirent à l'impossible de devenir réalité? J'en suis encore stupéfait. Le monde ne s'est pas converti à Jésus-Christ. Une deuxième guerre a recouvert la première comme une couche de limon et de sang. Le monde actuel semble à bout de souffle. Il ne croit pas en Jésus-Christ, et ne croit déjà plus à la prospérité, doublée de famines lointaines, qui

Between the creation of the "Fraternité" at Clamart in 1920 and its jubilee of 1970, much had happened, of course, but Trocmé's confidence in the "adventure" of trusting God who transforms the world, and who calls people to transform the world with him, was still alive. Was it intact? No. It had endured the loss of dear ones in his family and among his friends. But faith in the transformative power of love as manifested by Jesus, the call to become a peacemaker, were still at the center of his life.

André Trocmé was not present at the Jubilee of the "Fraternité." A year later, following a surgery on his back, he died in Geneva, unexpectedly, on June 5, 1971. He was buried in the cemetery of Le Chambon a week later. That same day, on June 12, in the Protestant church in Le Chambon, Magda Trocmé received the medal of the "Righteous among the Nations" awarded to her husband by Yad Vashem. André Trocmé had found out about that honor and was intent on declining it, wishing for the entire population to be associated in this honor conferred by the State of Israel. But Yad Vashem accepted his wish and decided to honor the entire population of Le Chambon. Magda Trocmé, who survived him until her death in 1996, was awarded the title of "Righteous" in 1986 and received the medal at a ceremony held at the Israeli embassy in Paris.

---

est sa marque de fabrique. Que pouvons-nous faire pour guérir ce monde? Retourner en arrière? Remettre en œuvre les méthodes de jadis? Non, mais courir vers celui qui est en avant de tout ce qui se fait en Amérique, en Russie ou en Chine. C'est à nous de le rattraper, en lui demandant par la prière de nous révéler où il faut le chercher, et quel est le chemin terrestre à parcourir, pour le retrouver, là où il est, non pas au Ciel, mais sur la terre, parmi les hommes de bonne volonté. La 'Frat' pourrait-elle être une base de départ, pour une nouvelle génération de croyants qui cherchent l'aventure? Pourquoi pas? Il n'est qu'un moyen de célébrer son Jubilé, c'est de mettre Dieu à l'épreuve. Il tient en réserve des exaucements inespérés pour ceux qui s'élancent vers le Christ de toute leur foi. André Trocmé." Trocmé papers, Swarthmore College, Series B, box 1.

Epilogue

> "The only privilege Christian social practices have themselves is the privilege of humility; their own claim to fame is always the ironic one of knowing their own full humanity and therefore their distance from the purity of the Word they witness to."
>
> KATHRYN TANNER[1]

FROM TOMMY FALLOT'S SERMONS in Paris in the late 1870s to Henri Nick's (and Élie Gounelle's) ministry among the workers of northern France, beginning at the end of the 19th century, to Jacques Kaltenbach's work as a pastor in Fives and Saint-Quentin, right before and during World War I, to André Trocmé's lifelong commitment to peace and solidarity, in Le Chambon and elsewhere, this book has presented a genealogy of the "Christianisme social" ("social Gospel") in French Protestantism, with an emphasis on its principled, non-violent strand, without ignoring its evangelistic and even revivalist dimensions.

There is little doubt that Henri Nick contributed, indirectly at first, through Jacques Kaltenbach, and later directly, to the kind of person André Trocmé became. Throughout his adult life, Trocmé displayed the two most important concerns of Henri Nick: a living, active faith and a concern for the moral and social implications of faith. Or, to put it another way, their passion for "salvation" and "conversion" never omitted the "earthly" dimension of "salvation" and "conversion." The motto of social Christians

---

1. *Theories of Culture. A New Agenda for Theology* (Minneapolis: Fortress, 1997) 114. Quoted in Jenny Daggers, "Thinking 'Religion': The Christian Past and Inter-religious Future of Religious Studies and Theology." *Journal of the American Academy of Religion* 78 (2010) 984.

Epilogue

all around the world, in the late 19th century and throughout the 20th century, was: "on *earth* as it is in heaven." In true social Christian fashion, Henri Nick, André and Magda Trocmé dedicated much energy during World War II in order to "save" lives on *this* earth. For their work, they have been honored with the title of "Righteous among the Nations" by Yad Vashem in Jerusalem: Magda and André Trocmé in 1971, Henri Nick in 1992 (the same is true of other people whose names are mentioned in this book. They are, among others: Édouard Theis and his wife Mildred, Pierre and Odile Nick, Simone Mairesse née Pévenage, Charles Guillon, Henri Roser, Jacques Martin, Madeleine Barot, Daniel Trocmé, Mireille Philip, Roger Darcissac, Marc Boegner, André Bettex, August Bohny, André Morel, Pierre Toureille, Daniel Curtet). The entire population of Le Chambon and the surrounding "Plateau" was awarded the same title in 1988.[2]

When Henri Nick died, on March 9, 1954, André Trocmé wrote a eulogy for the *Revue du Christianisme social*.[3] He recounted some of his recent encounters with Nick and aptly described the "Foyer du peuple" as a place where "one found, reconciled without effort, the most evangelical piety with the boldest form of social Christianity."[4] Because he was a "man of prayer," "hundreds of people found a direct knowledge of God thanks to him. A carnal man is dead: he always wanted to disappear, his wish has now been heard. An eternal ministry lives on, which follows Mr. Nick in his rest in God's presence."[5]

Several things are striking about these two lives:

First, what one may call their early socialization and formation. Small groups of young men shaped Nick and Trocmé for life: for Nick, it took place at the "Faculté de théologie" in Montauban, especially during his

---

2. On the French "Righteous," see Lazare, *Dictionnaire des Justes*. The only other similar case, on a smaller scale, of an entire village or town rescuing Jews during the war, is the Dutch village of Nieuwlande. All 117 inhabitants of the village were recognized as "Righteous among the Nations." The French town of Dieulefit must also be mentioned, as hundreds of people found refuge there. Suchon, *Résistance et liberté*. Other towns have not received the attention they deserve, including Vébron (Lozère) and Vabre (Tarn), where dozens of Jews were given shelter. But see Joutard, *Cévennes, terre de refuge*, 265.

3. Trocmé, "Henri Nick."

4. "On y trouvait, réconciliés jusqu'alors sans effort, la piété la plus évangélique et le christianisme social le plus hardi." Ibid.

5. "Et parce que M. Nick a été l'homme de cette prière, des centaines d'hommes ont trouvé, par son intermédiaire, une connaissance directe de Dieu. Un homme charnel est mort: il voulut toujours disparaître et son vœu est exaucé aujourd'hui. Une œuvre éternelle subsiste, qui suit M. Nick dans son repos auprès de Dieu." Ibid.

final year of studies (1889–90), when he experienced a personal conversion in true Pietist mode and discovered the "Christianisme social," then a burgeoning movement. Among his closest friends were Wilfred Monod and Élie Gounelle, two young men who would lead the "Christianisme social," and in some ways French Protestantism, in the first half of the 20th century.[6] In the case of André Trocmé, the "Unions chrétienne de jeunes gens" at the parish of Saint-Quentin during World War I was the place where he found the decisive orientation to which he would remain faithful, with an impressive coherence and consistence, until his death. Both Nick and Trocmé sustained these initial commitments to evangelization and social awareness through circular letters, to keep in contact with their friends despite geographical distances (as it turns out, the group Trocmé was a part of—the "groupe du Nord"—had Henri Nick himself as its hero and model, or "saint"!). For both Nick and Trocmé, the genesis of their lifelong values and commitments can be traced to these small groups of young men. The same was probably true for many of their colleagues in the pastoral ministry, since so many of them were part of various youth groups ("Unions chrétiennes," student associations etc.), which played decisive roles in shaping them. At a regional synod in Tournon during the war (November 12–13, 1940), Trocmé urged his colleagues never to lose sight that "our churches recruit their members in the works of the church among the youth. The ideals of the young member of a Union or

---

6. One of the goals of the present study was to emphasize the importance of Henri Nick *alongside* Wilfred Monod and Élie Gounelle, who are better-known. Some who participated in the events I am recounting were quite aware of Nick's role. Adolphe Sibleyras put it well at a congress of social Christians in Montpellier (Nov. 11–13, 1939): "Il y avait, à cette époque féconde des commencements, dans notre vieille Faculté des bords du Tarn, trois étudiants que rien, en apparence, ne distinguait de leurs camarades, mais qui avaient en eux l'étoffe des apôtres et des chefs, et qui étaient destinés à jouer un rôle de premier plan dans le développement du Christianisme social en France et dans le monde: j'ai nommé Élie Gounelle, Wilfred Monod et Henri Nick. Grâce à Dieu, ils sont tous les trois encore vivants et l'un d'eux préside et anime ce Congrès, mais cela ne m'empêchera pas de dire ici hautement tout le bien que je pense et que, tous, nous pensons d'eux: Élie Gounelle, dévoré du besoin d'agir, touchant à toutes les questions [. . .]. Henri Nick, l'apôtre des cités industrielles du Nord, tourné, lui, tout entier vers la pratique et la poursuivant avec autant de douceur que d'énergie, celui des trois qui, peut-être, a pénétré le plus près l'âme de l'ouvrier, qui a le mieux gagné sa confiance, si bien qu'il a pu faire acclamer par les foules socialistes de Lille et de Roubaix les devises des Fraternités inscrites sur leurs bannières: 'Un seul est notre Maître, le Christ, et nous sommes tous frères.' Élie Gounelle, Wilfred Monod, Henri Nick, nous saluons en eux les trois mystiques de l'action sociale." Sibleyras, "Les débuts de l'Association." Sibleyras had known Gounelle and Nick as a student in Montauban in the 1880's.

of a young boy scout, ideals we have shaped for these young people, will remain the ideals of the church member."[7] These words clearly apply to André Trocmé himself, as well as his wife Magda.

This early formation obviously had a deep spiritual component. But what is remarkable here is that spirituality was never disconnected from social action. As Élie Gounelle pointed out in 1933: "Future historians of the worldwide social Christian Movement, when they will examine the psychology of the social reformers and pioneers, will have to pay attention to the kind of intimate piety which leads to social action, to the kind of mystical dynamism which is at the root of the salvific rebellions and of the revolutions which have a lasting effect. . ."[8]

An impressive coherence runs through Nick and Trocmé's lives. From his beginnings in Mialet in 1890 to the almost six decades he spent at the "Foyer du Peuple" in Fives–Lille, Nick equated his pastoral ministry with evangelization, a ministry which included a strong moral and social dimension. Trocmé, since his youth, identified the message of the Gospel with revivalism, but also with the ideal and the practice of non-violence. After the war, it appears that Trocmé's action in favor of peace trumped more and more his initial commitment to revivalism. But his stance on the secularization of IFoR in 1968 and his message to his old friends from Clamart in 1970 show the resilience, in the face of personal and world tragedy, of his faith. Trocmé never ceased being a pastor.[9]

---

7. "Nos églises, ne l'oubliez pas, se recrutent parmi nos œuvres de jeunesse. L'idéal du jeune unioniste ou du jeune éclaireur, tel que nous l'aurons forgé à l'usage de nos jeunes, restera l'idéal du membre d'église." "Rapport sur les problèmes de l'indépendance de l'Église, et la mise au point des membres responsables," 14. Trocmé papers, Peace Collection (Swarthmore College), series B, box 5, 8th folder.

8. "Les futures historiens du Mouvement mondial du Christianisme social, quand ils approfondiront la psychologie des réformateurs sociaux et des pionniers, auront à rechercher quelle qualité de piété intime mène à l'activité sociale, quel dynamisme mystique est à la base des révoltes salutaires et des révolutions, qui ont une valeur de durée. . ." Gounelle, "Le Congrès du Chambon," 408–9. In some ways, my narrative resembles the story told by Smith, *Revivalism and Social Reform*, esp. ch. 10 ("The Evangelical Origins of Social Christianity").

9. It must be added that the "Fraternité" in Clamart still exists, in 2011. The same is true of the "Foyer du peuple" in Fives–Lille, which became an "Association cultuelle" in 1954, joining the "Église réformée de France" in 1961. Its official name is now "Association cultuelle de l'Église réformée de Fives, *Foyer du Peuple*."

THE SOCIAL GOSPEL AS A "VICTORIAN" MOVEMENT?

There is no denying the highly moralistic tendency of much of the social Christian movement, in France and elsewhere, from its struggle for temperance to the education of young men and women on moral purity. It is simply part of its legacy. But it would be a mistake to dismiss the entire movement because of this aspect, or to reduce it to this dimension, which might not be palatable to us today. One should also avoid anachronisms. Alcoholism, arguably, was a sort of social scourge in those years.

The patriarchal dimension of the social Gospel is also evident everywhere. There too looms the risk of anachronism, of projecting our values onto a past where they did not yet fully exist. Still, the English Brotherhoods and the French "Fraternités," in many ways, promoted what appears to be a classical Victorian vision of gender, gender relations, and the family. And yet that does not mean they defended the status quo: they called for deep transformations of social structures, in order to alleviate poverty, to defend the workers, to protect female prostitutes and children, to eliminate war, in short to implement justice.[10] We have seen the many "Men's Circles," "Men's Congresses" etc. which were organized in those years. In 1943, André Trocmé wrote the guidelines of a new group of men he wanted to form: the "Order of Servants" ("Ordre des Serviteurs"). The first principle was: "Our Order is masculine. Our Church, indeed, especially needs men."[11] At the same time, women played an important role in the "Christianisme social," often under the "tutelage" of the pastors and lay men to whom they were married (the first official "consecration" of a woman pastor in the "Église réformée de France" occurred in 1949, and that pastor, Elisabeth Schmidt, was the only female pastor of that Church until 1966.)[12] During the war, in Le Chambon, women such as Simone Mairesse, Mireille Philip and Madeleine Barot played a decisive role in

---

10. See Forsythe Fishburn, *The Fatherhood of God*, whose conclusions, mostly about Rauschenbusch, are negative. She states: "The Social Gospel defense of Christianity, democracy, and the family against the possibility that socialism might 'sweep away' the present social order was ultimately a defense of the social status quo." (120) To Fishburn, the "later Social Gospel" opposed not just militarism and feminism but also "internationalism and socialism" (126). See also Deichmann Edwards, *Gender and the Social Gospel*. On Tommy Fallot, the founder of the "Christianisme social" in France, and his defense of women, see Rochefort, "The Abolitionist Struggle."

11. A. Trocmé, "Ordre des Serviteurs." Trocmé papers, Swarthmore College, Series B, box 5, 8th folder. François Boulet quotes a different version, from a letter, in Bolle, *Le Plateau Vivarais-Lignon*, 411.

12. See Geneviève Poujol's pioneering work, *Une féminisme sous tutelle*.

Epilogue

the rescue effort, both locally and in humanitarian institutions such as the Cimade.

While, undeniably and unavoidably, the social Gospel in French Protestantism betrays attitudes which reflect the mentalities of the time, the movement sought to change society, through individual and collective conversion.

THE RHETORIC OF ABNEGATION AND SOLIDARITY

Both Nick and Trocmé shared the conviction that a pastor must fully give himself to his ministry. For them, a pastor is called to entirely commit himself to the service of the Gospel. "We are always seeking a more complete commitment, without ever reaching it," Trocmé wrote to his friends in France while a student at Union Theological Seminary in New York City.[13] Such conviction helps explain why Nick was so disappointed with Trocmé's decision to leave northern France in 1934.[14] What Nick could of course not foresee was that it was that decision, and the obstacles placed on Trocmé's way by his own Church leadership, which led him to Le Chambon-sur-Lignon, where his life would reach its culminating point. Trocmé often despaired when thinking about the distance between his prophetic ideals, his wishes for a life of complete dedication to others, and the reality of his daily life. There, in Le Chambon, that distance between ideals and reality was reduced to a minimum, as Magda and André Trocmé took part, with their parishioners and the people of "good will" in the area, in the rescue of hundreds of Jewish refugees who were persecuted. Whether one is in agreement with Trocmé's principled form of pacifism becomes secondary and irrelevant, here.[15] For, in those years of war, the rhetoric of solidarity, which was at the heart of the "Christianisme social," was not mere rhetoric: it was put into practice, to the point where one may consider what happened in Le Chambon as *the* high point of the entire history of the "Christianisme social" in French Protestantism.

---

13. "Bulletin" of the "Groupe du Nord," June–July 1926, 2. Samuel Cornier papers (Cornier family, Paris).

14. In his eulogy, Trocmé writes that Nick could be "terribly, sometimes almost unjustly, severe, but his severity always led to God." "Il lui arrivait d'être terriblement, parfois presque injustement, sévère; mais sa sévérité conduisait toujours à Dieu." Trocmé, "Henri Nick" 336–37.

15. The debate is, of course, ongoing. See for instance Wolterstorff, *Justice in Love*, 120–26, and, still worth reading: Barth, *Church Dogmatics* III/4, 450–70 (originally published in 1951).

Marcel Heuzé (parish bulletin, Reformed church in Marseille, 1945)

Appendix

Declaration Read by Pastors André Trocmé and Édouard Theis in the Church of Le Chambon on Sunday, June 23, 1940[1]

Brothers and sisters,

Yesterday on the radio the president of the Protestant Federation gave a speech to which we would like to add our voice. In that speech, Marc Boegner calls the Protestant Church to humble itself for the errors which have led our people to the state in which it finds itself today.

As in Israel's hours of great distress, we are now called to humble ourselves.

Let us humble ourselves for our share of responsibility in the general catastrophy; let us humble ourselves for the wrongs we have committed as well as for those we have allowed to be committed, for our passivity, our lack of courage; as a result, a recovery in the face of the impending storm was made impossible; let us humble ourselves for our lack of love as we see others suffer, for our lack of faith in God and our worship of riches

---

1. This translation of Trocmé and Theis's message follows the editions by P. Boismorand, *Magda et André Trocmé*, 125–9 and Patrick Cabanel, *Résister. Voix protestantes*, Nîmes, Alcide, 2012. The armistice had been signed the preceding day.

Appendix

and might, for tolerating or believing certain ideas which are not worthy of Christ; to put it succinctly, let us humble ourselves for the sin which we all bear and which is the only real cause of the untold adversity that has befallen us.

Let us humble ourselves before God, individually, as persons, as head or member of a household, as citizens and Christians, as pastors or elders, as youth leaders or members of youth groups, as Church faithfuls. It is God we implore, that God may forgive the sin of which we are personally guilty as well as the sin – which is not foreign to us – of our people, of humanity and of the Church today. From God alone may come the recovery we await.

And yet we need to beware of certain ways of humbling ourselves which would in fact be a disobedience to God.

First, let us not confuse our humbling of ourselves with being discouraged. Let us not think, and then spread it around us, that everything is lost. It is not true that everything is lost. The Gospel truth is not lost, it will be proclaimed freely from this pulpit as well as during gatherings and pastoral visits. The Word of God is not lost; in it lie all of the promises and possibilities of recovery for ourselves, our people and the Church. Faith is not lost: far from weakening faith, a true humbling of ourselves leads to a deeper faith in God and a growing desire to serve God.

Second, let us beware of humbling ourselves, in a spirit of bitterness and resentment, for the mistakes of others, rather than for ourselves and our own errors. These last days, during our home visits, we have heard many complaints coming from soldiers against their officers, from officers against their soldiers, from employers against their workers and from workers against their employers, from rich people against the poor and from poor people against the rich, from pacifists against patriots and from patriots against pacifists, from believers against non-believers and from non-believers against believers. Everyone is accusing others, everyone seeks to dodge one's own responsibilities in order to place the blame on fellow citizens or foreign nations, all the while forgetting that God alone can juge and evaluate each person's guilt. We do not believe such humbling of oneself is fruitful and may lead to the rebuilding of our country and our Church.

Third, as we humble our hearts, let us not humble our faith and our convictions which are based on the Gospel. Even though we have misused the freedom which was given to us, let us not renounce that freedom under the pretense of humility, so that we become enslaved by and cowardly surrender to the new ideologies. Let us not fool ourselves : the totalitarian doctrine of violence has gained, these past few days, a formidable prestige in the eyes of the world, for it has, by human standards, brilliantly succeeded [. . .][2]. To humble oneself does not mean bending before such a doctrine. We are convinced that the power of that doctrine is comparable to the authority of the Beast which is described in chapter eighteen of the book of Revelation. That doctrine is no less than anti-Christian. Saying that is for us a matter of conscience, today like yesterday. It is quite certain that the sons and daughters of our Church have given their lives while fighting that doctrine. To humble ourselves for our sins does not mean that we should now give in to it. It is by surrendering our lives to Jesus-Christ, in service of his Gospel and of his universal Church, that we will practice faithfulness and true humility.

To this appeal to the Christian humbling of oneself, we would like, brothers and sisters, to add several exhortations which we address to you in the name of our Lord Jesus-Christ.

First, let us abandon today all our divisions among Christians and all our bickering among French people. Let us stop labeling and designating each other with these words which are laden with contempt: right-wing and left-wing, farmers, workers, intellectuals, proletarians or business owners. Let us stop accusing each other of every possible misdeed. Let us begin once again to trust each other, to greet and welcome one another, remembering—as the first Christians did—each time we meet others that we are brothers and sisters in Jesus-Christ.

Then, having left behind such attitudes of distrust and hate as well as the political passions to which they give rise, let us gather decidedly around Jesus-Christ, the head of the universal Church, and let us take on, as the source of our thinking, of our obedience and action, his Gospel, and nothing but his Gospel.

Finally, let us understand that returning to obedience compels us to break with the world, with the ways of living which we deemed acceptable until now.

Formidable pagan pressures are going to be exerted, as we said, on ourselves and our families, tempting us to passively surrender to the totalitarian ideology. Even if it does not immediately manage to dominate our souls, it will at least seek to enslave our bodies. The duty of Christians is to counter the violence that will be applied on their conscience by using the weapons of the Spirit. We enjoin all our brothers in Christ to refuse

---

2. One sentence is undecipherable, the ink of the typed text has faded.

Appendix

collaborating with such violence, especially, in the coming days, as it is directed toward the English people.

Our duty is to love, to forgive, to render good to our adversaries. But we must do it without surrender, servility or cowardice. We shall resist, when our adversaries demand submission to orders which run counter to those of the Gospel. We shall do that without fear, but also without pride or hate. This moral resistance, however, will not be possible without a break from the inner servitudes which, since long, rule over us. A time of suffering, perhaps of famine, is beginning for us. We all have more or less lived in the service of Mammon, the worship of selfish well-being in our small families, of easy pleasure, of idle drinking. We are now about to be deprived of many things. And yet we will be tempted to play our own selfish game, to contine to enjoy what is left to us, or even to dominate our brothers. May we abandon our pride and our selfishness, brothers and sisters, our love of money and our trust in earthly possessions, may we learn to rely, today and tomorrow, on our Father who is in heaven, turning to God for our daily bread and sharing it with our brothers whom we must love as much as we love ourselves.

May God free us of our worries as well as our false securities, may God give us his peace, which nothing nor anyone can take away from his children, may God console us in our mourning as well as in all our trials, may God make us all humble and faithful members of the Church of Jesus-Christ, of Christ's body, as we await his kingdom of justice and love, the kingdom where his will will be done on earth as it is in heaven.

Magda and André Trocmé in 1938

Bibliography

UNPUBLISHED SOURCES

Bibliothèque de la Société de l'Histoire du Protestantisme Français (Paris):
  Papers of Élie Gounelle
  Mission populaire évangélique (Mission McAll)
  Papers related to Marcel Heuzé

Rockefeller Archive Center (Sleepy Hollow, New York):
  Documents related to André Trocmé: Rockefeller Family Archives, Record Group (RG) 2, Office of Messrs Rockefeller, Friends & Services Series, Box 129, Folder 958 I.
  LSR [Laurance S. Rockefeller] photographs, Photo Album (1924–1926).

Peace Collection, Swarthmore College (Pennsylvania):
  Magda and André Trocmé's papers (DG 107).

Private archives of Henri Nick's family, in the care of Grégoire Humbert (Paris)
Papers of Samuel Cornier, Cornier family (Paris)

PUBLISHED SOURCES

Andrieu, Claire et al. *Resisting Genocide. The Multiple Forms of Rescue*. New York [etc.]: Columbia University Press, 2011.
Appel, Rudy. "A Journey to Escape from the List of the Fallen." *Het Erasmiaans Gymnasium in de Tweede Wereldoorlog. Herinneringen van oud-leerlingen*, edited by Leen Stout et al., 59–66. Rotterdam–Rijswijk: Semper Floreat–Uitgeverij Elmar, 2003.
Association protestante pour l'étude pratiques des questions sociales, fondée en 1888. Paris: Fischbacher, 1889.
Azéma, Jean-Pierre, and François Bédarida. *La France des années noires*. Vol. 1: *De la défaite à Vichy*. Vol. 2: *De l'Occupation à la Libération*. Paris: Seuil, 1993 (2002).
Barde, Paul. *Sin-le-Noble. Histoire d'une œuvre parmi les mineurs du Nord*. Cahiers de l'évangélisation 2. Paris: Société centrale évangélique, 1927.

———. *La Société centrale évangélique, des origines à nos jours.* Neuilly-sur-Seine: Éditions de la Cause, 1925.
Barot, Madeleine. "La Cimade et le rôle des organisations internationales de jeunesse." In *Les protestants français pendant la seconde guerre mondiale*, edited by A. Encrevé and J. Poujol, 217–26. Paris: SHPF, 1994.
———. et al. *Itinéraires socialistes chrétiens. Jalons sur le christianisme social hier et aujourd'hui (1882–1982).* Geneva: Labor & Fides, 1983.
Barth, Karl. *Church Dogmatics. III/4: The Doctrine of Creation.* Translated by A. T. Mackey et al. Edinburgh: T. & T. Clark, 1961.
Batten, Alicia J., "Reading the Bible in Occupied France. André Trocmé and Le Chambon." *Harvard Theological Journal* 103 (2010) 309–28.
Baubérot, Jean. "L'action chrétienne sociale du pasteur Élie Gounelle à la 'Solidarité de Roubaix' (1898–1907) d'après des documents inédits." *BSHPF* 120 (1974) 229–56 and 401–37.
———. "Aspects du Christianisme social français jusqu'à la séparation de l'Église et de l'État." *RCS* 79 (1971) 605–41.
———. "Le Christianisme social français de 1882 à 1940. Évolution et problèmes." *RHPR* 67 (1987) 37–63 and 155–79.
———. "Le Christianisme social protestant et la libre pensée (1898–1914)." In *Libre pensée et religion laïque en France de la fin du Second Empire à la fin de la Troisième République, Journée d'étude tenue à l'Université de Paris XII, 10 novembre 1979*, 231–46. Strasbourg: Cerdic, 1980.
———. "L'espérance des temps futurs au début du christianisme social." *Itineris. Cahiers socialistes chrétiens* 7 (1982) 8–13.
———. "L'Évangélisation protestante et la classe ouvrière: les Solidarités." In *Christianisme et monde ouvrier*, edited by François Bédarida and Jean Maitron, 157–84. Paris: Éditions ouvrières, 1975.
———. "L'évolution des courants chrétiens-sociaux du protestantisme français de 1906 à 1914." *Parole et société* 1 (1974) 67–109.
———. "Libération sociale et Royaume de Dieu. L'exemple des socialistes chrétiens français (1882–1939)." In *Idéologie de libération et message du salut*, edited by René Metz et al., 87–119. Strasbourg: Cerdic, 1973.
———. "Le protestantisme roubaisien face au socialisme guesdiste et au courant libertaire (1898–1907)." In *Christianisme et pouvoirs politiques, de Napoléon à Adenauer*, edited by Claude Langlois, 121–56. Paris: PUF, 1974.
———. *Le retour des huguenots. La vitalité protestante 19e–20e siècle*, Paris–Geneva: Cerf–Labor & Fides, 1985.
———. *Un christianisme profane? Royaume de Dieu, socialisme et modernité culturelle dans le périodique 'chrétien social' l'Avant Garde (1899–1911)* Paris: PUF–Bibliothèque de l'École pratique des hautes études, 1978.
———. "Pacifismes du christianisme social," *Autres temps* 1 (1984) 20–28.
———. "Tommy Fallot et ses continuateurs Élie Gounelle et Wilfred Monod: la fondation du Christianisme social." In *Itinéraires socialistes chrétiens*, edited by Madelein Barot et al., 15–31. Geneva: Labor & Fides, 1983.
———. *Vers l'unité pour quel témoignage? La restauration de l'unité réformée (1933–1938).* Paris: Les Bergers et les Mages, 1982.
Bédarida, Renée. *Témoignage chrétien (1941–1944). Les armes de l'esprit.* Paris: Éditions ouvrières, 1977.

Besin, Suzanne. *Pierre Nick, médecin de campagne. Une page de la Résistance dans le Cambrésis*. Cambrai: Les Amis du Cambrésis, 1994.
Biéler, André. *Chrétiens et socialistes avant Marx*. Geneva: Labor & Fides, 1982.
Boegner, Marc. *L'Évangile et le racisme. Conférence donnée à l'Eglise Réformée de Passy*. Paris: Je sers, 1939.
———. *La vie et la pensée de Tommy Fallot*. Vol. 1: *La préparation (1844–1872)*. Paris: Fischbacher, 1914. Vol. 2: *L'achèvement (1872–1904)*. Paris: Fischbacher, 1926.
———. *Les Églises protestantes pendant la guerre et l'occupation. Actes de l'Assemblée générale du protestantisme français réunie à Nîmes, du 22 au 26 octobre 1945*. Paris: Messagerie évangélique, 1946.
———. *L'exigence oecuménique. Souvenirs et perspectives*. Paris: Albin Michel, 1968.
Boegner, Philippe. *Carnets du pasteur Boegner (1940–1945)*. Paris: Fayard, 1992.
———. *'Ici on a aimé les juifs,' récit*. Paris: Lattès, 1982.
Bois, Henri. "La Conférence générale des 'Fraternités.' Londres, 16–19 septembre 1911." *RCS* 24 (1911) 707–25.
Boismorand, Pierre. *Magda et André Trocmé. Figures de résistances*. Paris: Cerf, 2007.
Boissonnas, Madame Georges [Gabrielle Boissonnas, née Rogier]. *Expériences d'un évangéliste*. Strasbourg–Paris: Oberlin, 1966.
Bolle, Pierre. "Charles Guillon." In *Le Plateau Vivarais-Lignon. Accueil et Résistance (1939-1944)*, edited by Pierre Bolle, 42–53. Le Chambon-sur-Lignon: Société d'histoire de la Montagne, 1992.
———. "Paris été 40. Journal d'un pasteur." *BSHPF* 127 (1981) 457–96.
———. *Le Plateau Vivarais-Lignon. Accueil et résistance (1939–1944)*. Le Chambon-sur-Lignon: Société d'histoire de la Montagne, 1992.
———. "Les protestants français et leurs Églises pendant la Second Guerre mondiale." *Revue d'histoire moderne et contemporaine* 26 (1979) 286–97.
———. "Les protestants et leurs églises devant la persécution des Juifs en France." *ETR* 57 (1982) 185–208.
———. "Les réfugiés d'Europe centrale et les protestants français (1933–1939)." In *De l'exil à la résistance. Réfugiés et immigrés d'Europe centrale en France (1933–1945)*, edited by Karel Bartosek et al., 61–65. Paris: Presses Universitaires de Vincennes et Arcantère, 1989.
———. "Les thèses de Pomeyrol." In *Spiritualité, théologie et résistance*, edited by Pierre Bolle and Jean Godel, 182–97. Grenoble: Presses universitaires de Grenoble, 1987.
———. with Pierre Petit. *La vie des églises protestantes dans la vallée de la Drôme de 1928 à 1938*. Paris: Les Bergers et les Mages, 1977.
Bollon, Gérard. "Contribution à l'histoire du Chambon-sur-Lignon: le foyer universitaire des Roches." *Cahiers de la Haute-Loire* 96 (1996) 1–31.
Bonar, Horatius. *A Cry from the Land of Calvin and Voltaire. Record of the McAll Mission*. London: Hodder and Soughton, 1887.
———. *The White Fields of France, or the Story of Mr. McAll's Mission to the Working Men of Paris and Lyons*. London: James Nisbet, 1879[1] (1880[2]).
Boulet, François. "Étrangers et Juifs en Haute-Loire de 1936 à 1944." *Cahiers de la Haute-Loire* (1992) 302–21.
———. *Histoire de la Montagne-refuge. Aux limites de la Haute-Loire et de l'Ardèche, de la Réforme protestante à la Seconde Guerre mondiale. Le Chambon-sur-Lignon, Tence, Fay-sur-Lignon, Saint-Agrève, Le Mazet-Saint-Voy et leurs environs*. Polignac: Roure, 2008.

Bredemeier, Karsten. *Kriegsdienstverweigerung im Dritten Reich. Ausgewählte Beispiele*, Baden-Baden: Nomos, 1991.

Brémond, Arnold. "Une explication du monde ouvrier. Enquête d'un étudiant-ouvrier dans la banlieue parisienne." *RCS* 40 (1927) 729–885.

Cabanel, Patrick. "Les courants pacifistes dans le protestantisme français, 1860–1944." In *De la guerre juste à la paix juste. Aspects confessionnels de la construction de la paix dans l'espace franco-allemand (XVIe–XXe siècle)*, edited by Jean-Paul Cahn et al., 161–76. Villeneuve d'Ascq: Presses Universitaires du Septentrion, 2008.

———. *Juifs et protestants en France. Les affinités électives (XVIe–XXIe siècle)*. Paris: Fayard, 2004.

———. with Laurent Gervereau. *La Deuxième Guerre mondiale, des terres de refuge aux musées*. Le Chambon-sur-Lignon: Sivom Vivarais–Lignon, 2003.

———. with Philippe Joutard. *Itinéraires protestants en Languedoc du XVIe au XXe siècle*. Vol. 2: *Espace gardois*. Montpellier: Presses du Languedoc, 2000.

———. "Le pasteur Jacques Martin, de l'objection de conscience à la résistance spirituelle à l'antisémitisme." *Archives juives* 40 (2007) 78–99.

———. "Veillée d'armes face à l'antisémitisme: le mouvement du christianisme social (1933–1940)." In *Cévennes. Terre de refuge 1940–1944*, edited by Philippe Joutard et al., 213–29. Montpellier: Presses du Languedoc, 2006[4].

Casalis, Georges. "La jeunesse protestante en 'zone non-occupée' (1940–1942)." In Xavier de Montclos et al., *Églises et chrétiens dans la IIe guerre mondiale*, vol. 2: *La France. Actes du Colloque national tenu à Lyon du 27 au 30 janvier 1978*, 101–15. Lyon: Presses Universitaires de Lyon, 1982.

Chaline, Nadine-Joseph. "Le catholicisme social dans le Nord au début du XXe siècle." *Revue du Nord* 73 (1991) 305–14.

Chalmel, Loïc. "Jean-Luc et Daniel Legrand, des relais essentiels." In *Oberlin. Le pasteur des Lumières*, 180–84 and 230–31. Strasbourg: La Nuée Bleue, 2006.

Chastand, Emmanuel. *Une belle aventure de la foi. La Mission Populaire Évangélique, Mission McAll*. Paris: Mission Populaire Évangélique, 1952.

———. "La Conférence Constituante des Fraternités françaises. Strasbourg, 25 Juin 1922 – église St. Nicolas." *RCS* 35 (1922) 520–30.

———. "Le Mouvement des Fraternités Françaises." *RCS* 35 (1922) 426–31.

Chevandier, Christian, and Gilles Morin. *André Philip, socialiste, patriote, chrétien. Colloque "Redécouvrir André Philip" tenu à l'Assemblée Nationale les 13 et 14 mars 2003*. Paris: Comité pour l'histoire économique et financière de la France, 2005.

Cholvy, Gérard. *Mouvements de jeunesse chrétiens et juifs. Sociabilité juvénile dans un cadre européen (1799–1968)*. Paris: Cerf, 1985.

Cohen, Asher. *Persécutions et sauvetages. Juifs et Français sous l'occupation et sous Vichy*. Paris: Cerf, 1993.

Congrès de l'Évangélisation. Paris, 19–25 Mai 1913. Paris: Société centrale évangélique, 1913.

Cooper, Sandi E., "Pacifism in France (1889–1914): International Peace as a Human Right." *French Historical Studies* 17 (1991) 359–86.

Crespin, Raoul. *Des protestants engagés. Le Christianisme social (1945–1970)*. Paris: Les Bergers et les Mages, 1993.

DeBerg, Betty. *Ungodly Women: Gender and the First Wave of American Fundamentalism*. Minneapolis: Fortress, 1990.

Debiève, Roger. *Mémoires meurtries, mémoire trahie: Le Chambon-sur-Lignon.* Paris: L'Harmattan, 1995.

De Félice, Théodore. "Essai démographique sur la commune protestante du Chambon-sur-Lignon." *RCS* 46 (1933) vol. 2, 38–47.

Deichmann Edwards, Wendy J., and Carolyn De Swarte Gifford. *Gender and the Social Gospel.* Urbana: University of Illinois, 2003.

Delmaire, Danielle, and Yves-Marie Hilaire. "Chrétiens et juifs dans le Nord–Pas-de-Calais pendant la Seconde Guerre mondiale." *Revue du Nord* 237 (1978) 451–60.

———. "Christianisme social dans le nord de la France, vers 1900. Eléments de recherche." *Revue du Nord* 73 (1991) 329–38.

De Montclos, Xavier, et al. *Églises et chrétiens dans la Deuxième guerre mondiale.* Vol. 1: *La région Rhône-Alpes. Actes du Colloque tenu à Grenoble du 7 au 9 octobre 1976.* Lyon: Presses Universitaires de Lyon, 1978.

———. *Églises et chrétiens dans la Deuxième Guerre mondiale.* Vol. 2: *La France. Actes du colloque tenu à Lyon du 27 au 30 janvier 1978.* Lyon: Presses universitaires de Lyon, 1982.

De Visme, Roger. "Notre méthode d'évangélisation en Pas-de-Calais." In *Congrès de l'Évangélisation. Paris, 19–25 Mai 1913,* 61–90. Paris: Société centrale évangélique, 1913.

De Vries, Minke. *Vers une gratuité féconde. L'expérience œcuménique de Granchamp.* Paris: Parole et silence, 2009.

Diebolt, Évelyne. "Femmes protestantes face aux politiques de santé publiques (1900–1939)." *BSHPF* 146 (2000) 91–132.

Dolléans, Édouard. "La vocation religieuse d'André Philip." *RCS* 51 (1938) 57–61.

Duke, David Nelson. *In the Trenches with Jesus and Marx: Harry F. Ward and the Struggle for Social Justice.* Tuscaloosa: University of Alabama Press, 2003.

Églises et chrétiens pendant la Seconde Guerre mondiale dans le Nord-Pas de Calais. Actes du colloque de Lille, 1977. In *Revue du Nord* 237–8 (1978) 225–465 and 473–741.

Encrevé, André. *Dictionnaire du monde religieux dans la France contemporaine.* Vol. 5: *Les Protestants.* Paris: Beauchesne, 1993.

———. "Les Protestants et la Commune de Paris en 1871." *RCS* 79 (1971) 368–417.

———. with Michel Richard. *Les Protestants dans les débuts de la Troisième République (1871–1885). Actes du colloque de Paris, 3–6 octobre 1978.* Paris: SHPF, 1979.

———. *Les Protestants en France de 1800 à nos jours. Histoire d'une réintegration.* Paris: Stock, 1985.

———. *Protestants français au milieu du XIXe siècle. Les réformés de 1848 à 1870.* Geneva: Labor & Fides, 1986.

———. with Jacques Poujol. *Les protestants français pendant la seconde guerre mondiale. Actes du colloque de Paris, Palais du Luxembourg, 19–21 novembre 1992.* Paris: SHPF, 1994.

Evans, Christopher H. *The Kingdom is Always but Coming. A Life of Walter Rauschenbusch.* Grand Rapids: Eerdmans, 2004.

Fabre, Rémi. "L'émergence d'un mouvement: les premiers camps de vacances de la F.F.A.C.E. (1906–1914)." In Gérard Cholvy, *Mouvements de jeunesse chrétiens et juifs. Sociabilité juvénile dans un cadre européen (1799–1968),* 141–60. Paris: Cerf, 1985.

———. "Les étudiants protestants face aux totalitarismes dans les années trente." *Revue d'histoire de l'Église de France* 191 (1987) 269–84.

———. "Les pacifismes protestants français de l'entre-deux guerres." In *Le pacifisme en Europe des années 1920 aux années 1950*, edited by Maurice Vaïsse, 237–56. Bruxelles: Bruylants, 1993.

Fallot, Tommy. *Christianisme social. Études et fragments*. Paris: Fischbacher, 1911.

———. *Les Fraternités de demain. Cinq discours à mes paroissiens*. Valence: Ducros, 1904.

———. *Les pauvres et l'Évangile. Thèse à la Faculté protestante de Théologie de Strasbourg*. Strasbourg: Silbermann–Fischbacher, 1872.

———. *Pour aider à l'organisation de l'effort missionnaire en France*. Valence: Ducros, 1899.

———. "Pourquoi je m'occupe des questions sociales." *Revue de théologie pratique et d'homilétique* 2 (1889) 61–72.

———. *La religion de la solidarité*. Paris: Fischbacher, 1908.

Farrugia, Peter. "French Religious Opposition to War, 1919–1939. The Contribution of Henri Roser and Marc Sangier." *French History* 6 (1992) 278–302.

Fath, Sébastien. *Du ghetto au réseau. Le protestantisme évangélique en France (1800–2008)*. Geneva: Labor & Fides, 2005.

———. *Le protestantisme évangélique, un christianisme de conversion. Entre ruptures et filiations. Actes du colloque international organisé à Paris (Iresco, EPHE Sorbonne) par le Groupe de Sociologie des Religions et de la Laïcité (EPHE/CNRS) du 14 au 16 mai 2002*. Turnhout: Brepols, 2004.

———. "Rassembler ou multiplier? Le prophétisme des réveils de Drôme et d'Ardèche au début des années 1930." *BSHPF* 148 (2002) 217–33.

Fayol, Pierre. *Le Chambon-sur-Lignon sous l'Occupation (1940–1944). Les résistances locales, l'aide interalliée, l'action de Virginia Hall (O.S.S.)*. Paris: L'Harmattan, 1990.

Fivaz-Silbermann, Ruth. "Le sauvetage clandestin des enfants juifs à travers la frontière genevoise." In *Espaces savoyards: frontières et découpages. Actes du 39e congrès des sociétés savantes de Savoie. Archamps, 14 et 15 septembre 2002*, 171–81. Archamps: La Salévienne, 2004.

Flaud, Annick, and Gérard Bollon. *Paroles de Réfugiés. Paroles de Justes. La Montagne dans la guerre, terre d'exil, terre d'asile autour du Chambon-sur-Lignon*. Le Cheylard: Dolmazon, 2009.

Forsythe Fishburn, Janet. *The Fatherhood of God and the Victorian Family. The Social Gospel in America*. Philadelphia: Fortress, 1981.

Freychet, Yves. "Sully (1933–1944). Analyse politique d'un périodique protestant et monarchiste." In *Les protestants français pendant la seconde guerre mondiale*, edited by André Encrevé and Jacques Poujol, 469–78. Paris: SHPF, 1994.

Gagnebin, Laurent. *Christianisme social et christianisme spirituel. La prédication de Wilfred Monod (1894–1940)*. Geneva: Labor & Fides, 1987.

Gambarotto, Laurent. *Foi et patrie. La prédication du protestantisme français pendant la Première Guerre mondiale*. Geneva: Labor & Fides, 1996.

Gerdes, Uta. *Ökumenische Solidarität mit christlichen und jüdischen Verfolgten. Die Cimade in Vichy-Frankreich 1940–1944*. Göttingen: Vandenhœck & Ruprecht, 2005.

Gide, Charles, et al. *Le Congrès du Christianisme social, tenu à Strasbourg. Premier congrès de la Fédération protestante du christianisme social, 17e assemblée générale, 25–28 juin 1922*. Saint-Étienne: Bureau du Christianisme social, 1923.

Gounelle, Élie. *L'agnosticisme de M. Herbert Spencer. Étude critique.* Montauban: Granié, 1889.
———. "L'aventure prodigieuse du racisme hitlérien." *RCS* 46 (1933) 151–58.
———. "La Conférence constituante de Constance (1er–2 août 1914)." *RCS* 33 (1920) 638–47.
———. "Le Congrès du Chambon et le Mouvement du Christianisme Social." *RCS* 46 (1933) 245–51.
———. "Une Consultation théologique, à propos de l'Objection de conscience." *RCS* 48 (1935) 216–25.
———. "La conversion et la question sociale." *RCS* 7 (1894) 245–67.
———. "La défense du droit en cas d'agression. Une autre affirmation de l'esprit." *RCS* 43 (1930) 6.
———. "L'Église n'a ni le droit ni le pouvoir d'exclure les objecteurs." *RCS* 47 (1934) 483–86.
———. "La Fédération des P.S.A. Brotherhoods." *L'Avant-Garde* (August 15, 1908).
———. "Fondons des Fraternités." *Bulletin de la Fédération des Fraternités Françaises*, nr. 5 (May 1925) 3–4.
———. "Hommage à Tommy Fallot." *RCS* 17 (1904) 465–82.
———. *Mission chrétienne sociale de Roubaix et de Lille.* Vals-les-Bains: Aberlen, 1899.
———. "Une Mission chrétienne-sociale à Lille et à Roubaix." *RCS* 12 (1899) 197–211.
———. *Le Mouvement des Fraternités. Travail présenté au 'Congrès constituant de l'Action chrétienne sociale,' tenu à Saint-Quentin, les 25 et 26 Juin 1911; et à Messieurs les Membres de la Commission protestante évangélique d'action morale et sociale.* Vals-les-Bains: Aberlen, 1911.
———. "Le Pasteur Louis Comte, pionner du Christianisme social et de la Moralité publique et bienfaiteur de l'Enfance." *RCS* 39 (1926) 572–646.
———. "Pour Philippe Vernier and Jacques Martin." *RCS* 48 (1935) 111.
———. *Pourquoi sommes-nous Chrétiens Sociaux? Coup d'oeil historique, religieux et économique sur le Christianisme social français.* Saint-Blaise-Roubaix: Foyer solidariste de librairie et d'édition, 1909.
———. "Le premier congrès de 'L'Étoile blanche.' Roubaix, 15 juillet 1899." *RCS* 12 (1899) 289–94.
———. "Le premier Congrès des Fraternités à Roubaix (5–8 Mai)." *RCS* 36 (1923) 403–11.
———. "Christianisme social et Royaume de Dieu." *RCS* 45 (1932) 39–49.
———. "Réflexions sur la situation présente. Tribune libre: l'objection de conscience. Le cas de Jacques Martin." *RCS* 45 (1932) 253–57.
———. "Réforme sociale et réveil religieux." *RCS* 7 (1894) 22–51.
———. "La repentance sociale." *RCS* 7 (1894) 333–49.
———. "Réponse à quelques bienveillantes critiques de M. Maury sur l'œuvre des Solidarités du Nord." *L'Avant-Garde* (June 15, 1901).
Grotefeld, Stefan, *Friedrich Siegmund-Schultze. Ein deutscher Ökumeniker und christlicher Pazifist.* Gütersloh: Chr. Kaiser, 1995.
Grynberg, Anne. *Les camps de la honte. Les internés juifs des camps français (1939–1944).* Paris: La Découverte, 1992².
Guillon, Charles. "Le Plateau de la Haute-Loire." *RCS* 40 (1927) 221–28.
Halle, Gerhard. "Confession." *CR* (November 1932) 2–6.

Hallie, Philip. *Lest Innocent Blood Be Shed. The Story of the Village of Le Chambon and How Goodness Happened There.* New York: Harper & Row, 1979 (1994).

Harismendy, Patrick. "Les chrétiens-sociaux (1930–1939)." In *Les protestants français pendant la Seconde Guerre mondiale. Actes du colloque de Paris, Palais du Luxembourg, 19–21 novembre 1992*, edited by André Encrevé and Jacques Poujol, 57–72. Paris: SHPF, 1994.

———. "Les intellectuels protestants français dans les années 20." In *Intellectuels chrétiens et esprit des années 1920. Actes du colloque. Institut catholique de Paris, 23–24 septembre 1993*, edited by Pierre Colin, 51–82. Paris: Cerf, 1977.

Hartmann, Albrecht, and Hartmann, Heidi. *Kriegsdienstverweigerung im Dritten Reich.* Frankfurt: Haag-Herchen, 1986.

Henry, Patrick. *We Only Know Men. The Rescue of Jews in France During the Holocaust.* Washington: Catholic University of America Press, 2007.

Heuzé, Marcel. "Rouen - The Impressions of a Licentiate." *AMR* 41 (May 1923) 22–24.

Hilaire, Yves-Marie. "Les ouvriers de la région du Nord devant l'Église catholique (XIXe et XXe siècles)." *Le Mouvement Social* 57 (1966) 181–201.

Houghton, Louise Seymour. *Handbook of French and Belgian Protestantism.* New York: Federal Council of the Churches of Christ in America-Missionary Education Movement, 1919.

———. "The Mission Populaire of France. Known as the McAll Mission." *Methodist Review Quarterly* 64 (1915) 644–64.

Ingram, Norman. *The Politics of Dissent. Pacifism in France (1919–1939).* Oxford: Clarendon, 1991.

Joas, Hans. *The Genesis of Values.* Chicago: University of Chicago Press, 2000.

Jones, Peter d'Alroy. *The Christian Socialist Revival (1877–1914).* Princeton: Princeton University Press, 1968.

Joutard, Philippe, et al. *Cévennes. Terre de refuge 1940–1944.* Montpellier: Presses du Languedoc, 2006[4] (1987[1].)

———. *La légende des camisards. Une sensibilité au passé.* Paris: Gallimard, 1977.

Kaltenbach, Jacques. "Le camp de Camprieu." *Le Semeur* 10 (1907–1908) 56–65.

———. "L'Église locale et le poste d'évangélisation." In *Congrès de l'Évangélisation. Paris, 19–25 Mai 1913*, 99–119. Paris: Société centrale évangélique, 1913.

———. *L'Église réformée de Saint-Quentin pendant la guerre.* Marseille: Barlatier, 1919.

———. *L'étude personnelle de la Bible.* Paris: Comité national des Unions chrétiennes de jeunes gens, 1912.

———. *Étude psychologique des plus anciens réveils religieux aux États-Unis.* Geneva: W. Kündig & Fils, 1905.

———. "Les Étudiants Chrétiens à l'Université de Harvard." *Foi et Vie* 7 (1904) 275–76.

———. *Les protestants sur les galères et dans les cachots de Marseille de 1545 à 1750.* Marseille: Église réformée, 1953.

Kneubühler, Pierre. *Henri Roser. L'enjeu d'une terre nouvelle.* Paris: Les Bergers et les Mages, 1992.

Lazare, Lucien. *Le Livre des Justes.* Paris: Lattès, 1993.

———. *Dictionnaire des Justes de France.* Paris-Jérusalem: Fayard-Yad Vashem, 2003.

Le Forestier, Jean-Philippe. "Roger Le Forestier, mon père." In *Les Résistances sur le Plateau Vivarias-Lignon (1938–1945). Témoins, témoignages et lieux de mémoires. Les oubliés de l'histoire parlent*, 116–35. Polignac: Éditions du Roure, 2005.

Maarten, Johan. *Le village sur la montagne. Tableau de l'église fidèle sous le régime nazi.* Geneva–Paris: Labor–'Je Sers', 1939 (Paris: Les Bergers et les Mages, 1999).

Maillebouis, Christian. *La montagne protestante. Pratiques chrétiennes-sociales dans la région du Mazet-Saint-Voy (1920–1940).* Lyon: Olivétan, 2005.

Marrus, Michaël R., and Robert O. Paxton. *Vichy France and the Jews.* New York: Basic Books, 1981 (*Vichy et les Juifs.* Paris: Calmann-Lévy, 1981).

Martin, Jacques. *Élie Gounelle. Apôtre et inspirateur du Christianisme social.* Paris: L'Harmattan, 1999.

Mayeur, Jean-Marie, et al. *Dictionnaire du monde religieux dans la France contemporaine.* Vol. 4: *Lille–Flandres,* Paris–Lille: Beauchesne–Centre d'histoire de la région du Nord et de l'Europe du Nord-Ouest (Université Charles de Gaulle–Lille III), 1990.

[McAll, Elizabeth.] *R. W. McAll, Founder of the McAll Mission, Paris. A Fragment by Himself, a Souvenir by his Wife.* London: The Religious Tract Society, 1896 (*La vie et l'œuvre de Robert-W. Mac-All, fondateur de la Mission populaire évangélique de France. Fragments et souvenirs rassemblés par Mme Mac-All, traduits et complétés par son ami Eug. Réveillaud.* Paris: Fischbacher, 1898).

The McAll Mission in France (Mission Populaire Évangélique de France). [28th–33rd annual reports] Paris, Office of the Mission, 1900–1905.

Mehl, Roger. *Le pasteur Marc Boegner (1881–1970). Une humble grandeur.* Paris: Plon, 1987.

Ménégoz, Eugène. "Un côté faible du Christianisme Social." *Revue chrétienne* 50 (1903) 161–78.

Merle d'Aubigné, Jeanne, et al. *Les clandestins de Dieu. Cimade (1939–1945).* Geneva: Labor & Fides, 1989 (1968[1]). ET: *God's Underground. Accounts of the Activity of the French Protestant Church During the German Occupation of the Country in World War II.* Trans. William and Patricia Nottingham. Saint Louis: Bethany Press, 1970.

Miller, Robert Moats. *Harry Emerson Fosdick. Preacher, Pastor, Prophet.* Oxford–New York: Oxford University Press, 1985.

Monnier, Henri. *Daniel Le Grand et la législation internationale du travail.* Paris: Société générale d'impression, 1908.

———. *Édouard Monnier (1829–1900). Souvenirs de sa vie et de son œuvre.* Paris: Fischbacher, 1904.

———. "Sur l'objection de conscience." *Le Semeur* (July 1, 1934) 571–88.

Monod, Paul. "Visite des 'Fraternités' anglaises à Lille. Une prophétie." *RCS* 23 (1910) 369–74.

Monod, Wilfred. *Après la journée. Souvenirs et visions (1867–1937).* Paris: Grasset, 1938.

———. *Les bases psychologiques du dogme de la rédemption.* Montauban: Granier, 1891.

———. *Comment on devient chrétien social.* Paris: Fischbacher, 1914.

———. "L'Église et l'Objection de Conscience." *RCS* 46 (1933) 192–210.

———. *L'espérance chrétienne. Le Roi.* Vals-les-Bains: Aberlen, 1899.

———. *L'espérance chrétienne. Le Royaume.* Vals-les-Bains: Aberlen, 1901.

———. "Que signifie le Message à la Chrétienté? L'Église' et le 'Royaume de Dieu' à Stockholm." *RCS* 38 (1925) 866–908.

———. "La SDN et le Royaume de Dieu." *Foi et Vie* 15–16 (Sept. 1922) 253–88.

———. *La Solidarité de Rouen. Les buts et les principes de l'œuvre.* Rouen: Blondel, 1900.

Monsieur Nick. Cinquante-sept ans d'une vie dans un faubourg ouvrier de Fives–Lille (1897–1954). Paris: Mission populaire évangélique de France, 1982.
Morley, Jean-Paul. *La mission populaire (1871–1984). Les surprises d'un engagement.* Paris: Les Bergers et les Mages, 1993.
Mours, Samuel. *Le protestantisme en Vivarais et en Velay*. Valence: Imprimeries réunies, 1949.
———. *Un siècle d'évangélisation en France (1815–1914)*. Vol. 2: *1871–1914*. Flavion: Éditions de la librairie des éclaireurs unionistes, 1964.
Munos-du Peloux, Odile. *Passer en Suisse. Les passages clandestins entre la Haute-Savoie et la Suisse (1940–1944)*. Grenoble: Presses universitaires de Grenoble, 2002.
Neury, Laurent. "La banalité du bien. Devenir passeur de Juifs à la frontière franco-suisse (1939–1945)." *Relations internationales* 118 (2004) 169–84.
Nick, Hélène. "Du rôle social de la jeune fille, ou la jeune fille et la question sociale." *RCS* 12 (1899) 336–47.
Nick, Henri. "L'anniversaire des Fraternités." *Bulletin de la Fédération des Fraternités Françaises* nr. 9 (1926) 2.
———. "Autre son de cloche: Généreuse protestation de M. le pasteur H. Nick, au Conseil de la Fédération protestante de France." *RCS* 36 (1923) 346–49.
———. "Congrès abolitionniste de Genève." *RCS* 12 (1899) 429–36.
———. "Difficultés spéciales de l'Évangélisation de la classe ouvrière. Comment entrer en contact avec les ouvriers? Comment assurer le progrès d'une œuvre parmi les ouvriers tout en maintenant son contact avec le milieu?" In *Congrès de l'Évangélisation. Paris, 19–25 Mai 1913*, 17–46. Paris: Société centrale évangélique, 1913.
———. *Evangelization in Northern France*. Philadelphia: American McAll Association, 1906.
———. "Fives-Lille, 1919–1920. A Brief Resumé of the Year's Work." *AMR* 39, nr. 1 (1920) 7–11.
———. with Élie Gounelle and Emmanuel Chastand, "Formons le faisceau! Fédérons les Fraternités françaises!" *RCS* 35 (1922) 432–35.
———. "Le général Booth." *RCS* 25 (1912) 541–50 and 637–49.
———. "Guerre et Fraternité." *Bulletin de la Fédération des Fraternités Françaises* nr. 2 (April 1923) 3.
———. *Notion de la metanoia d'après le Nouveau Testament et l'expérience chrétienne. Thèse publiquement défendue devant la Faculté de théologie protestante de Montauban en juillet 1890*. Montauban: Granié, 1890.
———. *Parmi les ouvriers*. Saint-Blaise-Roubaix: Foyer solidariste de librairie et d'édition [no date].
———. "Pastor Nick Tells of the Work at Fives-Lille." *AMR* 42, nr. 2 (1924) 16–22.
———. *Pendant la guerre. Abstinents et abstinence anti-alcoolique*, Paris: Agence de la Croix Bleue, 1920.
———. "Le pionnier de Roubaix." *RCS* 60 (1952) 112–15.
———. "Remontons à la source." *L'Espoir du Monde* 2, nr. 8 (1909) 125–27.
Nick, Jeanne. "Un hôpital-école en région libérée." *RCS* 35 (1922) 362–63.
———. "Lille in the Early Days of Peace." *AMR* 37, nr. 2 (1919) 9–11.
Nusslé, Henri. "In Northern France. A History of the Foyer du Peuple at Fives-Lille." *AMR* 41, nr. 1 (1923) 21–25; 41, nr. 2 (1923) 10–17.

Offenstadt, Nicolas. *Les fusillés de la Grande Guerre et la mémoire collective (1914–1999)*. Paris: Odile Jacob, 1999.

Peschanski, Denis. *La France des camps. L'internement (1938–1946)*. Paris: Gallimard, 2002.

Pfender, René. "Le Bassin Houiller du Pas-de-Calais." In *Congrès de l'Évangélisation. Paris, 19–25 Mai 1913*, 47–60. Paris: Société centrale évangélique, 1913.

Philip, André. *Le christianisme et la paix*. Paris: Je sers, 1932.

———. *Socialisme et christianisme*. Paris: Fédération des socialistes chrétiens, 1934.

Phillips, Paul T. *A Kingdom on Earth. Ango-American Social Christianity (1880–1940)*. University Park: Pennsylvania State University Press, 1996.

Pierrard, Pierre. *L'Église et les ouvriers de France (1840–1940)*. Paris: Hachette, 1984.

———. *Lille. Dix siècles d'histoire*. Lille: Arctica, 1972.

Poujol, Geneviève. *Une féminisme sous tutelle. Les protestantes françaises (1810–1960)*. Paris: Éditions de Paris-Max Chaleil, 2003.

———. "Présences protestantes." In *Les centre sociaux (1880–1980). Une résolution locale de la question sociale?*, edited by Dominique Dessertine et al., 63–73. Villeneuve d'Ascq: Presses universitaires du Septentrion, 2004.

———. "Les Unions chrétiennes de jeunes filles (1891–1920)." *BSHPF* 143 (1997) 335–69.

Poujol, Jacques. "André Philip, les années de guerre (1939–1945)." *BSHPF* 138 (1992) 181–241.

———. "Documents et pistes de recherches sur les protestants de zone occupée pendant la Seconde Guerre mondiale." *BSHPF* 139 (1993) 391–498.

———. *Protestants dans la France en guerre (1939–1945). Dictionnaire thématique et biographique*. Paris: Les Éditions de Paris, 2000.

Quiévreux, Aquilas. "Le Congrès de Rouen." *RCS* 14 (1901) 485–98.

———. with Élie Gounelle. *Guerre à l'immoralité! Un projet d'action morale*. Vals-les-Bains: Aberlen, 1899.

Ragaz, Leonhard. [Report on the conference of IFoR in Bad Boll.] *Neue Wege* 18 (Sept. 1924) 387–92.

Rauschenbusch, Walter. *Christianizing the Social Order*. New York: MacMillan, 1912.

Ricœur, Paul. "André Philip, économiste, protestant et socialiste." In *André Philip, socialiste, patriote, chrétien. Colloque 'Redécouvrir André Philip' tenu à l'Assemblée nationale les 13 et 14 mars 2003*, edited by Christian Chevandier and Gilles Morin, 1–2. Paris: Ministère de l'Économie, des Finances et de l'Industrie, 2005.

———. "Le Yogi, le Commissaire, le Prolétaire et le Prophète. À propos de 'Humanisme et Terreur' de Maurice Merleau-Ponty." *RCS* 57 (1949) 41–54.

Rivet, Victor. "L'individualisme social de Vinet." *RCS* 11 (1898) 77–96.

Robert, Daniel. *Les Églises réformées en France (1800–1830)*. Paris: PUF, 1961.

———. with Samuel Mours. *Le protestantisme en France du 18e siècle à nos jours (1685–1970)*. Paris: Librairie protestante, 1972.

———. "Les protestants français et la guerre de 1914–1918." *Francia* (1974) 415–30.

Rochefort, Florence. "The Abolitionist Struggle of Pastor Tommy Fallot. Between Social Christianity, Feminism and Secularism (1882–1893)." *Women's History Review* 17 (2008) 179–94.

Roger, Jean-Pierre. *De la pierre polie à nos jours. Liévin (-3000 – +2000)*. Liévin: Imprimerie artésienne, 1970.

Roser, Henri. "Affirmation de Conscience." *Bulletin de la Fédération Française des Fraternités* nr. 16 (1929) 16–18.

———. "Le Congrès du Mouvement international de la Réconciliation (Lyon, 2–9 août)." *RCS* 42 (1929) 955–58.

———. "L'objection de conscience, affirmation de l'esprit." *RCS* 43 (1930) 2–4.

———. "La Réconciliation de 1923 à 1944." *CR* 50 (January 1983) 2–9.

———. "Vacation Colonies—Their Real Value. Report of the Colony at Aubengue in 1922 (Boys from Fives–Lille and Amiens)." *AMR* 41, nr. 3 (1923) 6–8.

Roussel, Bernard. "R. W. McAll, évangéliste auprès des prolétaires parisiens, entre la légende et l'histoire: le 18 août 1871." *RHPR* 61 (1981) 389–411.

Ryan, Donna F. "Vichy and the Jews. The Example of Marseille (1939–1944)." PhD diss., Georgetown University, 1984.

Schenkel, Albert F. *The Rich Man and the Kingdom. John D. Rockefeller, Jr. and the Protestant Establishment*. Minneapolis: Fortress, 1995.

Schloesing, Émile, et al., *Le centenaire de la Société Chrétienne du Nord (1843–1943)*. Saint-Quentin, 1–2 mai 1943. Le Cateau: E. Roland et Delcroix, 1943.

Sémelin, Jacques. *Sans armes face à Hitler. La Résistance civile en Europe (1939–1943)*. Paris: Payot, 1989.

Sibleyras, Adolphe. "Les débuts de l'Association protestante pour l'étude pratique des questions sociales." *RCS* 52 (1939) vol. 1, 86–104.

Smith, Timothy L., *Revivalism and Social Reform. American Protestantism on the Eve of the Civil War*. Baltimore-London: Abingdon, 1957 (New York: Harper & Row, 1965.)

Smyth-Florentin, Françoise. *Pierre Maury, prédicateur d'Évangile*. Geneva: Labor & Fides, 2009.

Spiero, Claude. *Innocents et pourchassés. Histoire d'une famille juive dans la tourmente*. Société des écrivains, 2001.

Stevenson, Lilian. *Towards a Christian International. The Story of the International Fellowship of Reconciliation*. London: International Fellowship of Reconciliation, 1941³ (1929¹).

Stott, George Raymond. "The History of the Modern Pentecostal Movement in France." PhD diss., Texas Tech University, 1973.

Suchon, Sandrine. *Résistance et liberté. Dieulefit. 1940–1944*. Die: Éditions A Die, 1994.

Thonger, William G. "Le premier Congrès international des Fraternités." *RCS* 33 (Dec. 1919) 36–37.

"Tommy Fallot: Notes, impressions, souvenirs." *Le Semeur* (May 15, 1905).

Travaux du congrès de Genève, 12e assemblée générale de l'Association protestante pour l'étude pratique des questions sociales, 19–22 juin 1906. Paris: Fischbacher, 1906.

Travaux du congrès du Havre. Cinquième assemblée générale de l'Association protestante pour l'étude pratique des questions sociales, 7 et 8 juin 1893. Paris: Fischbacher, 1894.

Travaux du congrès de Marseille. Quatrième assemblée générale de l'Association protestante pour l'étude pratique des questions sociales, 29 et 30 octobre 1891. Paris: Fischbacher, 1892.

Travaux du congrès de Nîmes, 9e assemblée générale de l'Association protestante pour l'étude pratique des questions sociales, 13–15 mars 1900. Paris: Fischbacher, 1900.

Travaux du congrès de Paris, 13e assemblée générale de l'Association protestante pour l'étude pratique des questions sociales, 18–20 juin 1908. Paris: Fischbacher, 1908.

Travaux du congrès de Roubaix, dixième assemblée générale de l'Association protestante pour l'étude pratique des questions sociales, 21–22 octobre 1902. Paris: Fischbacher, 1902.

Travaux de la deuxième assemblée générale de l'Association protestante pour l'étude pratique des questions sociales, Lyon, 11, 12, 13 novembre 1889. Paris: Fischbacher, 1890.

Travaux de la troisième assemblée générale de l'Association protestante pour l'étude pratique des questions sociales, Montbéliard, 14–15–16 juillet 1890. Paris: Fischbacher, 1891.

Trocmé, André. "Le chrétien et les haines politiques." *CR* (Dec. 1937) 8–11; (March-April 1938) 12–28.

———. "Deux valent mieux qu'un." *ÉM* 28, nr. 3 (Feb. 1936) 1.

———. "Henri Nick." *RCS* 62 (1954) 336–37.

———. *Jésus et la révolution non-violente.* Geneva: Labor & Fides, 1961. (*Jesus and the Nonviolent Revolution.* Trans. Charles E. Moore. Maryknoll: Orbis, 2003).

———. "Un pont de bonne volonté. France–Afrique du Nord." *RCS* 63 (1955) 493–507.

———. "La Réconciliation depuis la guerre." *CR* (November 1960) 12–20.

———. "Le Scandale de la Ferme-Ecole." *ÉM* 37, nr. 1 (Christmas 1944–January 1945) 4.

———. "Les tâches actuelles des Églises pour la paix." *RCS* 55 (1947) 256–77.

Trocmé, Hélène. "Un modèle américain transposé: les foyers du soldat de l'union franco-américaine (1914–1922)." In *Les Américains et la France (1917–1947), Engagements et représentations*, edited by François Cochet et al., 5–23. Paris: Maisonneuve et Larose, 1999.

Vallée, Charles. "Solidarité de Roubaix." *L'Avant-Garde* (December 15, 1902).

Vermeil, André. "Entreprises communes." In *La vie des Églises protestantes de la vallée de la Drôme de 1928 à 1938. Actes du colloque tenu à la Faculté de théologie de Montpellier du 25 au 28 avril 1974*, edited by Pierre Bolle and Pierre Petit, 101–13. Paris: Les Bergers et les Mages, 1977.

Vernier, Philippe. "Avez-vous connu. . . le pasteur Henri Nick?" *Le Christianisme au XXe siècle* (July 14, 1960) 334.

Vernier-Escande, Lucie. *Infirmières et pionnières: Thérèse Matter (1887–1975), Eva Durrleman (1891–1993). Deux vies. . . une œuvre. . .* Le Fontanil-Cornillon: Alzieu, 2000.

Vincent, Gilbert. "The Engagement of Protestantism in Solidarism." *Ethical Theory and Moral Practice* 4 (2001) 401–21.

Wallis, Jill. *Valiant for Peace. A History of the Fellowship of Reconciliation (1914 to 1989).* London: Fellowship of Reconciliation, 1991.

Ward, Reginald W. "The Way of the World: The Rise and Decline of Protestant Social Christianity in Britain." *Kirchliche Zeitgeschichte* 1 (1988) 293–305.

Ward, William. *Brotherhood and Democracy.* Birmingham: Eld & Blackham, [1910].

———. "Les 'Fraternités' de Grande-Bretagne." *RCS* 22 (1909) 157–66.

Weiss, Raymond. *Daniel Le Grand (1783–1859). Son œuvre sociale et internationale.* Paris: Marcel Rivière, 1926.

Wells, Samuel. *Transforming Fate into Destiny. The Theological Ethics of Stanley Hauerwas.* Carlisle: Paternoster, 1998

Winter, Thomas. *Making Men, Making Class. The YMCA and Workingmen (1877–1920).* Chicago: University of Chicago Press, 2002.

Wolterstorff, Nicholas. *Justice in Love*. Grand Rapids–Cambridge: Eerdmans, 2011.
Yagil, Limore. *Chrétiens et Juifs sous Vichy (1940–1944). Sauvetage et désobéissance civile*. Paris: Cerf, 2005.
———. *La France, terre de refuge et de désobéissance civile (1936–1944)*. 3 vols. Paris: Cerf, 2010–2011.
Zasloff, Tela. *A Rescuer's Story. Pastor Pierre-Charles Toureille in Vichy France*. Madison: University of Wisconsin Press, 2003.

Index Nominum

NB: the names of Henri Nick and André Trocmé are not included

Aeschimann, Albert, 70, 99
Aeschimann, André, 118
Albaric, Maurice, 170
Allier, Raoul, 31
Amiotte-Suchet, Laurent, 105
Andrieu, Claire, 143
Anet, Henri, 31
Appel, Rudy, 156–57
Ayles, Walter, 79–80
Aymard, Mr. and Mrs., 164
Azéma, Jean-Pierre, 141

Babut, Charles, 31
Babut, Henry, 31, 64
Babut, Jacques, 70–71, 78, 90, 92, 101–2, 106, 115, 127, 135
Bach, Robert, 141–42, 148–50
Balter, Jacques, 166
Barde, Paul, 52, 72, 91, 97–98
Barot, Madeleine, 139–41, 158, 183, 186
Barth, Karl, 76–77, 84, 102, 107, 115, 170, 187
Bass, Joseph, 154–55
Batten, Alicia J., 146
Baubérot, Jean, 13, 19, 26–27, 29, 31, 34, 36, 64, 170
Bédarida, Renée, 136
Benoit, Jean-Paul, 70, 103
Berman, Léon, 163
Bertrand, Louis, 123
Besin, Suzanne, 135, 163–64

Beskow, Natanael, 81
Bettex, André, 155, 183
Beuve-Méry, Hubert, 135, 173
Bion, Pierre, 97
Biville, Raoul, 33
Blackham, John, 32
Blanc, Maurice, 166
Blanc, Philippe, 166
Blum, Léon, 135
Blumhardt, Christoph, 79–80
Blumhardt, Johann Christoph, 13–14, 79–80
Boegner, Marc, 13–15, 17, 22, 38, 111–12, 118, 132–33, 137, 140–42, 148–49, 157–58, 183, 189
Boegner, Philippe, 140, 142, 147–48, 157–58
Bohny, August, 138, 148, 155–56, 160, 162, 183
Bois, Henri, 35
Bois, Jacques (?), 170
Boismorand, Pierre, 125, 136, 150, 170, 172, 174–75, 189
Boissonnas, Georges, 23, 97–99
Bolle, Pierre, xvi, 91, 107, 125, 137, 144–45, 148, 154–55, 186
Bollon, Gérard, xvi, 139–40, 142, 147–49, 154–55, 166
Bollon, L., 127
Bonifas, Aimé, 167
Bonte, Florimond, 99–100
Booth, William, 8

Index Nominum

Bosc, Mr., 152
Boulet, François, xvi, 125, 130, 132, 134–35, 138–39, 141–43, 145, 147, 149, 155, 159, 162, 186
Boumédiène, Houari, 173
Bousquet, René, 148, 157
Boyve, Édouard de, 19, 31
Braemer, Henri, 138
Bredemeier, Karsten, 110
Brémond, Arnold, 93, 104, 127
Bresch, Jean, 113
Bretegnier, Léon, 90
Bucke, Emory Stevens, 175
Bugajski, David, 164
Bury, Charles, 167
Butler, Josephine, 15, 27
Butte, Antoinette, 131, 154

Cabanel, Patrick, xvi, 63, 111–12, 139, 143, 160, 189
Cadier, Jean, 118
Calvin, Jean, 2, 127, 144
Carrière, Georges, 24
Casalis, Georges, 158
Casalis, Roger, 115, 118, 121–23, 127
Catrice, abbé Paul, 163
Cérésole, Pierre, 80, 138, 173
Cerisier, E., 31
Chabut, Mr., 152
Chalmel, Loïc, 13
Chalmers, Burns, 137
Chapal, Odette, 155
Chapal, Paul, 155
Charreyron, Gilles, 139
Chastand, Emmanuel, 92, 113–14, 166
Chastand, Gédéon, 12, 31, 42, 114
Chaudier, Albert, 148
Chéradame, Daniel, 70–71, 91, 102, 104, 107, 163
Chéradame, Robert, 70–71, 101–3, 107, 114, 127, 163
Chouraqui, André, 175
Christen, Marcel, 86
Coe, George Albert, 53, 82
Comte, Louis, 17, 19, 31, 126, 145
Conord, Paul, 91, 94, 127
Cornier, Samuel, 70–74, 76, 79, 90, 92, 103, 106–7, 166–67

Couchoud, Paul-Louis, 103
Coutris, André, 120
Couve, Jean-Baptiste, 71, 101
Crombez, Jean, 164
Cullmann, Oscar, 174
Curtet, Daniel, 144, 155, 183
Curtet, Suzanne, 155
Cyboulle, Mlle, 25

Daggers, Jenny, 182
Dallière, Louis, 71, 166
Darby, John Nelson, 137
Darcissac, Roger, 127, 147–48, 151, 183
Davaine, Édmond, 8
de Boyve: see under "Boyve"
Decoppet, Auguste, 66
de Gaulle, Charles, 135, 142, 172
Deichmann Edwards, Wendy J., 186
Dejarnac, Jules, 31
Delanno, 127
Delaporte, André, 48, 56
Delaporte, Maurice, 56
Delattre, Samuel, 31
de Lattre de Tassigny, Jean, 159
Delmaire, Danielle, 162–65
Delory, Gustave, 33
Delpech, François, 140
de Pressensé: see under "Pressensé"
Deransart, 103
Deschamps, Jean, 159
Dickinson, Willoughby H., 69
Diebolt, Évelyne, 95
Diény, Jacques, 56–57, 69–71, 78, 92, 135, 179
Dieterlen, Christophe, 13–14
Dieterlen, Robert (?), 31
Dolléans, Édouard, 113
Dominicé, Max, 174
Donadille, Marc, 139
Dryer, Oliver, 77, 80, 89
Ducros, Pierre, 70–71, 127, 170
Duhamel, Georges, 172
Duke, David Nelson, 82
Dumas, Louise (née Trocmé), 73
Durand, André, 90
Durand, Émile, 31, 37, 42
Durand-Gasselin, Pierre, 121

Index Nominum

Durrelman, Eva, 95
Durrleman, Freddy, 31, 36, 38, 41, 66, 95, 99

Eichmann, Adolf, 140
Encrevé, André, 52, 70, 126, 141, 143, 167
Estoppey, Henri, 151
Évrard, Édmond, 101

Fabre, Émile, 70-71, 90, 96, 98-100, 127
Fabre, Louis, 9
Fabre, Rémi, 93
Fabreguettes, Polydore, 116
Fallot, Jenni, 111
Fallot, Louis, 13
Fallot, Tommy, 12-19, 22, 27, 30, 35-36, 44, 63, 67, 83-84, 111-12, 126, 182, 186
Fargues, Paul, 31
Farrugia, Peter, 112
Fath, Sébastien, 31, 39, 105
Fayol, Pierre, 155
Félice, Marguertie de, 130
Félice, Théodore de, 126
Ferrière, Louis (?), 31
Finet, Albert, 119-21
Finney, Charles, 8
Fivaz-Silbermann, Ruth, 155
Flaud, Annick, 143, 156
Folliet, abbé, 155
Forsythe Fischburn, Janet, 186
Fosdick, Harry Emerson, 88-89
Freychet, Yves, 143
Frommel, Gaston, 82
Fulliquet, Georges, 31

Galland, Pierre, 155
Gandhi, Mohandas Karamchand, 89, 113
Gauthier, René, 179
Gerdes, Uta, 139, 141
Geymonat, Paolo, 86
Ghesquières, Henri, 33
Gide, Charles, 12, 19, 23, 31, 36, 42, 52
Goguel, Maurice, 61, 63, 103
Gonin, Louis, 119

Gonin, Mrs., 119
Gontaudier, 114-16
Gounelle, Édmond, 31
Gounelle, Élie, 1-2, 5-13, 17-24, 27, 29-37, 42-44, 52, 63-64, 66-68, 71, 82, 99, 108, 116-18, 126, 138, 170, 182, 184-85
Gounelle, Gédéon, 6
Gounelle, Paul, 31
Gounelle, Théodore, 170
Gouth, Louis, 12, 31
Graaf, Hannes de, 177
Granier, Guillaume, 7
Gratry, Alponse, 12, 64
Grauss, Charles, 31
Greig, Charles-É., 7, 28, 104
Grilli di Cortona, Oscar, 85
Grilli, Magda: see under "Trocmé"
Grosjean, Georges, 118
Grotefeld, Stefan, 80
Grünhut, Bertha, 140
Grünhut, Egon, 140
Grynberg, Anne, 140
Guéhenno, Jean, 111
Guex, Henri, 5, 119
Guex, Mrs., 119
Guignebert, Charles, 61
Guillon, Charles, 122, 130, 132, 136-38, 145, 155, 183
Gumbel, Robert W., 90
Guth, Émilie, 155
Guyonnaud, André, 150

Halle, Gerhard, 110
Hallie, Philip, xvi
Harder, Milton J., 173
Hardie, Keir, 32, 34, 36
Harmegnies, Jacques, 110-111
Harmegnies, Jean, 111
Hartmann, Albrecht and Heidi, 110
Hatzfeld, Olivier, 132
Hauerwas, Stanley, xv
Heinemann, Gustav, 172
Henderson, Arthur, 32
Henry, Simone, 120
Heuzé, Marcel, 70-71, 94, 101, 104, 106, 155, 166-68
Heuzé, Simone, 71

Index Nominum

Hilaire, Yves-Marie, 162–65
Hirsch, Emanuel, 77
Hirsch, Hanne, 155–56
Hirsch, Maurice, 15
Hitler, Adolf, 109–10, 114, 135, 160, 166
Hodgkin, Henry, 162
Hoefert, Mrs., 132
Holland, Aug., 31
Hollard, Henri, 31
Hollard, Roger, 31
Honig, Eliyahu, 175
Houghton, Louise Seymour, 34
Huchet-Bishop, Claire, 176
Humbert, Grégoire, 2

Ingram, Norman, 114
Isaac, Daniel, 176
Isaac, Jules, 41, 176

Jalla, Aimée, 86
James, William, xv, 35, 47
Jeannet, Marcel, 127, 154
Jézéquel, Jules, 31, 69
Jispa: see under "Reynier"
Joas, Hans, xv
Jolivet, abbé Marius, 155
Jospin, Albert, 120
Jospin, D., 120
Jospin, H., 120
Jospin, Lionel, 55
Jospin, Marc, 127
Jospin, Robert, 55, 170
Joutard, Philippe, xv, 146, 155, 183
Jouve, G., 127
Julien, Claire, 139

Kaltenbach, Elizabeth, 95
Kaltenbach, Jacques, 31, 33–35, 38, 44, 46–51, 53, 56, 60, 62, 95, 107, 182
Kaspar, G., 31
Kastler, Alfred, 172
Kaufmann, Elizabeth, 143
Kindler, 54–55
King, Martin Luther, Jr., 170, 178
Kneubühler, Pierre, 61, 78
Kohn, Mr., 140
Kutter, Hermann, 36, 80

Lacordaire, Henri, 12
Lafon, Louis, 31
Lamennais, Félicité de, 12
Lamirand, Georges, 141
Lamotte, Mr. and Mrs., 164
Lançon, Joseph, 155
Lange, Halvard, 77
La Pira, Giorgio, 176
Lasserre, Georges, 170
Lasserre, Jean, 127
Lauga, Georges, 31, 71, 170
Lauriol, Élie, 170
Laval, Pierre, 148
Lavondès, Antoinette, 160
Lazare, Lucien, 134, 162–65, 183
Lecerf, Auguste, 118
Ledermann, E., 31
Leenhardt, Frantz, 2
Leenhardt, Roland, 175
Le Forestier, Jean-Philippe, 159
Le Forestier, Roger, 159
Le Goff, R., 104
Legrain, Maurice, 25
Legrand, Daniel, 13
Legrand, Louise-Émile, 13
Lenoir, Émile, 7
Leser, Mr., 164
Lester, Muriel, 109, 162
Liebmann, Max, 155–56
Liénart, Achille, 41, 163
Lipszyc (or Lif), Avraham, 163
Lipszyc, Haya, 163
Lipszyc, Perla, 163
Lods, Adolphe, 63, 118
Louis XIV, 127
Luther, Martin, 144

Maillebouis, Christian, 125–26, 130–31
Mairesse, Simone (née Pévenage), 95, 154, 183, 186
Malan, Adolphe, 7
Marcel, Gabriel, 135
Marrot-Fellag Ariouet, Céline, 101
Martin, Jacques, 1, 11, 63, 111–15, 127, 133, 145–46, 170, 176, 183
Marx, Karl, 29
Matile, A., 123, 127
Mattmüller, Markus, 68

Index Nominum

Mauriac, François, 172
Maury, Léon, 29, 31
Maury, Pierre, 115, 118, 127
McAll, Elizabeth, 18
McAll, Robert W., 17–18, 34, 51, 63, 65
Mehl, Roger, 112, 158, 170
Mendès France, Pierre, 172
Ménégoz, Eugène, 29
Merle d'Aubigné, Henri, 36, 66
Merle d'Aubigné, Julia, 35
Merz, Ernst, 68
Meunier, Arthur, 48, 56
Meuron, Alfred de, 27, 31
Meyer, Hubert, 139
Minault, Paul, 7, 12, 17, 21–22
Molines, Louis, 7
Monnier, André, 170
Monnier, Édouard, 54
Monnier, Henri, 13, 31, 52, 63, 90, 98, 118
Monod, Adolphe, 13, 65–66
Monod, Dorina, 65
Monod, Ernest, 21
Monod, Gabriel, 14
Monod, Jean (†1907), 2
Monod, Jean (†1836), 65–66
Monod, Paul, 31, 33
Monod, Théodore, 6, 14, 63, 65
Monod, Wilfred, 1–2, 5–8, 10, 20–21, 33, 36, 38, 44, 63–70, 84, 112, 184
Monod, William, 65
Montclos, Xavier de, 140
Montet, Ferdinand, 2
Moody, Dwight L., 8, 14, 50
Moore, Charles E., 174
Morel, André, 156, 183
Morel, Élie, 70, 92
Morley, Jean-Paul, 18
Morsier, Auguste de, 31
Mott, John R., 74
Mounier, Emmanuel, 135
Mours, Samuel, 18, 23, 35, 38, 52, 72, 97
Mülinen, Hélène de, 31
Munos-du Peloux, Odile, 155
Mussolini, Benito, 136
Muste, Abraham Johannes, 162
Néel, [James-]Élie, 17, 31

Nestler, Waldus, 80
Neury, Laurent, 155
Newell, William W., 18
Nick, André, 56, 165
Nick, George-Henri, 1
Nick, Héléna, 165
Nick, Héléna (née Roussel), 1, 6
Nick, Hélène (née Lèques), 10, 22, 39, 165
Nick, Jeanne, 40, 95, 165
Nick, Madeleine, 165
Nick, Odile, 163, 165, 183
Nick, Paul, 165
Nick, Pierre, 56, 134–35, 163–65, 183
Niebuhr, Reinhold, 82
Niemöller, Martin, 172
Nougat, Noël, 143
Nusslé, Henri, 22

Oberlin, Jean-Frédéric, 13, 77
Offenstadt, Nicolas, 55
Olgiati, Rodolfo, 138
Olivès, Paul, 168
Ollier, François, 22
Orsi, Hermine, 155

Paradon, Émile (?), 31
Passy, Paul, 19, 31, 33–34
Pélissier, L., 127
Perret, Paul, 91–94, 96, 103
Perrotte, Françoise, 139
Peschanski, Denis, 140
Pestalozzi, Rudolf, 32
Pétain, Philippe, 135, 148, 158, 160
Petit, Pierre, 70
Pévenage, Simone: see under "Mairesse"
Pfender, René, 97
Philip, André, 79, 111–13, 126–27, 135, 139, 154, 160, 170
Philip, Mireille, 135, 154, 183, 186
Pieczynska-Reichenbach, Emma, 31
Pierre, abbé (Henri Grouès), 172
Piton, Pierre, 155
Plantet, Eugène, 24
Poggio, Alexander, 85
Poinsot, Georges, 90
Poivre, Noël, 151
Poliakov, Léon, 143

Index Nominum

Poujol, Geneviève, 186
Poujol, Jacques, 135, 139
Poujol, Pierre, 170
Praly, Léopold, 149
Pressensé, Édmond de, 82, 90
Pury, Roland de, 151

Quiévreux, Aquilas, 21–24, 29, 31, 37, 65, 70, 116, 126

Ragaz, Christine, 68, 80
Ragaz, Leonhard, 36, 64, 68, 79–81, 83, 89, 162
Rauschenbusch, Walter, 34, 186
Reinhardt, Myriam, 31
Réveillaud, Eugène, 38
Reynier, Alice ("Jispa"), 154, 174
Rich, Arthur, 68
Ricœur, Paul, 160, 171
Riou-Bollon, Mrs., 127
Rivet, Victor, 84
Roberty, Jules-Émile, 31
Rochat, Louis-Lucien, 49
Rochefort, Florence, 15, 186
Rockefeller, David, 88–89
Rockefeller, John D., 86, 88, 109, 132
Rockefeller, Laurance, 88
Rockefeller, Winthrop, 88
Roger, Jean-Pierre, 70, 98
Rohr, Maurice, 151
Rombaut, Camille, 111, 114–15, 127
Roosevelt, Franklin D., 135
Rosay, Father Jean, 155
Roser, Henri, 23, 61, 69, 77–79, 81, 104, 112–14, 117, 127, 133, 162, 170, 176, 178, 183
Rosowsky, Oscar, 155
Rostand, Jean, 172
Roth, Jean, 31
Roussel, Bernard, 18
Roussel, Héléna – see under "Nick"
Rousselle, Jeanne, 163
Roussiez, G., 26, 29
Roux, Hébert, 107
Roux, Th., 118
Ryan, Donna F., 167
Saillens, Ruben, 38
Sangnier, Marc, 111–12

Sautter, Emmanuel, 74
Sautter, Louis, 23, 29
Sauvage, Pierre, xvi, 136, 154
Sauzède, Albert, 31
Sayre, John Nevin, 80, 109, 114–15, 178
Schering, Ernst, 51
Schiebel, 149
Schleiermacher, Friedrich, 13
Schlœsing, Émile, 52
Schmidt, Élisabeth, 186
Schoen, Jean-Marie, 150
Schweitzer, Albert, 159
Scott, Clarice, 105
Scott, Douglas R., 105–7, 128, 166
Sibleyras, Adolphe, 31, 184
Siegmund-Schultze, Friedrich, 64, 69, 79–80
Siekerski, Denise, 155
Silvani, Sébastien, 147
Smith, Robert Pearsall, 14
Smith, Timothy L., 185
Smyth-Florentin, Françoise, 115
Söderblom, Nathan, 44, 64, 67–69
Sogne, Mrs., 127
Spiero, Claude, 154
Stahl, abbé, 164
Stevenson, Lilian, 81, 109
Stott, George Raymond, 105
Straube, Paul, 142
Suchon, Sandrine, 183

Tagore, Rabindranath, 89
Tamar, Mr., 152
Tanner, Kathryn, 182
Tarrou, Louis (?), 31
Tec, Nechama, 143
Teule, Édmond, 7
Theis, Édouard, 63, 88, 101, 127, 131–32, 134–36, 147–49, 151, 155, 160, 176, 183, 189
Theis, Mildred, 132, 183
Thich Nhất Hạnh, 178
Tholuck, August, 13
Thomas, Frank, 31, 127
Thonger, William G., 42, 104
Thurneysen, Eduard, 77

Index Nominum

Toureille, Pierre[-Charles], 127, 139, 183
Treister, Guy, 164–65
Trial, Louis, 31
Tricot, Henri, 19
Trocmé, Daniel (son of André Trocmé) 99, 118, 172
Trocmé, Daniel (cousin of André Trocmé), 138–39, 148–51, 167, 183
Trocmé, Hélène, 74
Trocmé, Henri, 151
Trocmé, Jacques, 99, 118, 152–54
Trocmé, Jean-Pierre, 99, 118, 152–53, 159, 169
Trocmé, Louise, 73
Trocmé, Magda (née Grilli), xvi, 85–89, 91–96, 99, 106, 118–19, 125, 128–30, 132, 136–37, 147–50, 152–54, 159, 169, 171–74, 178, 181, 183, 185, 187
Trocmé, Marguerite, 111
Trocmé, Marie (née Walbaum), 54, 91
Trocmé, Nelly, 95, 99, 118, 123, 156
Trocmé, Paul, 48–49, 51–54, 56, 60, 89, 91, 94, 134
Trocmé, Paula (née Schwerdtmann), 51, 53, 84, 136
Trocmé, Robert, 54

Usach, Juliette, 138

Valynseele, Joseph, 70
Vallée, Charles, 25, 31, 41, 113, 127
Vallée, Marguertie, 127
Vermeil, André, 101
Vernier, Daniel, 71
Vernier, Frédéric, 112
Vernier, Jacques, 63
Vernier, Philippe, 63, 104, 112, 114–15, 133, 176
Vernier, Pierre, 133
Vernier-Escande, Lucie, 95
Vesper, Noël: see under "Nougat"
Villon, François, 159
Vincent, Philémon, 38
Vinet, Alexandre, 13, 67, 82–85
Vismes, Roger de, 52, 66, 90
Visser 't Hooft, Willem, 140, 172–73
Voge, Maurice, 170
Vries, Minke de, 131

Wabnitz, Auguste, 1–2
Waegner, Frü, 77
Wagner, Charles, 10, 31
Walbaum, Ferdinand, 91
Ward, Harry F., 82, 88
Ward, William, 32–34, 36, 42
Weber, Hans-Ruedi, 160
Weil, Simone, 135
Weiss, Raymond, 13
Weisser, Paul, 120
Wells, Samuel, xv
Williams, Leighton, 34
Winitzer, 149
Wissotzky, Nelly, 85
Wissotzky, Varia, 85
Wolfradts, 149
Wolterstorff, Nicholas, 187
Wrede, Mathilda, 162

Yagil, Limore, 155, 163

Zasloff, Tela, 139.

www.ingramcontent.com/pod-product-compliance
Lightning Source LLC
Chambersburg PA
CBHW062023220426
43662CB00010B/1453